HISTORIC PHOTOS OF
TAMPA
IN THE 50s, 60s, AND 70s

Text and Captions by Steve Rajtar

TURNER
PUBLISHING COMPANY

Dominating the Tampa skyline in this 1975 photo is the Park Tower, the city's first substantial modern skyscraper. This 36-floor building was built in 1972–73, and stood as Tampa's tallest until 1981, when One Tampa City Center was built. Park Tower opened as the home of First National Bank of Tampa. For a time, the 458-foot-tall building at 400 North Tampa Street was owned by the Lykes Brothers Corporation. In 2006, it was purchased for $50 million by P. T. Associates, L.P.

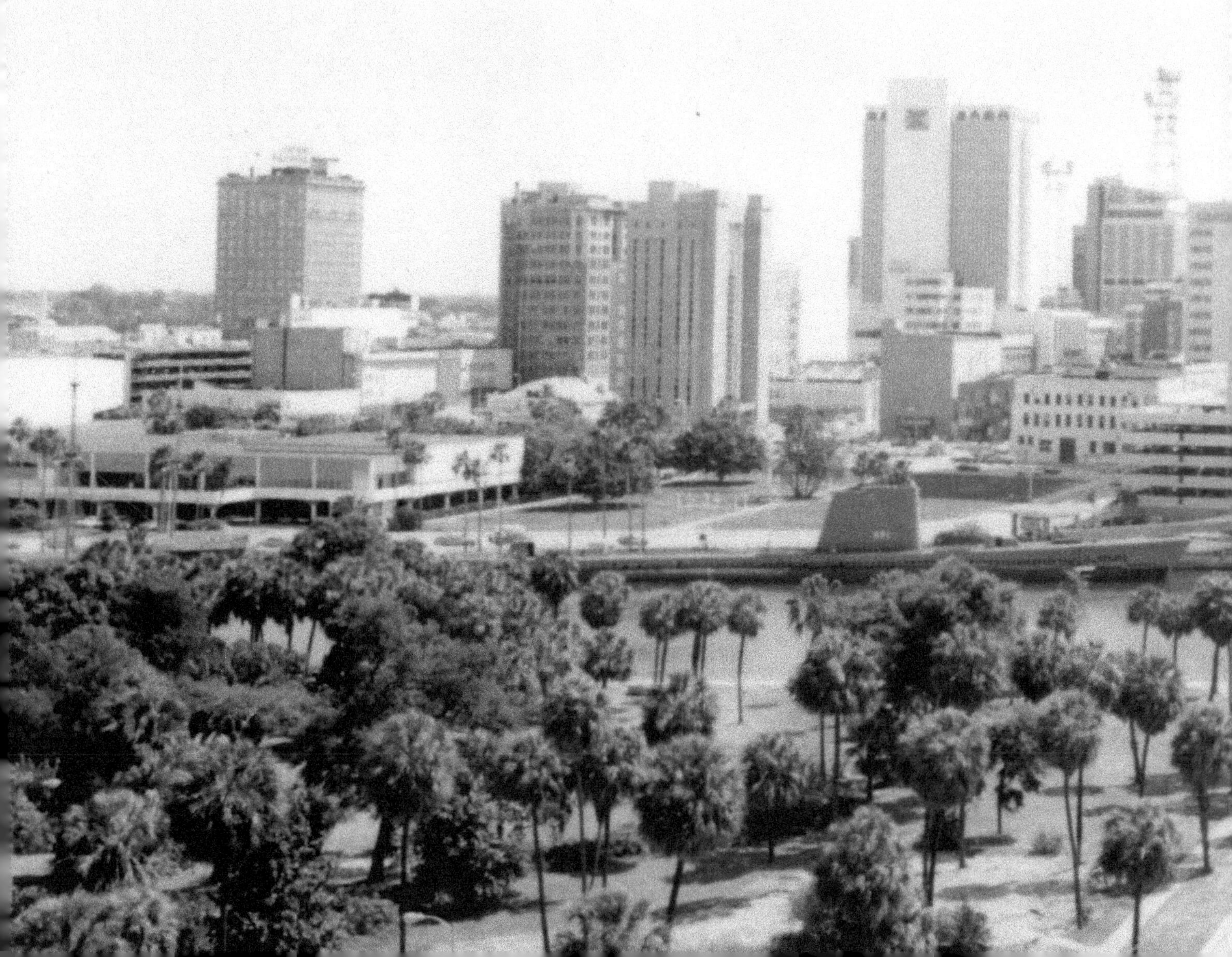

HISTORIC PHOTOS OF TAMPA IN THE 50s, 60s, AND 70s

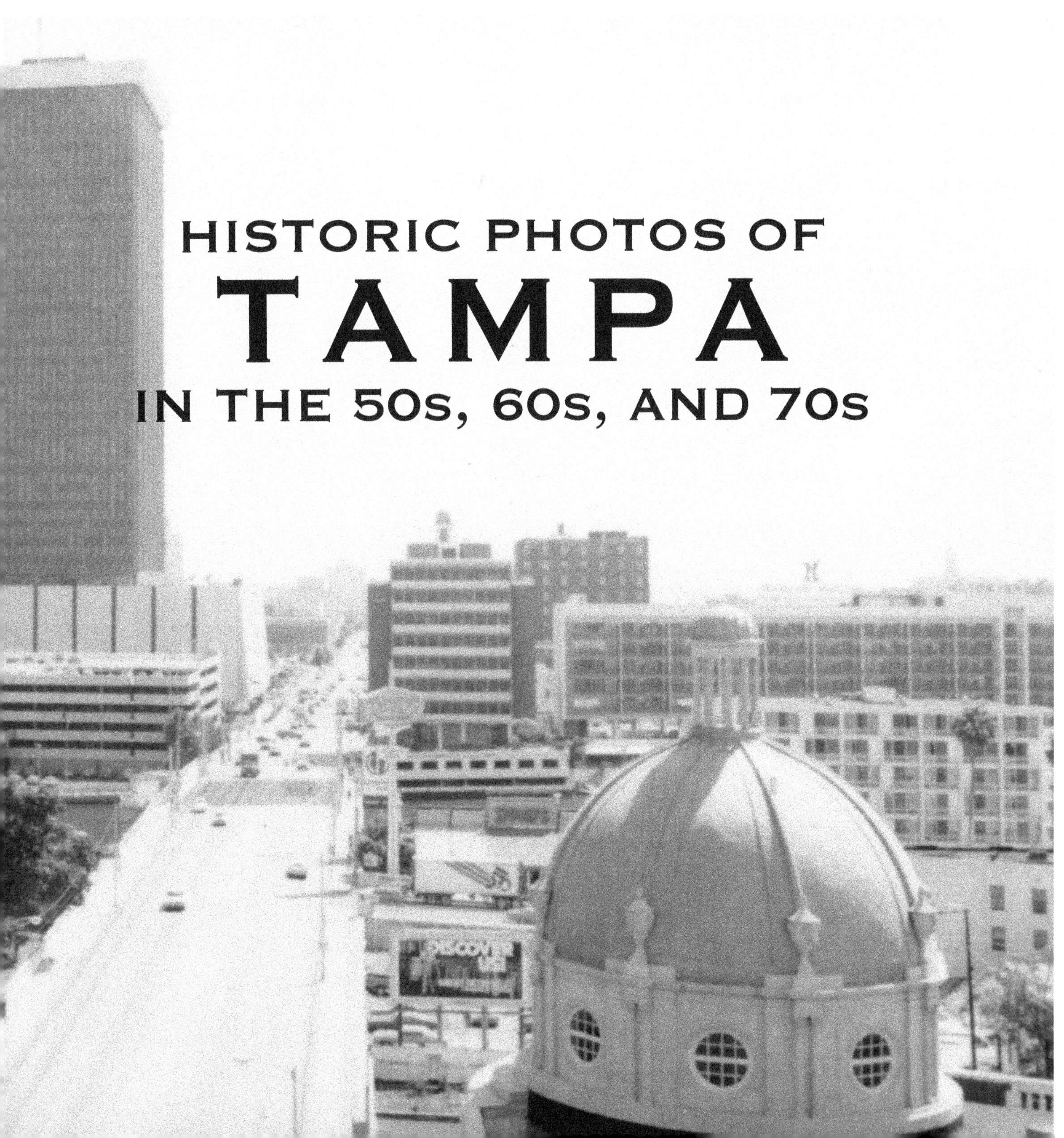

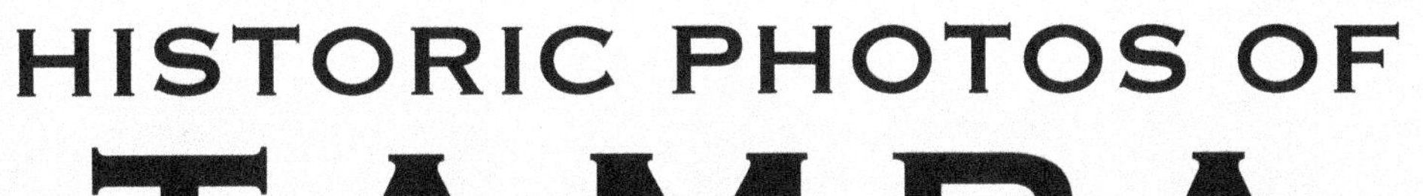

Turner Publishing Company
4507 Charlotte Avenue • Suite 100
Nashville, Tennessee 37209
(615) 255-2665

www.turnerpublishing.com

Historic Photos of Tampa in the 50s, 60s, and 70s

Library of Congress Control Number: 2011943136

ISBN: 978-1-59652-810-9
ISBN-13: 978-1-68442-133-6 (hardcover)

Printed in the United States of America

07 08 09 10 11 12 13 14—0 9 8 7 6 5 4 3 2 1

Contents

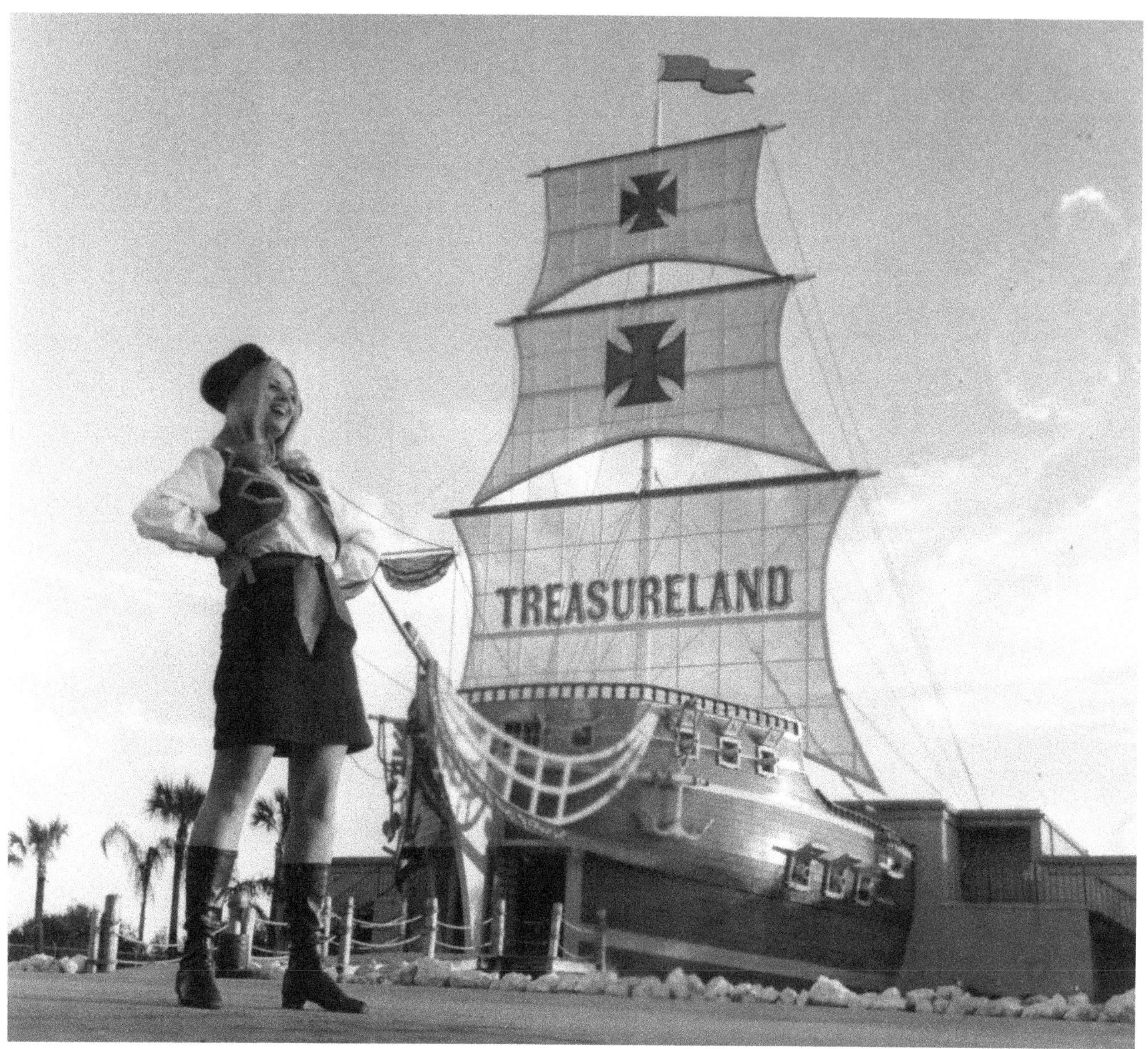

Along Busch Boulevard, not far from Busch Gardens, was the Treasureland amusement park, which opened in the mid-1960s. It was advertised as "All Indoors…Air Conditioned" and claimed to be "an exciting adventure in piracy." Pirate mannequins moved stiffly until the early 1970s, when Walt Disney World and other theme parks with better technology and effects put Treasureland and many other simpler parks out of business.

Acknowledgments

This volume, *Historic Photos of Tampa in the 50s, 60s, and 70s,* is the result of the cooperation and efforts of many individuals, organizations, and corporations. It is with great thanks that we acknowledge the valuable contribution of the following for their generous support:

Hillsborough County Public Library, Burgert Brothers Photographic Collection
Florida State Archives

With the exception of touching up imperfections caused by the damage of time and cropping where necessary, no other changes have been made. The focus and clarity of many images is limited to the technology and the ability of the photographer at the time they were taken.

Preface

Today's Tampa did not start out, as many other cities have, with the single central core such as a railroad station, port, or major manufacturer. Instead, it's a consolidation of several distinct neighborhoods, each of which was established with its own reason to be, and which, as the region grew, expanded to the borders of the others to create a patchwork whole which retains a variety of cultures, looks, and characters.

The downtown area started with a 16-square-mile Fort Brooke military reservation on a site suggested in 1818 by Andrew Jackson. Around it were built homes and businesses, and as it expanded it assumed the role of the commercial center. Nearby, the cigar manufacturing industry grew, the separate towns of Ybor City and West Tampa were established in 1885 and 1894.

The most aristocratic section, Hyde Park, came into being in 1886 south of downtown, followed by the upscale neighborhood of Bayshore. In the 1920s, more residences for the well-to-do appeared as Palma Ceia and Beach Park.

During the 1890s, Port Tampa (not to be confused with the Port of Tampa, located miles closer to downtown) was founded as a commercial and industrial center, and an ocean port. Its growth was supported by its proximity to the Gulf of Mexico in 1898, when it was connected to downtown with a railroad line for the transport of soldiers. They came from across the country to depart from Port Tampa on steamers to fight in Cuba during the Spanish-American War.

Another cigar-producing area, Palmetto Beach, came into being in about 1897. Not far away, DeSoto Park became popular in the 1920s with "tin-can tourists" who visited and often decided to settle in the vicinity. New growth occurred in a very literal way on Davis Islands, where two small islands were merged and greatly enlarged by a huge amount of sand dredged from the bottom of Tampa Bay, and then formed into one of the most sought-after places to live in Tampa.

By the time the photos on the following pages were taken, the individual parts of Tampa had spread in all directions and there was essentially no physical separation between any pair of them. However, that does not mean that the whole city has turned into a homogeneous urban place. On the contrary, one can wander through the city and experience a rich variety of architectural styles, businesses, languages, and traditions, all mixed in with first-class universities, hospitals, museums, and everything else which you might expect in a modern city that hasn't forgotten its historical roots.

—Steve Rajtar

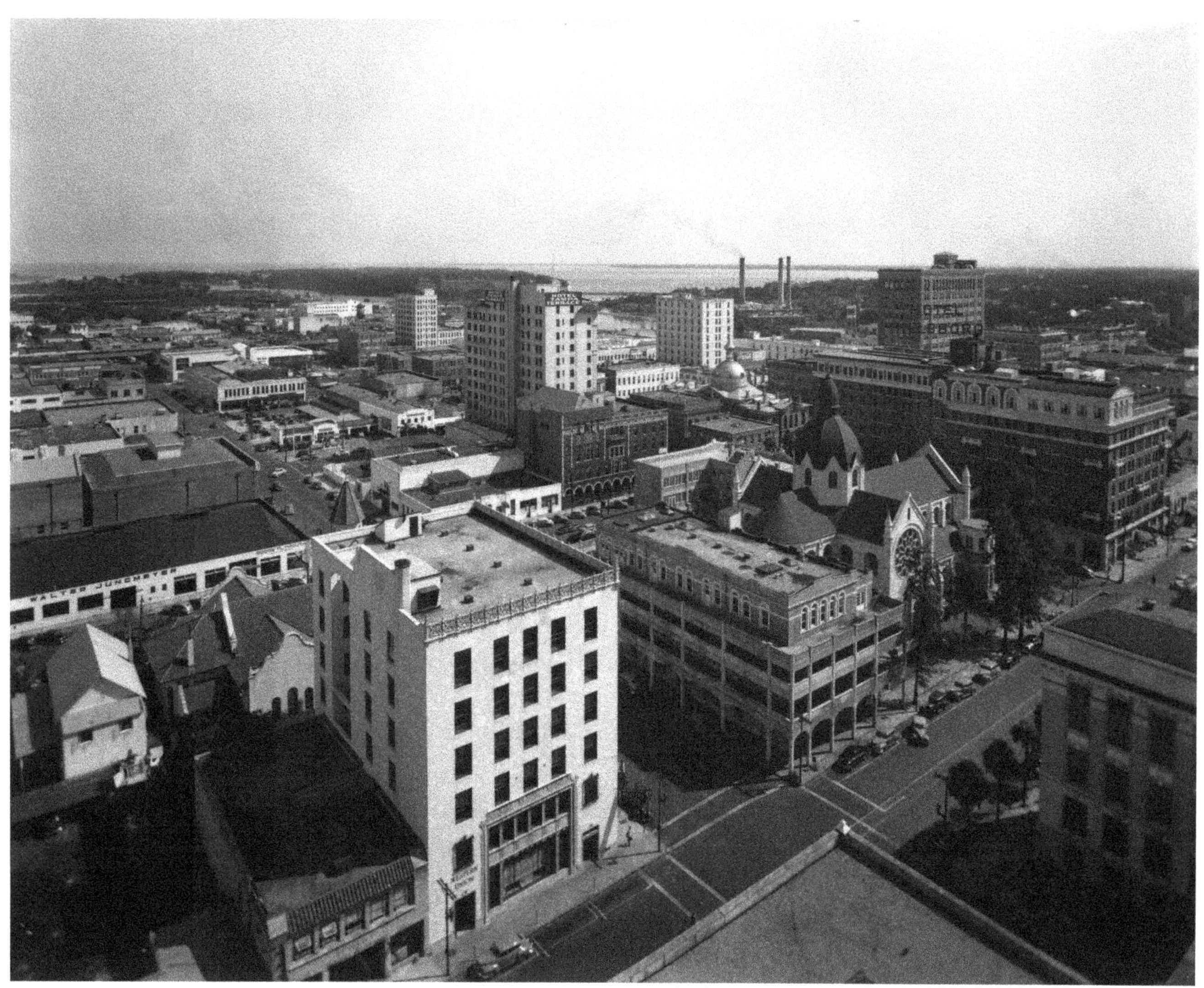

In 1950, this was the view looking out over Twiggs Street and downtown Tampa toward Tampa Bay in the distance. Just to the right of center is the domed Sacred Heart Catholic Church, whose congregation acquired land for its first sanctuary at 507 North Florida Avenue in 1853. Originally named St. Louis Catholic Church for King Louis IX of France, it was renamed Sacred Heart and its second sanctuary (shown here) was dedicated at the same site in 1905.

Crime, Education, and Tourists

(1950–1959)

In the middle of the twentieth century, Tampa was not as well known in the rest of the country as were other Florida cities such as Miami, Orlando, or Key West, but during the 1950s the federal government's actions introduced the city to many. Unfortunately, it was not the type of publicity the Chamber of Commerce would have preferred.

Since the 1880s, the workers of Tampa supported a thriving gambling industry, especially the game of bolita, which had been imported from Cuba. Workers could bet as little as a penny on a numbered ball which was placed in a bag with 99 others and shaken. If the bettor's ball was chosen, he won eight times the amount of his bet. Often, the game was rigged, but they still played. By 1927, there were about 300 bolita houses just within the Ybor City neighborhood.

Other crimes were rampant in the area, and when Prohibition was repealed, those who had engaged in bootlegging shifted to gambling and other organized crimes. Crime bosses including Charlie Wall and Santo Trafficante Sr. wielded great power in Tampa, and Trafficante's son in the mid-1950s allied with New York crime families to expand the scope of illegal activities to include the rest of Florida and Cuba.

During this decade, the federal government became concerned about the Tampa crime problem and hearings were conducted under the leadership of U.S. Senator Estes Kefauver. The extent of the crime problem was put on public display. Formerly prominent crime boss Charlie Wall testified against the mob then in power, and was rewarded with a severed throat, blunt force trauma to the back of his head, and nine knife wounds to his face. The discovery of his corpse helped to emphasize the severity of the problem and a campaign to repair the city's image was begun.

The decade also saw the establishment of two major institutions in the city. The University of South Florida was founded and Busch Gardens opened. The university has grown tremendously and, with the older University of Tampa, makes the city a destination for students seeking either private or state-supported higher education. Busch Gardens started small, but quickly grew to be the state's major theme park, as opposed to the smaller tourist attractions which had previously drawn visitors to the state. Busch Gardens remained as Florida's most popular tourist attraction until the opening of Walt Disney World in 1971.

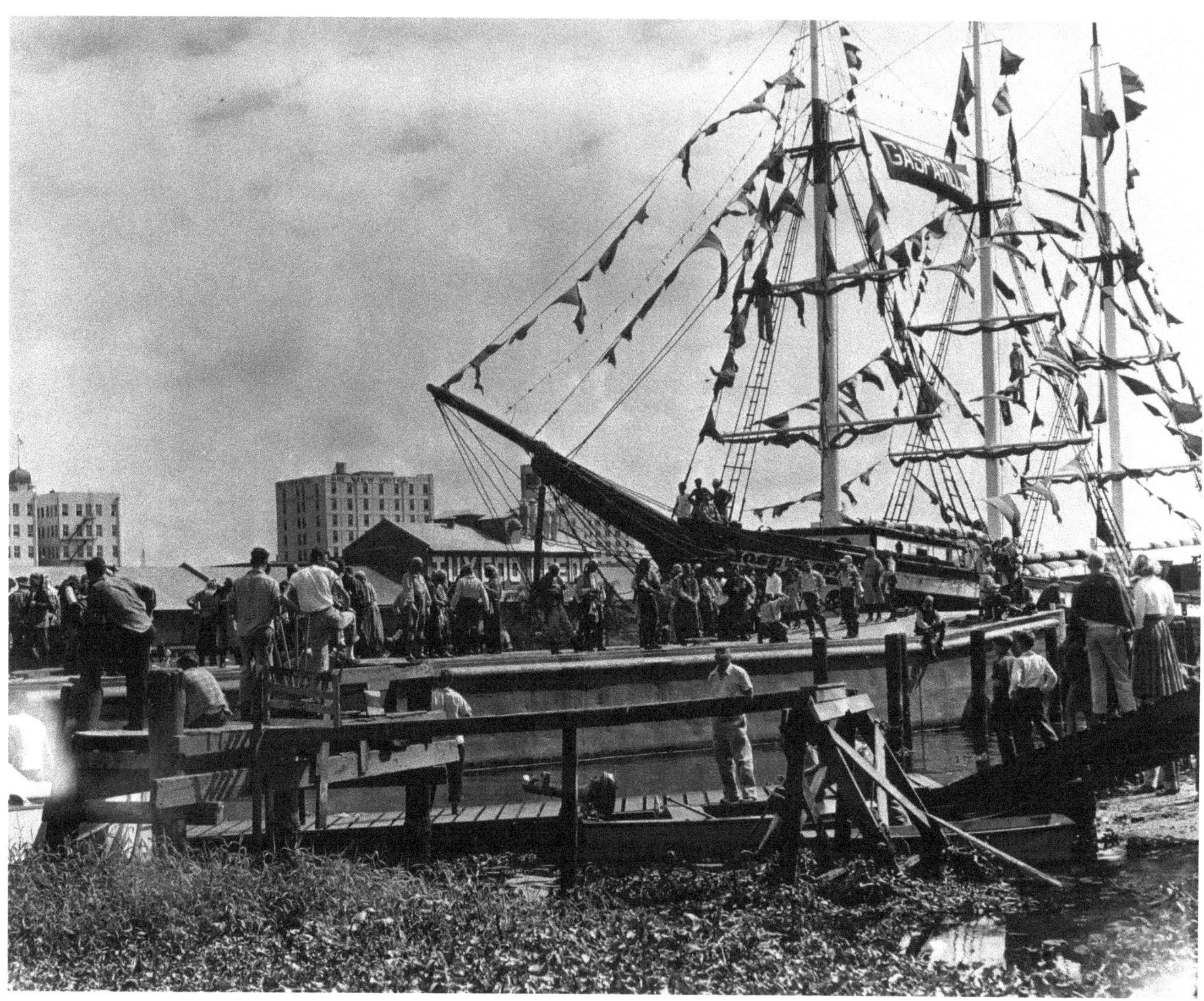

In the late 1700s and early 1800s, Jose Gaspar was a pirate who roamed the Gulf of Mexico, preying on merchant ships. In his last attack, he picked on a disguised U.S. Navy warship, and rather than be captured, he jumped into the sea and drowned. More than 80 years later, he was chosen as a symbol for a Tampa festival by Louise Frances Dodge, who had been hired as the society editor of the *Tampa Tribune* newspaper in 1903. This is a ship used in the 1950 Gasparilla Festival.

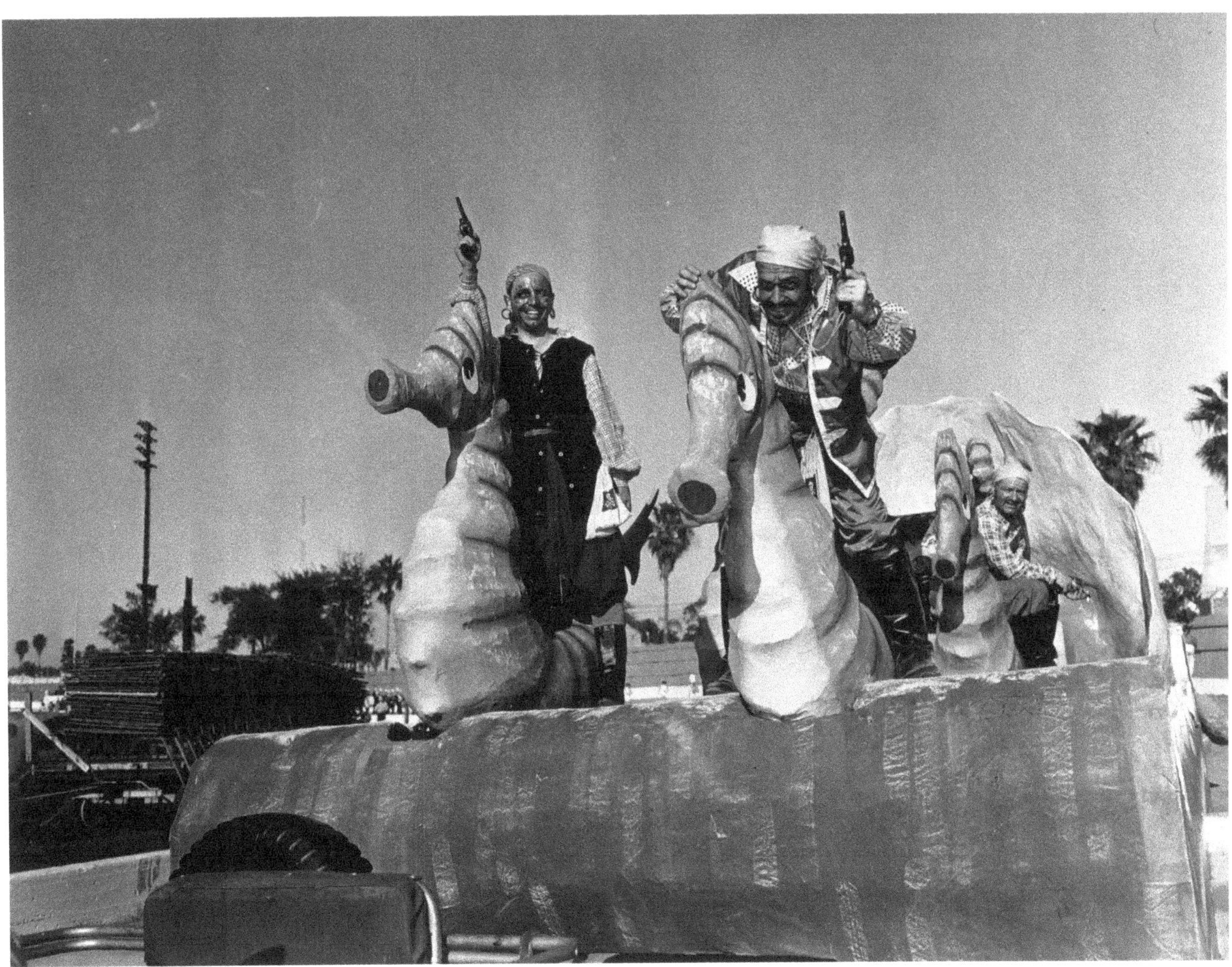

Editor Wallace F. Stovall assigned Louise Dodge the task of creating a winter event to attract tourists to Tampa. She was helped by Louisiana visitor George W. Hardee, and they came up with a festival similar to New Orleans' Mardi Gras. A highlight of the event is a parade, including floats such as the one shown here in 1950. The festival is still held annually and is known as the Gasparilla Festival, the Gasparilla Pirate Festival, and the Gasparilla Pirate Fest. The latter is the official name.

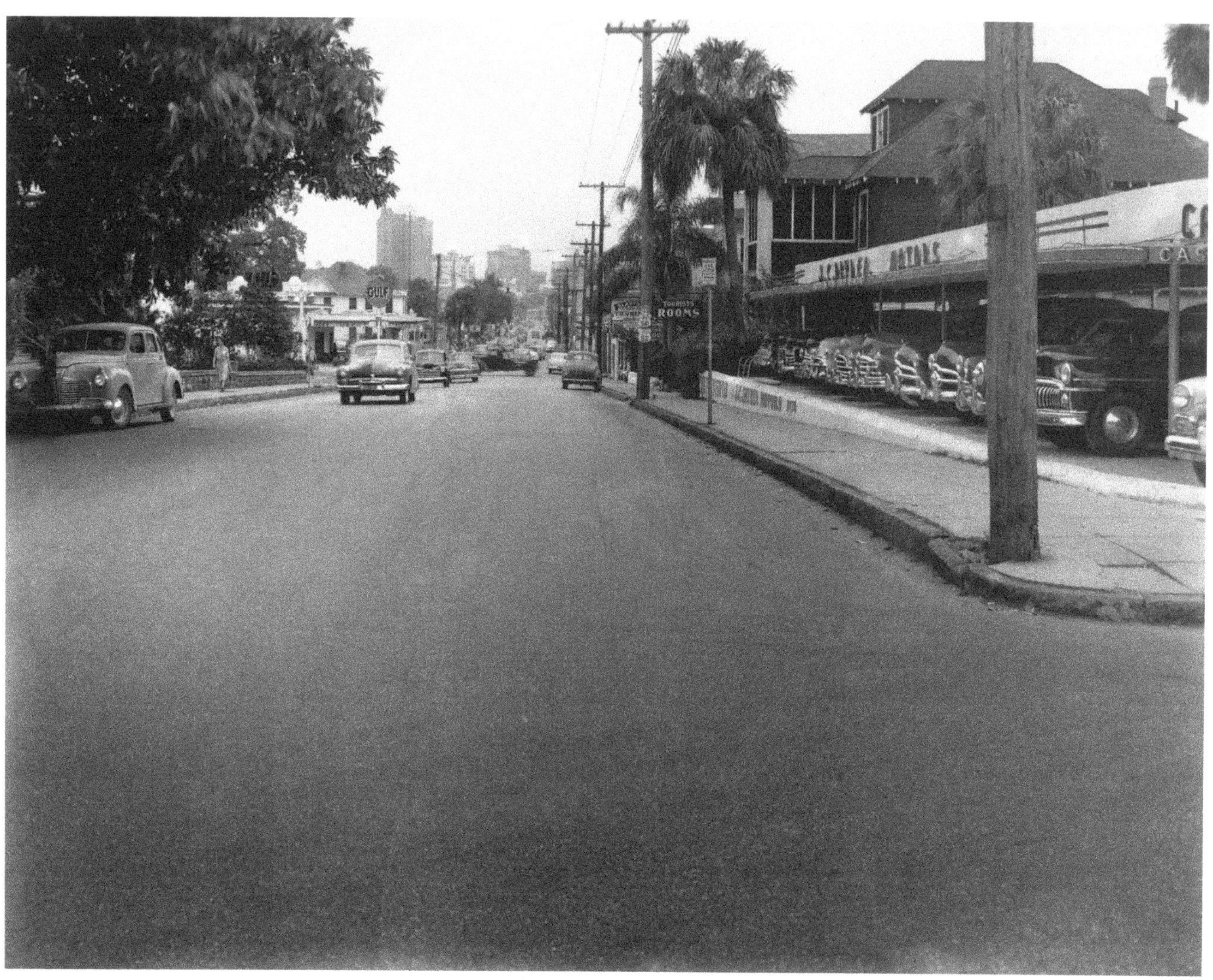

The skyline of downtown Tampa appears in the distance in this photo of North Florida Avenue taken on February 22, 1950. You can see a slight downward slope of the pavement here at the 1700 block, near the southern end of the area known as Tampa Heights. Just a few feet of elevation give it the name of "Heights," but it was enough to attract many who believed the low-lying area near Tampa Bay was less healthy. In 1886–87, they moved to the Heights because they believed the higher elevation would protect them from a deadly yellow fever epidemic. In fact, what protected them was getting away from infected individuals who had caught the disease from infected steamboat passengers.

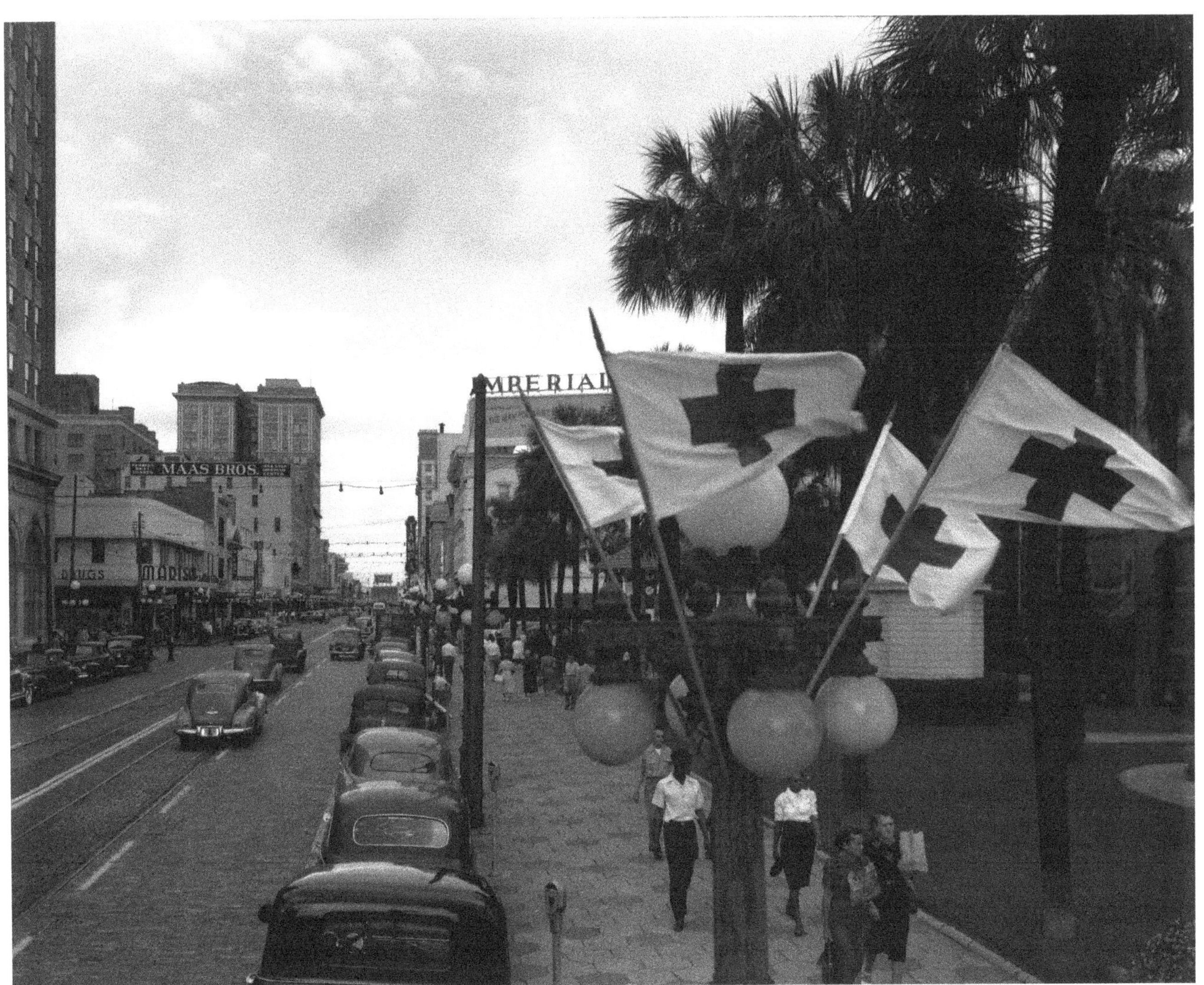

Red Cross flags are flying in front of the Hillsborough County Courthouse on March 7, 1950, with Mass Brothers in the distance. That eight-story tower located at 610-616 North Franklin Street was built for the department store to replace its outgrown Krause Building at the southeast corner of Franklin and Zack streets. The business began in 1898 when brothers Abe and Isaac Maas began to expand the Abe Maas Dry Goods Palace into Tampa's only complete department store.

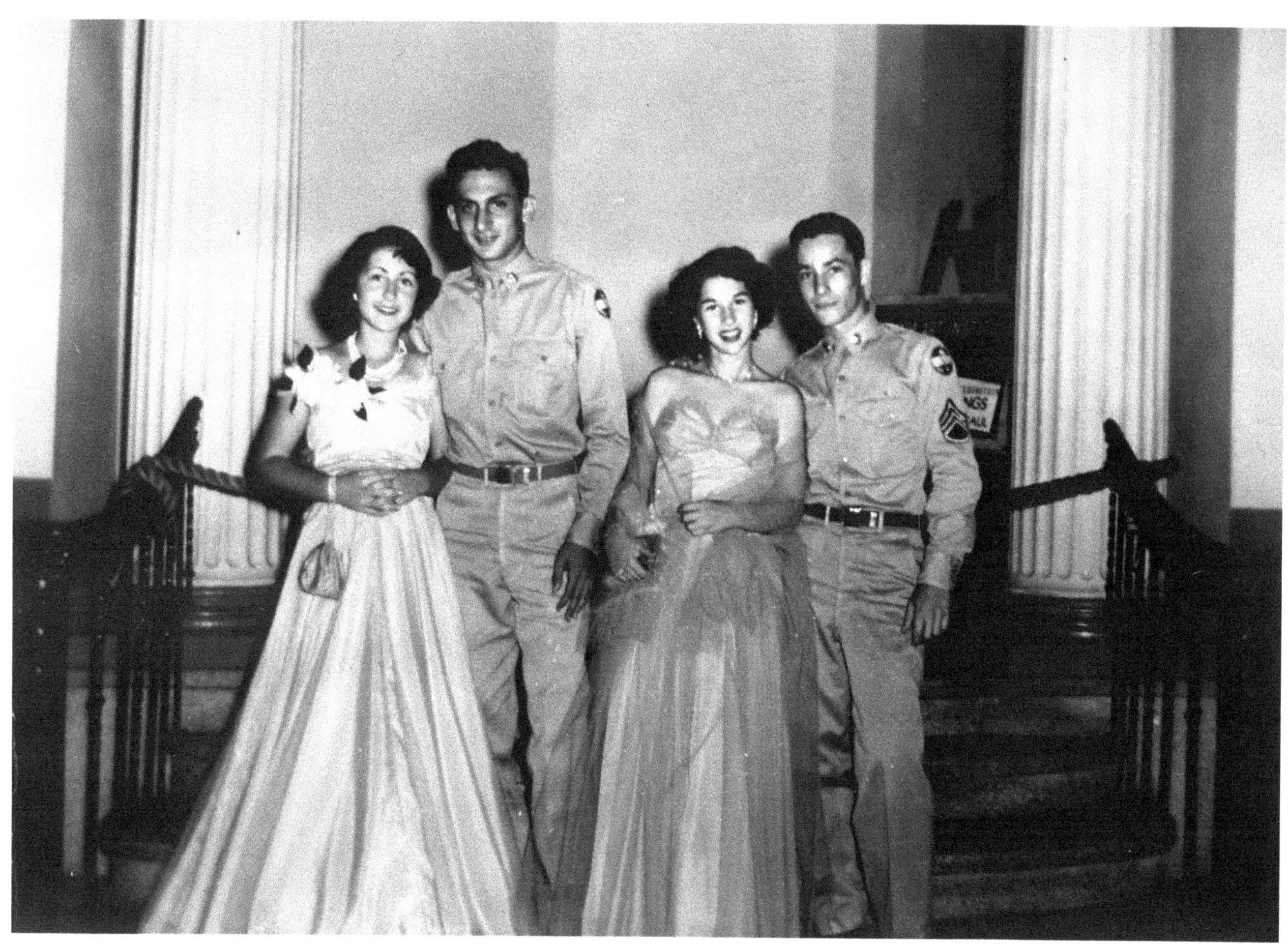

Two Jewish couples are pictured at an ROTC Ball in 1950. The students are Hannah Soman, Myrna Leonard Rubeleman, Bob Turkel, and one who is unidentified. They may be from Hillsborough High School, which established its Army Cadet ROTC program in 1935.

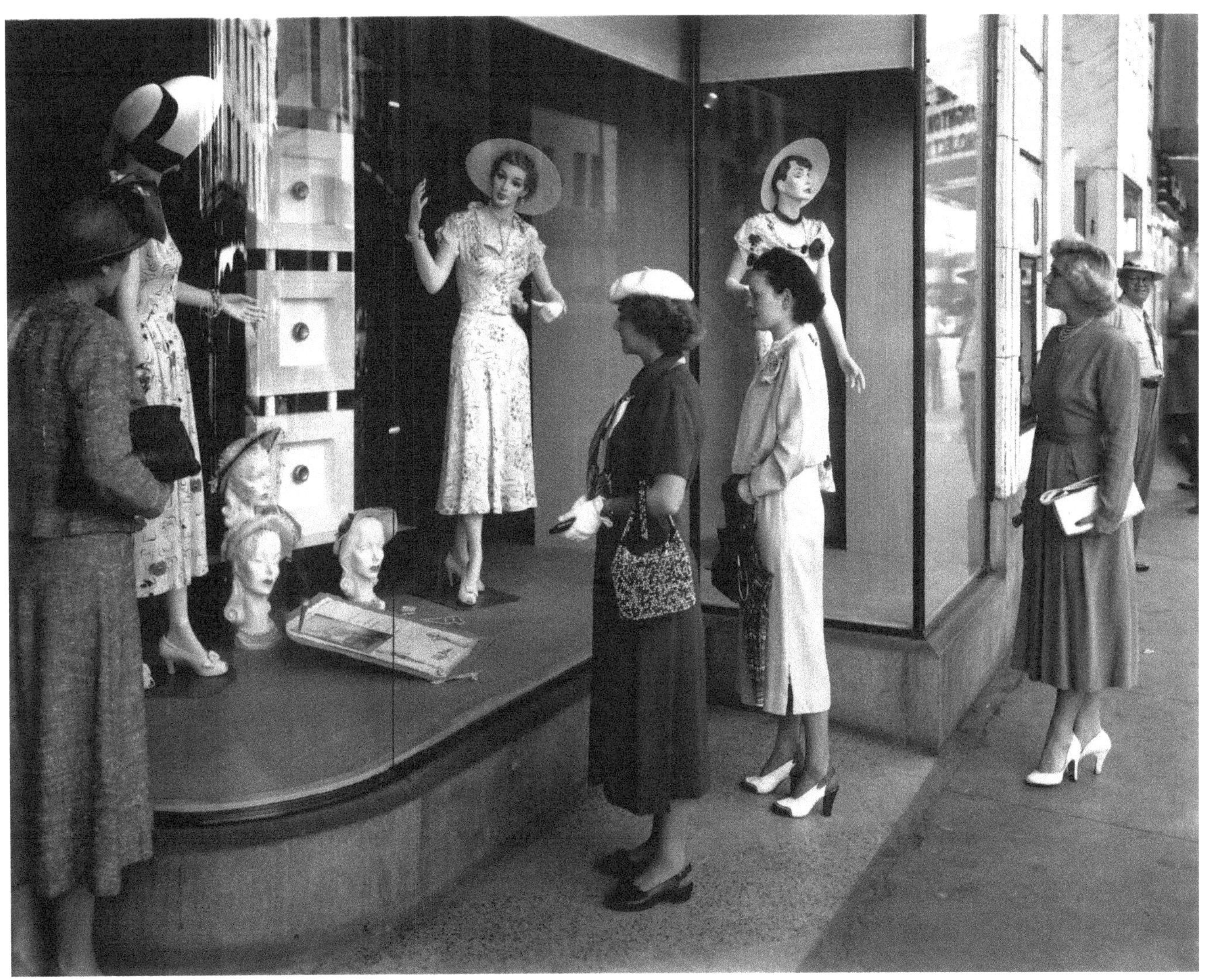

Women stop by the window display at Wolf Brothers on May 16, 1950. The clothing store at 808-810 Franklin Street was founded in 1899 by Morris Wolf of Germany and his brother Fred as the Wolf Brothers Men's Clothing Store. Morris served as a director of the Tampa Board of Trade and the president of the Florida Retail Clothiers Association.

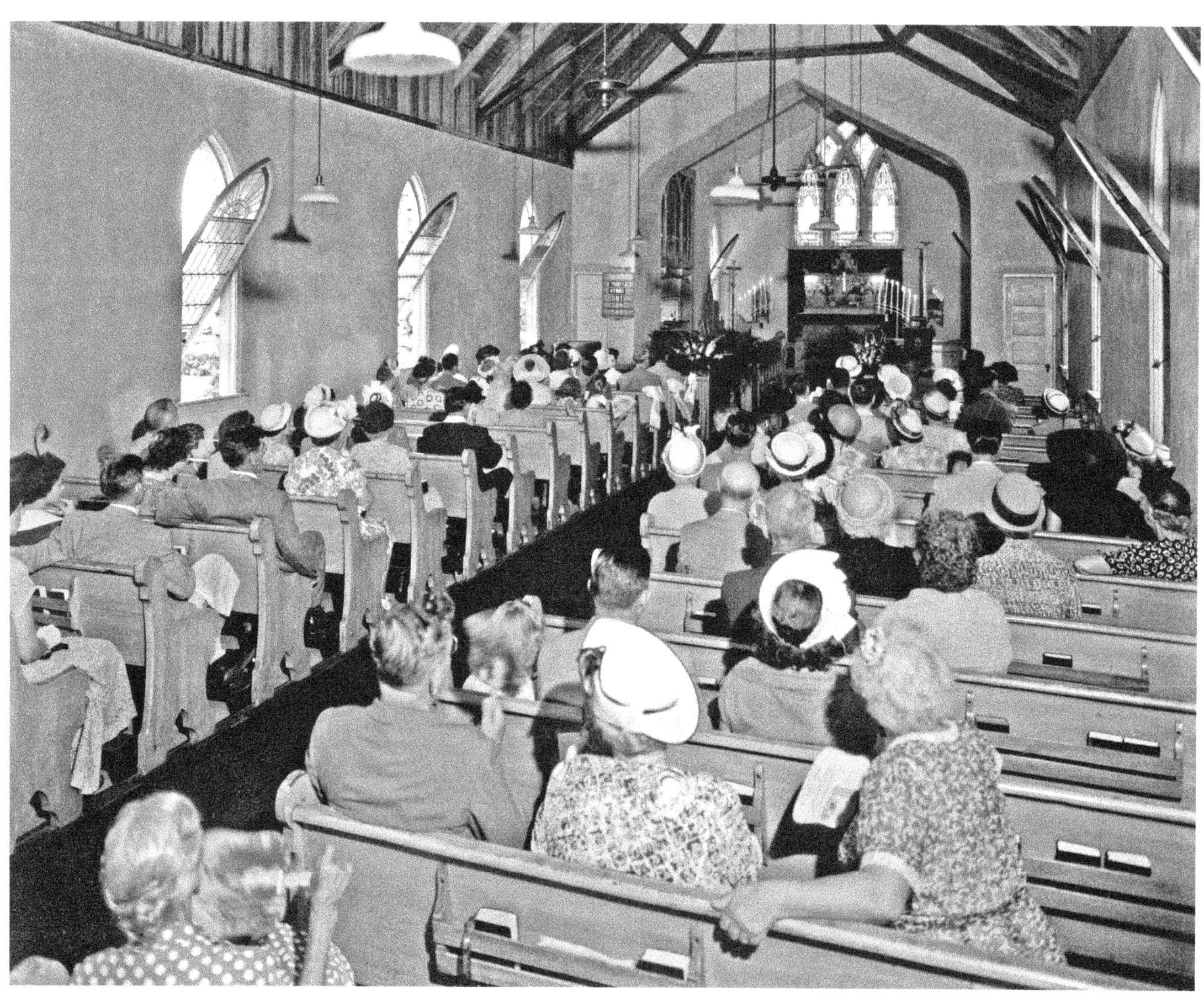

This wedding took place on June 25, 1950, inside the Episcopal House of Prayer. Located at the corner of Columbus Drive and Central Avenue in Tampa Heights, the congregation started out as a place of worship for black cigar workers who were not allowed in St. Andrew's Episcopal Church. The sanctuary, designed by Louis A. Fort, was built by members of the congregation in 1922 with rubble stone dredged from Hillsborough River.

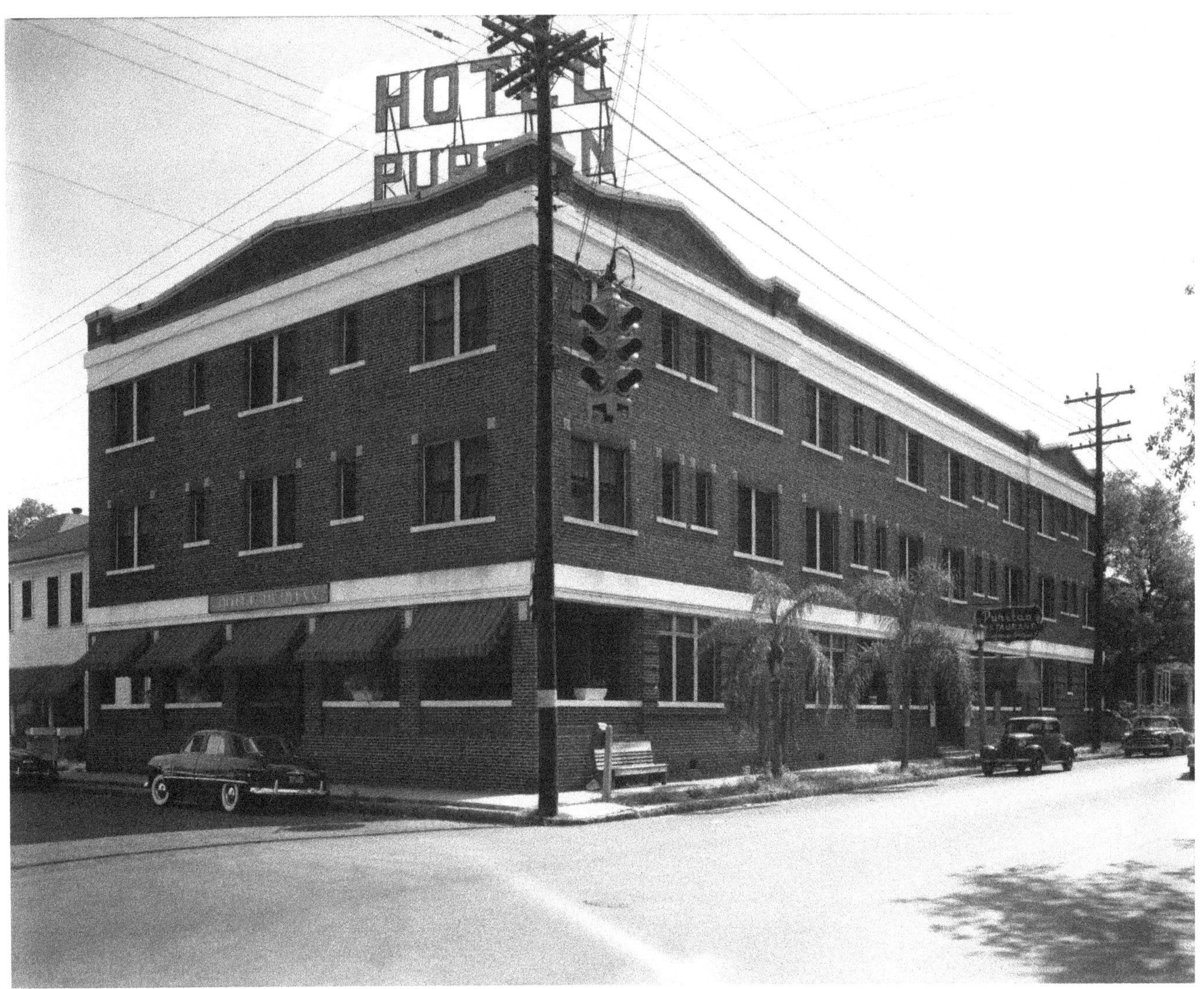

This building at the corner of Plant Avenue and Platt Street in Hyde Park had two entrances. The one on the left, with an address of 301 Plant, led to the lobby of the Hotel Puritan. The other, on the right opening onto Platt, was for the popular Puritan Restaurant. The hotel was advertised as modern with steam heat, excellent food, friendly service, and a homey atmosphere.

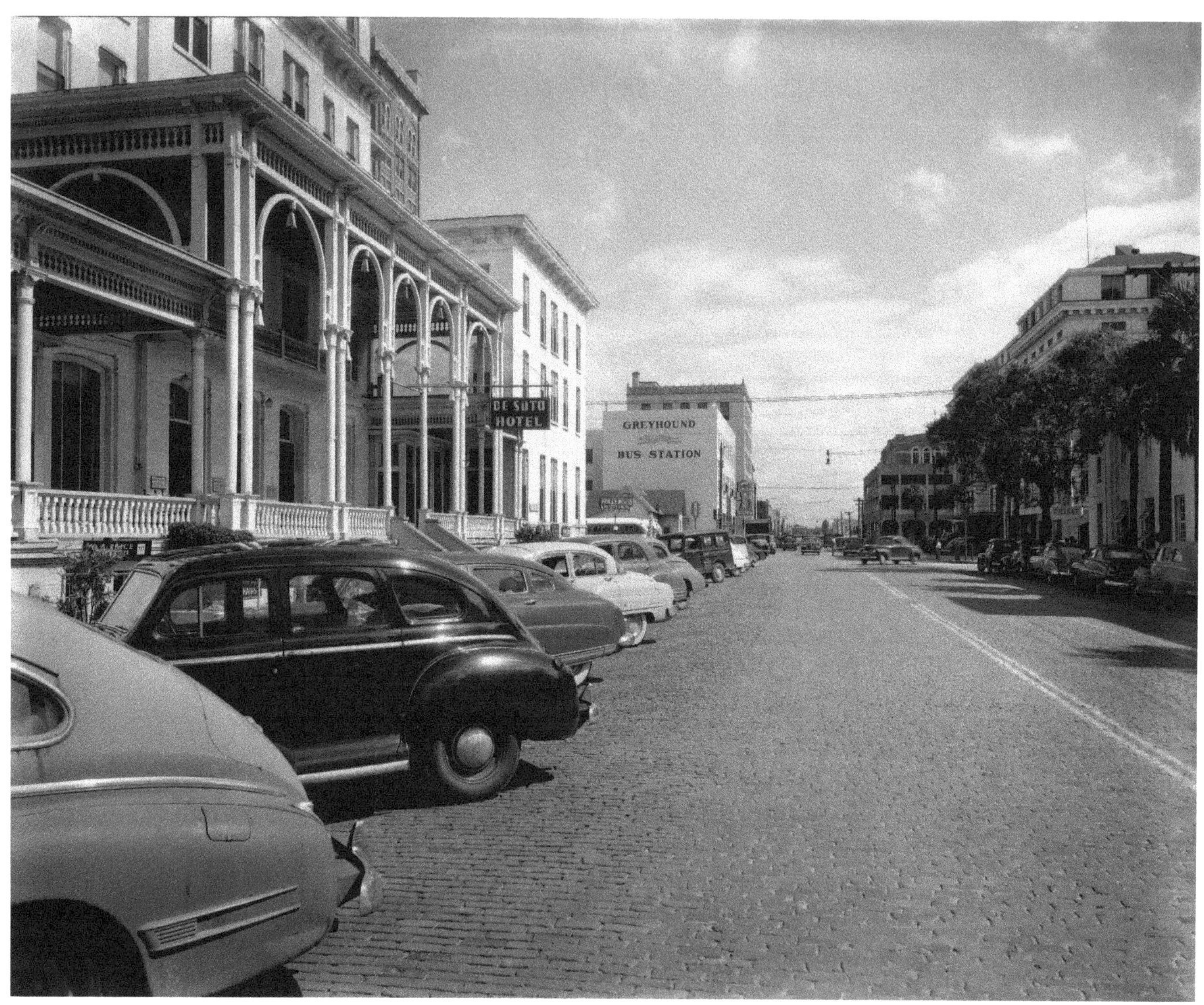

This was the view down Marion Street from the intersection with Polk Street. On the left is the arched façade of the De Soto Hotel. A few buildings beyond that was the station of the Greyhound Bus Company, which was one of several means of transportation which connected Tampa with the rest of Florida. The De Soto was torn down in about 1955, five years after this photo was taken, and in its place is the Robert L. Timberlake Jr. Federal Building.

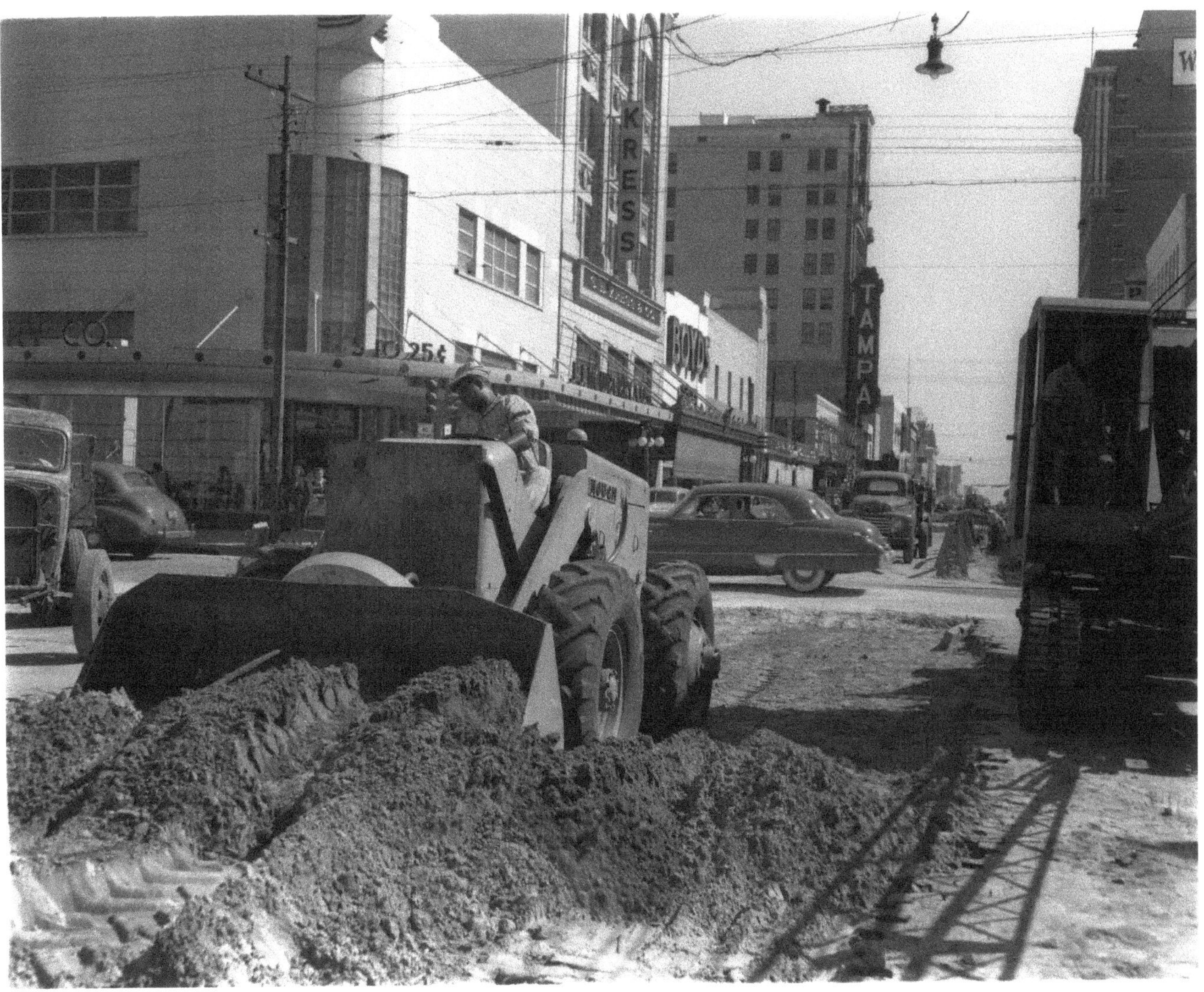

Traffic was disrupted at the intersection of Franklin and Cass Streets when this photo was taken on October 13, 1950. Three of the first four buildings on the left at times housed "dime stores." The one on the corner was J. J. Newberry, then Kress, and then F. W. Woolworth (with Boyd's in between).

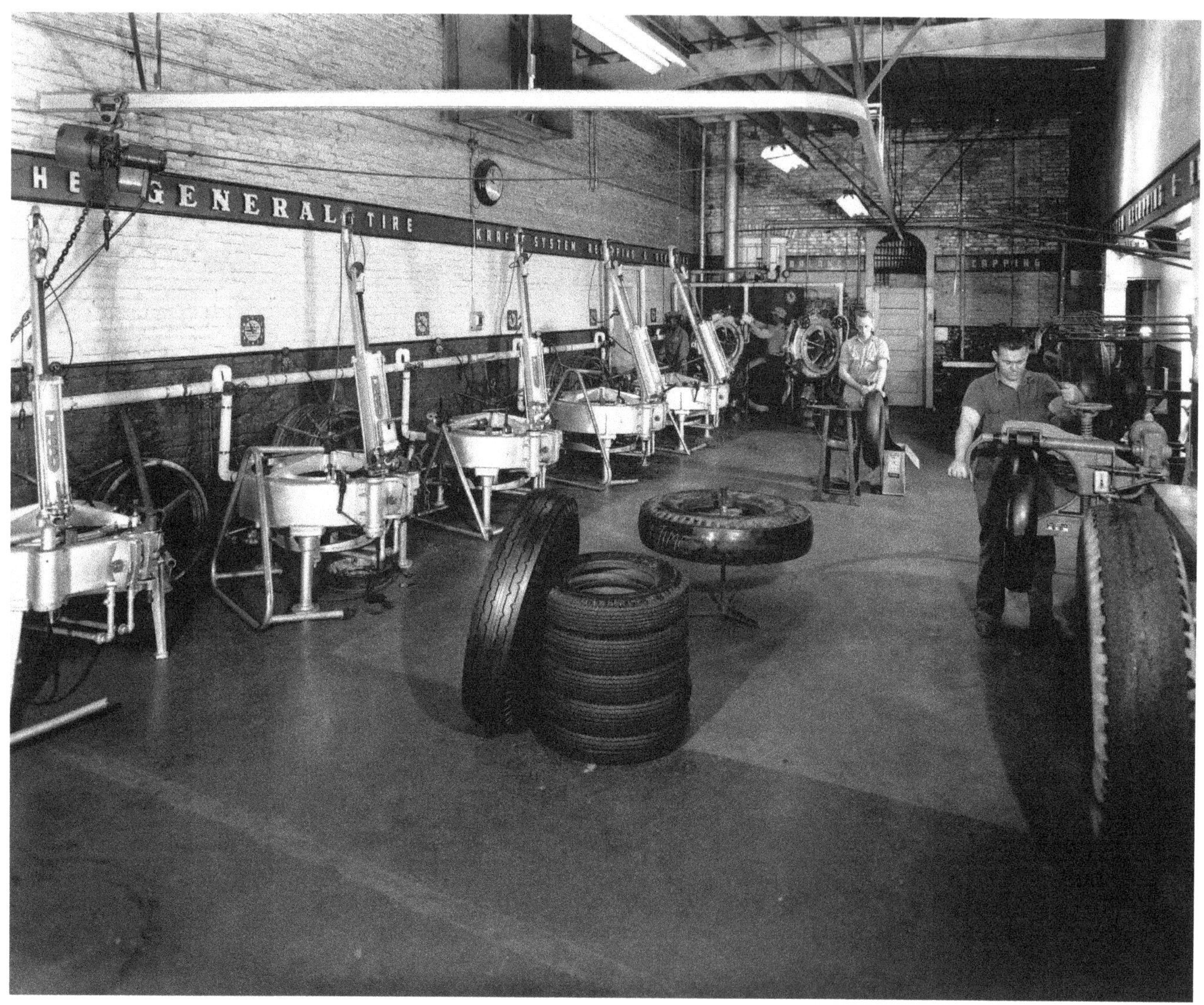

General brand tires were featured at Tampa's Pioneer Tire Company. Shown here on November 1, 1950, are employees working in its recapping and repair department. The company was owned by banker William Howard Frankland, who also owned about 20 acres along Old Tampa Bay. During this decade, as a member of the state road board, he pushed for the construction of a bridge from there to Pinellas County. The bridge, which was named for him, now carries Interstate 275 across the water.

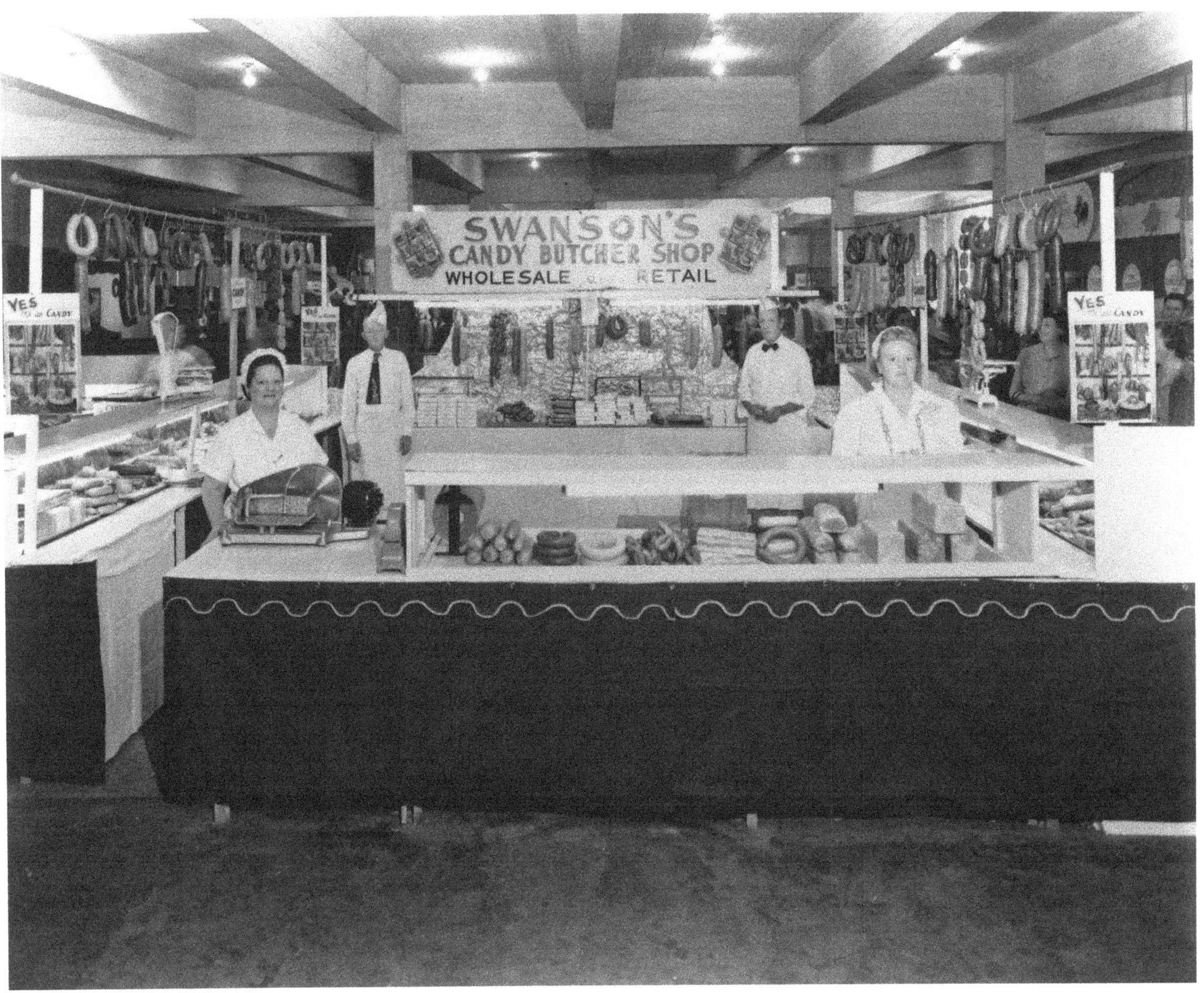

In 1905, a major fair was held in Tampa and took up an exhibition building, stock stalls, and a stadium. It became known as the Mid-Winter Festival, and then the Florida State Fair. Except for the World War II years, the fair was held every year, initially on a crowded site close to the campus of the University of Tampa. At the one held in 1950, Swanson's Candy Butcher Shop was one of many retailers to host displays of its products.

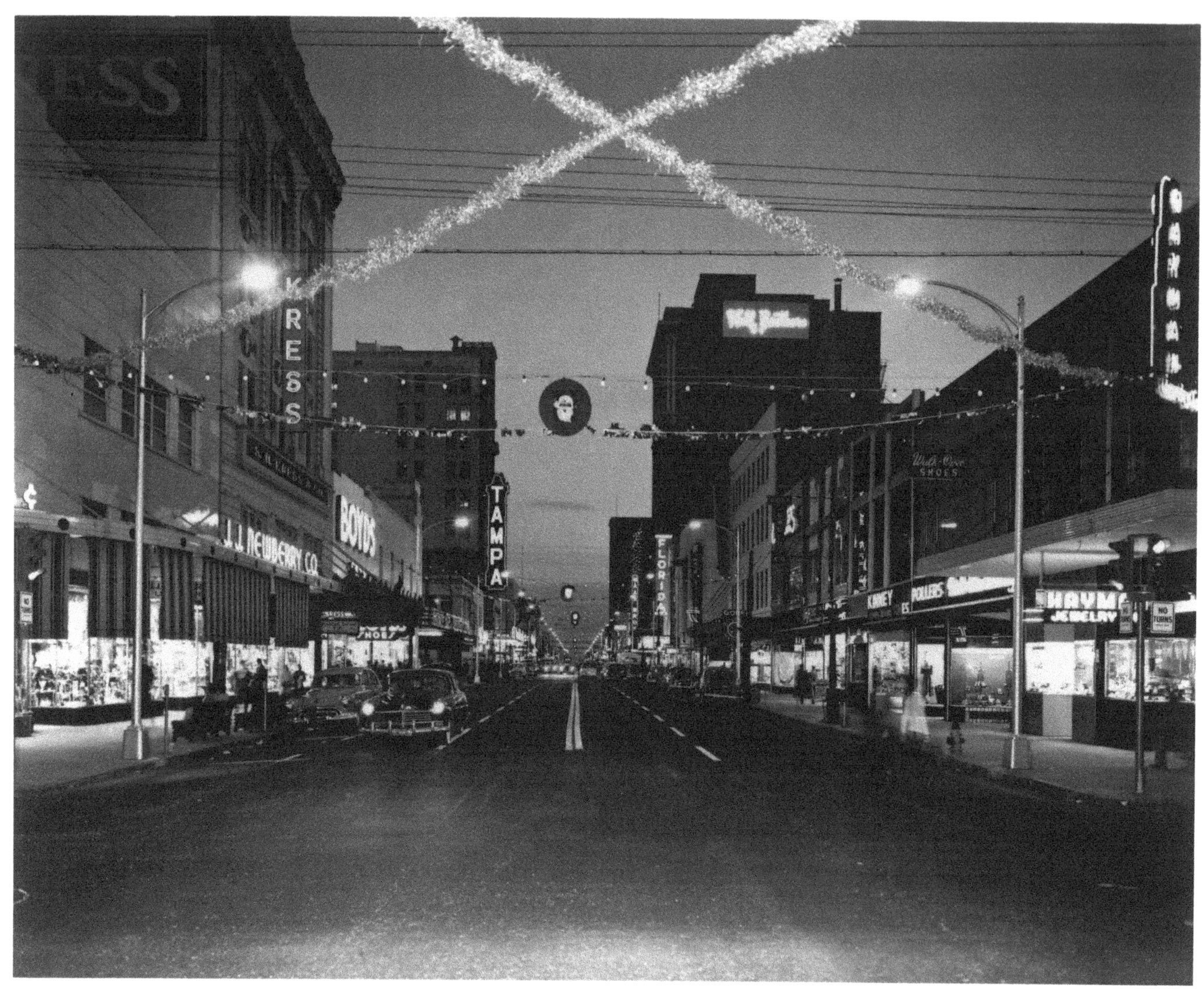

Just south of the intersection with Cass Street, these Christmas lights and decorations were strung across Franklin Street. The first building on the left was J. J. Newberry's, a five and dime store of a chain founded in Pennsylvania in 1911 by John Josiah Newberry. When he died in 1954, the chain had 475 stores and was still growing. In the 1970s, Newberry's was sold to Rapid-American Corporation, which merged with another of its subsidiaries, McCrory's. The last J. J. Newbery's store closed in 2001.

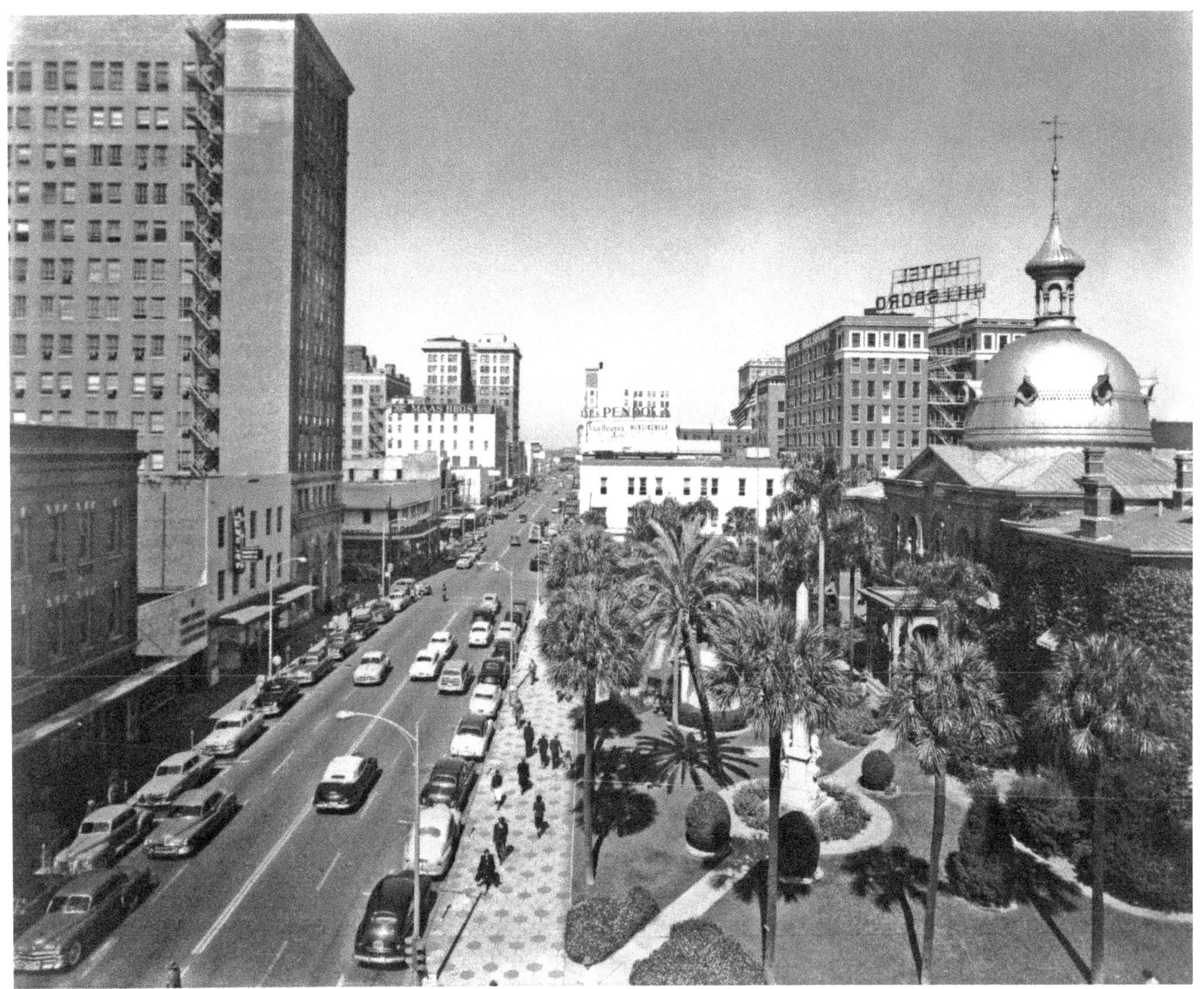

In the 400 block of Franklin Street, the domed Hillsborough County Courthouse was constructed in 1891–92 and served the area's judicial needs until it was replaced in the early 1950s by a much more modern building. The older structure's onion-shaped dome resembled those of the Tampa Bay Hotel located across the Hillsborough River.

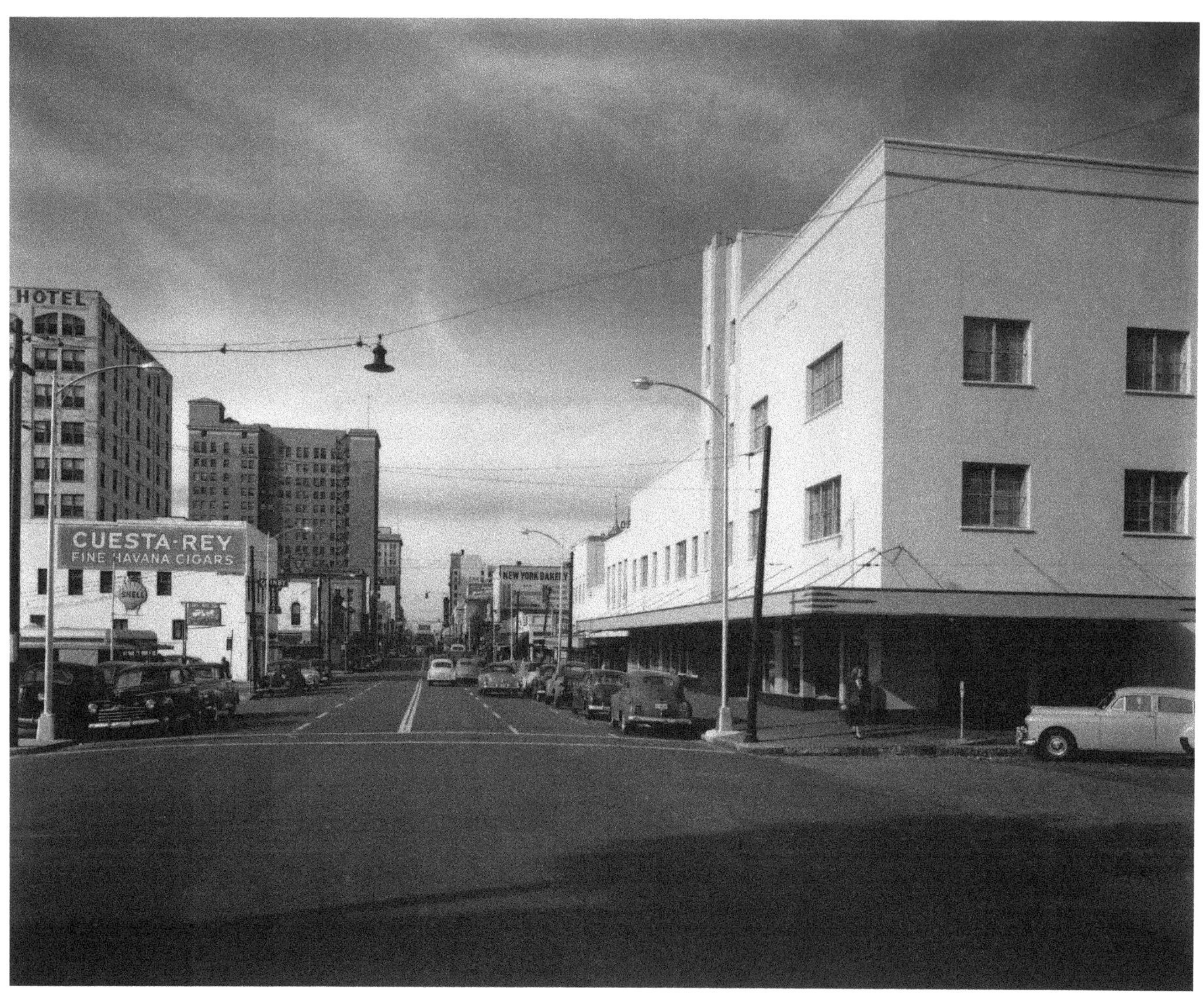

On the left, just north of the intersection of Franklin and Washington Streets, is an advertisement for a cigar manufacturer. Cuesta-Rey and Company was founded in 1895 by Angel L. Cuesta, Sr., and Pergrino Rey. The company was located in a cigar factory with an unusual octagonal tower which still stands at 900 North Howard Avenue in West Tampa. In 1959, the Cuesta-Rey brand was sold to M&N Cigar Manufacturers and the company moved out of the factory.

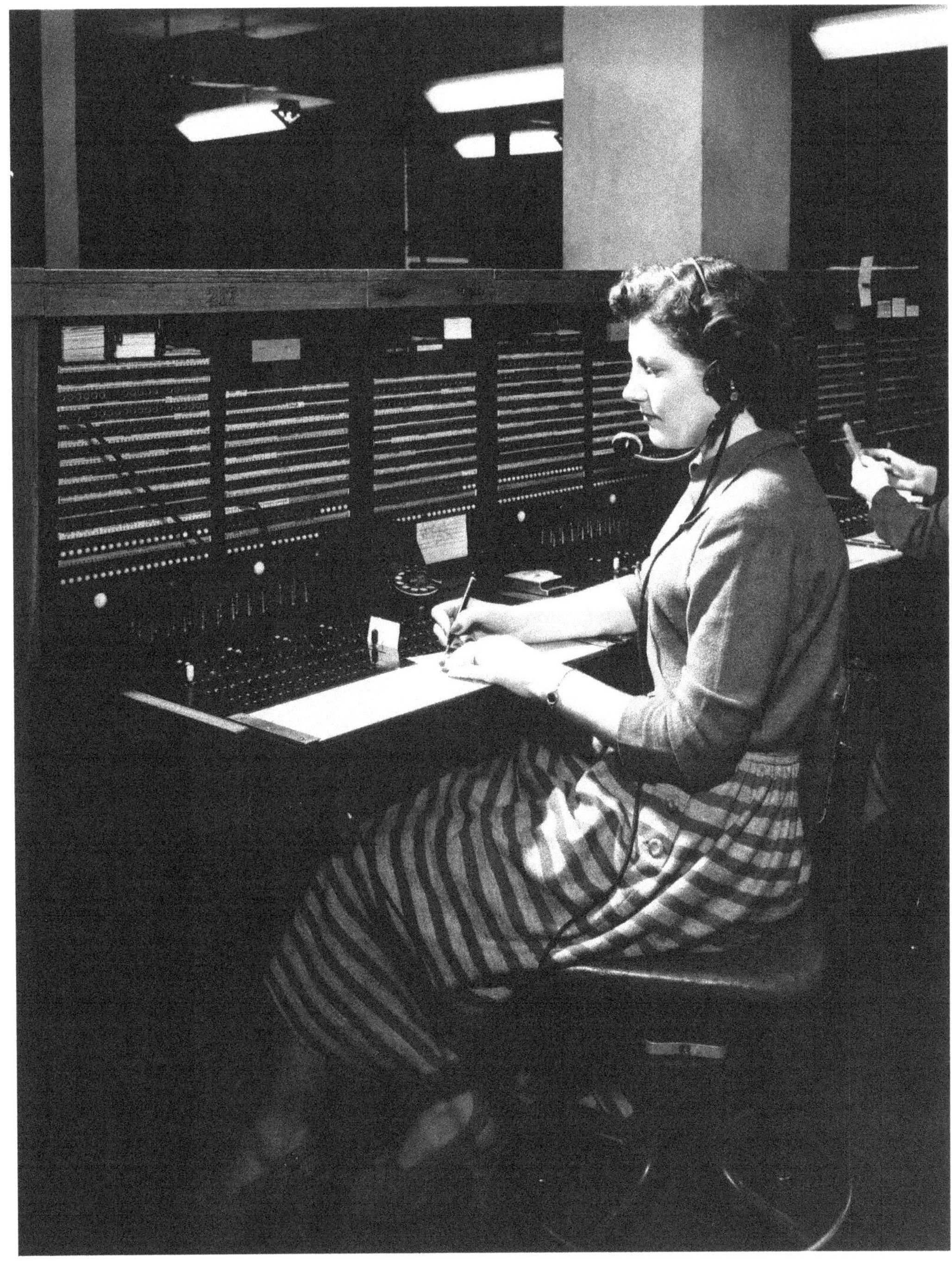

This operator in 1951 worked for the Peninsular Telephone Company which had opened in the Roberts Building in 1901. It was founded by William G. Brorein of Ohio, who had financial backing from his friends in that state, which allowed him to initially obtain a 30-year franchise for his company. He also served as the president of the Florida State Telephone Association and lobbied the legislature for regulation of services and rates.

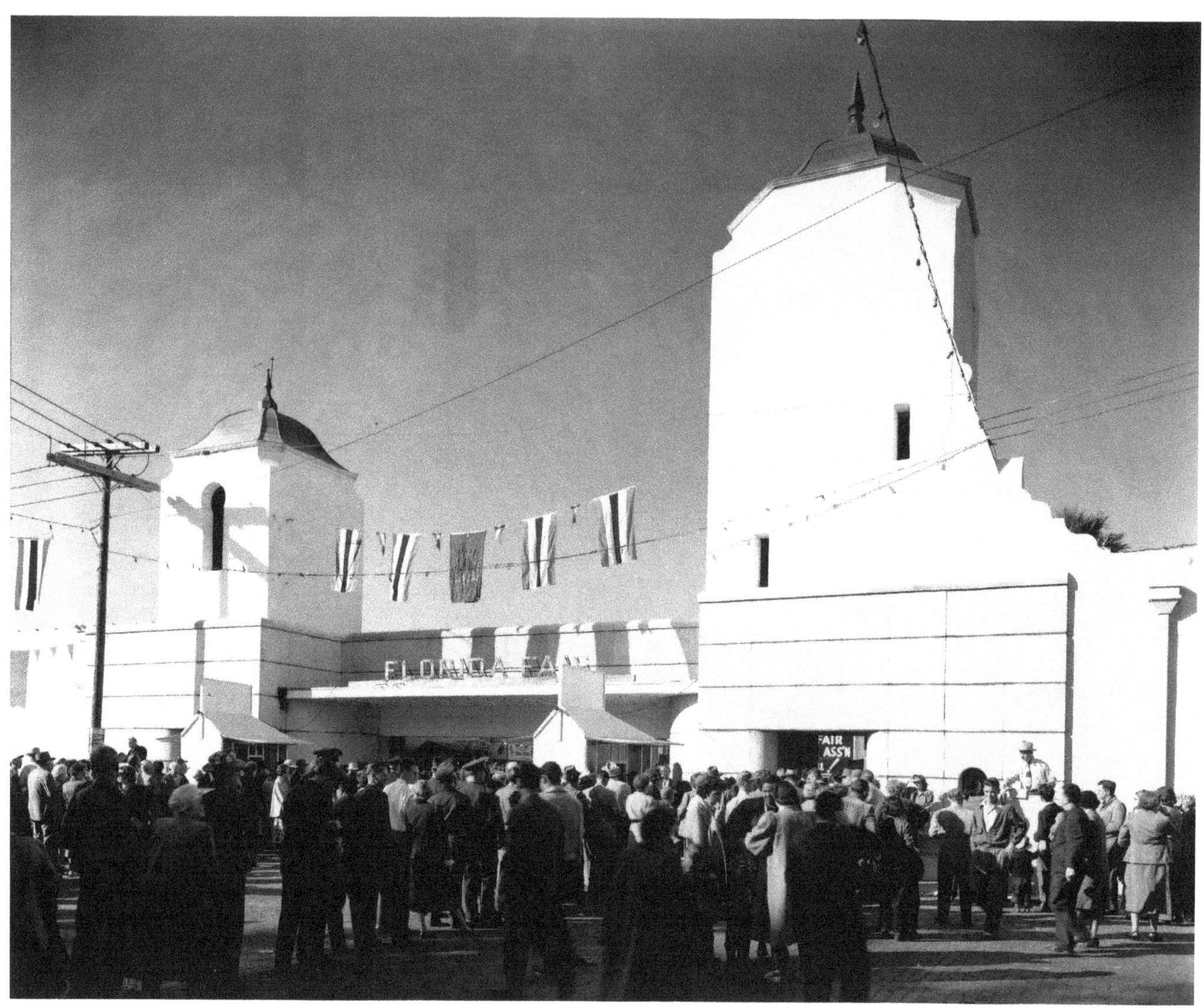

This was part of the crowd entering the 1951 Florida State Fair, held near the former Tampa Bay Hotel. A high stuccoed wall surrounded the area, and it still remains even though the fair moved away in 1973 to a larger site along Interstate 4. When it did, the field became the property of the University of Tampa, which uses it as a sports venue.

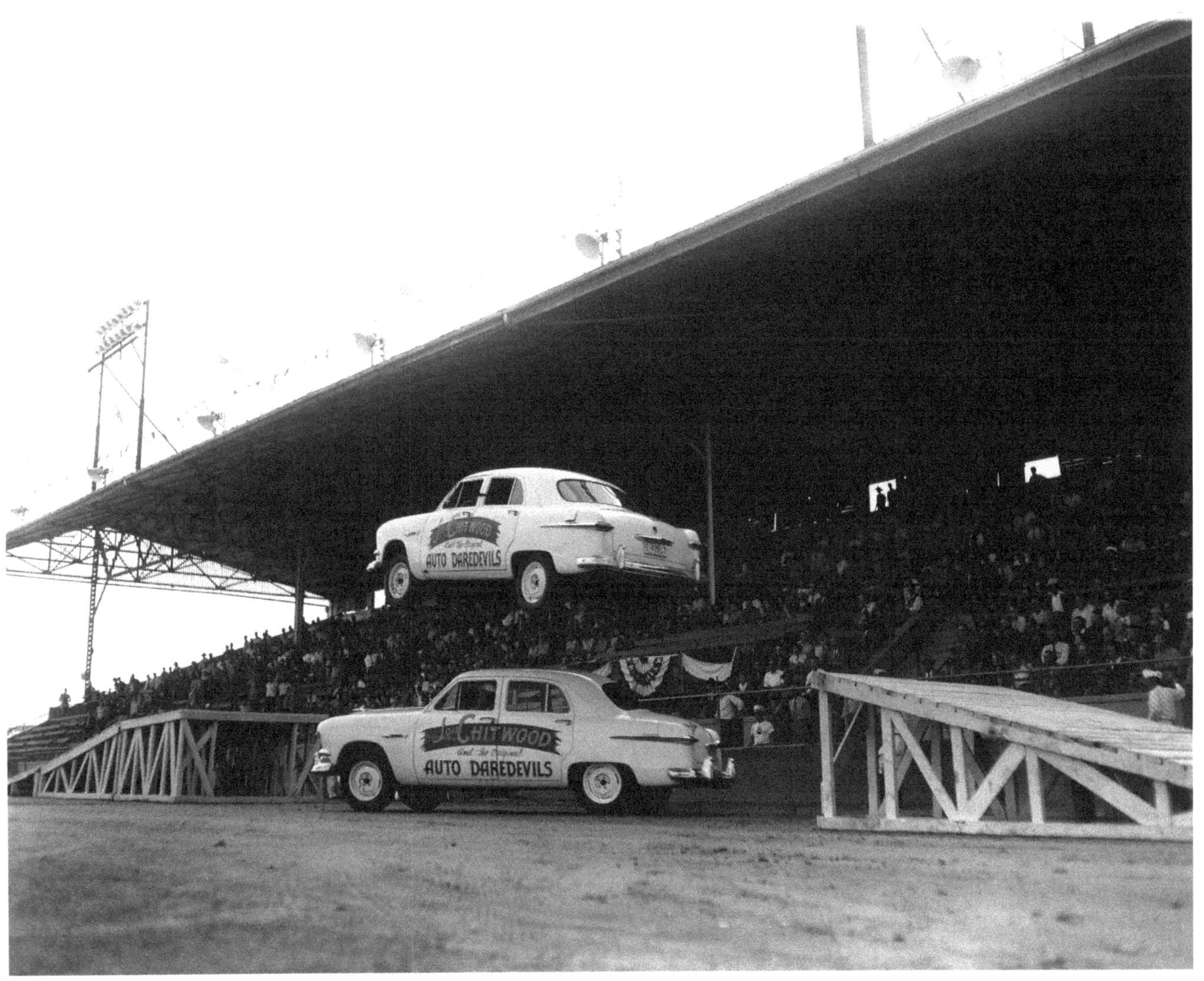

A perennial favorite show at the Florida State Fair was the Joie Chitwood Auto Daredevils stunt driving team. George Rice "Joie" Chitwood was a Tampa native who finished fifth three times in seven runnings of the Indianapolis 500 race between 1940 and 1950. When his stunt driving show became successful, he gave up racing and for 40 years toured the country, putting on death-defying performances.

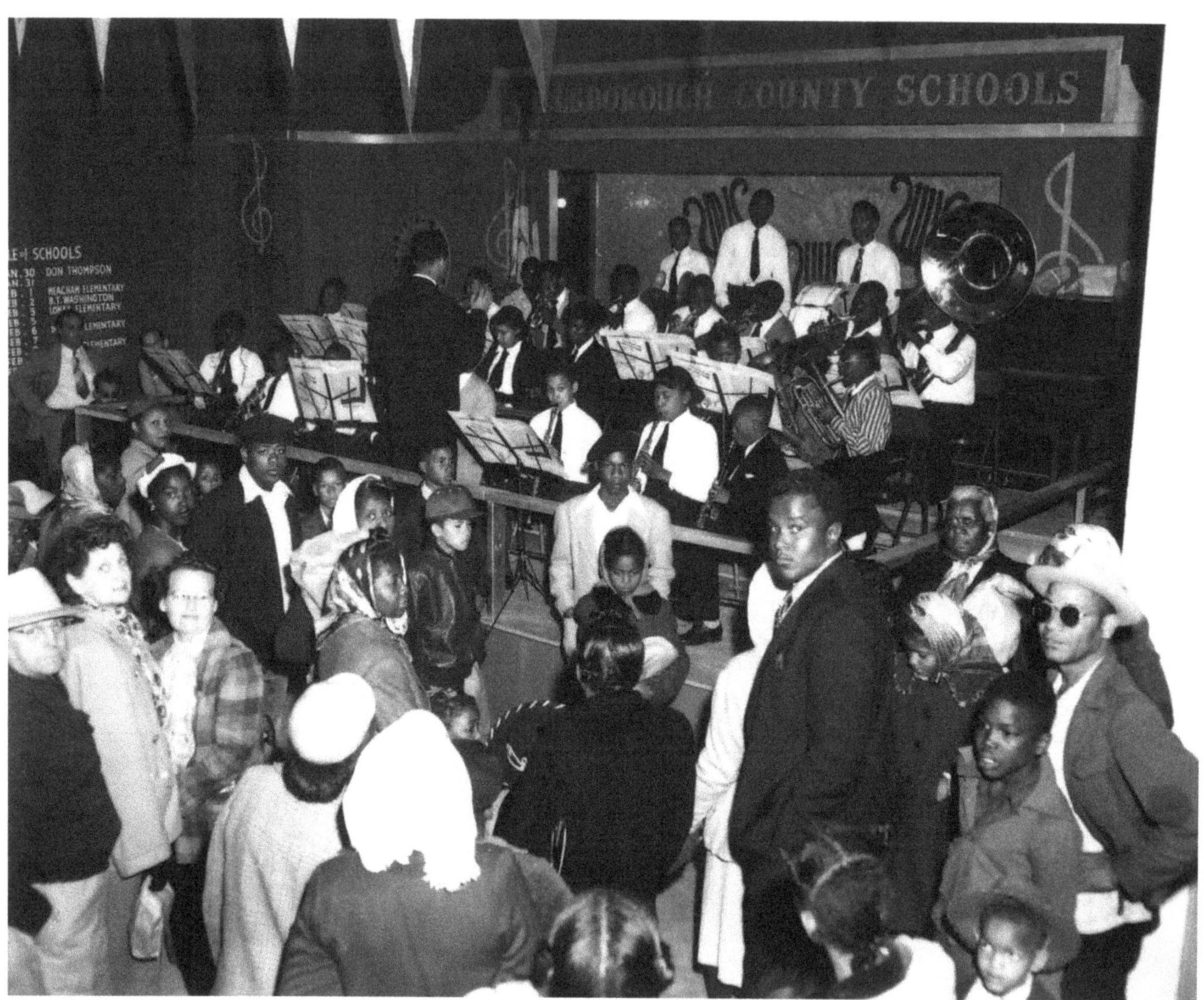

Musical performances at the 1951 Florida State Fair drew crowds. Here, a student band from one of the county's schools entertained the audience. They were likely from George S. Middleton High School, the school for black students founded in 1934–35. A second black high school, Howard W. Blake High School, opened in 1956.

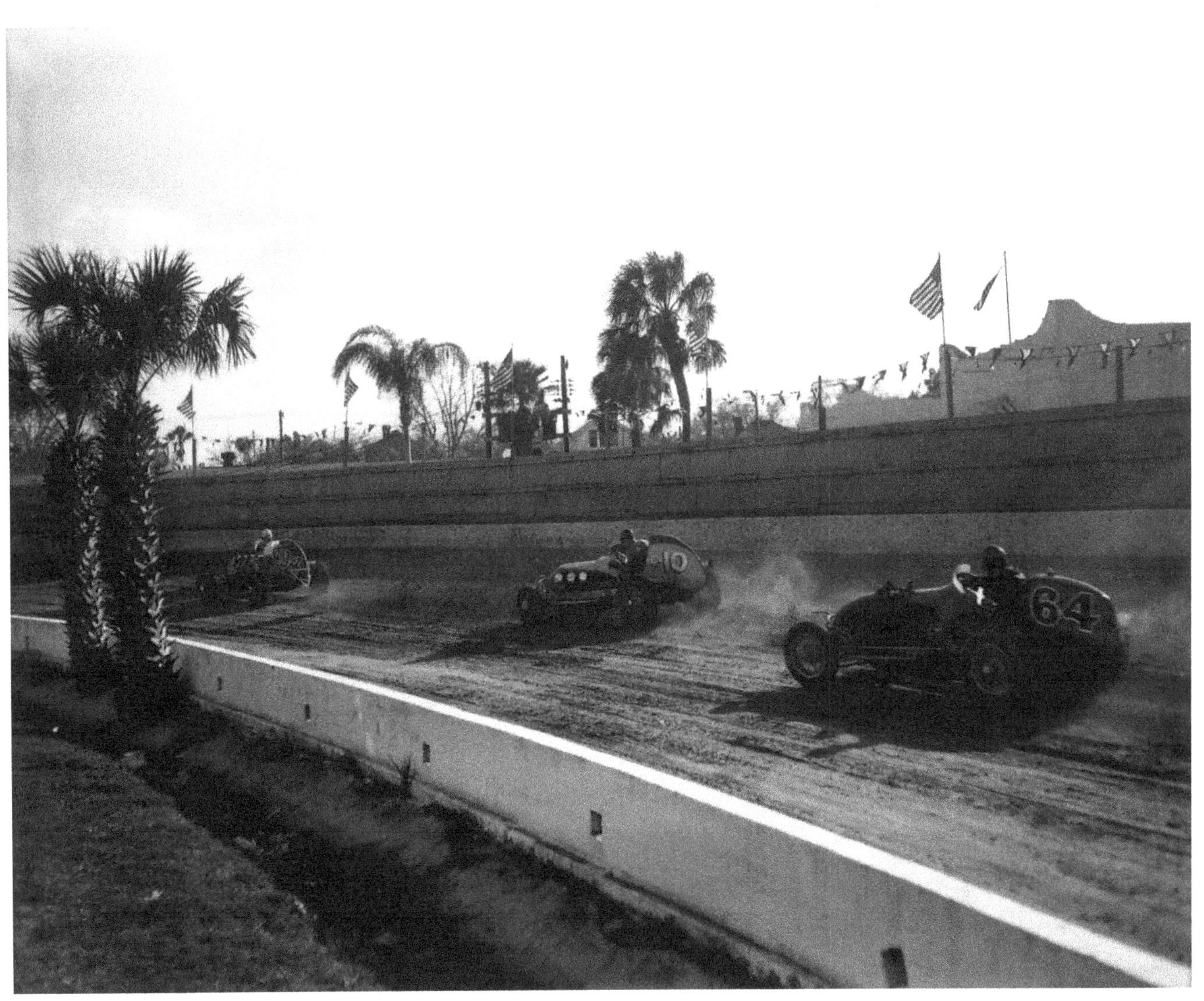

The grandstand at the Florida State Fairgrounds provided a good view of auto races. The fairgrounds were limited by the small amount of available land, so the racetrack was a short oval. That afforded the spectators a close view of entire races.

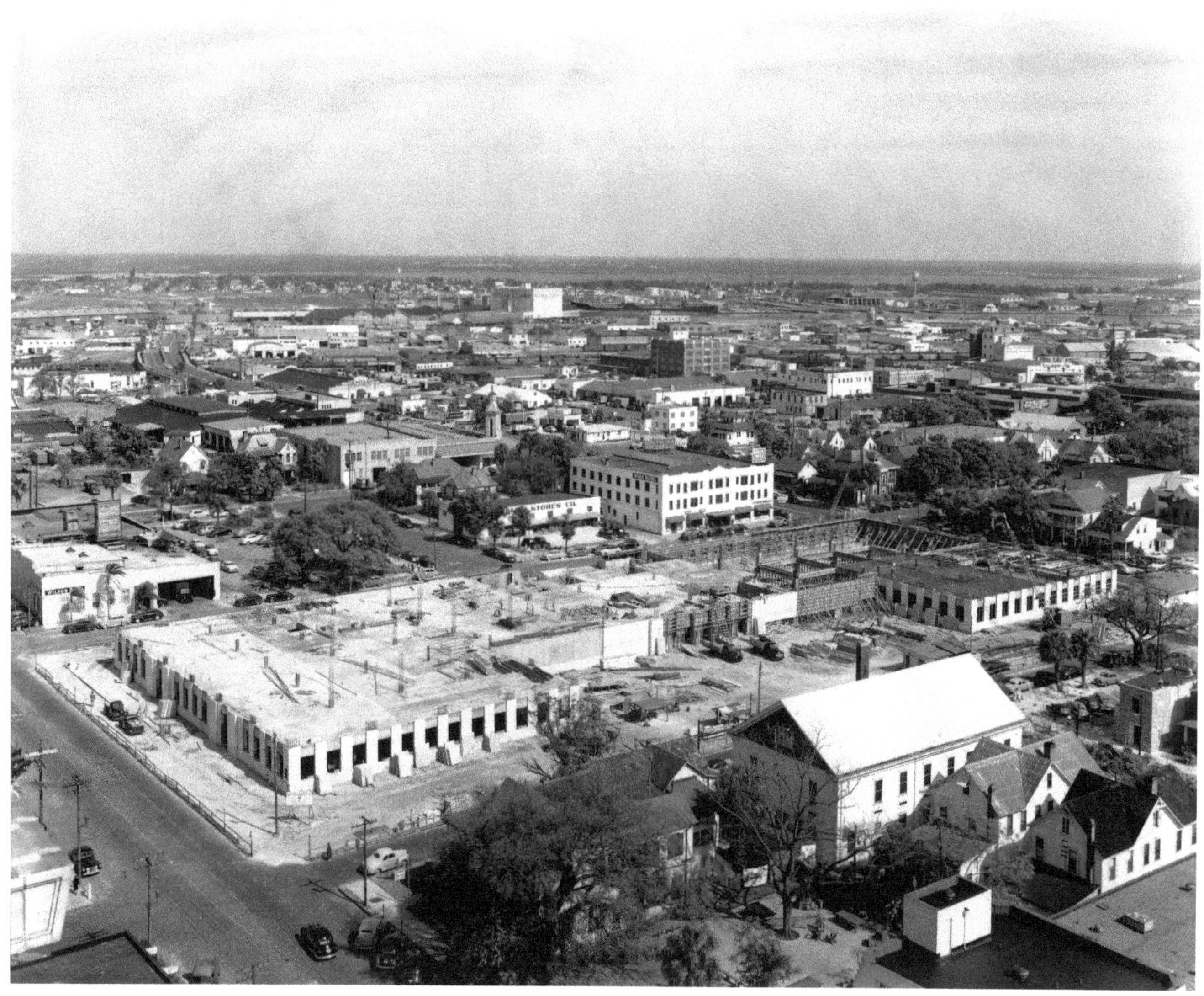

Shown here in March 1951 is the early phase of construction of the new facility, which opened in 1952 and served as the Hillsborough County Courthouse for 51 years. Behind it, the three-story building near the center of the photo is the Knox Hotel, which was later torn down to make room for the construction of a courthouse annex.

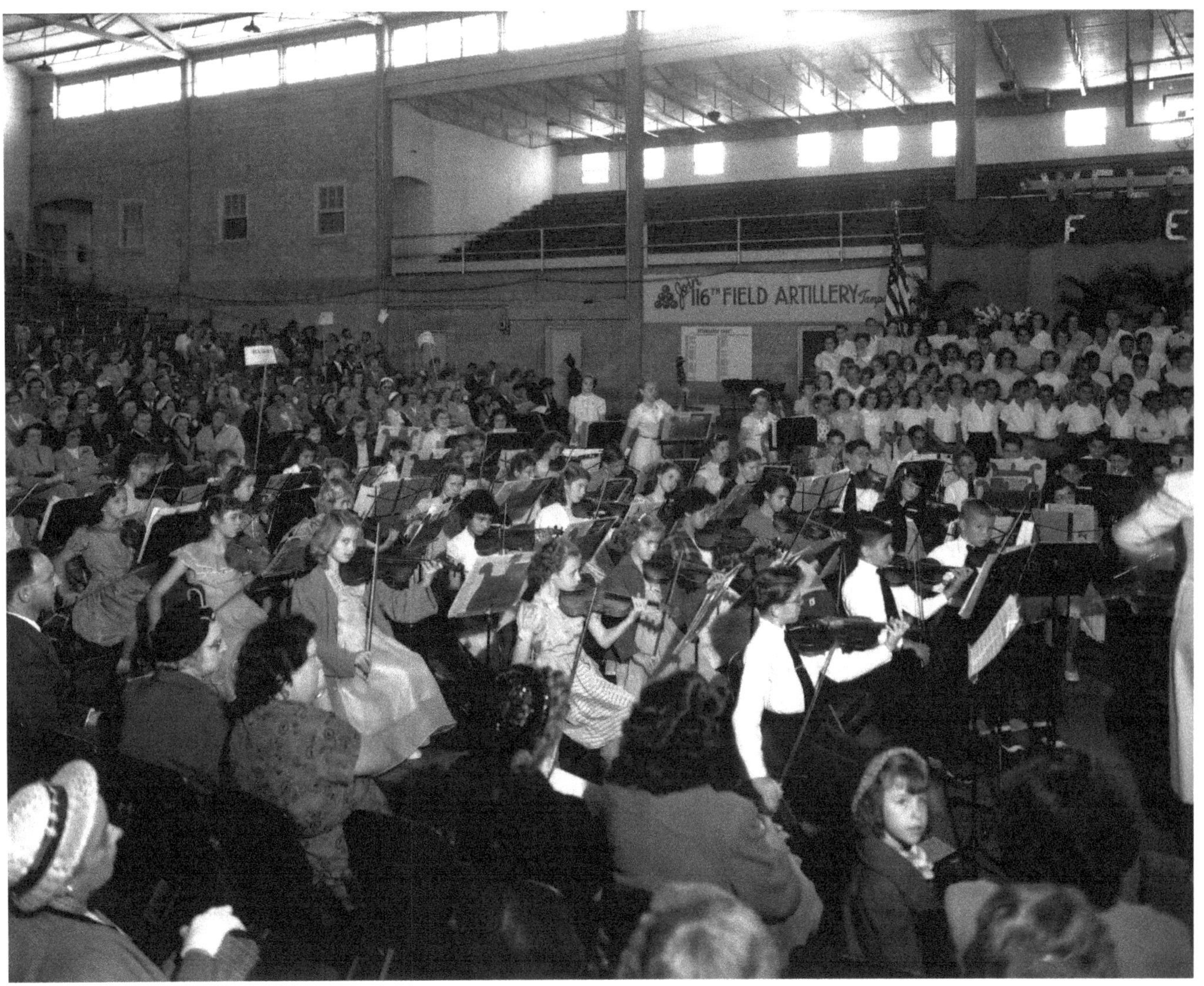

The large Fort Homer W. Hesterly Armory hosted this concert by a children's orchestra on March 31, 1951. The building was constructed during the Great Depression as a Works Progress Administration project as a National Guard facility, on land which in 1898 had been the campground of Theodore Roosevelt's Rough Riders and other soldiers awaiting deployment to Cuba in the Spanish-American War. The Armory was used by the National Guard until 2005, and the land has been considered for redevelopment for a luxury hotel.

At the corner of Franklin and Zack Streets stands the Citizens Bank Building. It was constructed in 1913 at a cost of $600,000 for the Citizens Bank and Trust Company, which had operated in Tampa since 1895. It was the home of the bank until it went out of business in 1929. Much later, its major tenant was Lydian Bank and Trust.

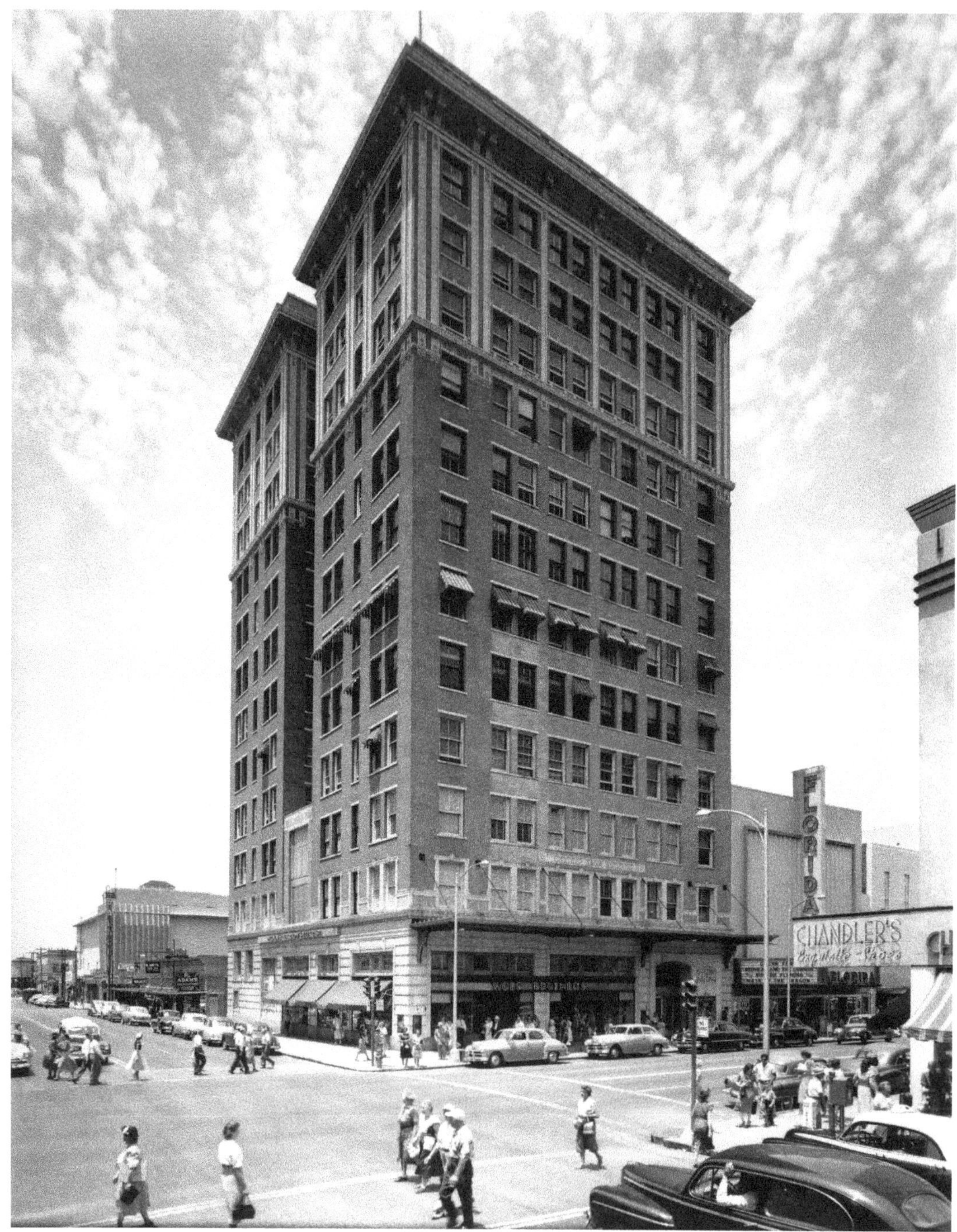

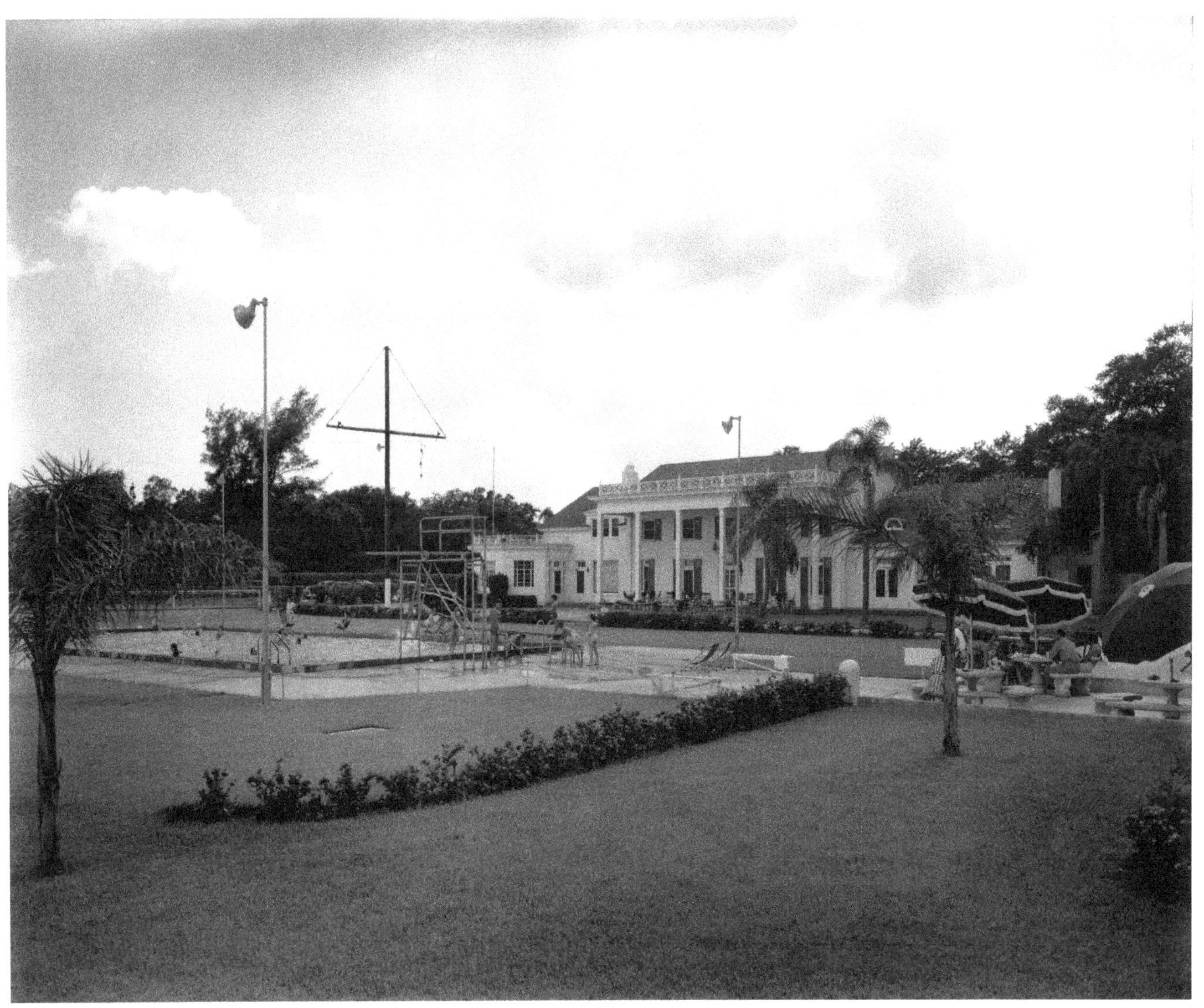

This view of the Tampa Yacht and Country Club features the swimming pool and some of the landscaping performed by the Culbreath Landscape Nursery in the mid-1950s. The club was founded in 1904 by professionals and businessmen who desired a place to socialize, sail boats, and ride horses.

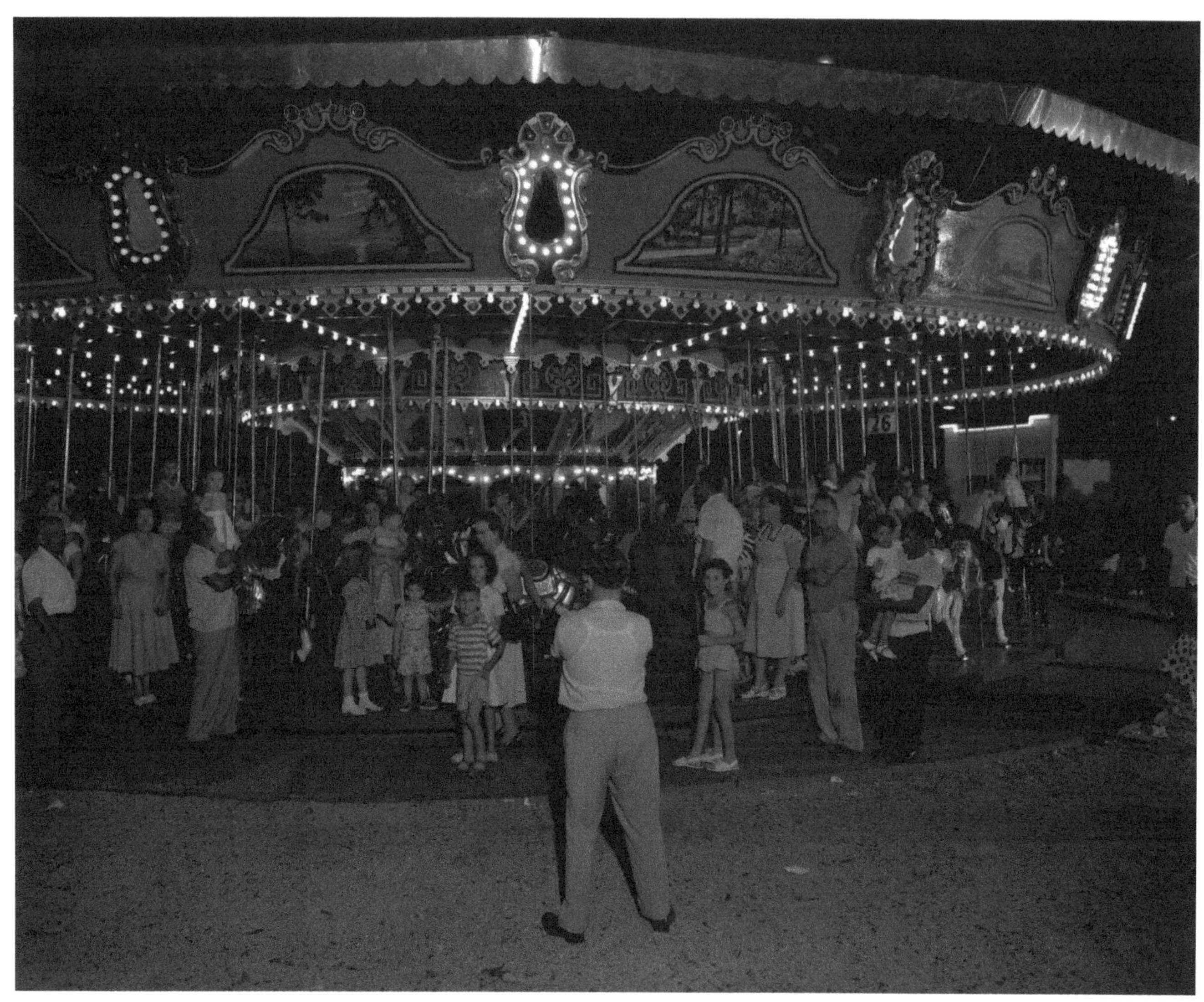

Pictured here, on August 17, 1951, are families having fun on a merry-go-round on the grounds of the Super Test Oil Company gas station. It was located across the street from today's American Victory Ship Mariners Memorial Museum (705 Channelside Drive), but in the 1950s before the street was renamed, the gas station's address was 704 13th Street.

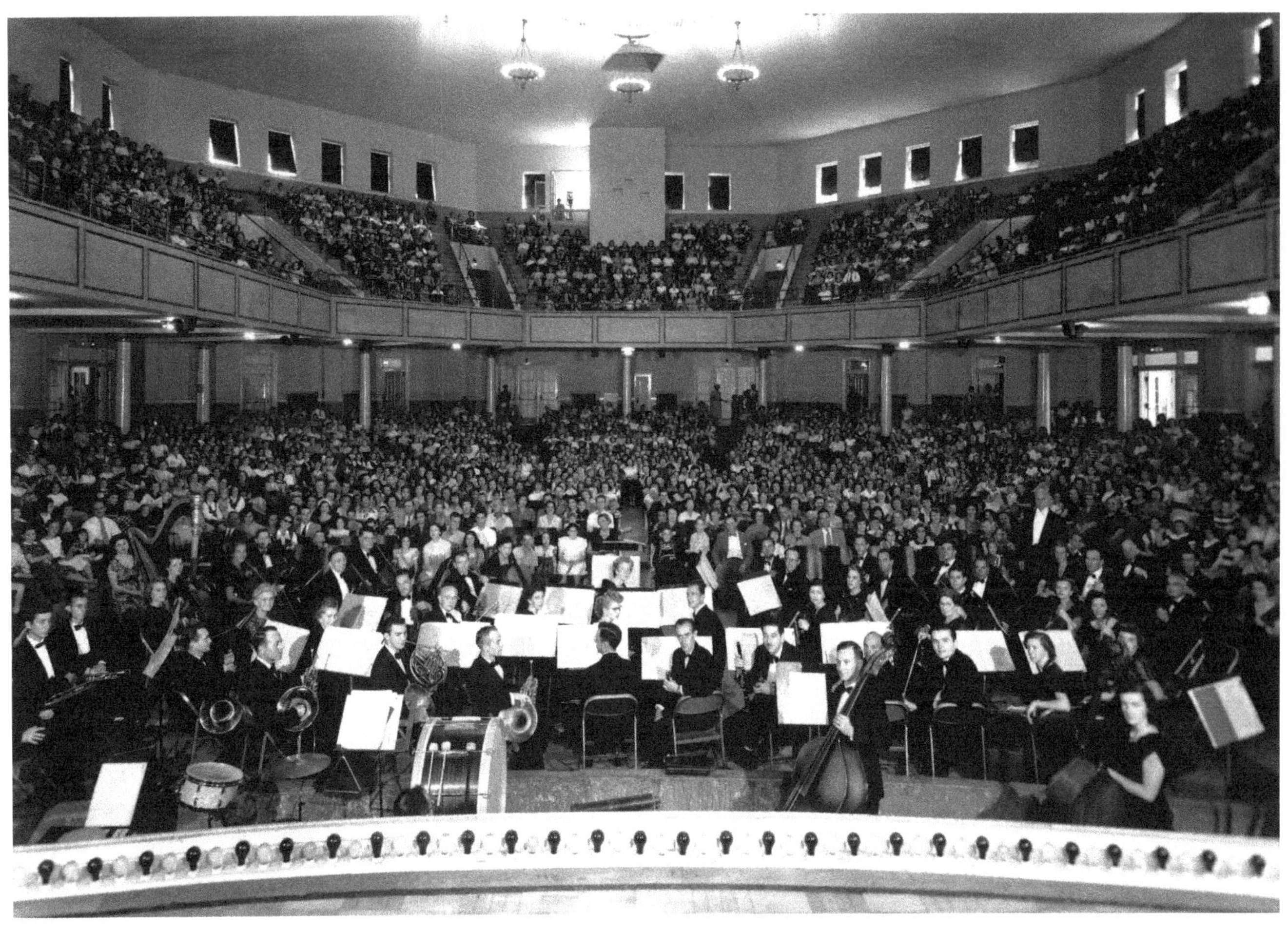

The City of Tampa Municipal Auditorium located behind the Tampa Bay Hotel, now the campus of the University of Tampa, was built in 1925–26. It was the venue for this concert by the Tampa Symphony Orchestra, held on December 8, 1951. The building was dedicated as the McKay Auditorium following the 1960 death of Donald B. McKay, the publisher of the *Tampa Times* newspaper, who served as the city's mayor during the 1910s, 1920s, and 1930s. The auditorium building is now the home of the university's John H. Sykes College of Business.

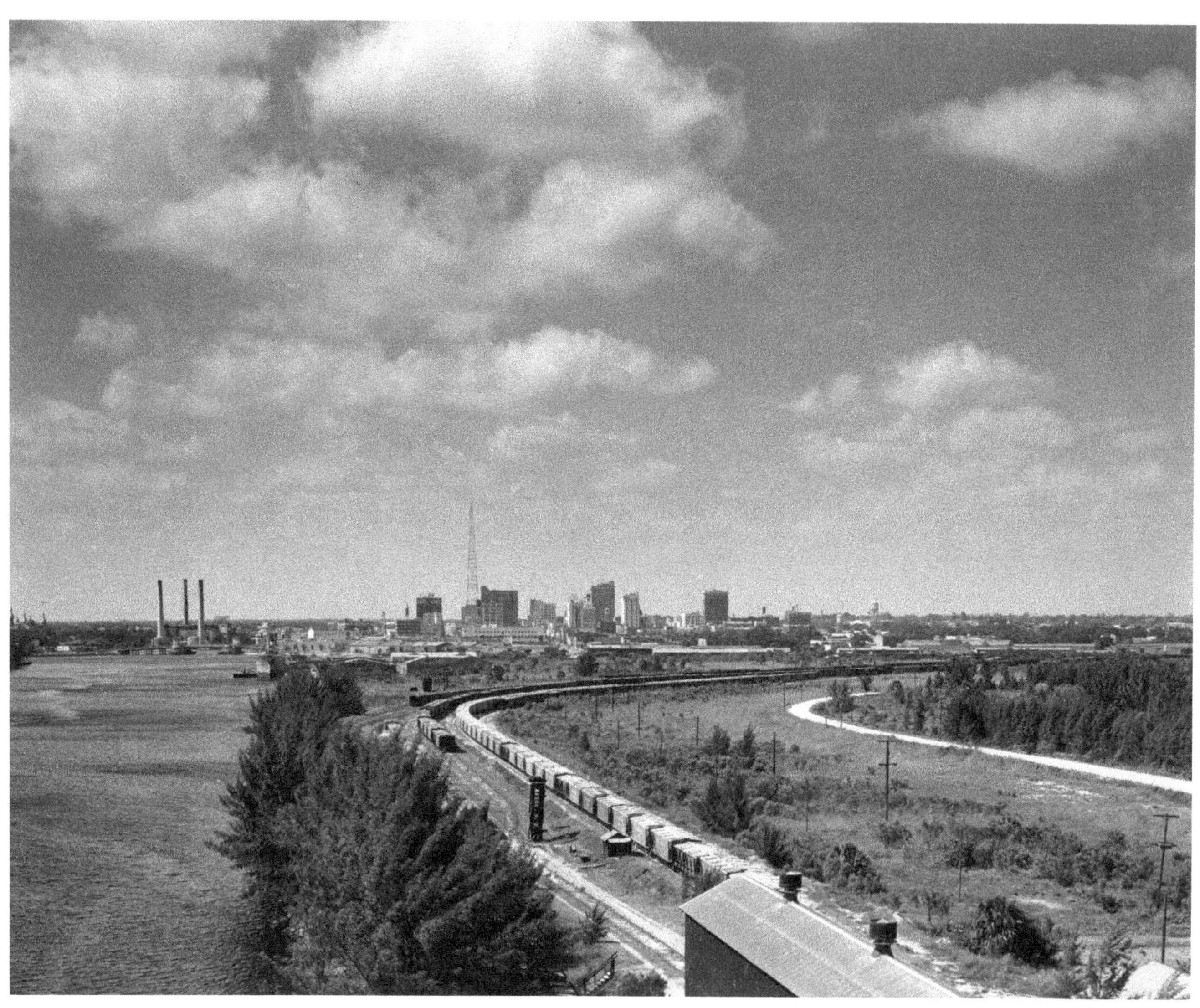

Looking north along the shore of the Seddon Channel and the railroad tracks of Seddon Island (now called Harbor Island) is the skyline of Tampa as it appeared in 1952. In the distance is the trio of smokestacks of the Tampa Electric Company power plant.

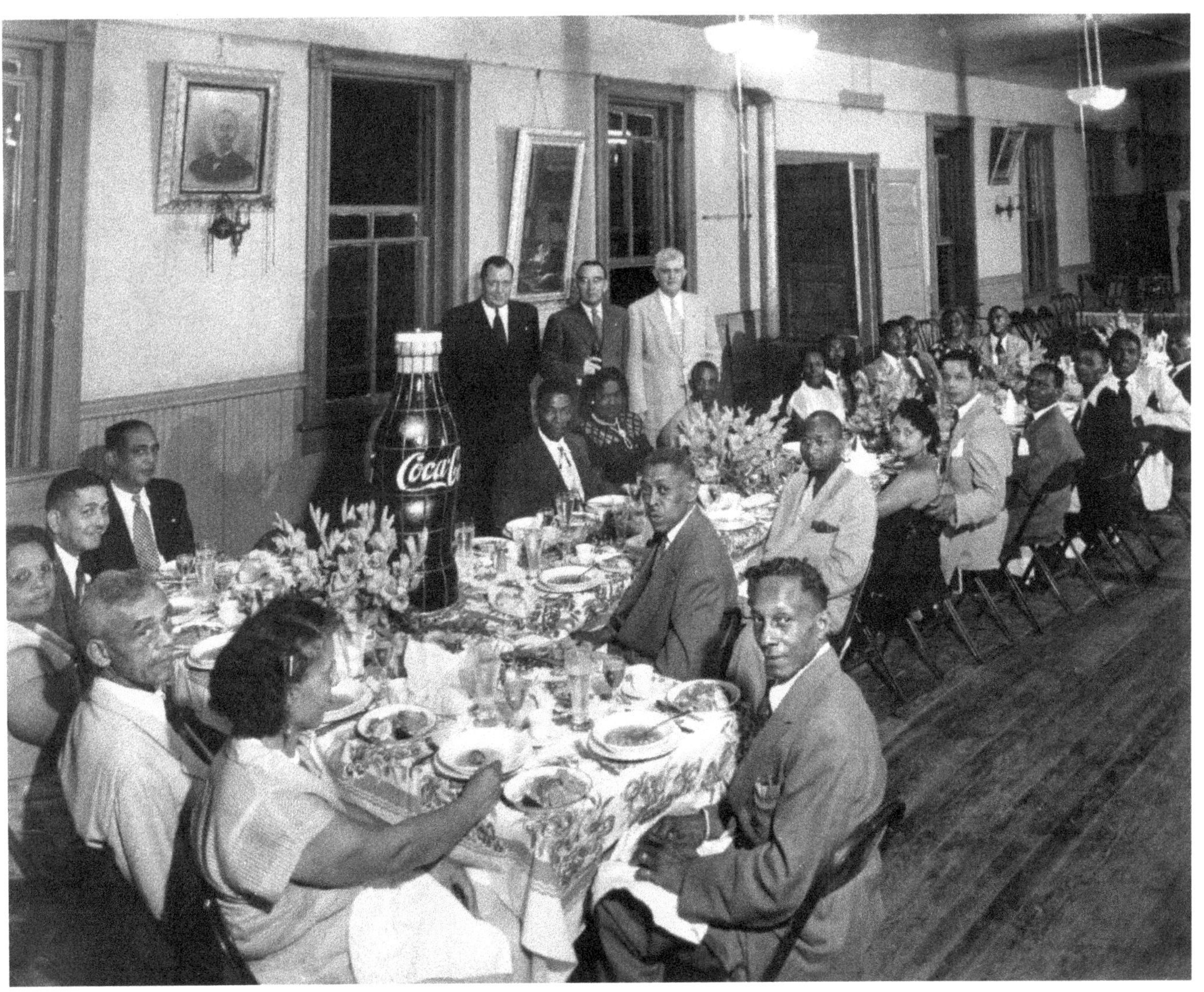

On July 3, 1952, the Tampa Coca-Cola Company held this banquet for its employees. The company, which began granting franchises in 1899, had about 400 independent bottling plants in 1952, including the one in Tampa.

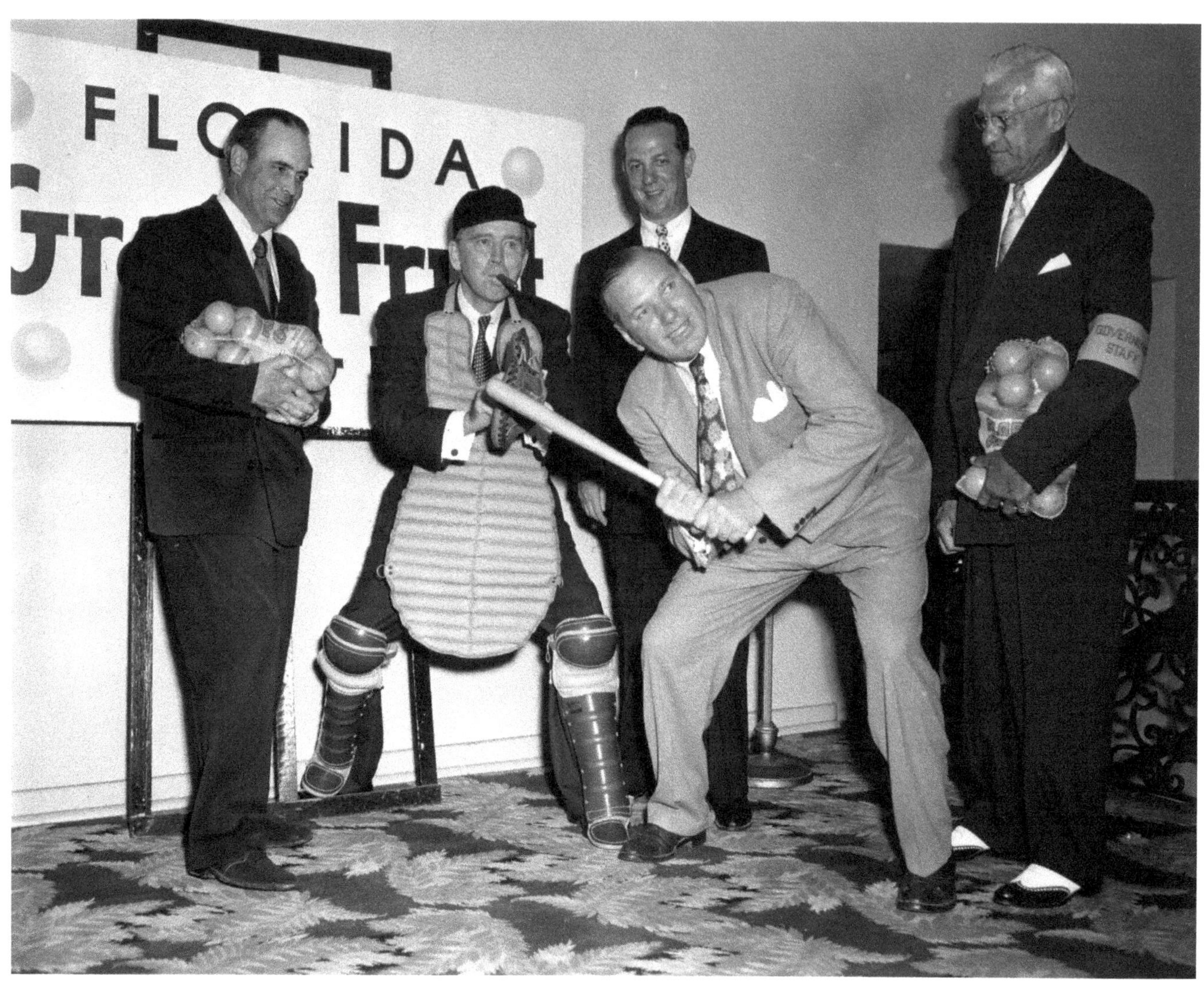

In 1952, Governor Fuller Warren hosted this baseball-themed dinner in Tampa. He is the one wearing catcher's equipment and smoking a cigar. The man at the right is American League president Will Harridge, probably thinking that it's a good thing the man with the unconventional batting stance is not a player on any of his teams.

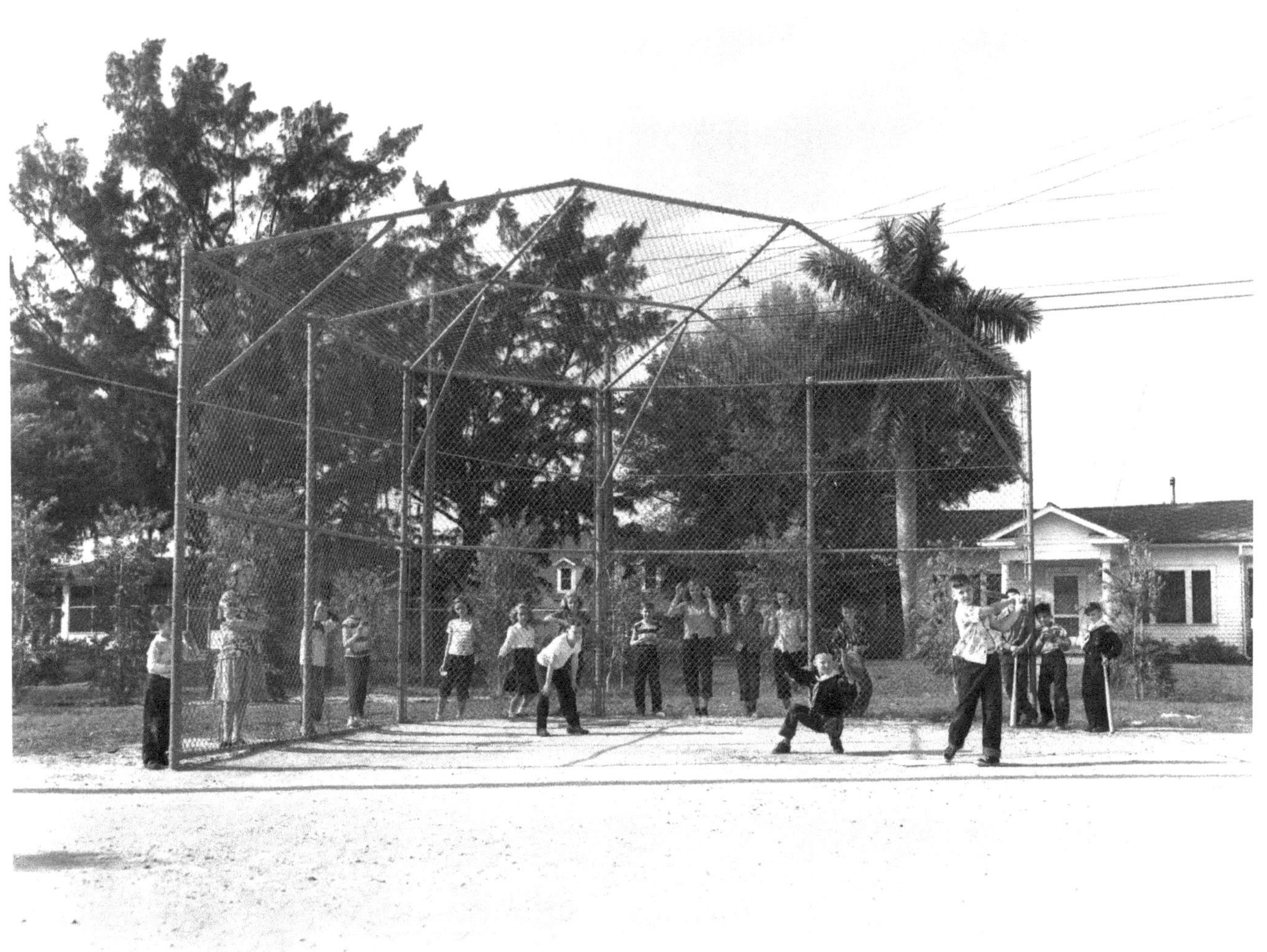

Despite the Tampa area not having a Major League team to call its own until the Tampa Bay Devil Rays began to play in 1998, baseball has always been an immensely popular pastime for local children. However, there is a major difference between today's games and those played in 1952, such as the one shown here. Back then, it was a sport for boys only and the girls were relegated to standing behind the backstop as onlookers.

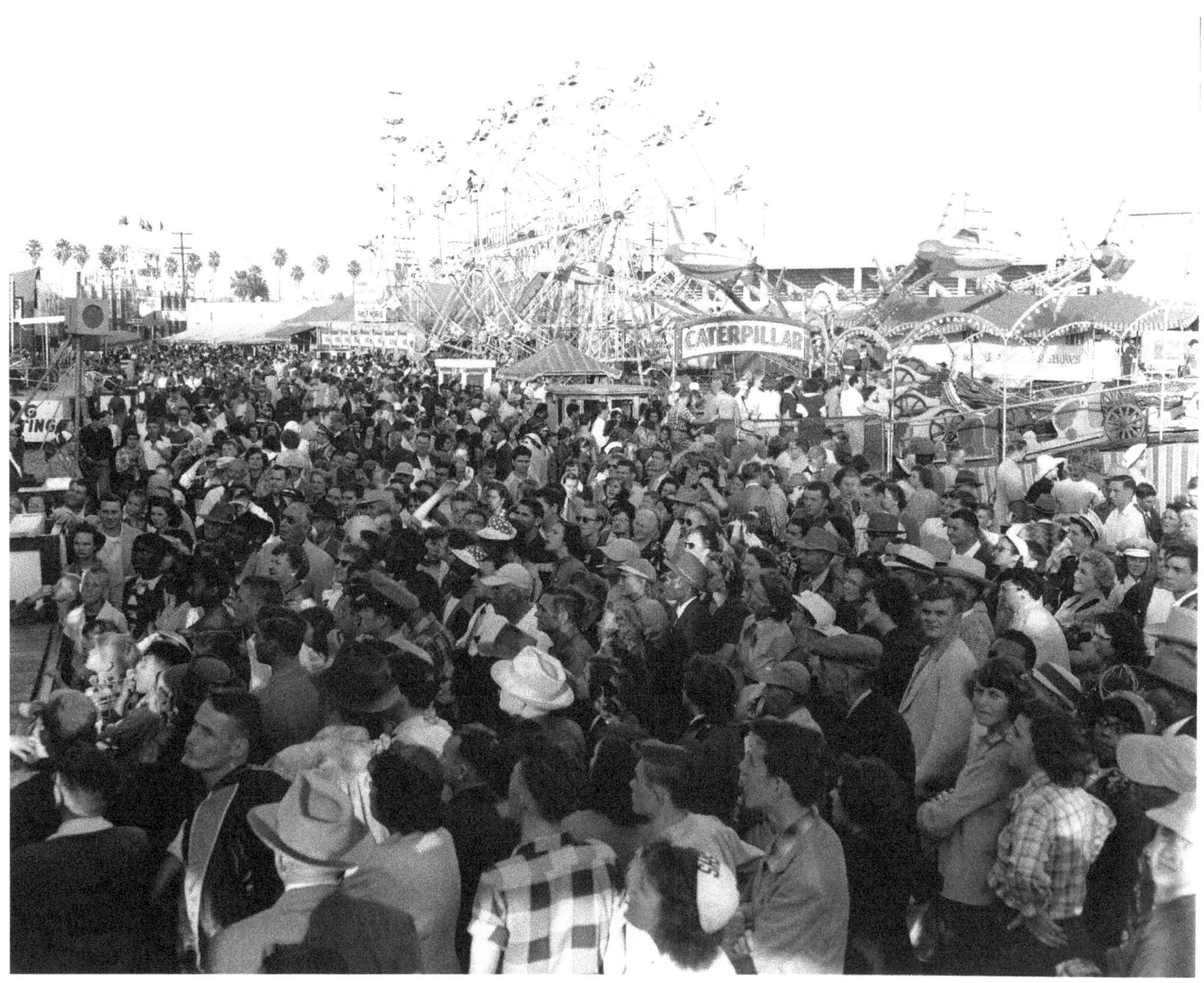

This was part of the throng at the 1952 Florida State Fair held in Tampa. The crowded fairgrounds were often on the verge of overflowing, but it would be another 23 years before the Florida legislature would create the Florida State Fair Authority, designate the event as the official Florida State Fair, and seek a larger site where it could expand.

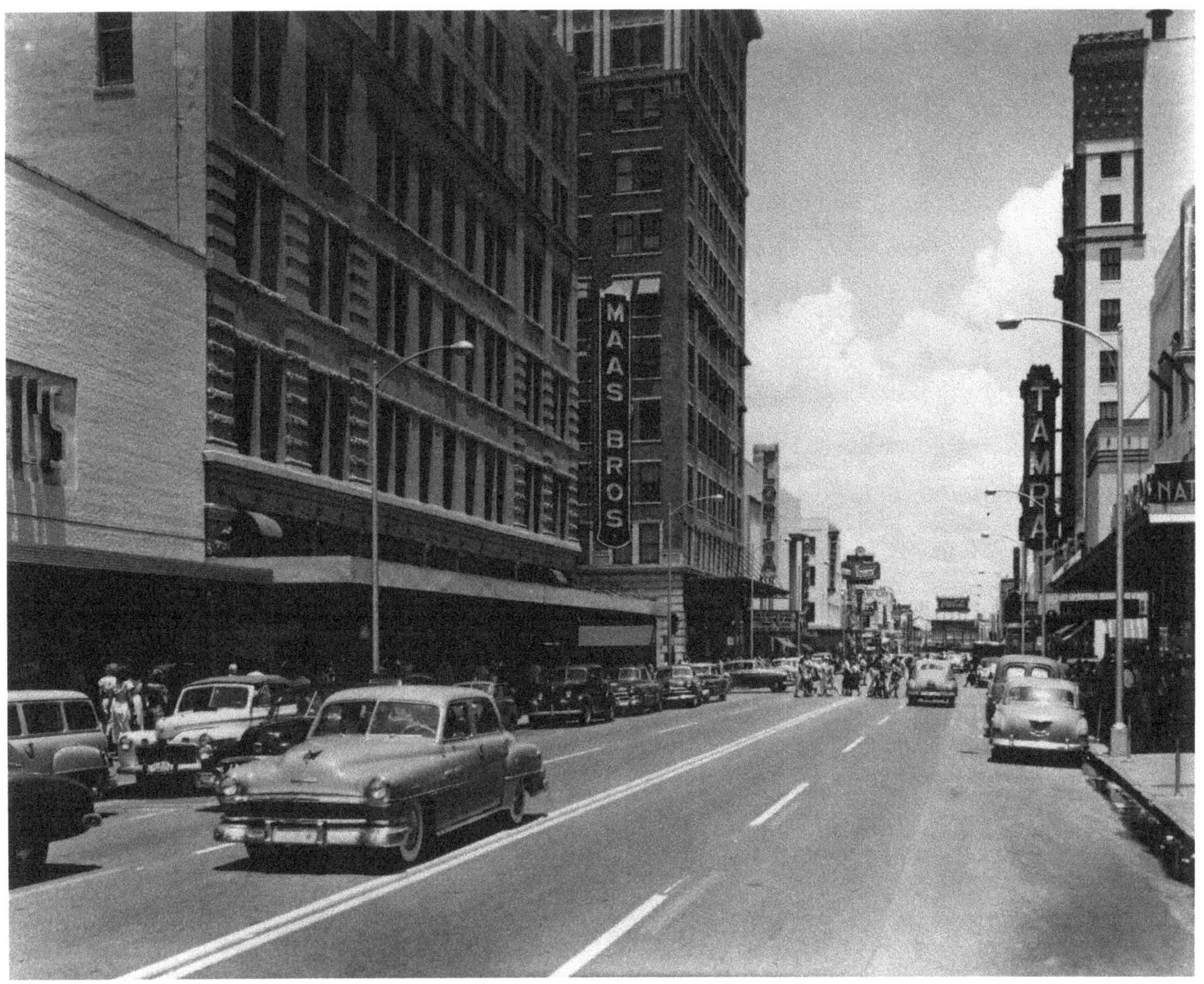

The view of Franklin Street in 1952 includes a good view of one side of the Maas Brothers Department Store. What can't be seen around the corner at 200 Twiggs Street is the former Strand Theater. It sat 850 for movies and opened in 1918, and its streetside entrance included a pair of Spanish Colonial-style towers. Its business was hurt by the 1926 opening of the fancier Tampa Theatre, and the Strand closed in the late 1940s and was absorbed into the Maas Brothers building to house its women's wear department. The entire block was torn down after 2000.

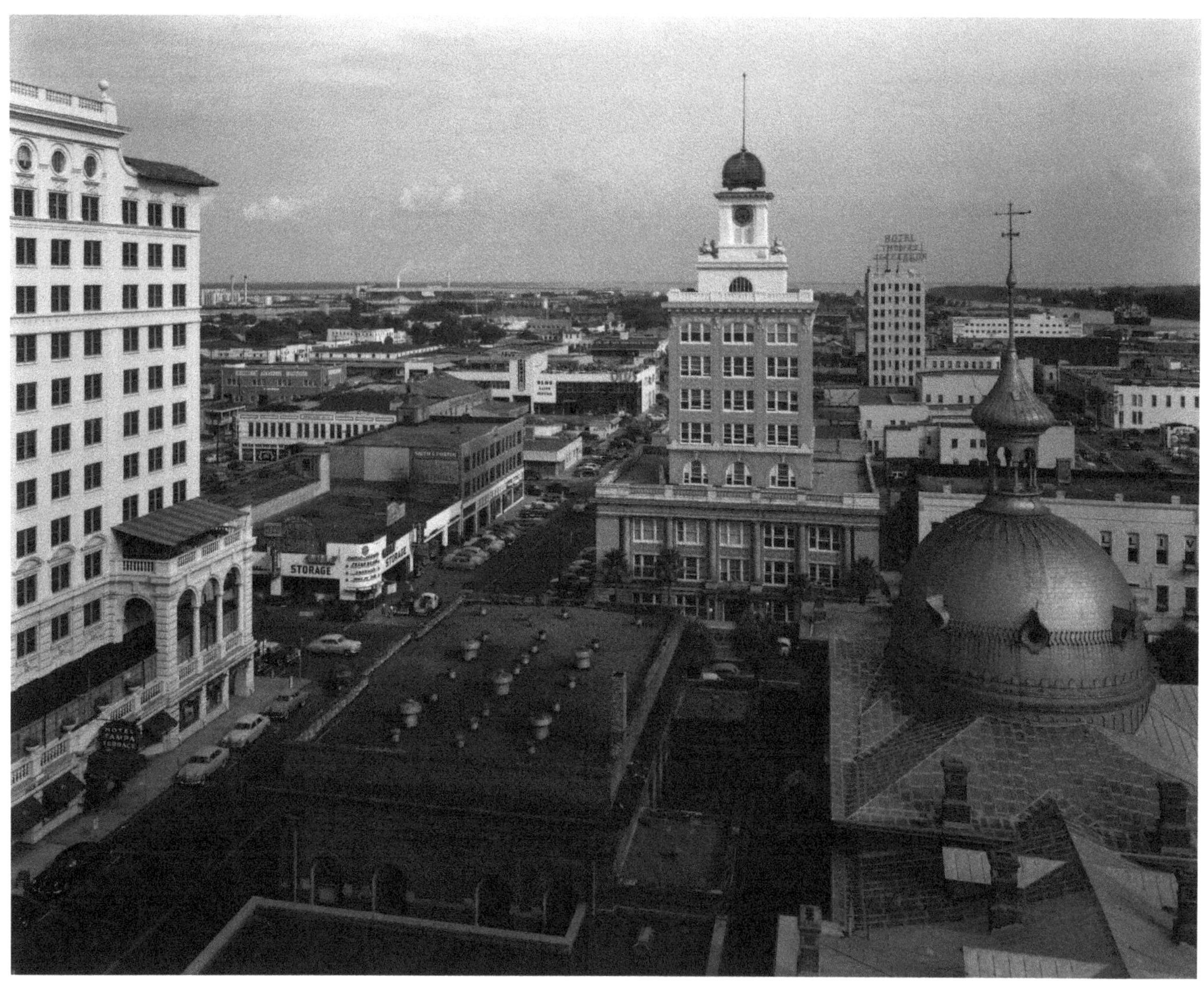

The tall building in the center of this 1952 photo is the City Hall, built in 1914–15. It was designed by B. C. Bonfoey and M. Leo Elliott with a "wedding cake" shape, Doric columns, terra-cotta details, and a balustrade encircling the main block. An elevator was installed in it in 1927. Atop the copper dome is a 27-foot-tall flagpole. The city hall was added to the National Register of Historic Places in 1974.

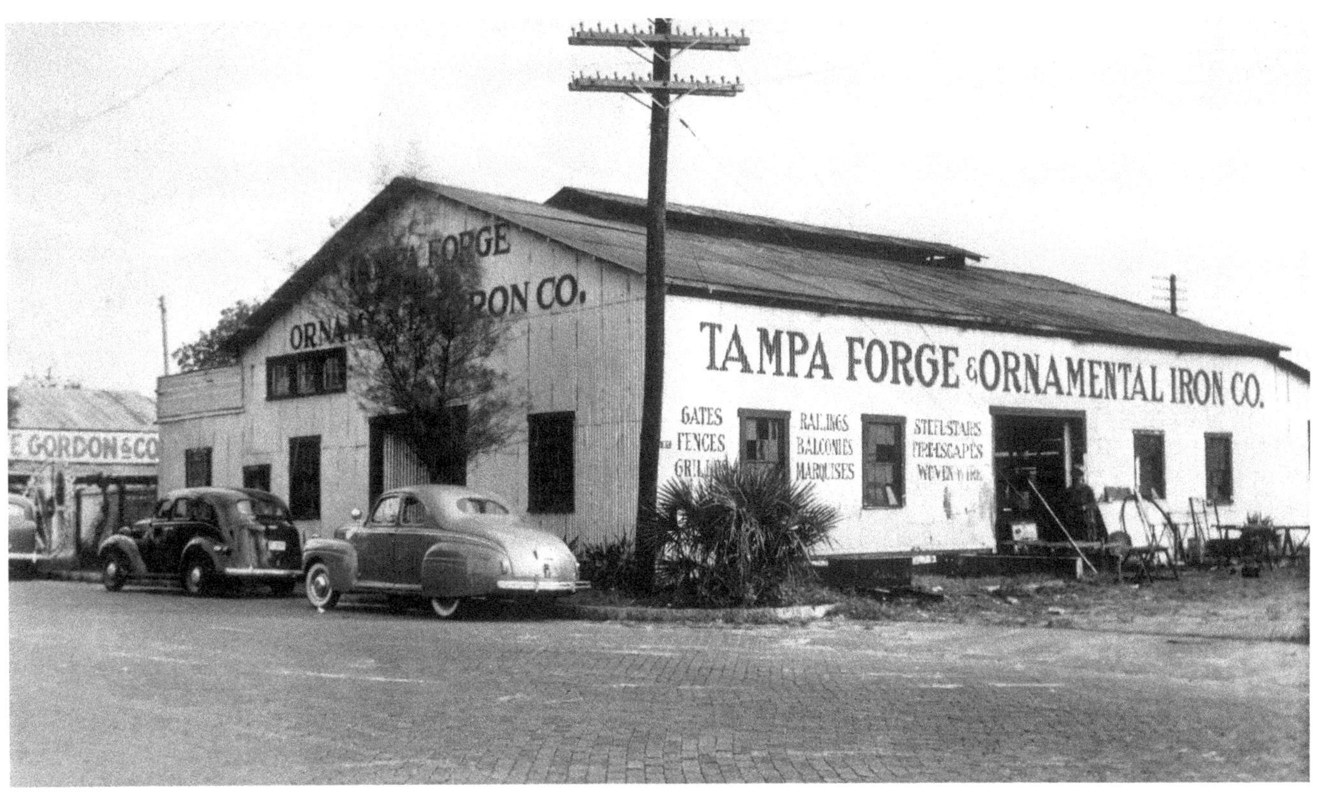

In about 1925, the shop of Tampa Forge & Ornamental Iron Works was established at the corner of 2nd Avenue and 19th Street in the southern part of Ybor City. Joseph C. Christ and Joseph G. Christ started the company.

Reporter Sol Fleischman was photographed as he interviewed a customer at Florida National Bank of Tampa's sidewalk service window. WDAE was founded in 1922 by the *Tampa Daily Times* newspaper, and erected its transmitter atop the Times Building at the corner of Franklin and Washington Streets. Fleischman had been an all-around broadcaster since the 1920s, and was best known as a sportscaster. In 1957, he left WDAE and went to work for WTVT.

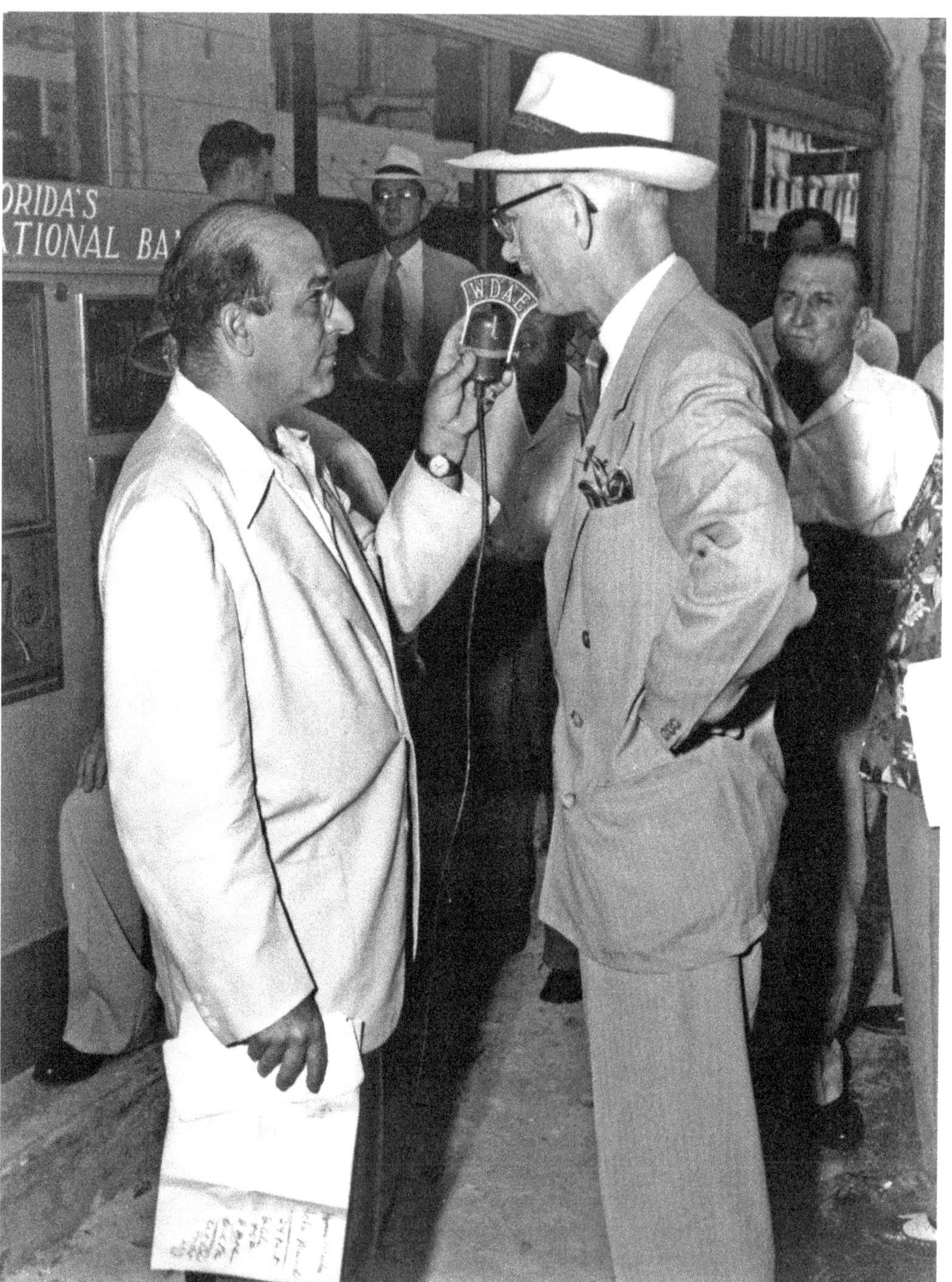

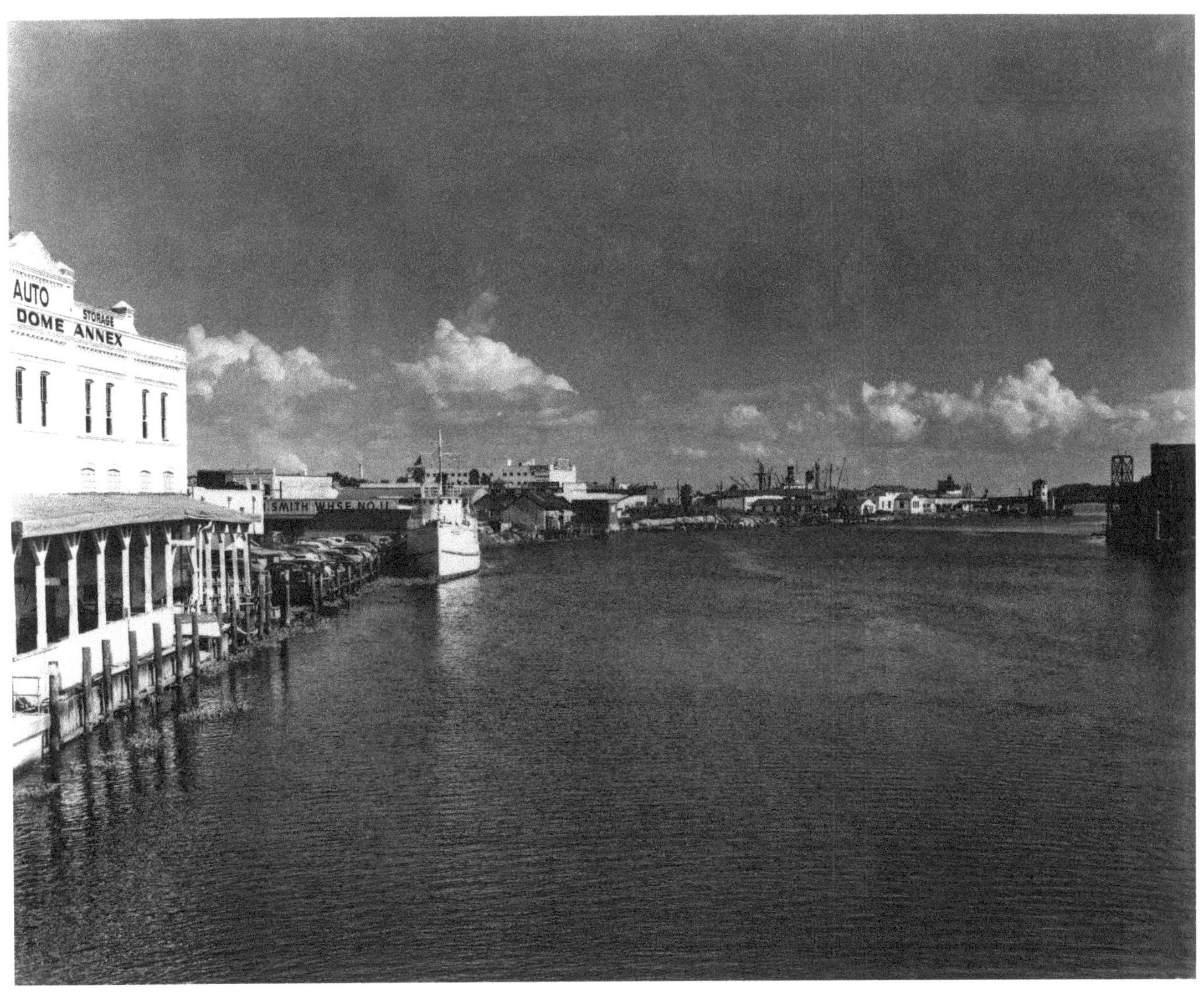

This is a view of the Hillsborough River waterfront from the vantage point of the Lafayette Street Bridge, which connects Hyde Park and the Tampa Bay Hotel to downtown Tampa. The river was first explored by Europeans when Don Pedro Menendez de Aviles arrived at 1566–67. It was named in 1772 for Wills Hill, Viscount Hillsborough of England. He was in charge of collecting information about English overseas possessions for the king.

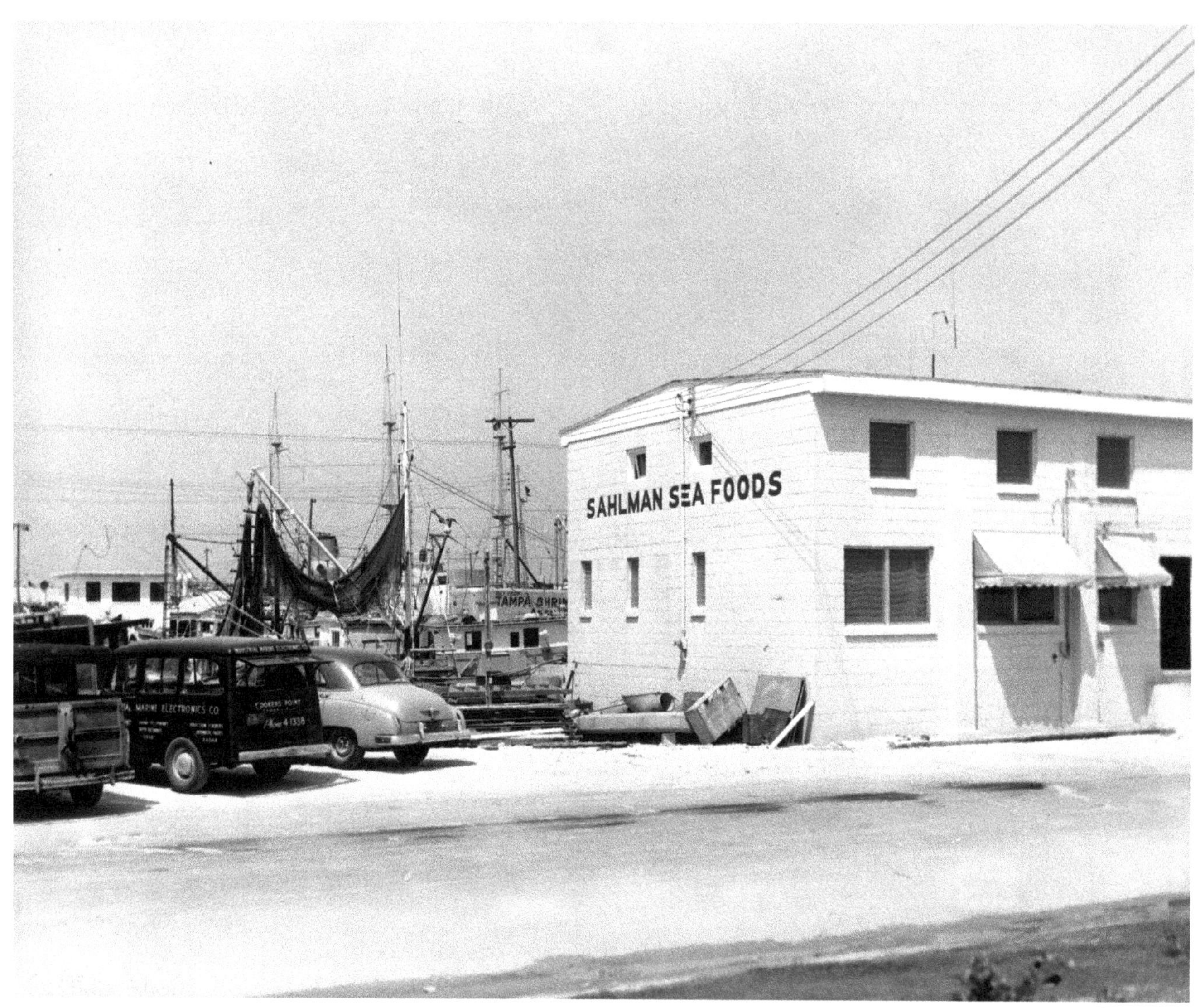

Located at Hookers Point, east of Seddon Island and Sparkman Bay, is the shrimp processing plant of Sahlman Sea Foods. Beyond it, in McKay Bay, are seen some of the more than 200 shrimp boats operating out of Tampa during the 1950s.

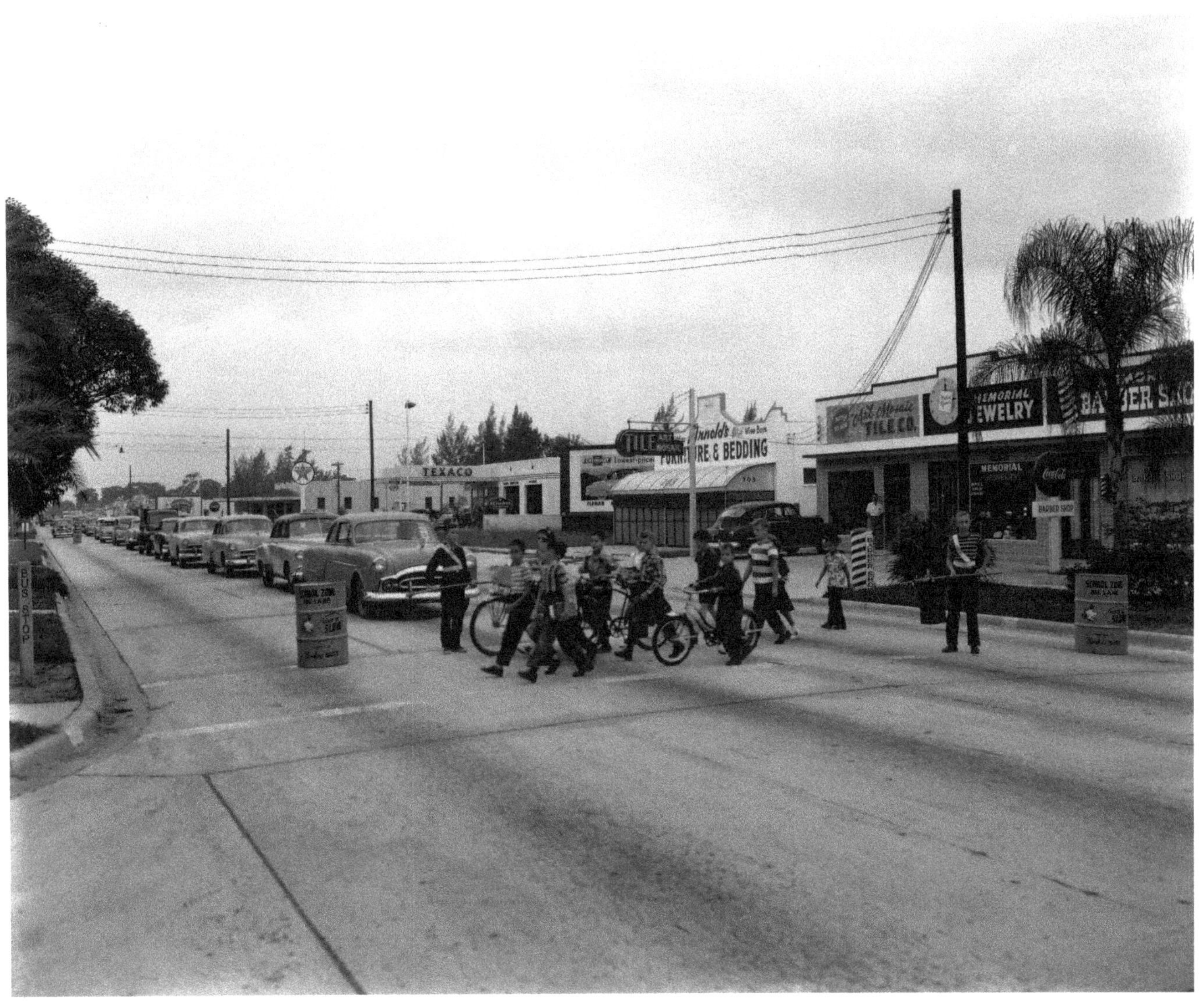

A school crossing guard stops traffic so these students can cross Memorial Highway,just west of Gomez Avenue at the northwestern corner of Hyde Park. They likely attended nearby Mitchell Elementary School, built in 1915 and named for Henry Laurens Mitchell, state supreme court justice, governor of Florida in the 1890s, and court clerk in Hillsborough County.

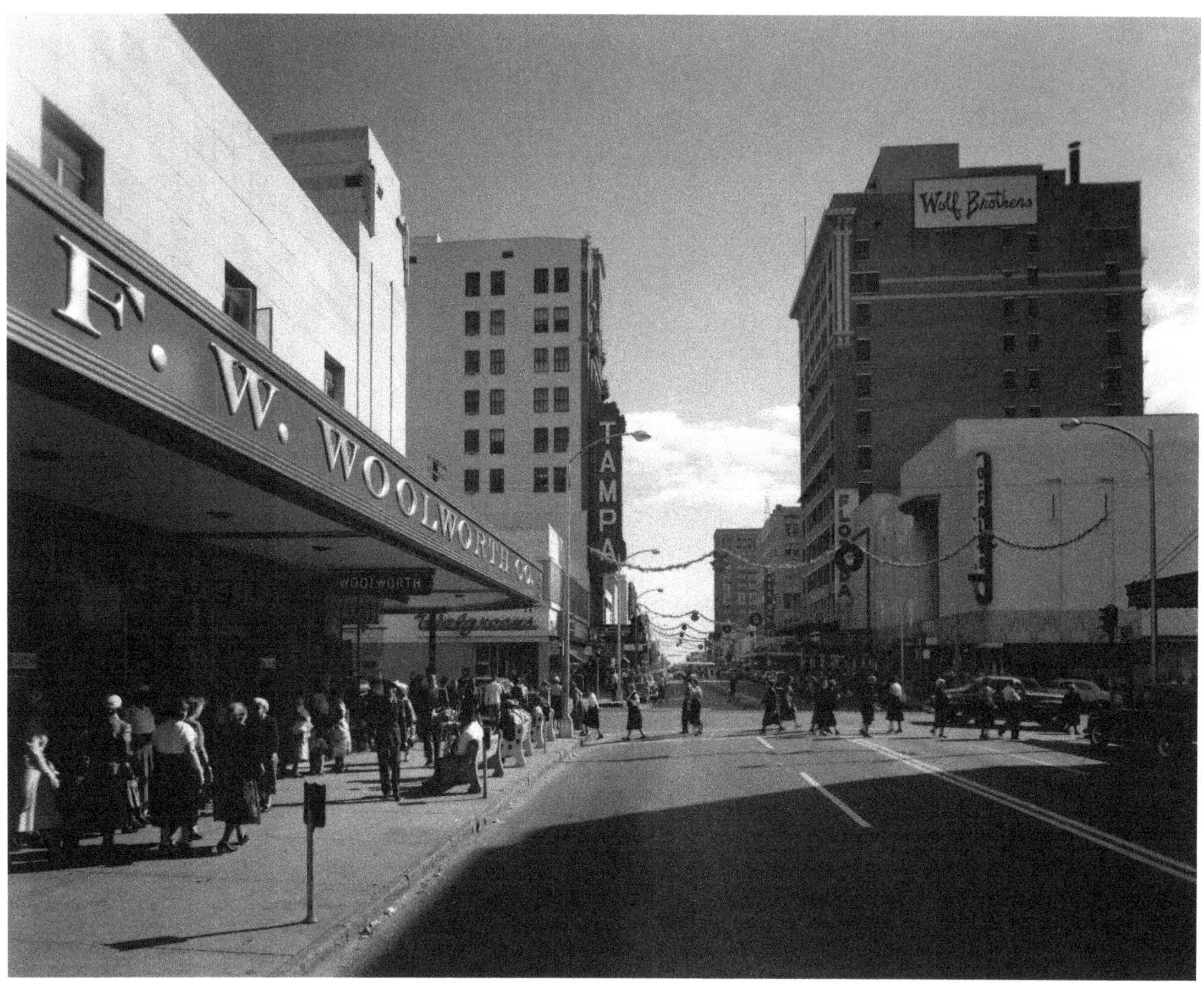

The building of the F. W. Woolworth Co. at 801 North Franklin Street was constructed in 1927 with an Art Deco style. Its Franklin Street side was covered with stucco and the rear was much simpler, with uncovered brick. The store extended through this building to an adjacent three-story one built in 1920 facing Florida Avenue, which also included the Woolworth offices. In the mid-1990s, the Woolworth corporation closed all of its stores and the Tampa building stood vacant for more than a decade.

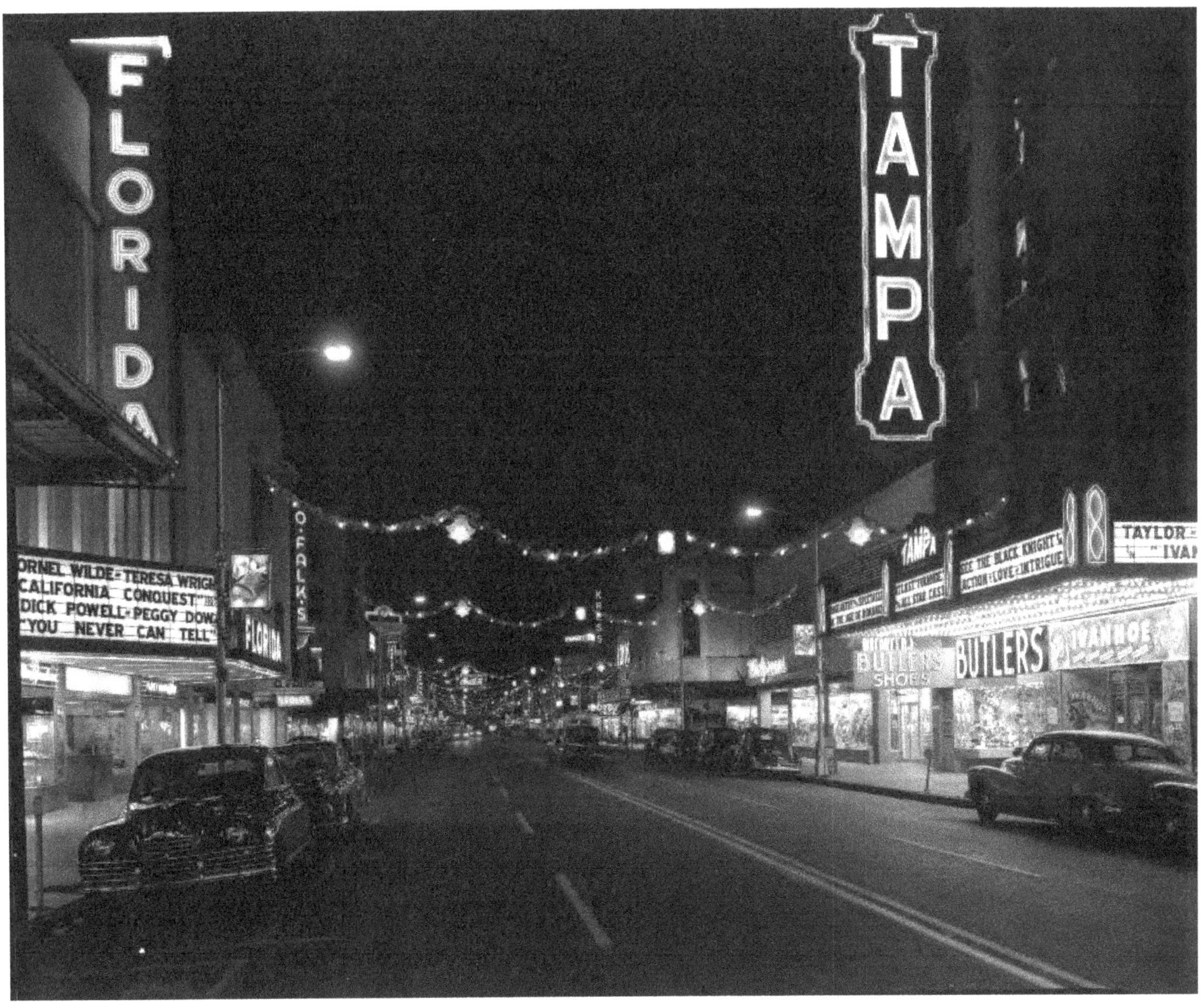

Franklin Street, just north of the intersection with Zack Street, featured two major movie theaters, the Florida and the Tampa. The Florida Theatre was open by the mid-1920s, and sometime later changed its name to the Franklin Theatre. By the early 1940s, it was the Florida Theatre again. It sat 900 moviegoers and was rather plain-looking when compared to the ornate Tampa Theatre across the street It closed in the mid01970s and was demolished in about 1978.

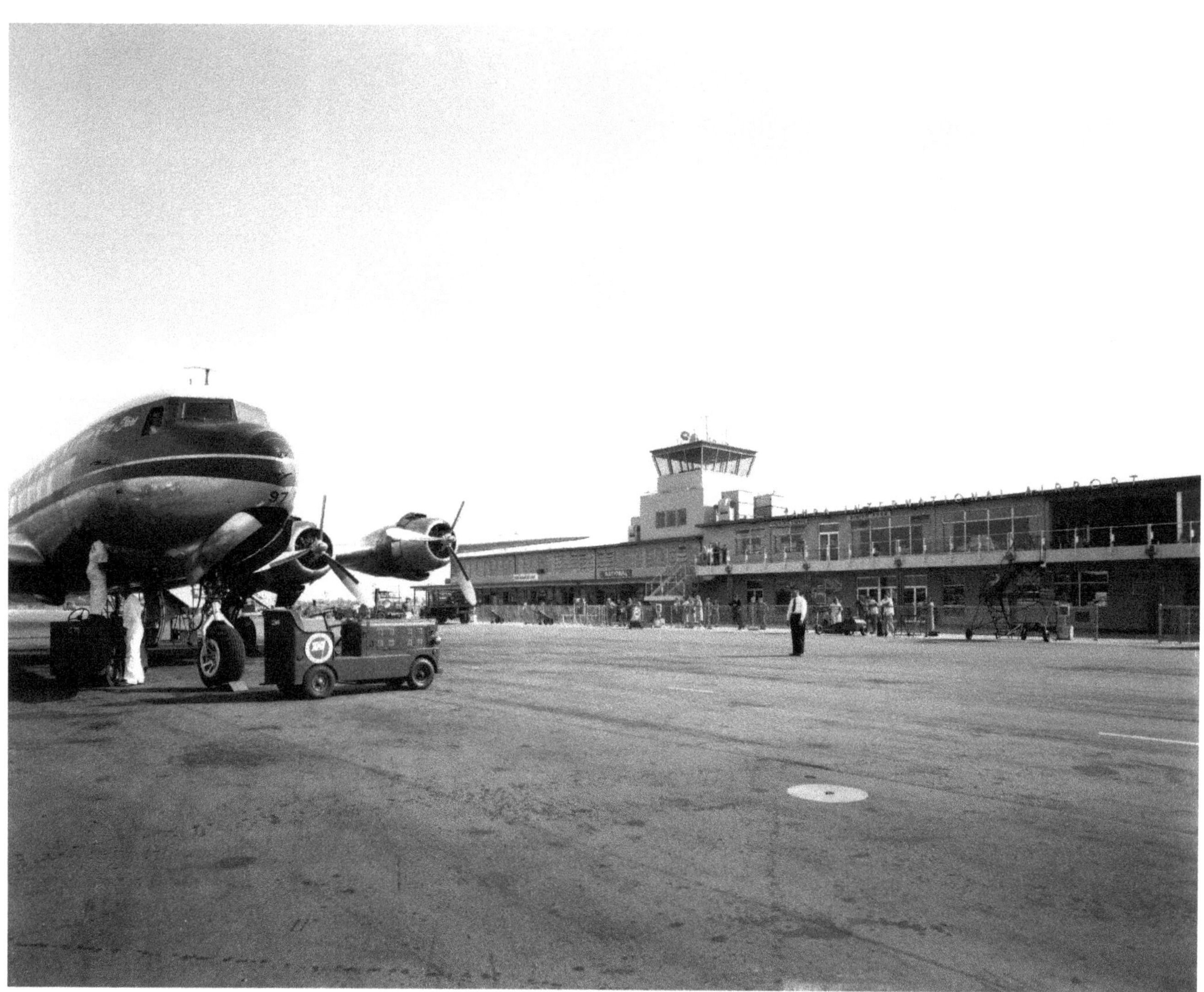

Today's Tampa International Airport opened in 1928 as Drew Field Municipal Airport and served as a military training facility during World War II. In 1945, it was transferred back to the city and soon became the predominant municipal airport, taking over that position from the Peter O. Knight Airport located on Davis Islands. It was renamed as Tampa International Airport in 1952, the year this DC-6 was photographed in front of the terminal.

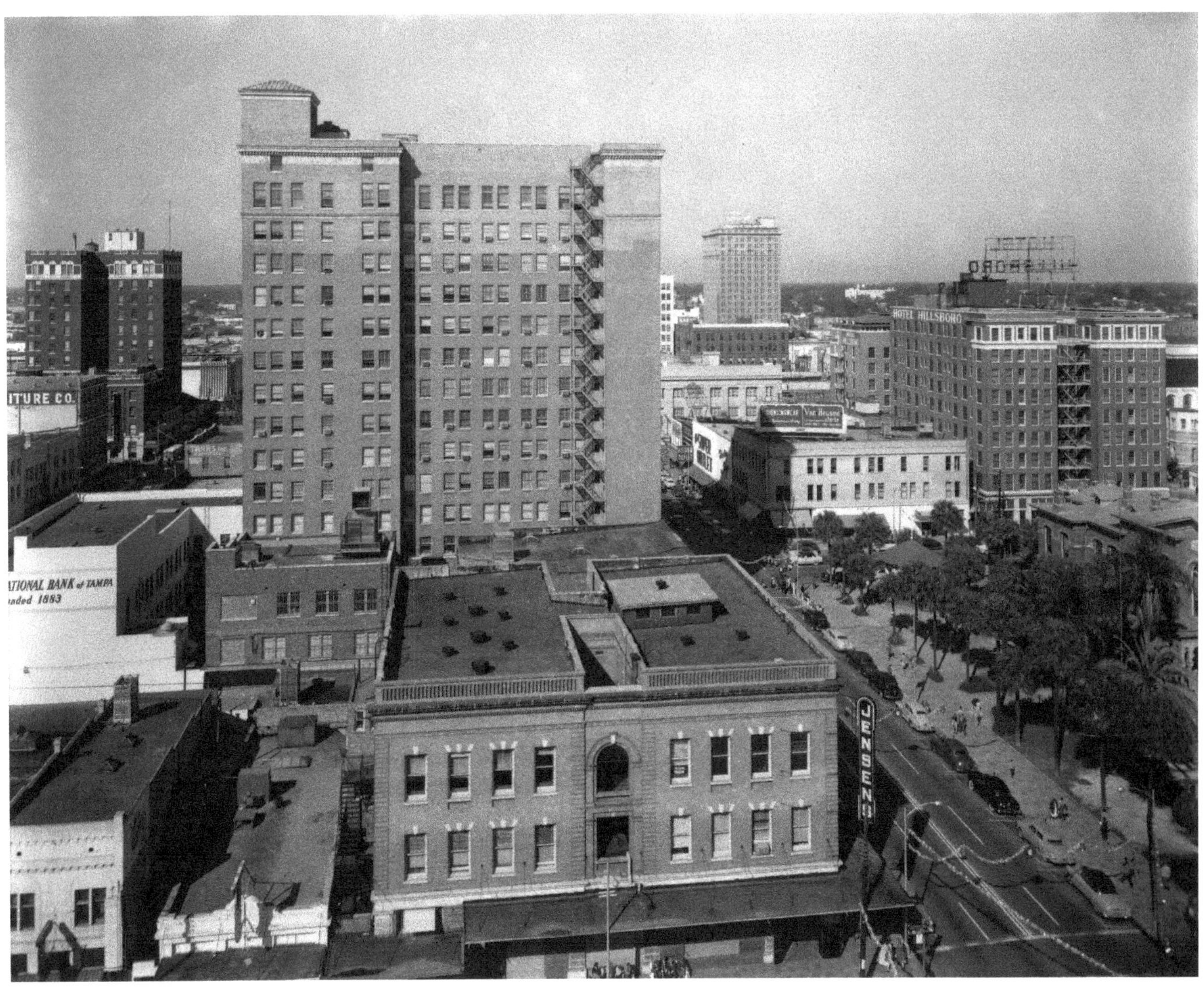

This view of downtown features Jensen's at the northwest corner of Franklin and Lafayette Streets, the tall First National Bank Building, and, on the extreme right, the Hotel Hillsboro. The hotel was building 1912 and for a time was the state's largest commercial hotel. Located at 512 North Florida Avenue, the nine-story brick building replaced the previous Hotel Hillsboro, which was only three stories tall.

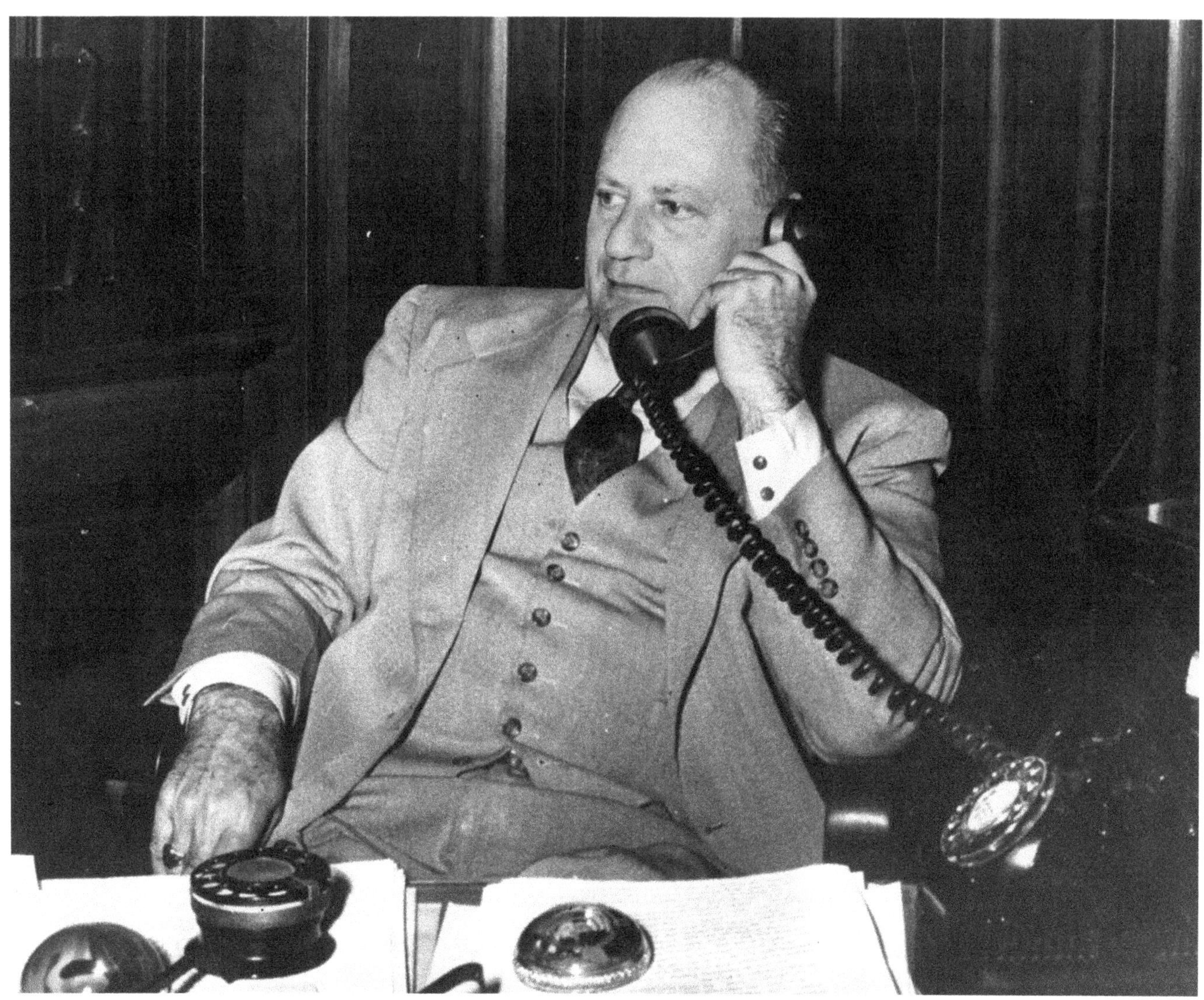

Carl D. Brorein, Sr., is shown here in December 1952, making the first telephone call on the new coaxial cable which linked Tampa with Orlando. He was the president of Peninsular Telephone Company which, in 1957, became General Telephone Company of Florida. Founded in 1901, it competed with Southern Bell and each company had separate phone lines in the city. Peninsular eliminated the need for subscribers to have two telephones by purchasing Southern Bell in 1906. Carl became the president of the company upon the death of his uncle, founder William G. Brorein, in 1937.

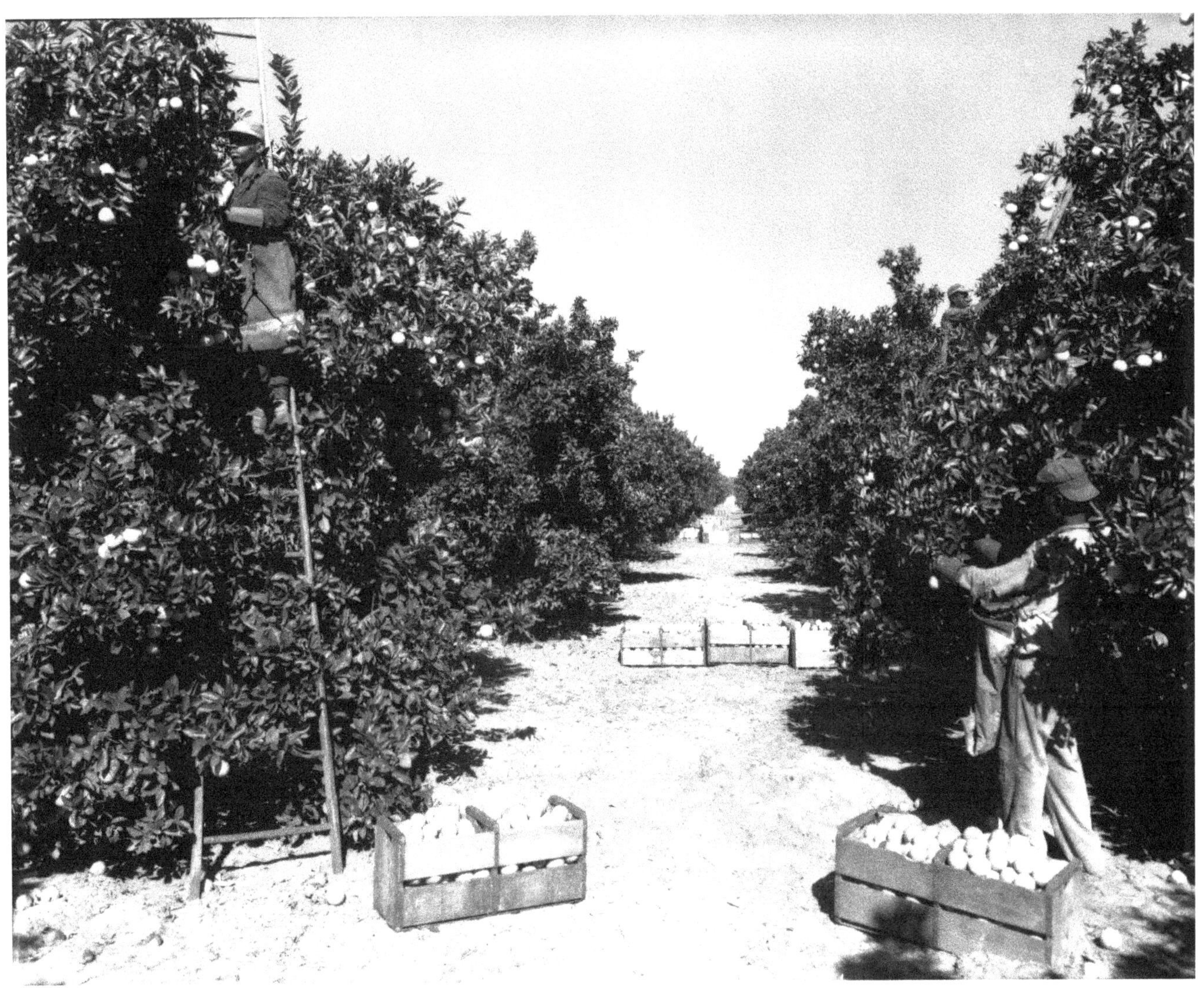

In December 1952, this was a Tampa citrus grove owned by Stokely-Van Camp, Incorporated. The company has its roots in canned beans and other fruits and vegetables, dating back to the Civil War and the Indianapolis grocery store of Gilbert and Hester Van Camp, Inc. The Van Camp company was acquired in 1933 by James and John Stokely, who had been canning tomatoes in Tennessee, resulting in Stokely-Van Camp, Inc. The company was acquired by the Quaker Oats Company in 1983.

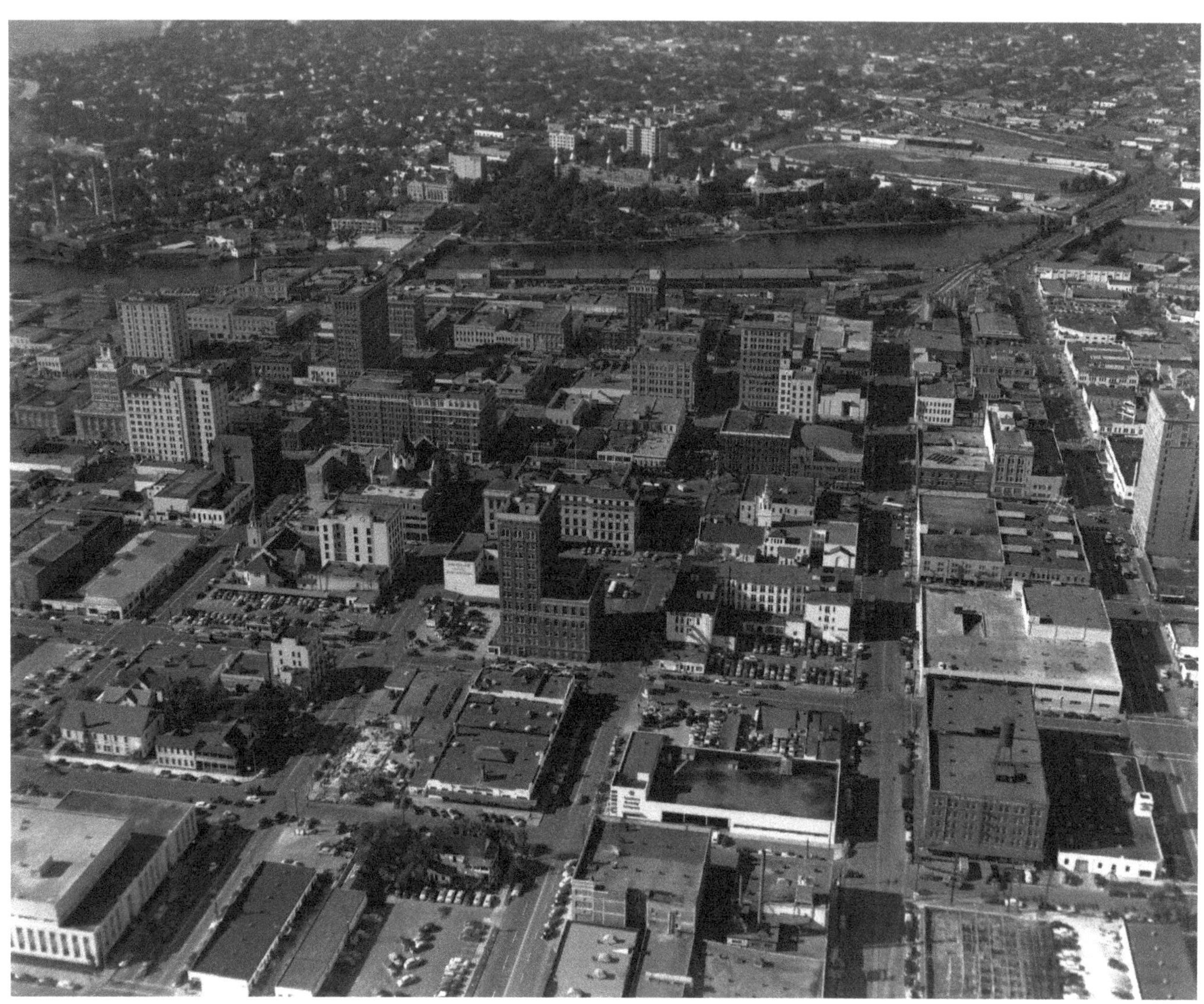

Here, looking west over downtown Tampa, the Lafayette Street and Cass Street bridges are visible, and between them on the western short of the Hillsborough River the onion-shaped towers of the Tampa Bay Hotel and the racetrack of the Florida State Fairground.

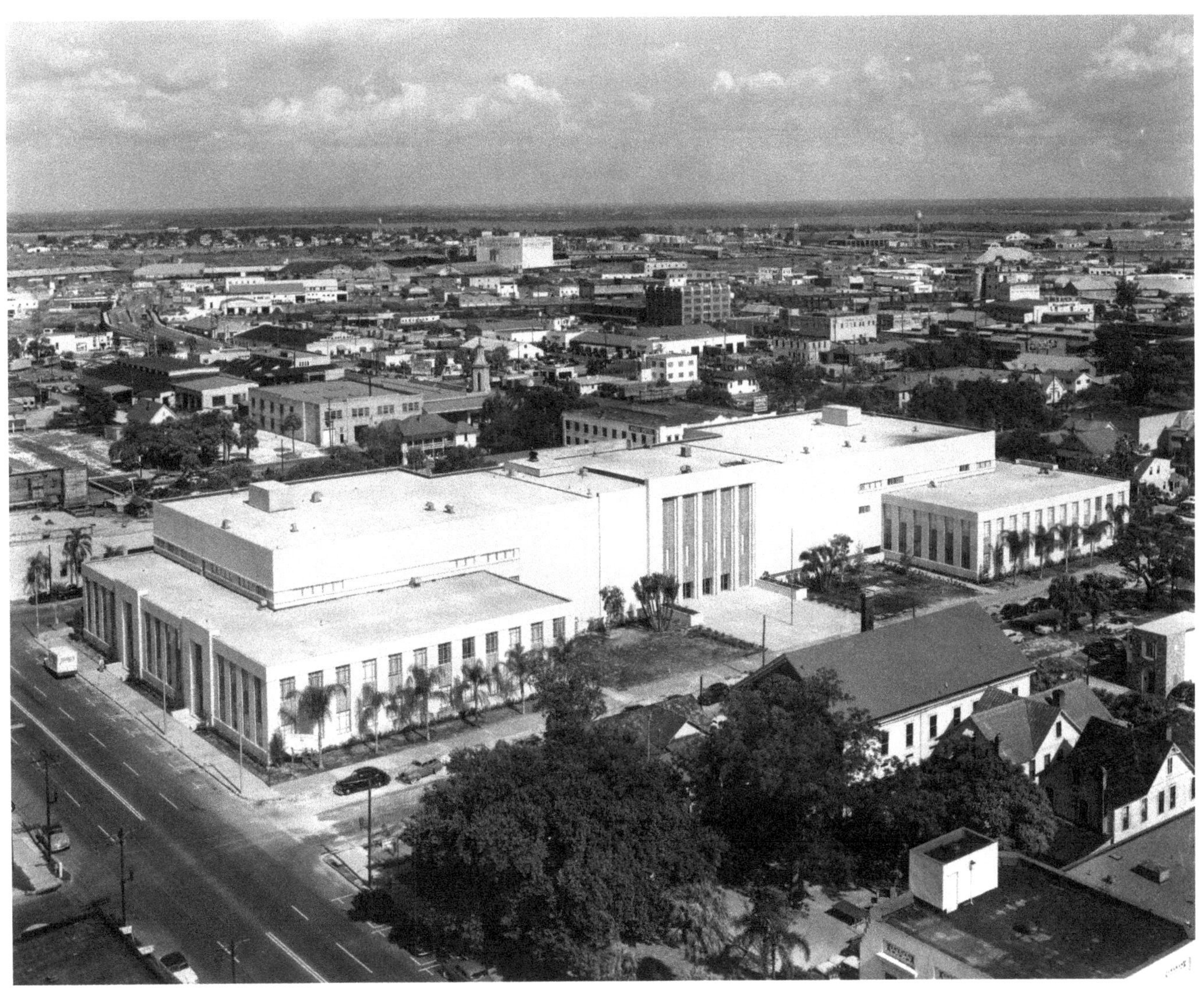

Photographed on March 26, 1953, this was the new Hillsborough County Courthouse. It served the country's judicial needs until the end of the twentieth century, when the building was deemed to be too small and outdated. To replace it, the George E. Edgecomb Courthouse was built at 800 Twiggs Street, with a construction cost of $43 million, and opened in 2003.

Although a quick glace at a map of Florida might lead one to think that Tampa is a coastal town, it lies several miles form the Gulf of Mexico. It is bordered by Tampa Bay, Old Tampa Bay, and Hillsborough Bay, which form a large, sheltered body of water frequented by boaters such as the ones in this sailboat in 1953.

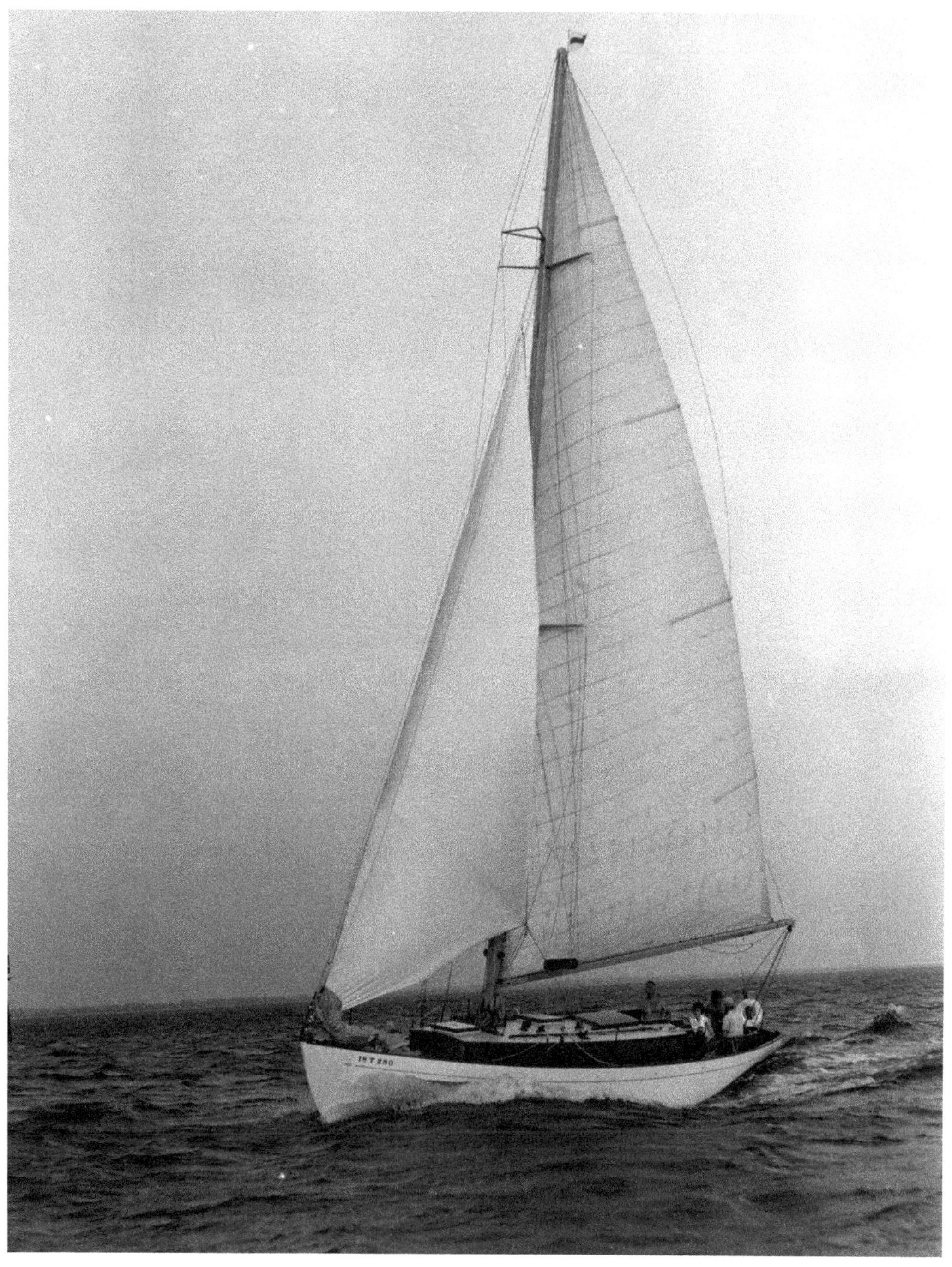

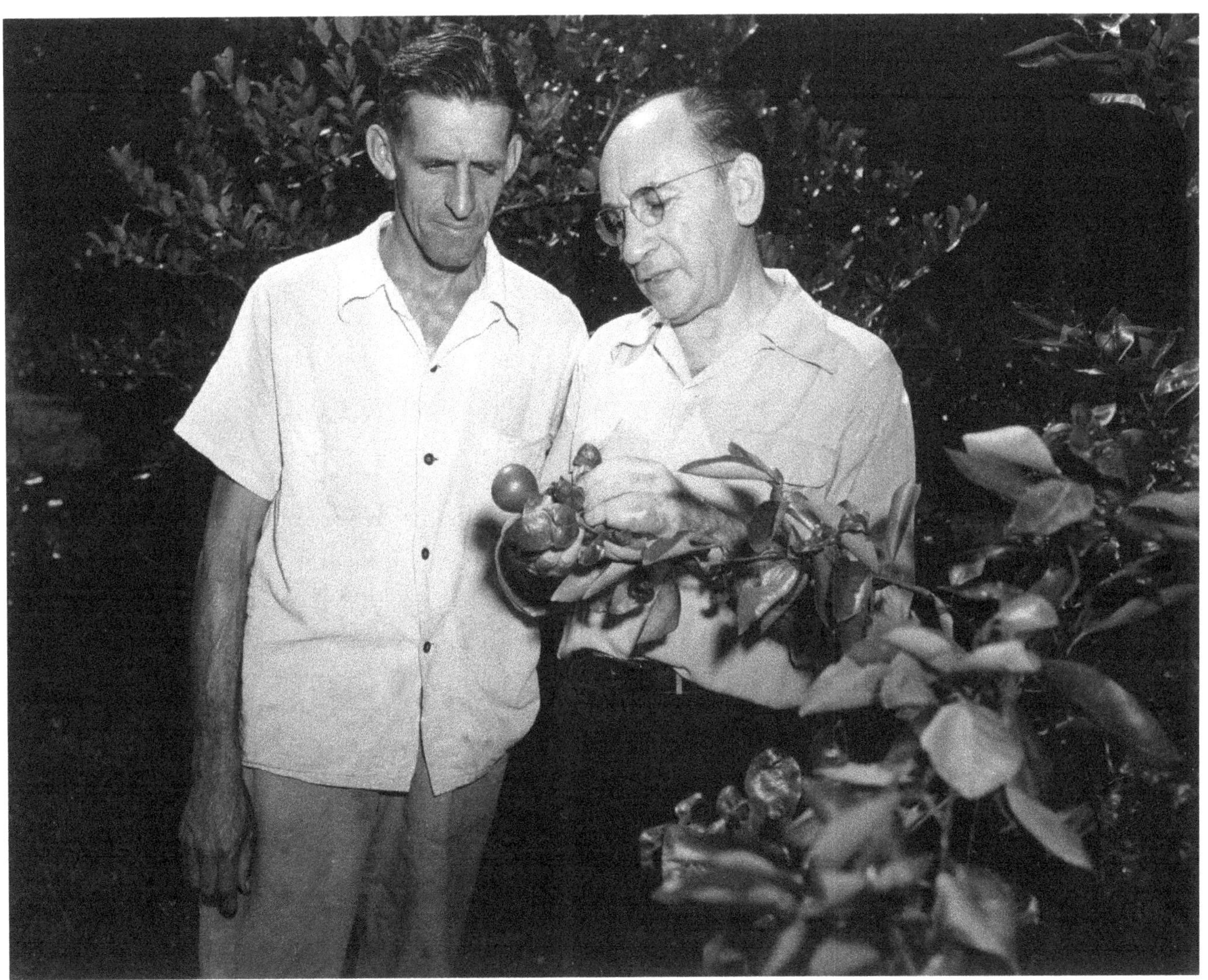

Tampa's climate and rich soil have long provided a fertile venue for raising citrus and tropical plants. When the Temple variety of orange was discovered in Winter Park, cuttings were brought to the Tampa area and propagated in groves, and today's city of Temple Terrace near the University of South Florida is named for the fruit. Shown here in 1953 are men studying a plant in one of the greenhouses of Tampa's Everglades Tropical Nursery.

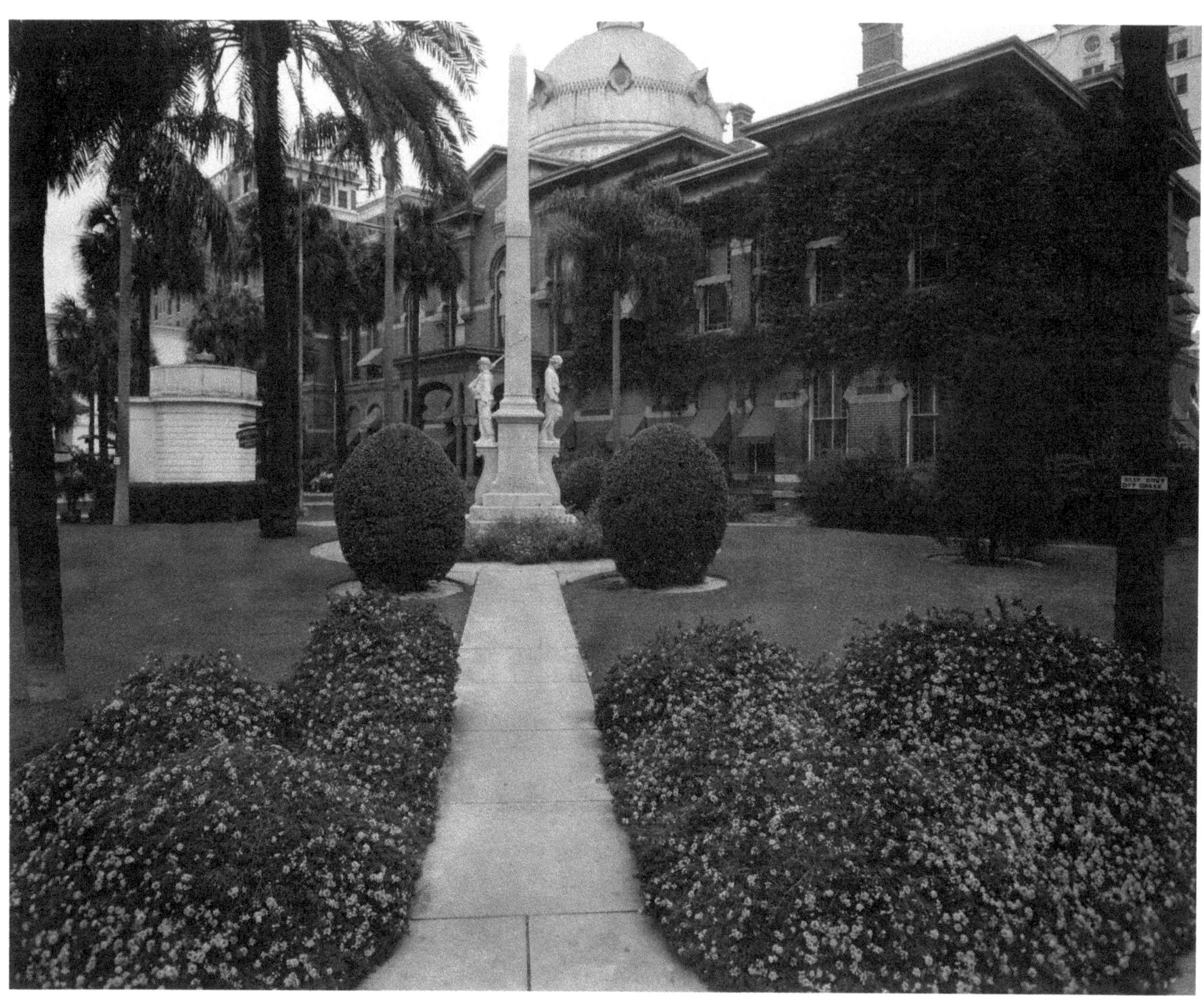

The obelisk on the grounds of the Hillsborough County Courthouse was erected in 1911 to commemorate the men from the county who died in the Civil War. It is the result of a fund-raising campaign begun in 1910 by the Tampa chapter of the United Daughters of the Confederacy, and was formally accepted by Tampa Mayor D. B. McKay. Named "Memoria in Aeterna," it is fashioned of Italian marble and is engraved with a poem by Sister Esther Carlotta, president of the Florida U.D.C. in 1911.

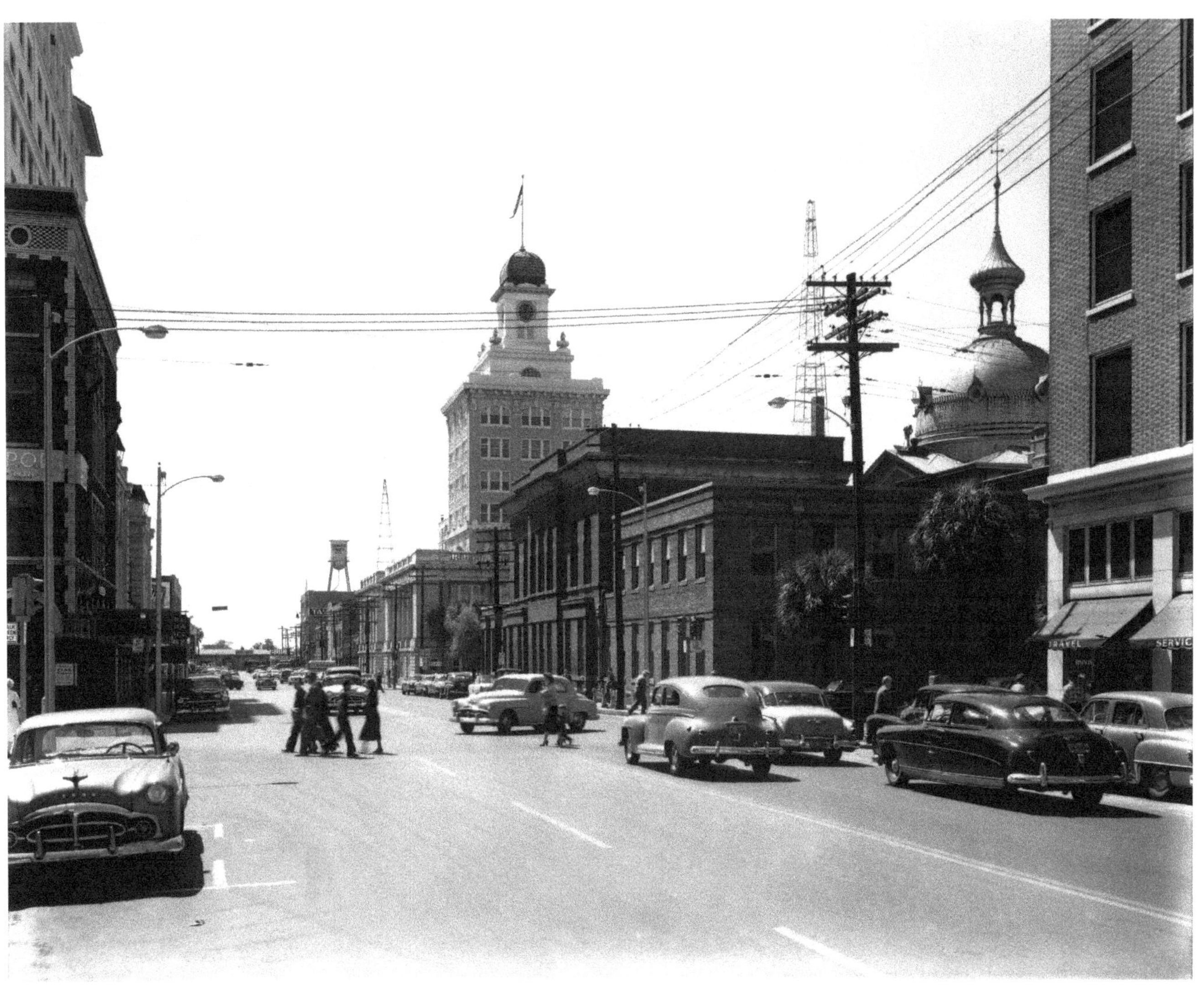

Looking south from the intersection with Madison Street are the 400 and 500 blocks of Florida Avenue. The two buildings topped with domes are the City Hall in the center and the 1991 Hillsborough County Courthouse on the right. The courthouse was designed by J. A. Wood, who also designed the Tampa Bay Hotel for Henry Plant. The large silver onion dome shown here is similar to those across the river on the former hotel building.

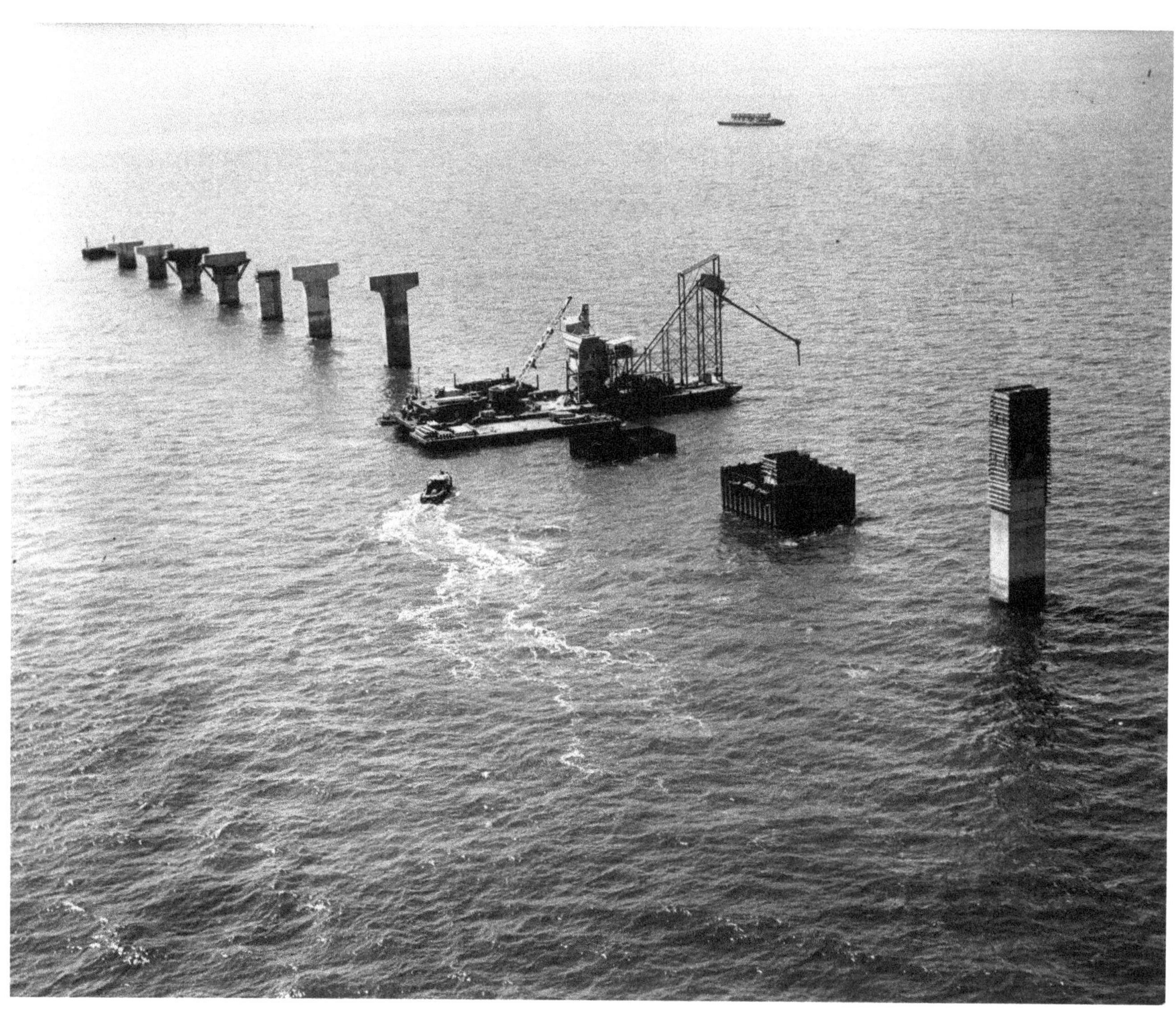

On March 26, 1953, construction of a second span of the Gandy Bridge can be seen in the water of Old Tampa Bay. The older span was purchased by the government in 1944, and at the urging of U.S. Senator Claude Pepper, President Franklin Roosevelt exercised his war powers and eliminated the toll to drive to or from St. Petersburg so military personnel could more easily use it.

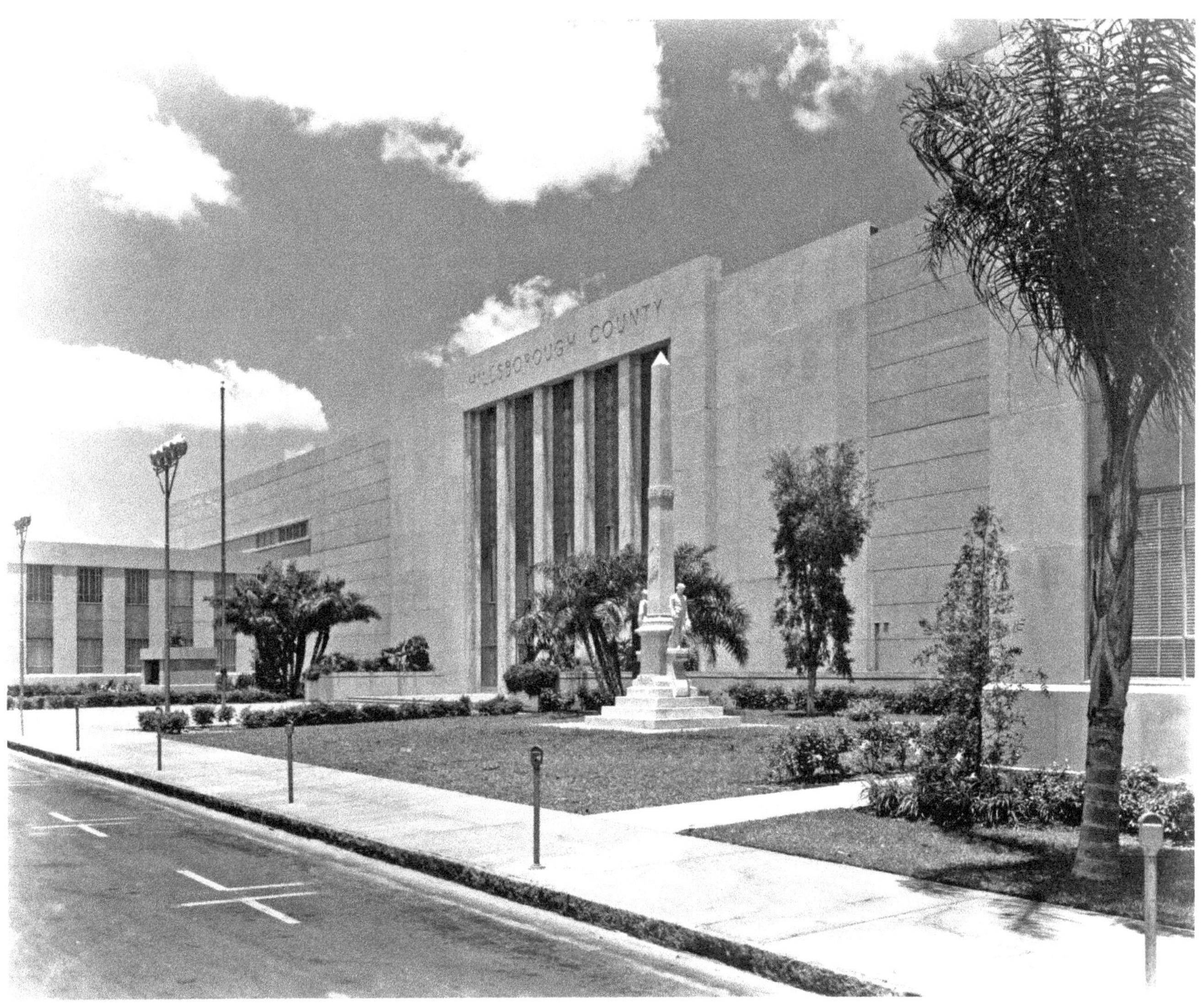

This May 1953 photo of the west façade of the new Hillsorough County Courthouse also provides a look at the Confederate Monument, which had just been moved from the grounds of the old courthouse. On the monument are two figures—one represents a determined warrior headed north, and the other a heroic youth facing south, returning home from battle.

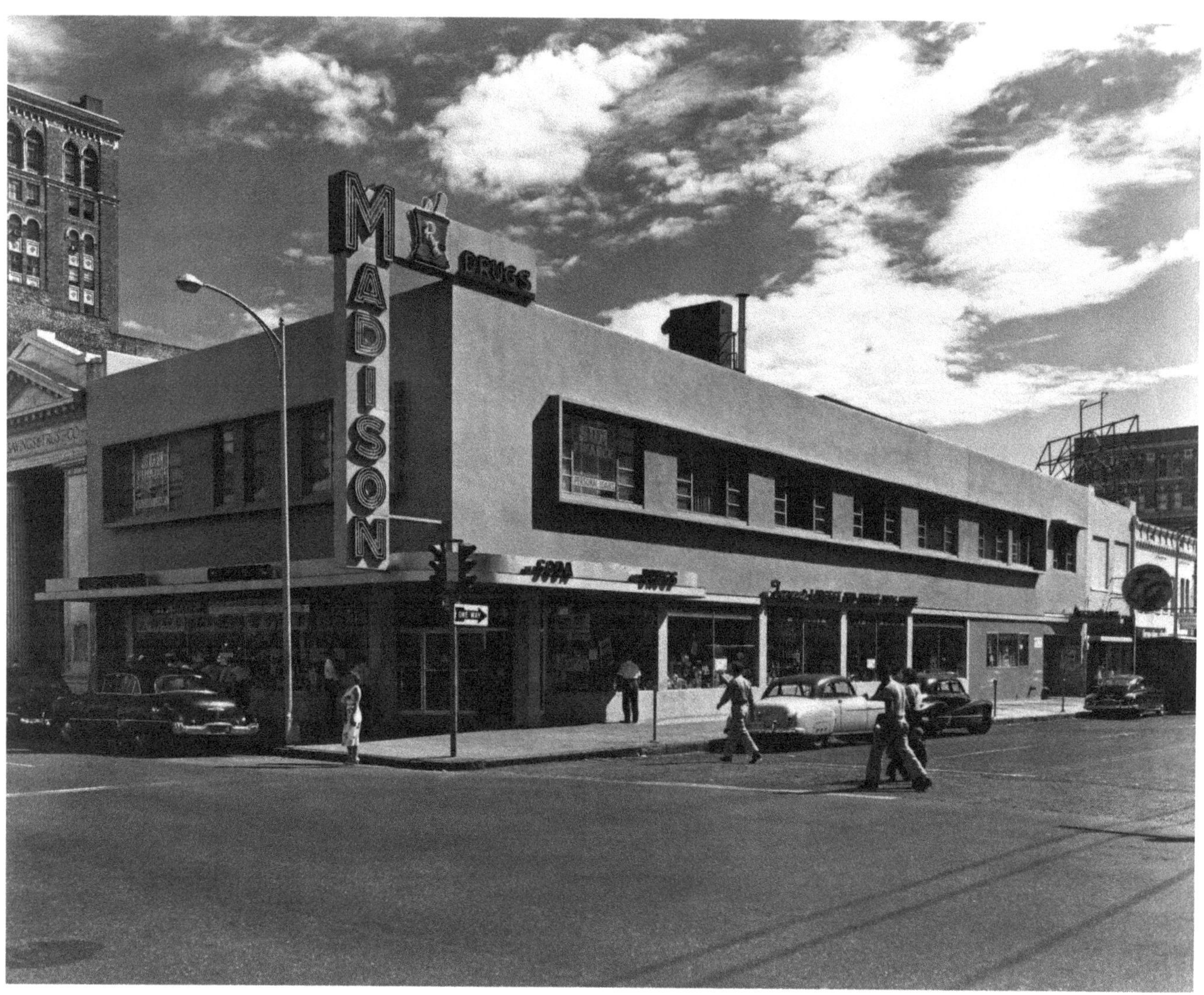

Mike Markes owned this building at the southwest corner of the intersection of Franklin and Twiggs Streets, and he opened the Commercial Hotel in the building. In 1913, it was renamed as the New Commercial Hotel, and by 1917, the Rex Billiard Parlor was also located inside it. Before this photo was taken in June 1953, the building was substantially remodeled, including the covering of the brick facing and modernization of the windows. Located at 514 North Franklin Street, it was the home of the Madison Drug Store, and later was acquired by Walgreens.

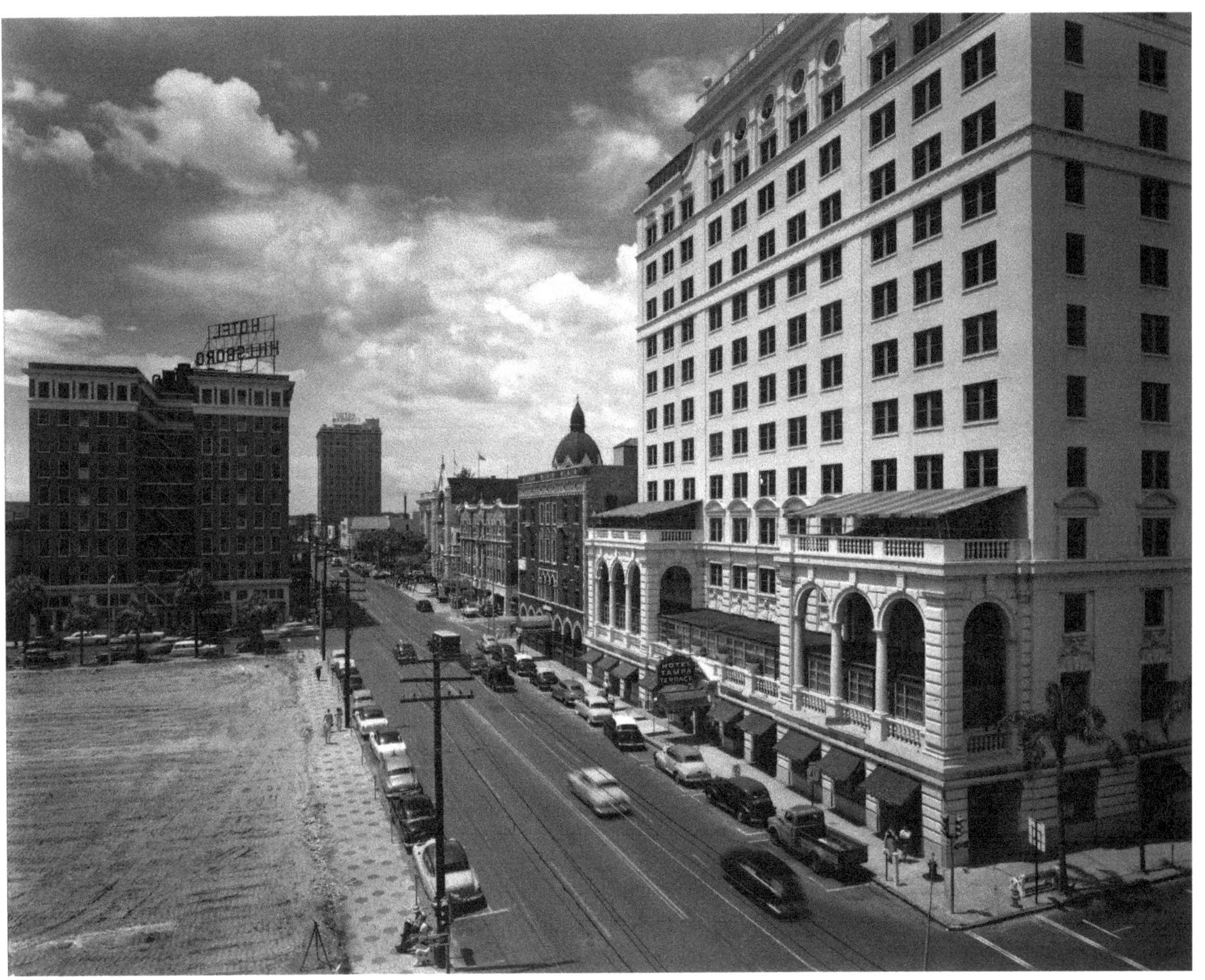

The 12-story white building on the right is the Tampa Terrace Hotel, located at 411 North Florida Avenue, at the intersection with Lafayette Street. It was financed by a group of 40 investors and opened for business in 1926. It went out of business and ceased to serve guests in 1965, and later that year it was torn down.

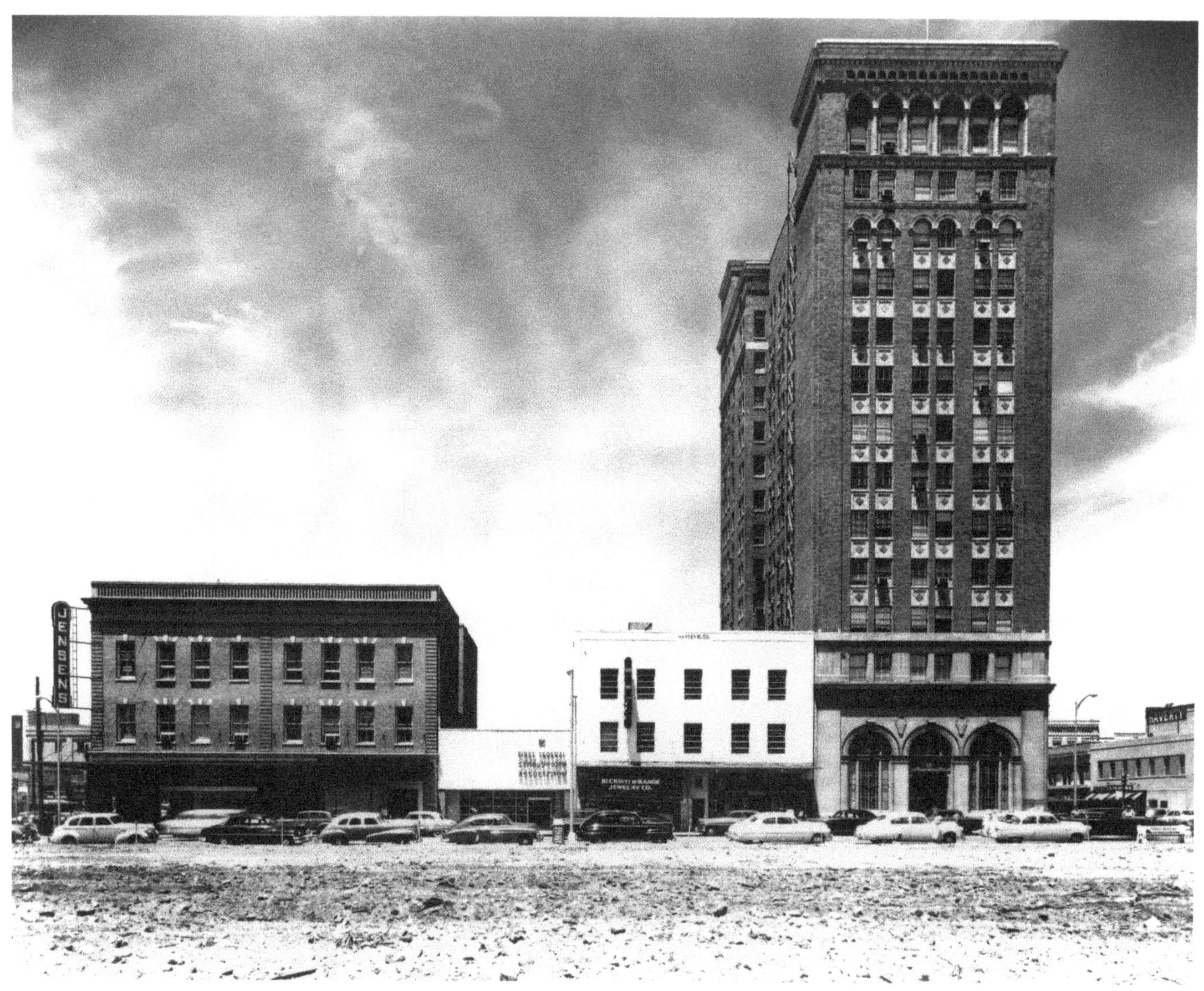

Between Lafayette and Madison Streets, across from the cleared courthouse square are seen the tall First National Bank Building, the white Hayden Building, and the Giddens Building. The latter, shown in August 1953 with a sign for Jensen's, was still known as "Giddens Corner." This three-story structure housing the Giddens Clothing Company replaced an 1880s two-story building that housed the Emery, Simmons and Emery Shoe Store.

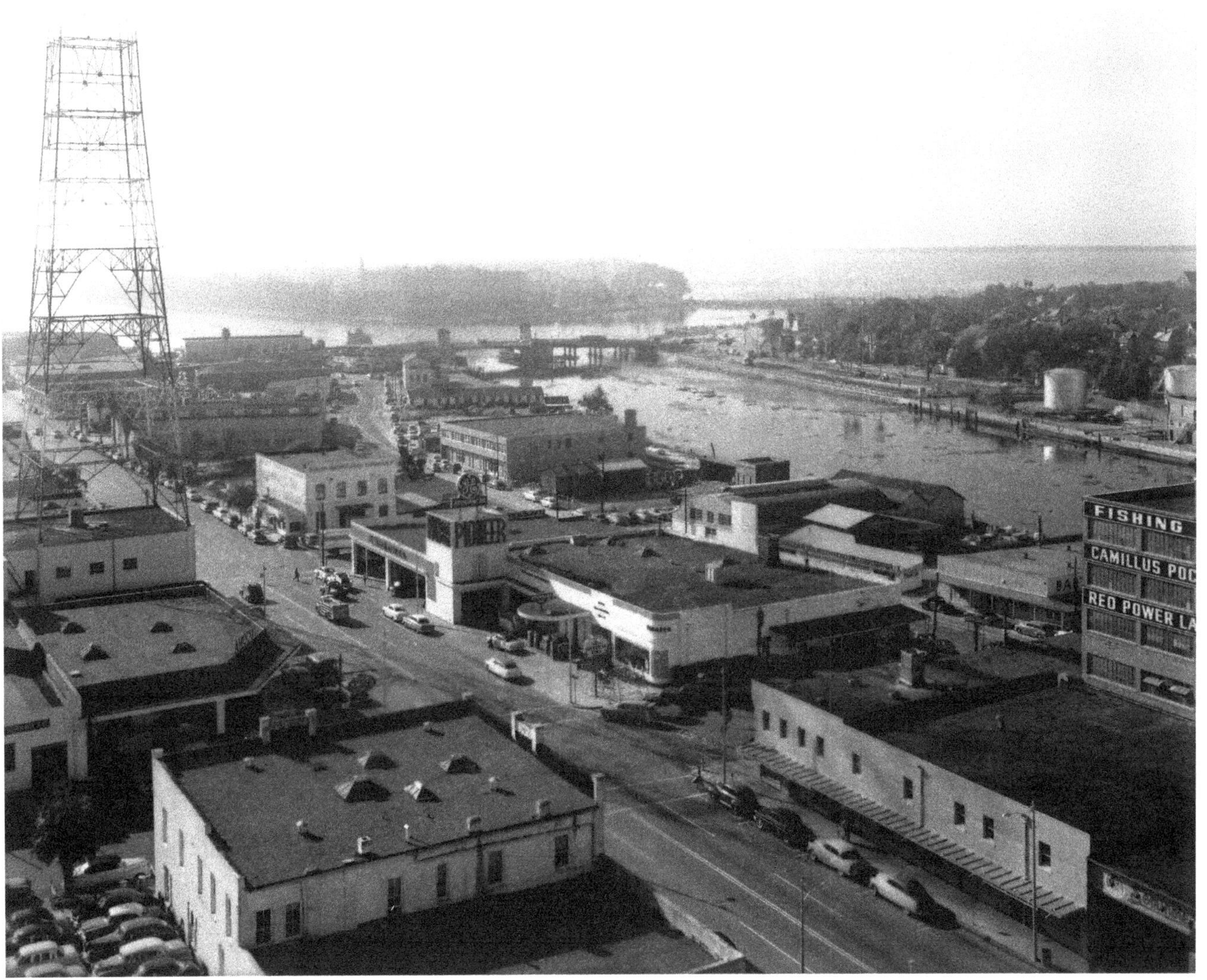

Looking southwest over the 100 and 200 blocks of North Tampa Street and the Pioneer Tire Company, we see the Hillsborough River and the Platt Street Bridge, Beyond that is the causeway connecting Hyde Park on the mainland to the right with Davis Islands to the left. To the right is the Knight & Wall Co. fronting on Ashley Drive, advertising, among other things, the sale of REO Power Lawn Mowers.

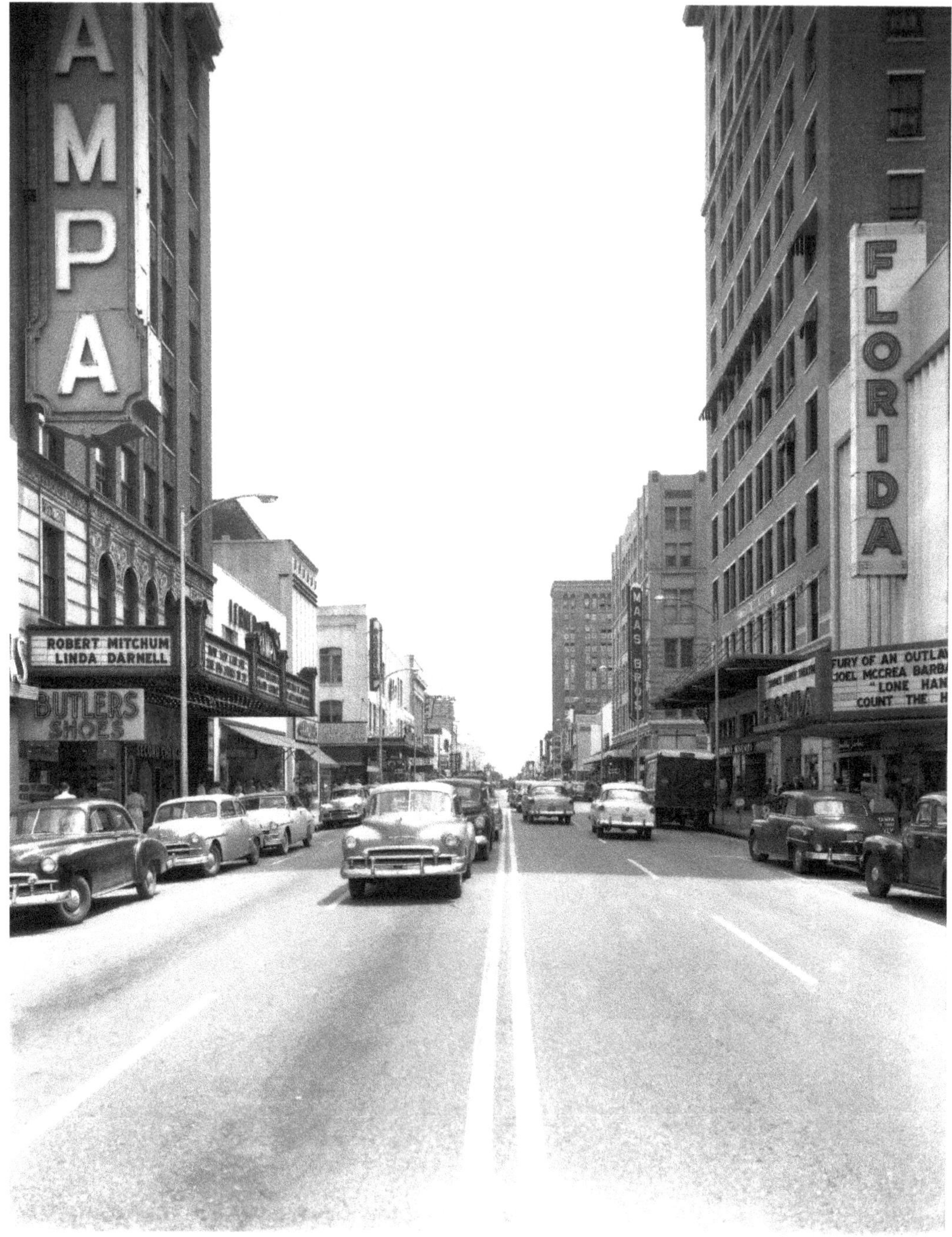

The 700 block of Franklin Street on September 18, 1953, features the marquees of the Tampa Theatre and Florida Theatre. Both were doing business in the same locations during the late 1920s, but the Florida was then known as the Franklin Theatre. The Florida claimed to be "Air Conditioned—Always Cool and Comfortable." Initially, before it obtained an air conditioning system of its own, it received its cool air from the Tampa Theatre, through pipes running under Franklin Street.

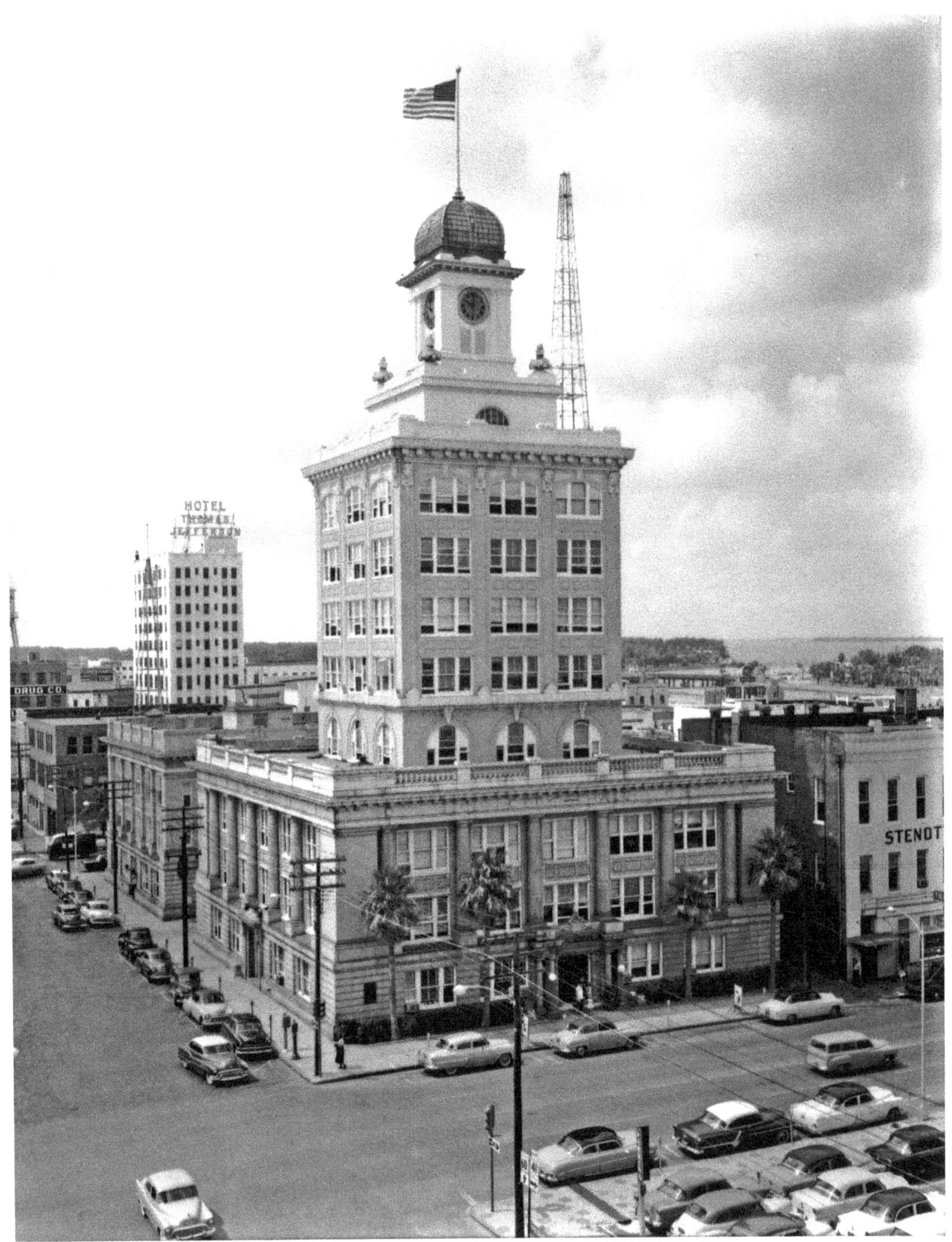

Just below the copper dome of Tampa's city hall is a 2,840-pound clock donated by the W. H. Beckwith Jewelry Company. Because it was installed after intense lobbying by a group led by Hortense Oppenheimer Ford, the Tampa Times nicknamed it "Hortense the Beautiful," and the clock is still known as Hortense. Hortense Ford and her four sisters were involved in the cultural affairs of the city, including the Friday Morning Musicale and the Tampa Civic Musical Association.

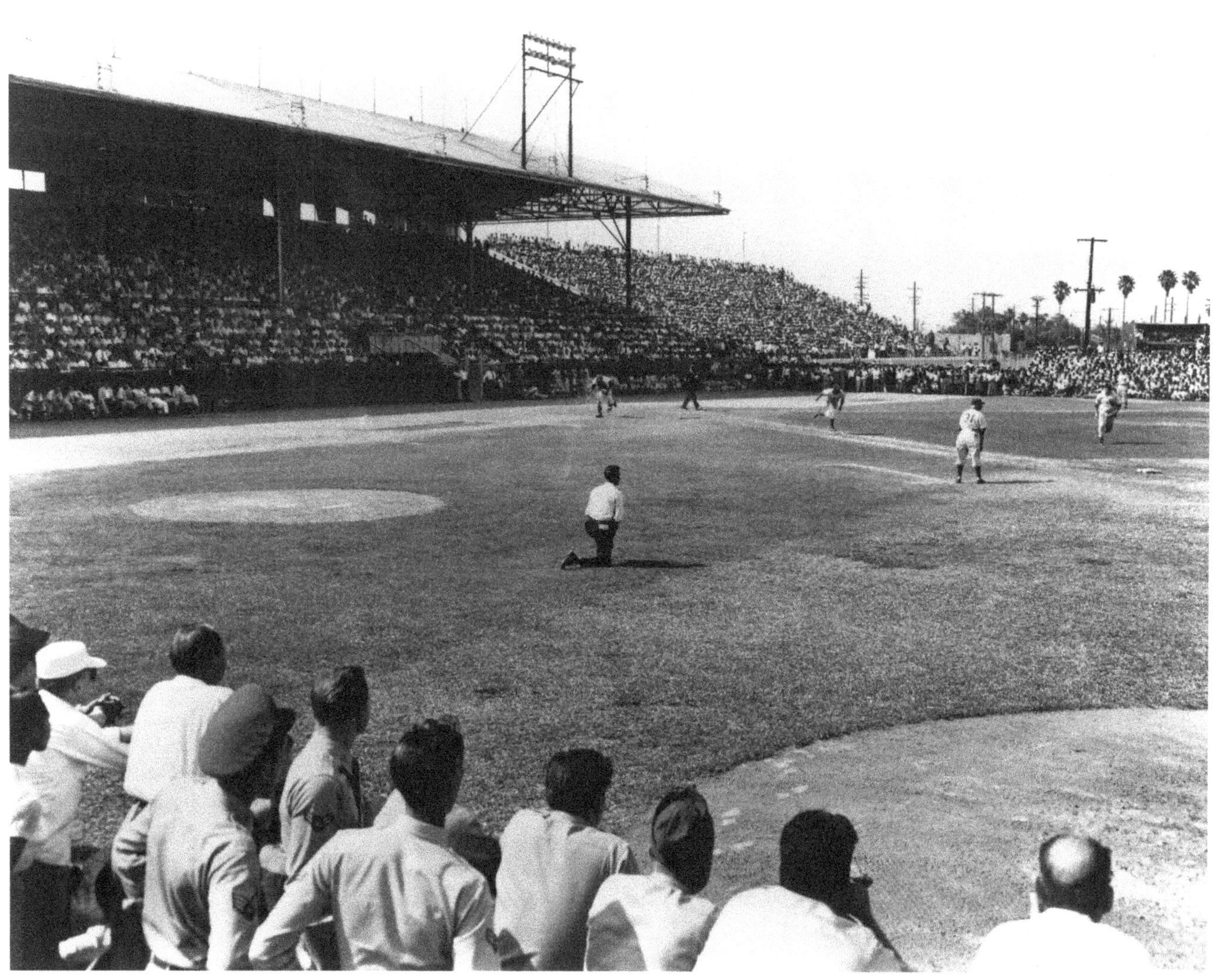

The teams in this spring training game on March 28, 1954, at Plant Field are the Brooklyn Dodgers and the Chicago White Sox. The baseball diamond is gone, but there is a historical marker commemorating a home run hit on April 5, 1919, by a pitcher for the Boston Red Sox. It was measured to have traveled in 579 feet, and the pitcher who hit it was in the process of transitioning to playing right field and became the greatest home run hitter of his era. His name was Babe Ruth.

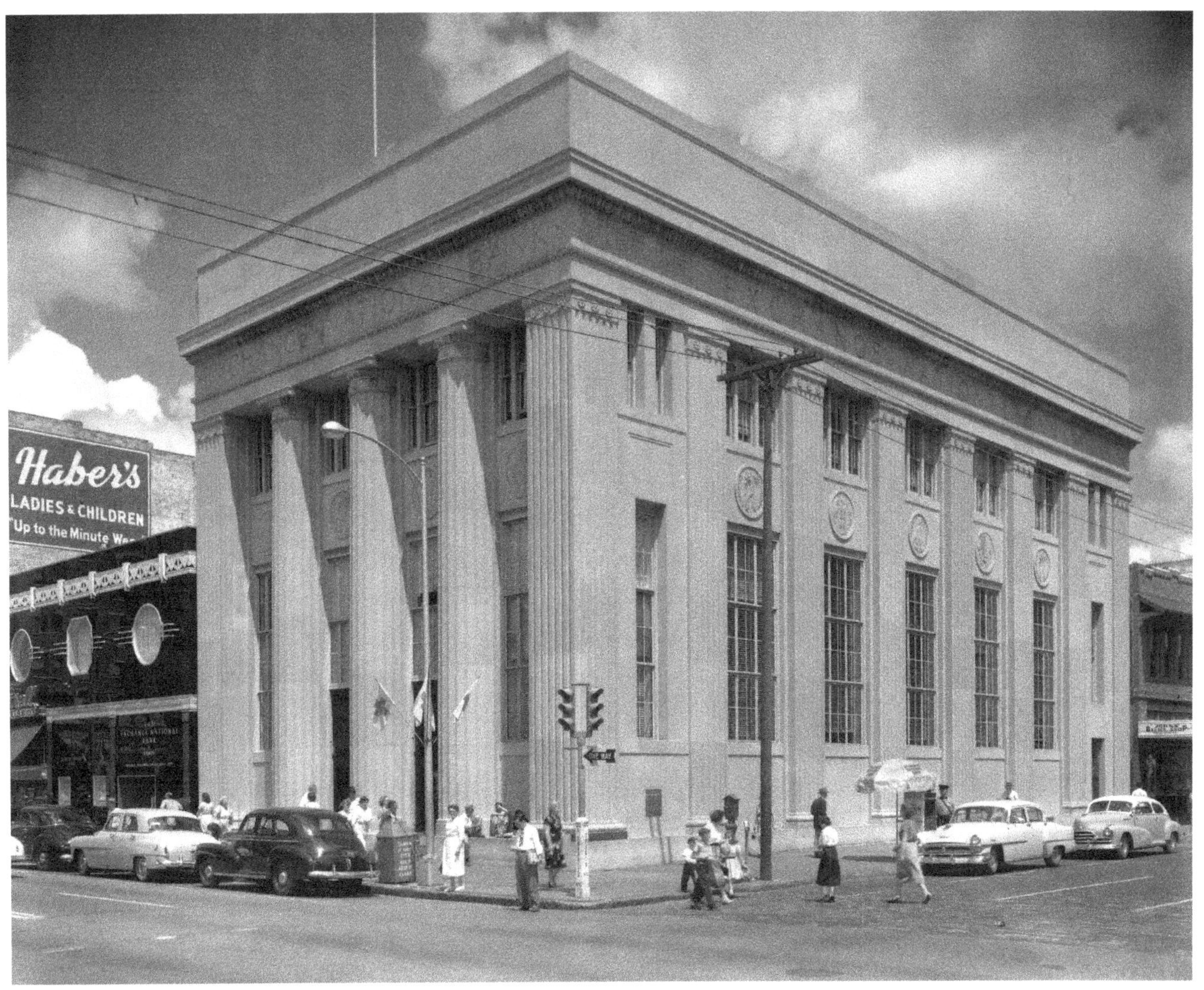

Exchange National Bank was founded in 1894 and survived the major freezes which hit the area at the end of that year and the beginning of the next. One of its principals was cashier Col. J. B. Anderson, who also served as the fiscal agent for Tampa's city government. In 1914, Exchange Bank became Florida's sole charter member of the Sixth District Federal Reserve Bank. Shown here, on April 1, 1954, is the bank at the northwest corner of Franklin and Twiggs Streets.

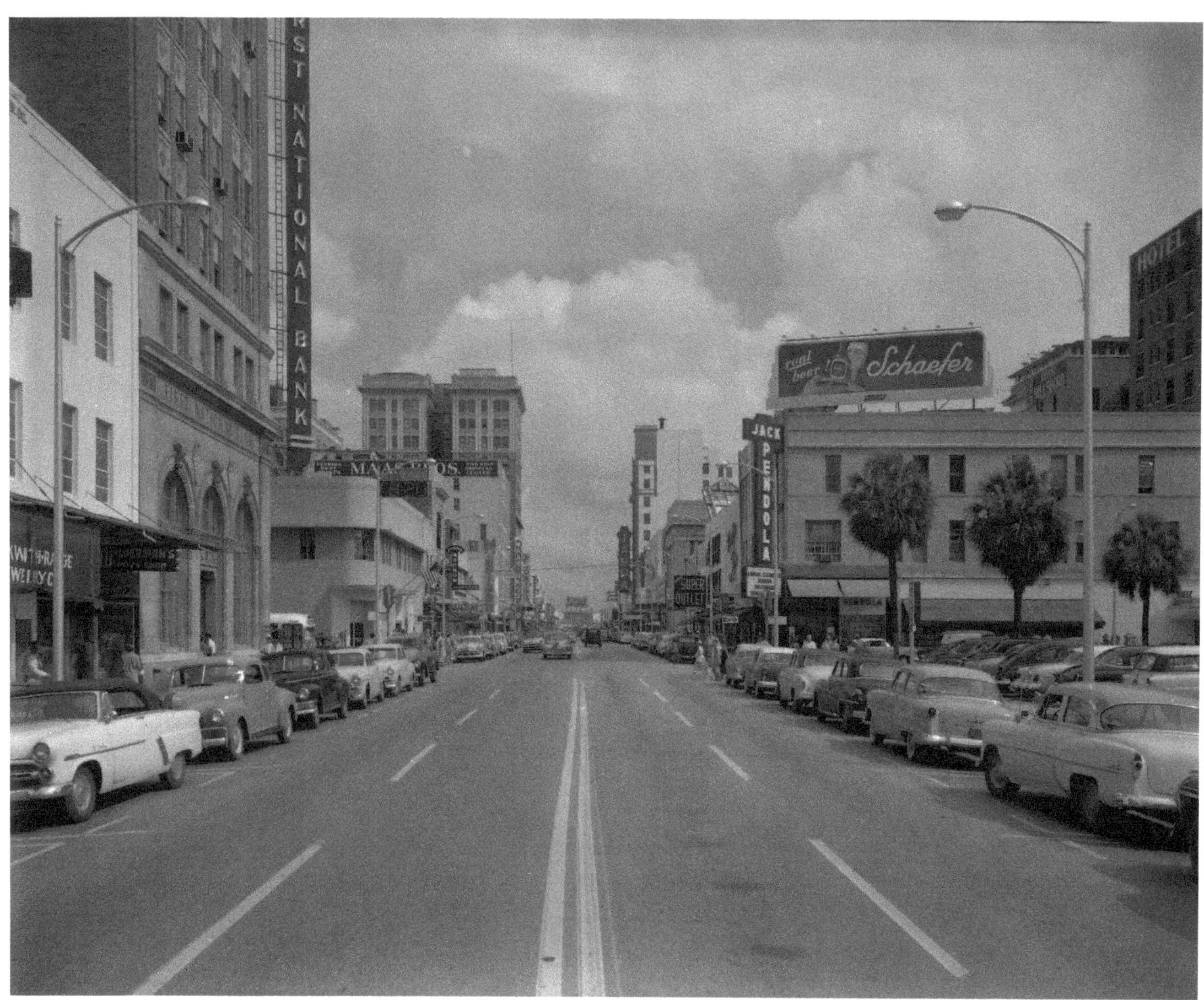

Heading north from Lafayette Street on Franklin Street are several business blocks. One prominent structure is the First National Bank Building, the home of the bank founded by Thomas C. Taliaferro in 1883. It was initially called the Bank of Tampa and was an affiliate of the Jacksonville private banking firm of Ambler, Marvin & Stockton. In 1886, it moved into the first brick building in downtown Tampa, a two-story structure at the corner of Franklin and Washington Streets.

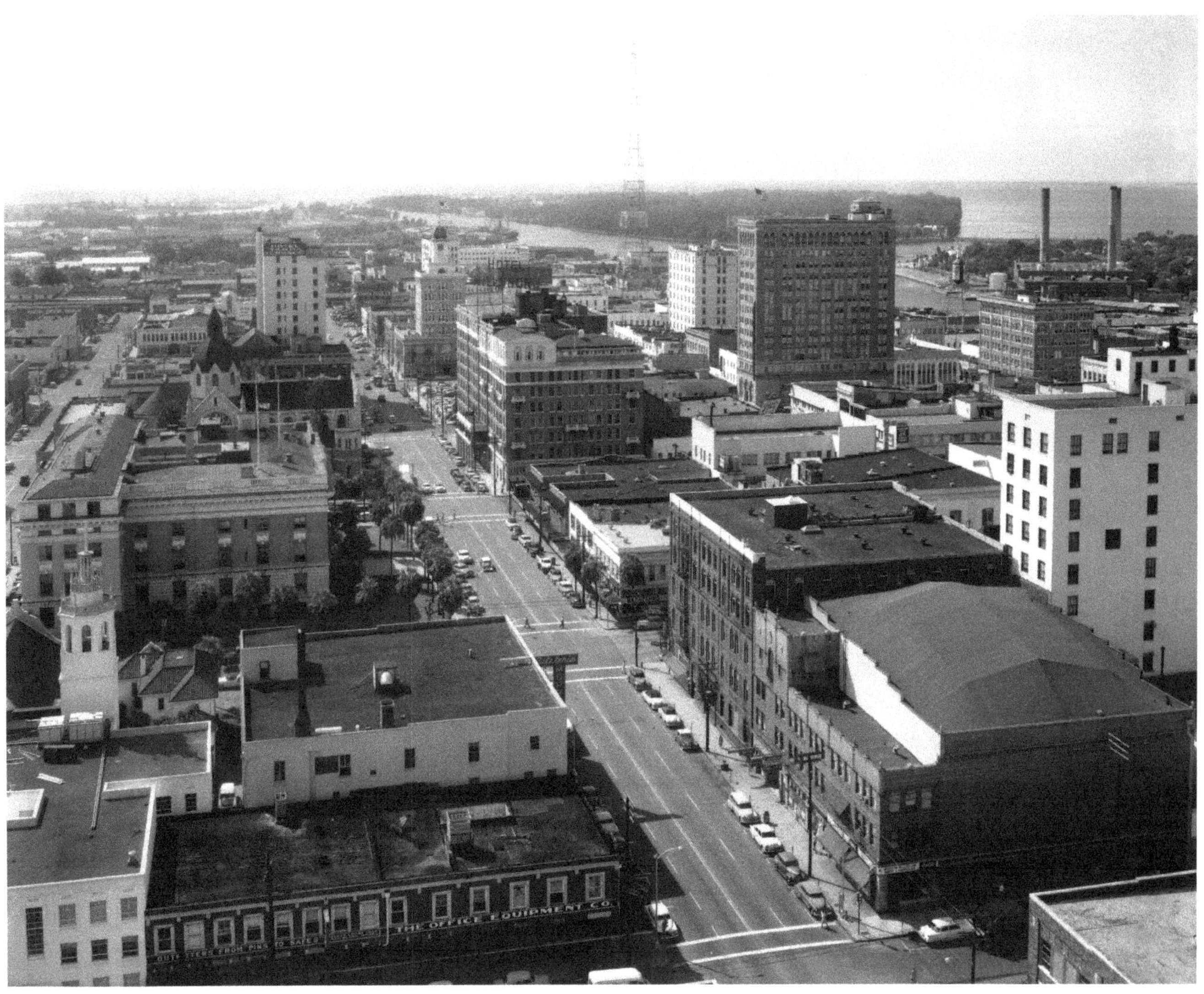

Looking south along the 500 to 700 blocks of Florida Avenue, the five-story brick building seen here to the right of the avenue (just beyond the building with the slightly domed roof) is the YMCA building at the northwest corner of the intersection with Zack Street. To its right is a tall white building which includes offices and the Tampa Theatre. The YMCA corner was later turned into a parking lot, but the theatre is still hosting shows.

South of Lafayette Street, Franklin Street continues over the Garrison Channel to turn into Harbor Island Drive on Harbor (formerly Seddon) Island. In the foreground is Stenotype Institute Business College, next door to the City Hall. The Bay View Hotel is all the way to the right edge of this image.

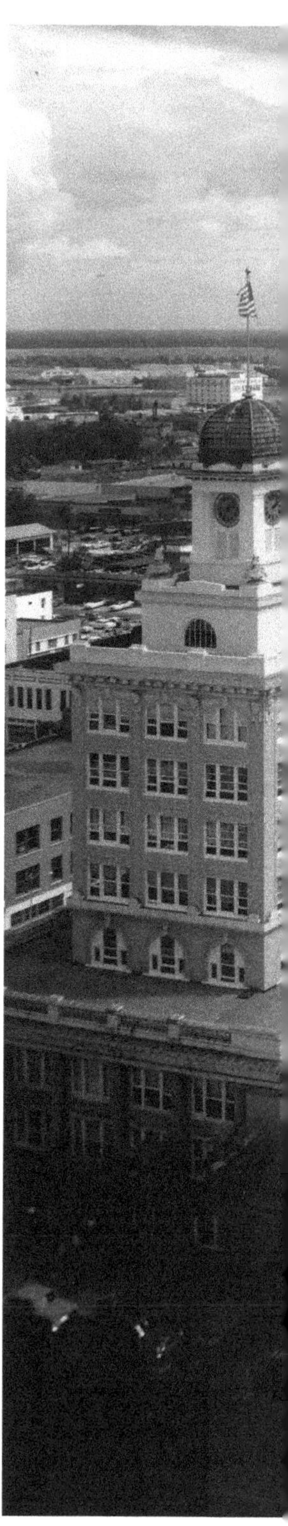

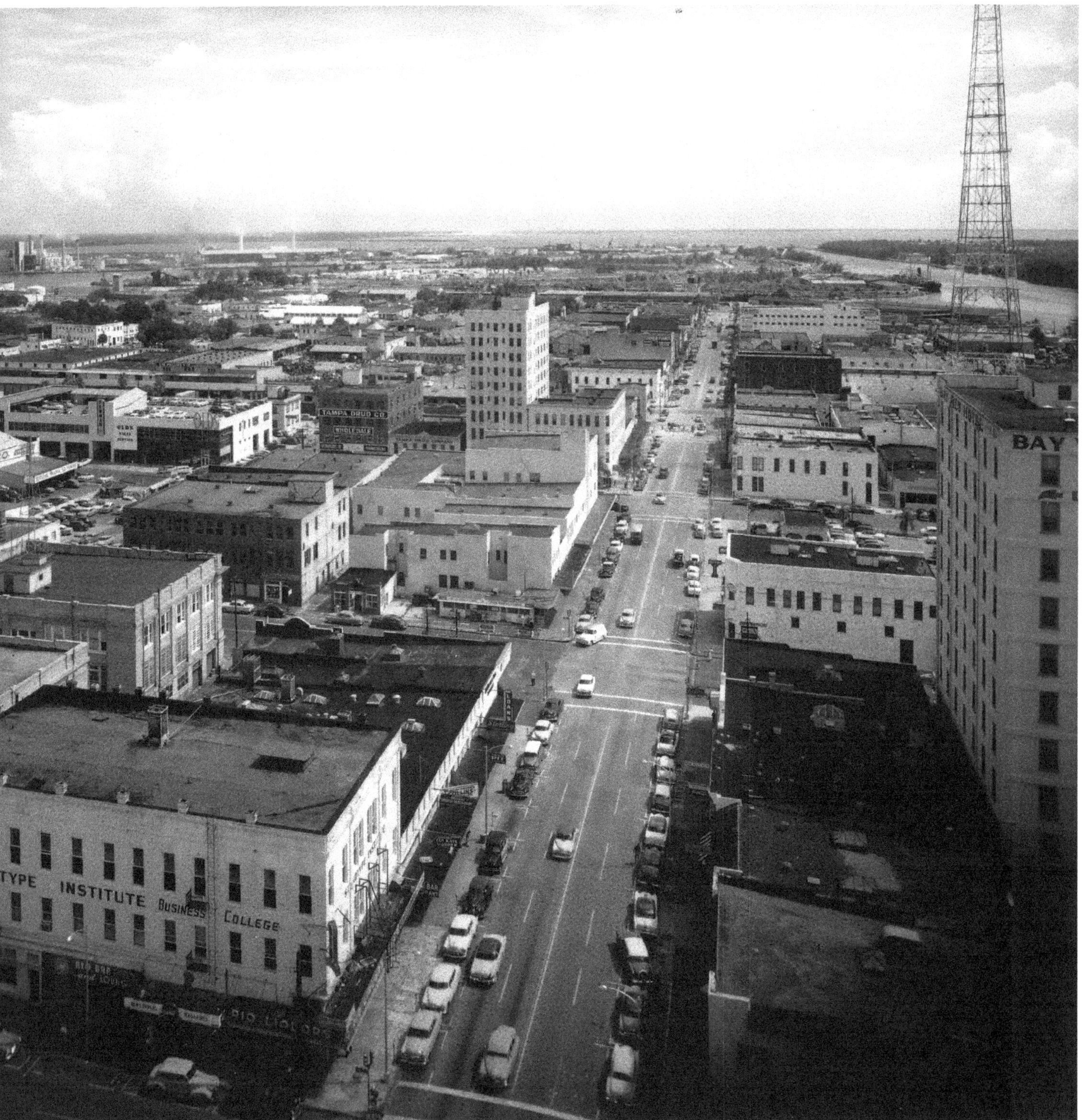
TAMPA DRUG CO.
WHOLESALE
BAY
TYPE INSTITUTE BUSINESS COLLEGE

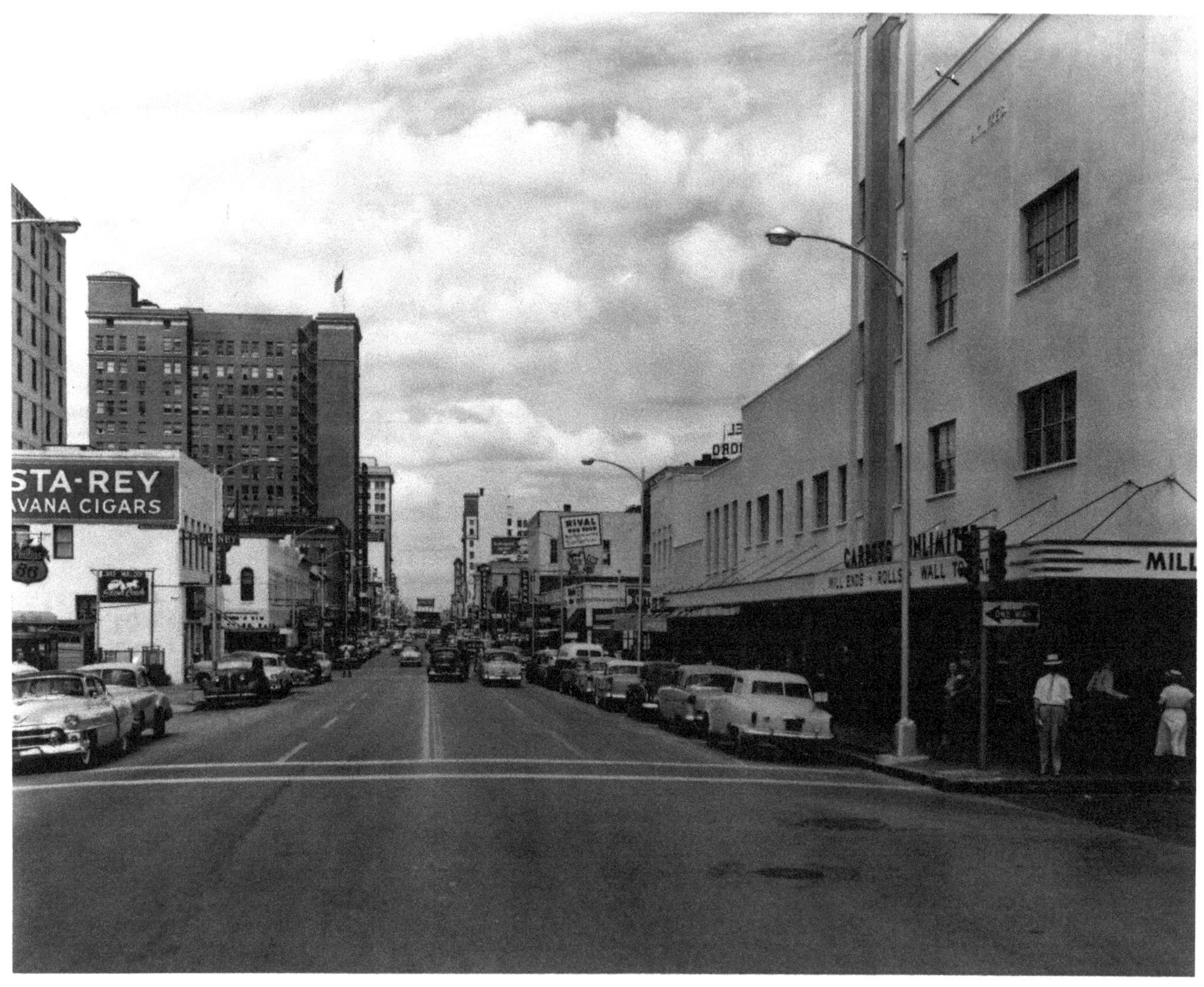

The 200 and 300 blocks of Franklin Street, looking north from the intersection with Washington Street, look nothing like this today. This stretch of Franklin has been replaced by a pedestrian mall. The white building on the right, the site of a series of hotels beginning with the Almeria in 1886, was replaced by the 38-story One Tampa City Center in 1981.

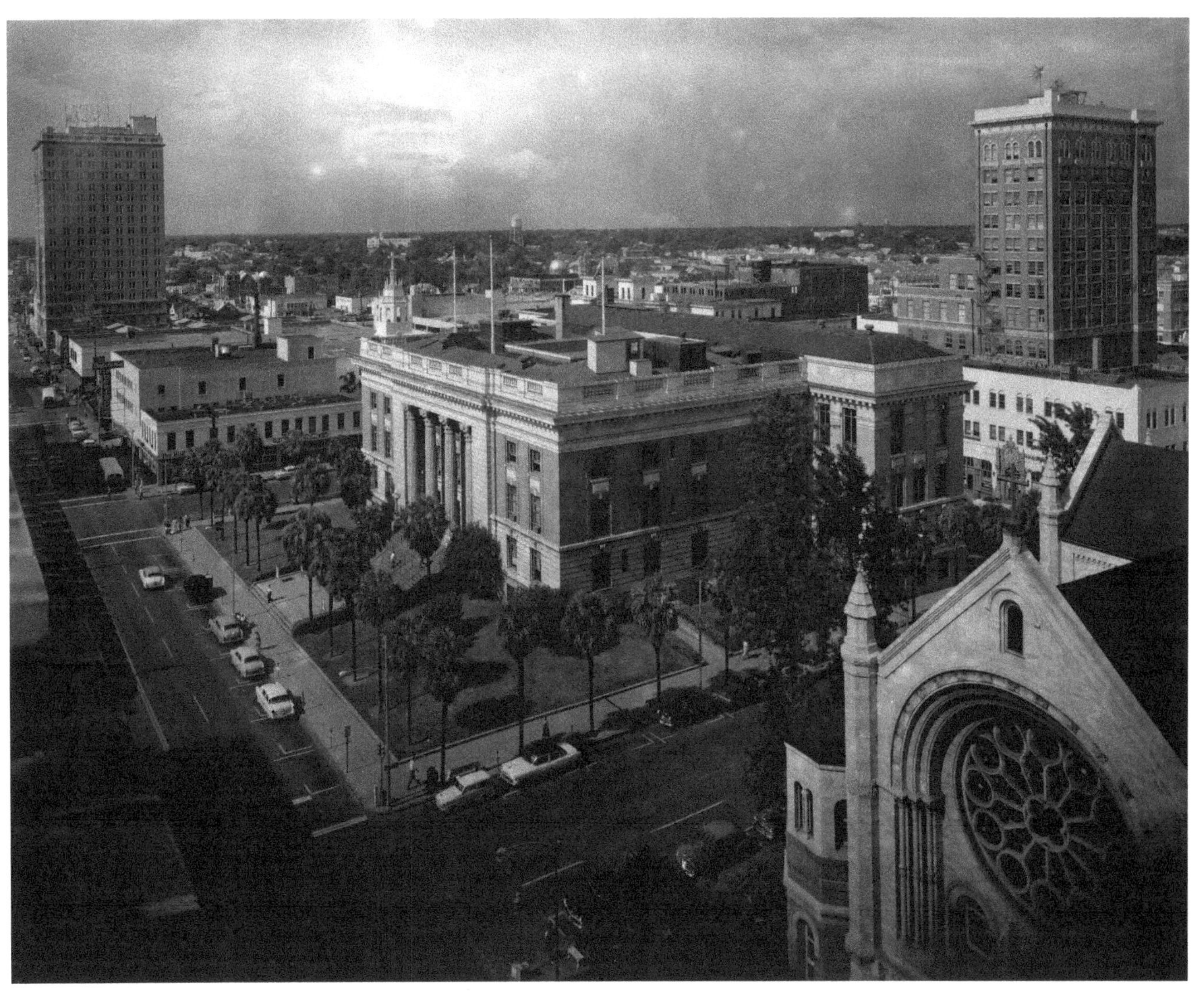

At 601 North Florida Avenue stands the Federal Building, which served as the post office and federal courthouse from 1905 until 1965. In the foreground is the large rose window of Sacred Heart Catholic Church.

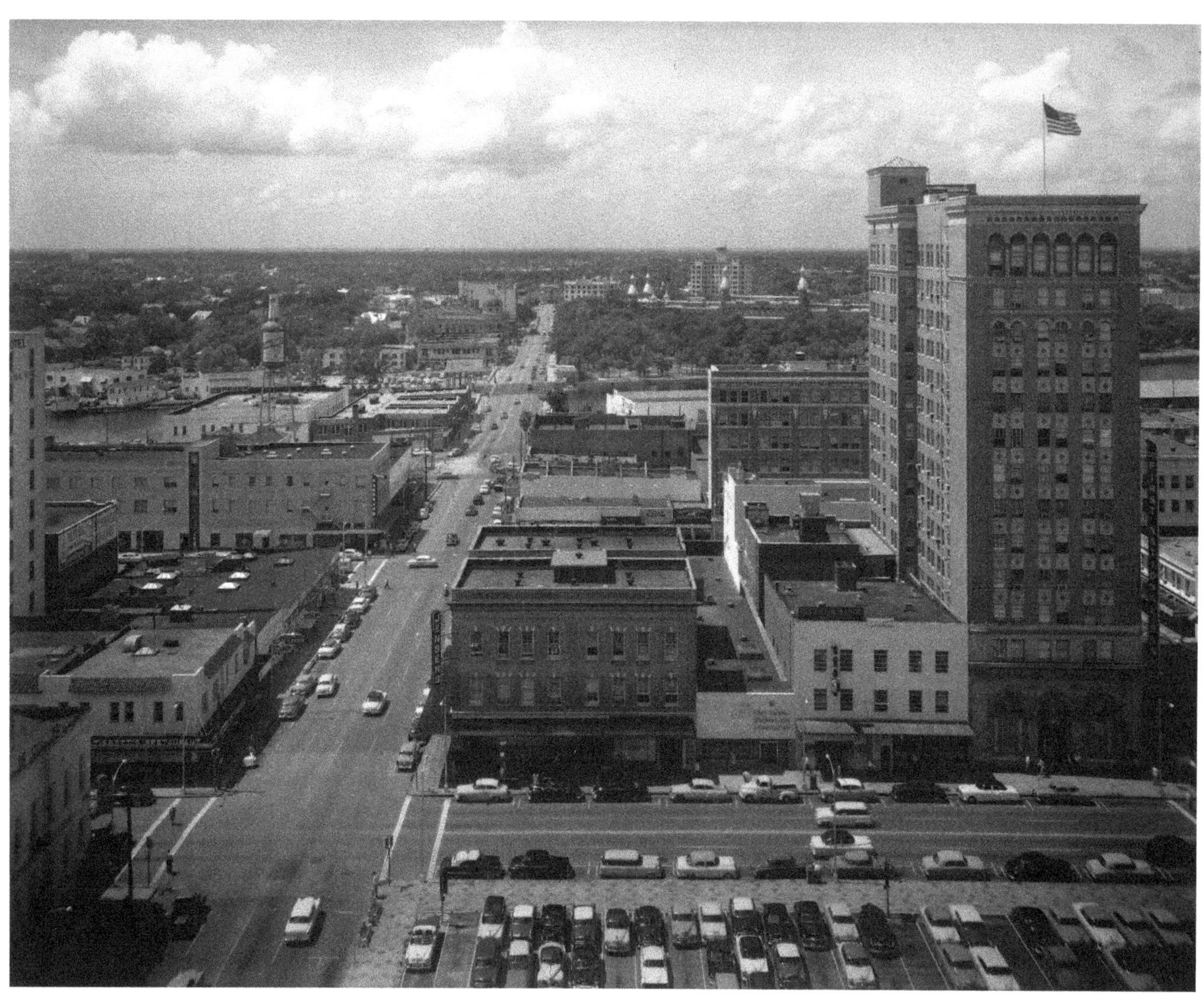

Lafayette Street heads westward toward the horizon, crossing over the Hillsborough River before passing by the former Tampa Bay Hotel. The tall tower topped by the flag is the First National Bank. This is a good view of an architectural method which was popularized in this country by Louis Sullivan in his designs of the earliest skyscrapers—the lower floors are covered with light-colored stone, and are set off from the darker upper floors by a projecting band.

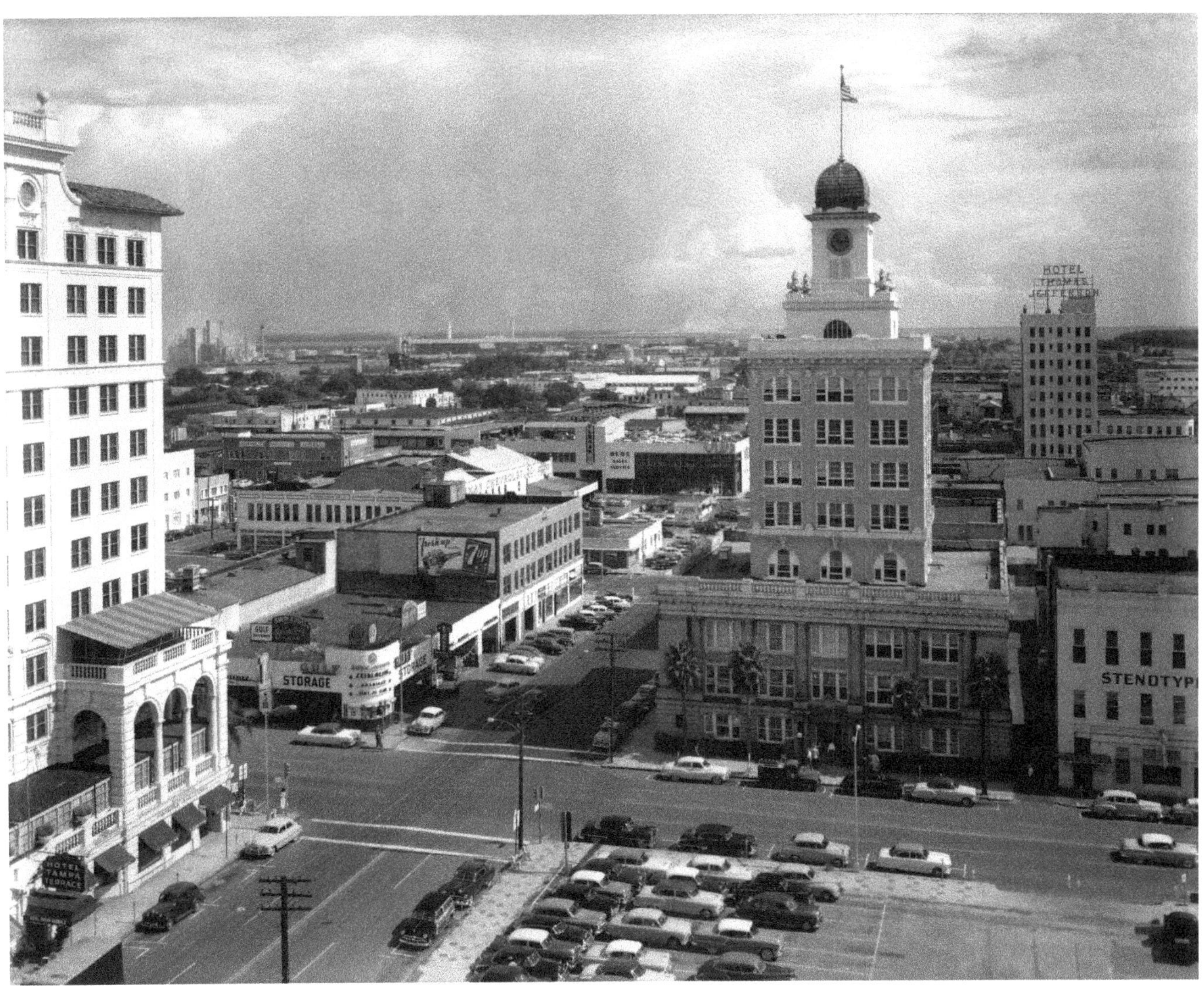

Standing north of the City Hall and facing south toward Tampa Bay, the most prominent building in sight is the Hotel Thomas Jefferson, located at the corner of Franklin and Washington Streets. It originally opened as the four-story Olive Hotel, and was expanded with the addition of a ten-story tower. This is how it appeared on September 17, 1954. It was torn down in 1969.

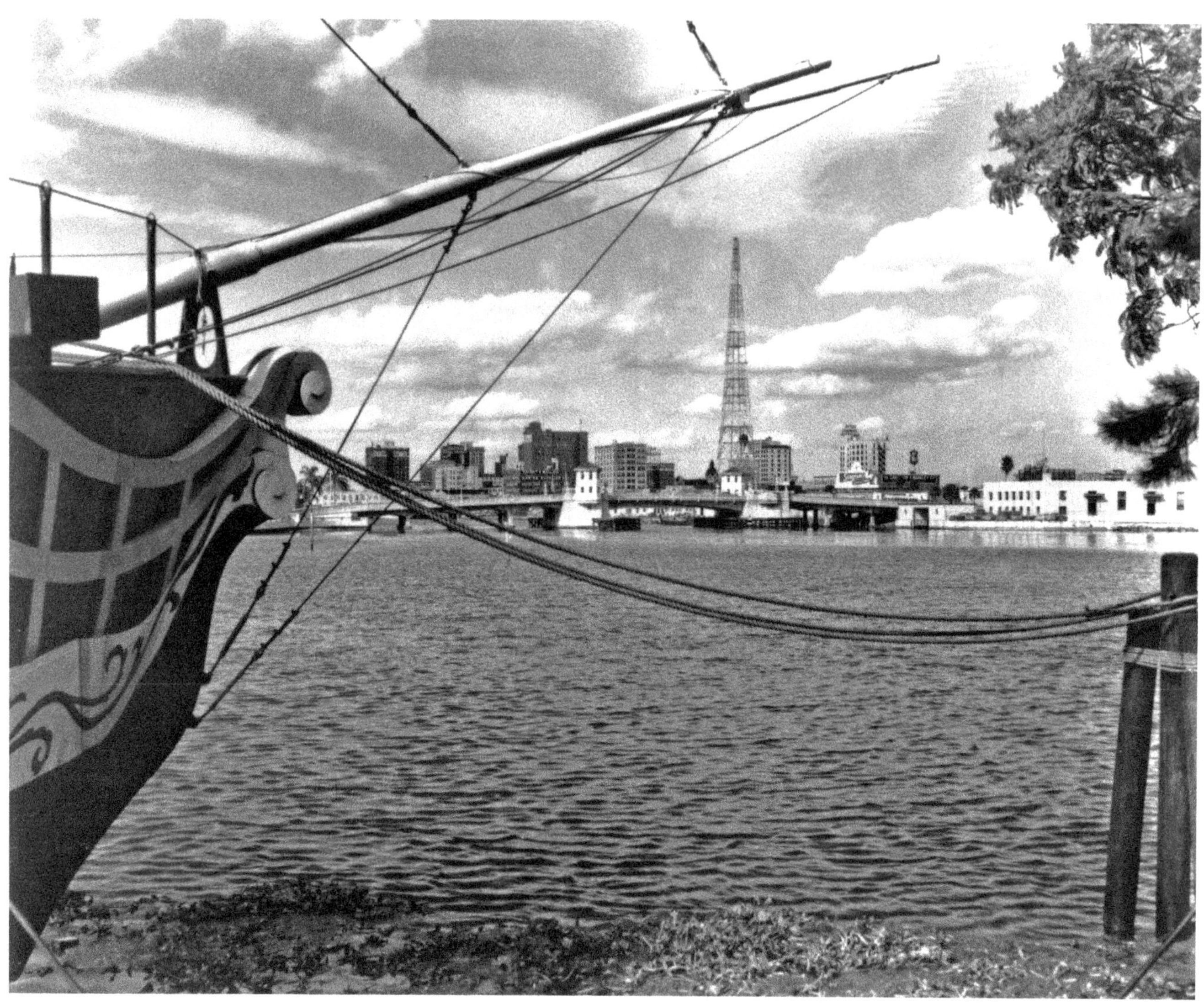

Separating the water of the Hillsborough River and the skyline of downtown Tampa is the Platt Street Bridge. Above the bridge in this view is the spar of the *Jose Gaspar*, a reproduction of a pirate ship. When it is not in use during the annual Gasparilla Festival, it is moored along Bayshore boulevard between Hyde Park Place and Beach Place, just south of the Tarpon Weigh Station.

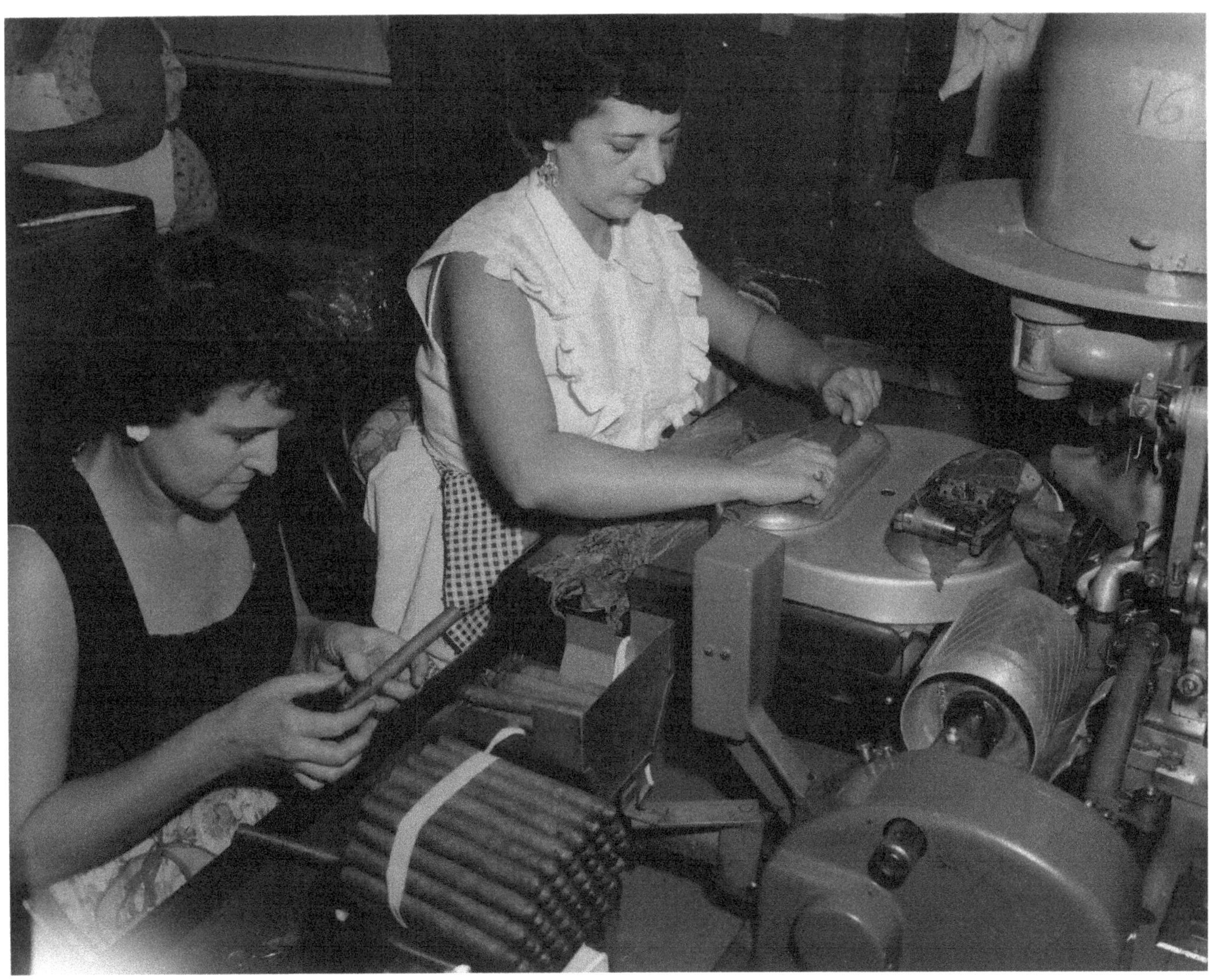

At least since the 1920s, Corral, Wodiska and Company was producing cigars in Tampa. One of the brands it produced was the "Julia Marlowe." By the time this photo was taken on November 13, 1954, there were two major changes in the company's manufacturing methods. Instead of a crew made up solely of men, women comprised a significant portion of the work force. Also, instead of being hand-rolled, the cigars were made on machines, including those shown here.

On its first day of business in 1883, what would become the First National Bank received only $5,636 in deposits. Within two years, Tampa entered the recession that was affecting the entire country, and business diminished even further. However, the Board of Trade encouraged cigar makers to move to Tampa, and their activities required large amounts of money in the form of gold and silver, so there was soon much banking activity. Tampa continued to grow, and with it the First National Bank. Shown here is its lobby in spring 1955.

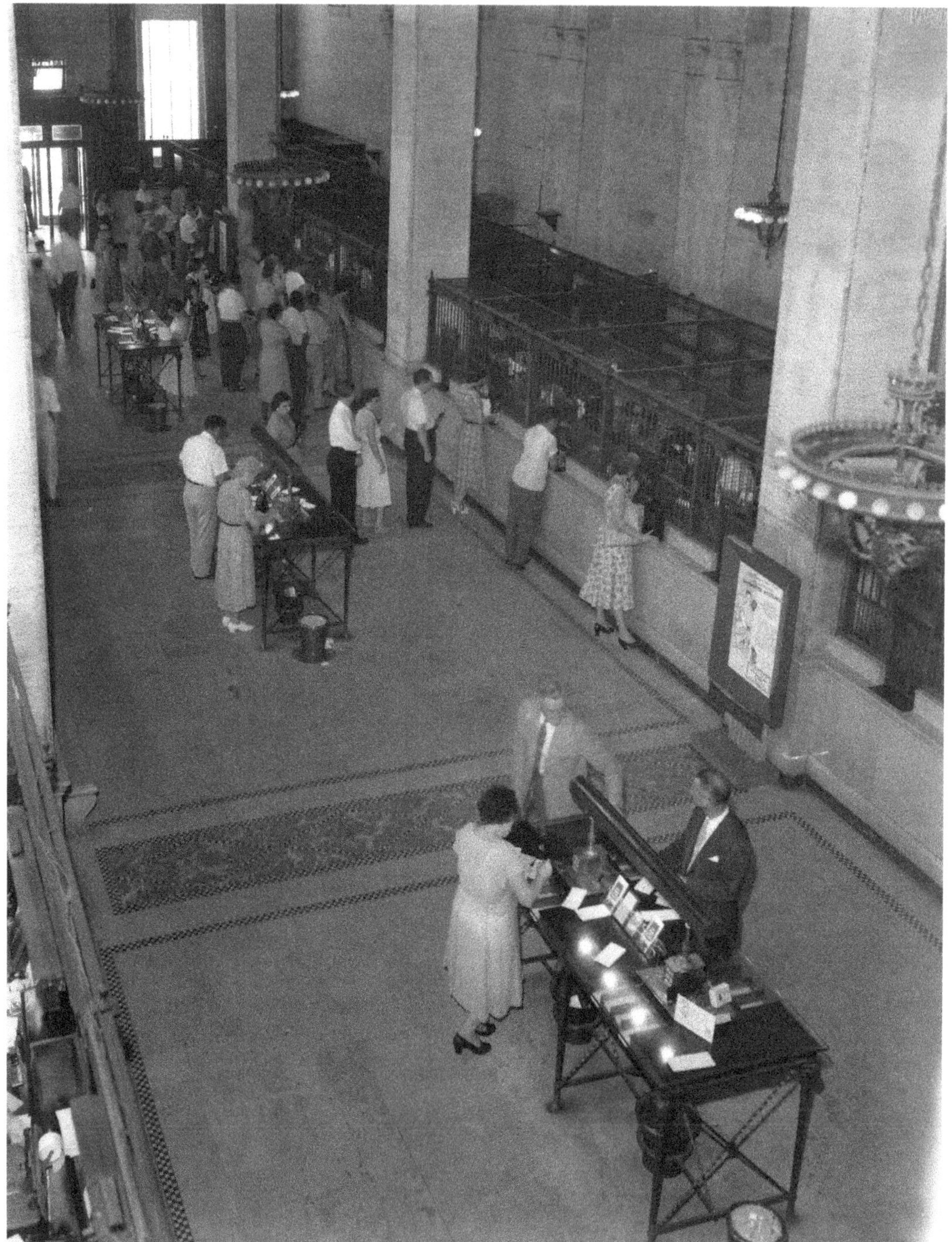

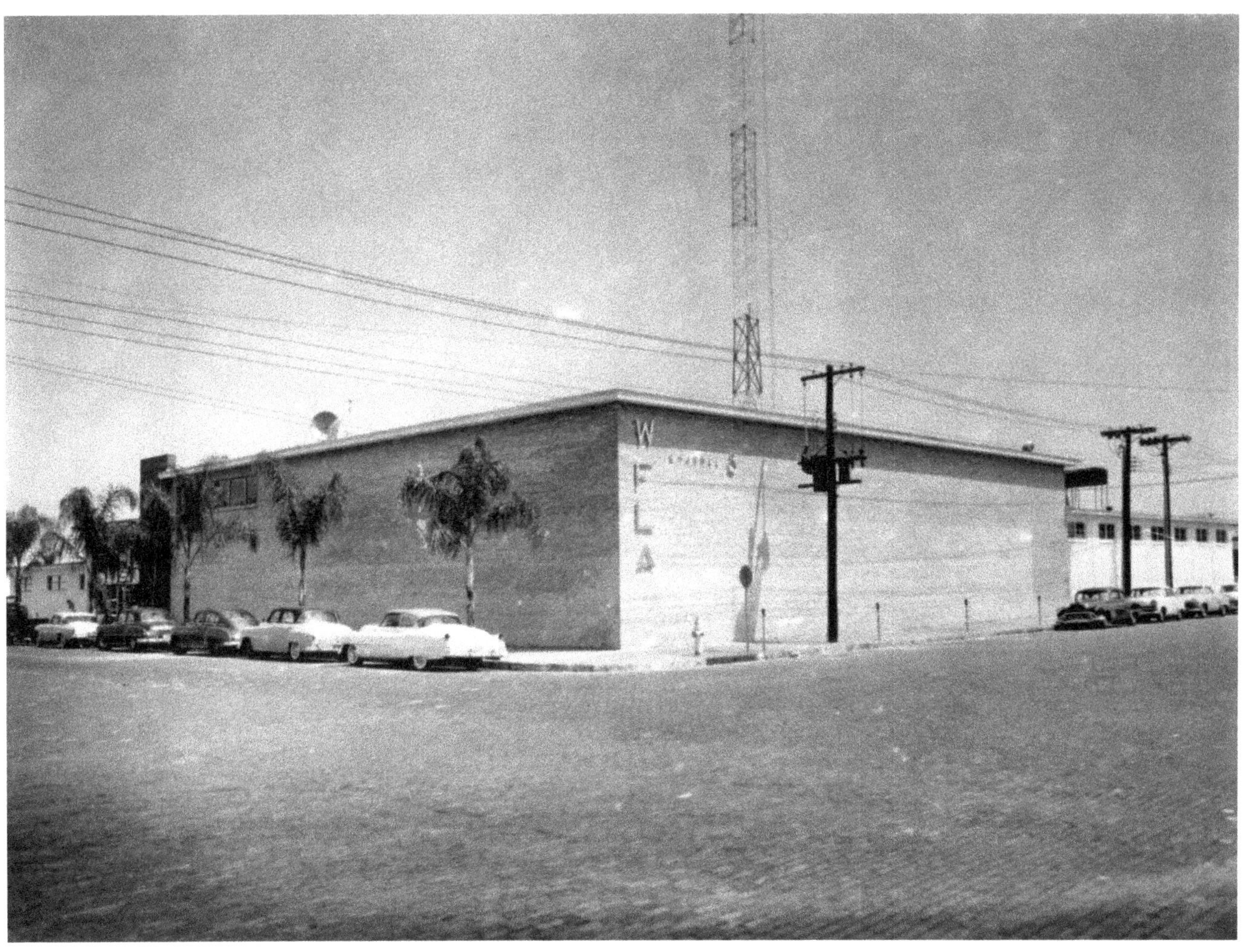

The *Tampa Tribune* newspaper took over an existing radio station and began using the call letters WFLA in 1941. The same call letters were used on Tampa's first VHF television station, pictured here on April 5, 1955. Its first broadcast was of the Gasparilla parade on Febraury 14 of that year. As Channel 8, it was an NBC affiliate with early shows including *The Medic, Robert Montgomery Presents,* and *The Tonight Show.* Later, the station's call letters were changed to WXFL.

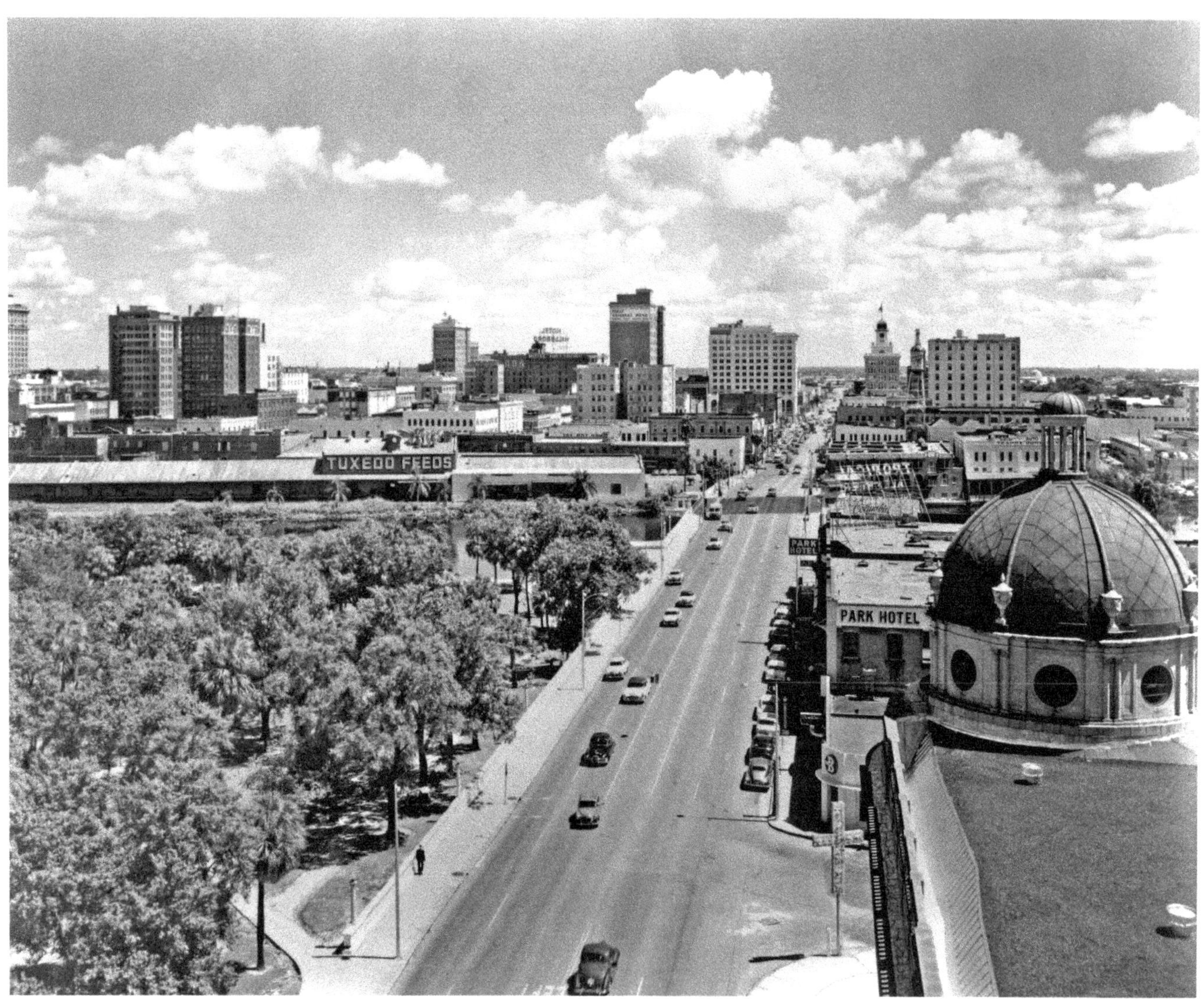

The beautifully landscaped Plant Park is seen on the north side of Lafayette Street, just west of the Hillsborough River. It was named for Henry B. Plant, the developer of the adjacent Tampa Bay Hotel. Across the street is the domed First Baptist Church, built in 1925 at the southwest corner of Lafayette Street and Plant Avenue to replace that congregation's 1896 brick church.

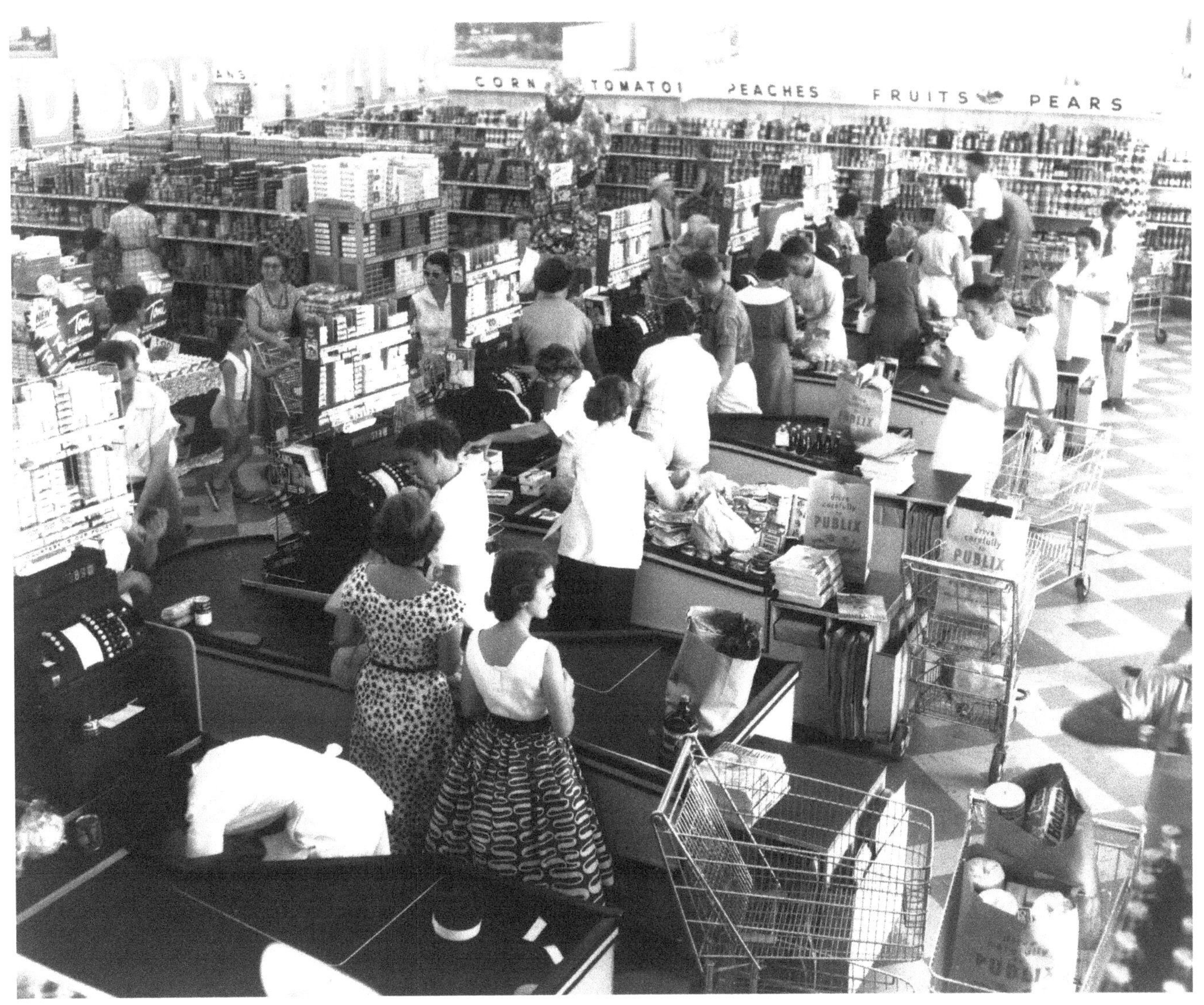

This was the scene inside the Publix Supermarket at 1313 South Dale Mabry Highway in July 1955. George W. Jenkins, Sr. founded the chain of stores and chose the name because of its sound, previously the name of a movie theater chain. He had worked in his family's grocery store in Harris, Georgia, and moved to Florida at age 17 to seek his fortune. A year later in 1925, he was the manager of a Piggly Wiggly store in Tampa. He opened his first Publix store in Winter Haven, later moved his headquarters to Lakeland and expanded its coverage with large, bright supermarkets throughout the Southeast.

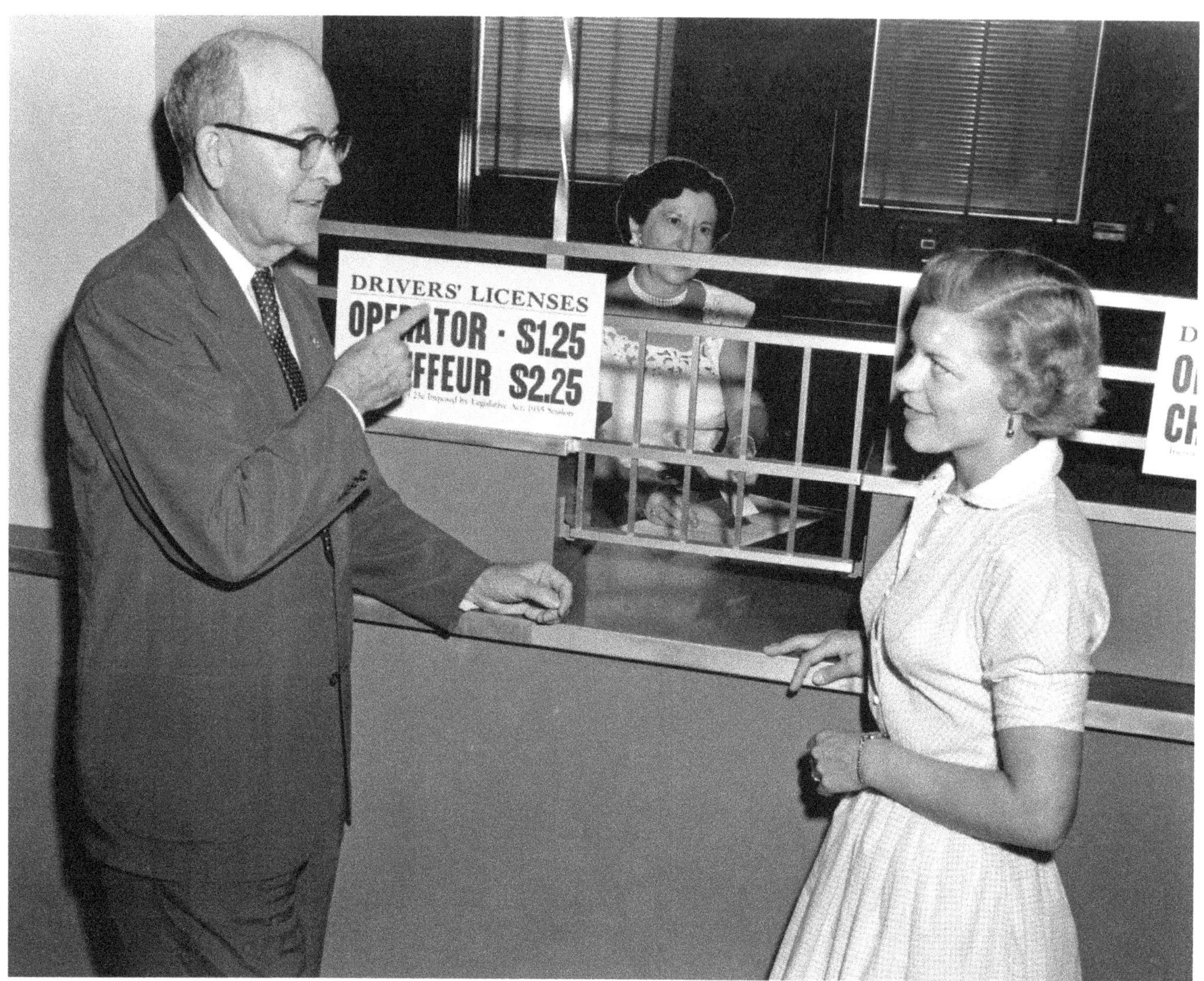

Seen here with a customer and a clerk at the auto license bureau is County Judge William C. Brooker. In addition to serving as a judge, Brooker was the president of the Tampa Exchange Club in 1942. In 1970, he made it into the news when he upheld the county's denial of marriage licenses to a pair of lesbian couples on the grounds that homosexual marriage—even though not then prohibited by statute—was contrary to public policy.

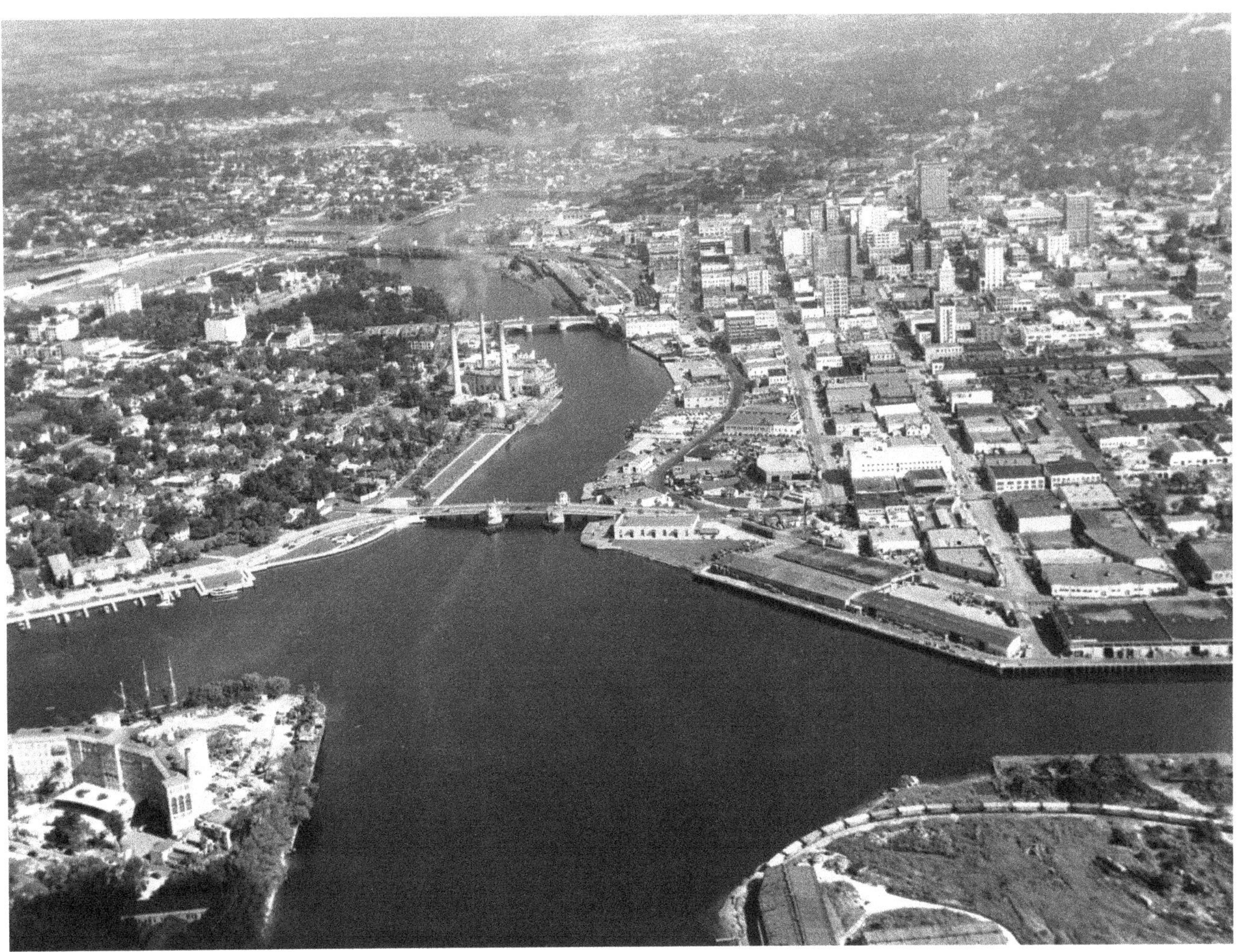

This aerial photo taken on September 28, 1956, shows how the city is split by the Hillsborough River. Downtown is the portion in the upper right, the upscale homes of Hyde Park appear among trees on the left, Seddon Island is in the lower right, and in the lower left is the northern end of Davis Islands. There, the tall Tampa General Hospital can be identified. It was built in 1926–27 and included the Gordon Keller Nursing School.

On Tampa Street, covering most of the block from Lafayette to Madison Streets, stood this seven-story office building. It was one of the projects of Wallace F. Stovall, who moved to Tampa from Kentucky in 1893 and founded the *Tampa Morning Tribune* newspaper. When he sold the newspaper in 1925 for $1.2 million, he invested his profits in real estate, including this lot at 416 North Tampa Street where he built the Stovall Office building. By the mid-1950s when this photo was taken, it was called the Flagler building. It was replaced by the 36-story Park Tower in 1972.

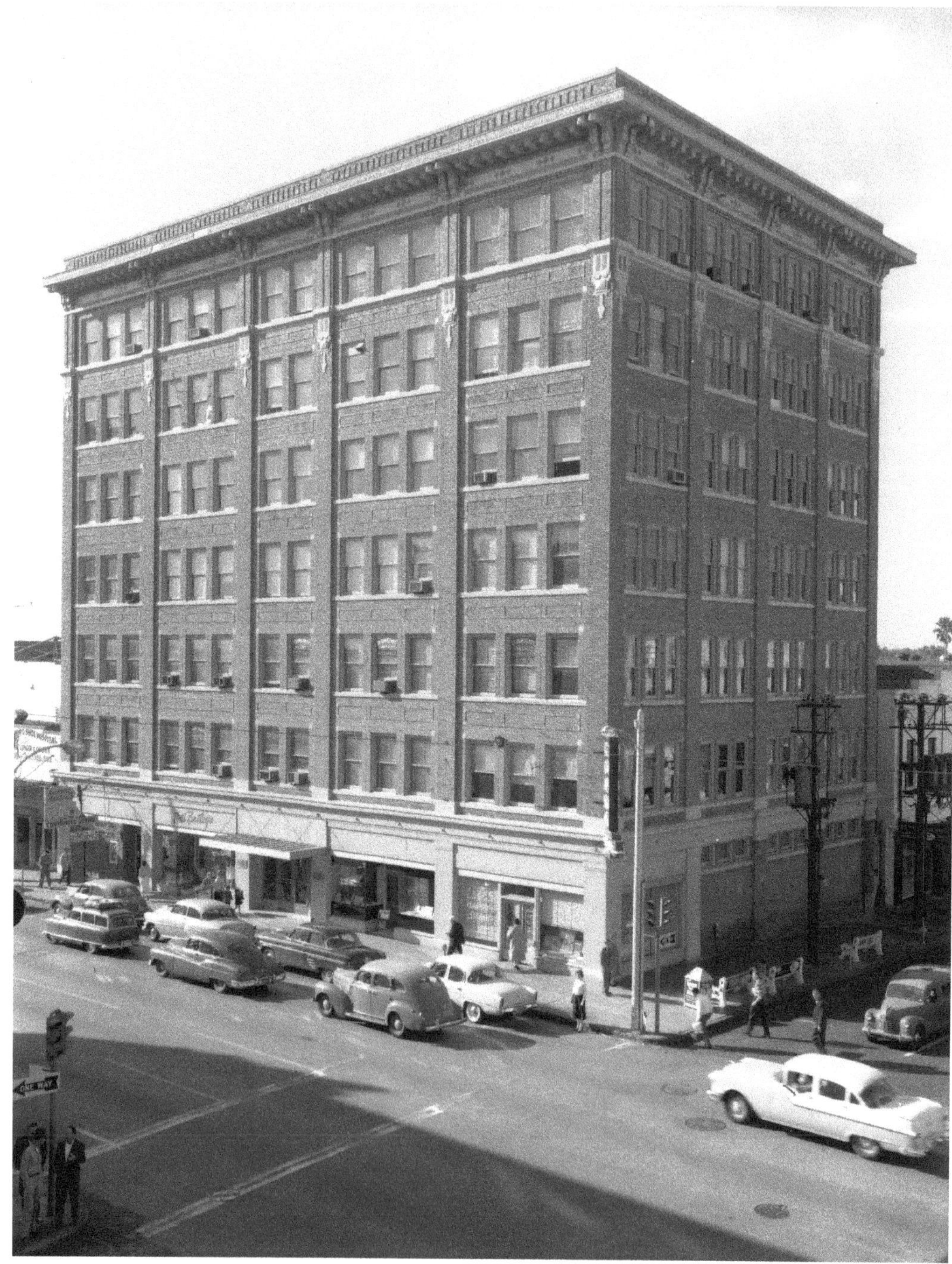

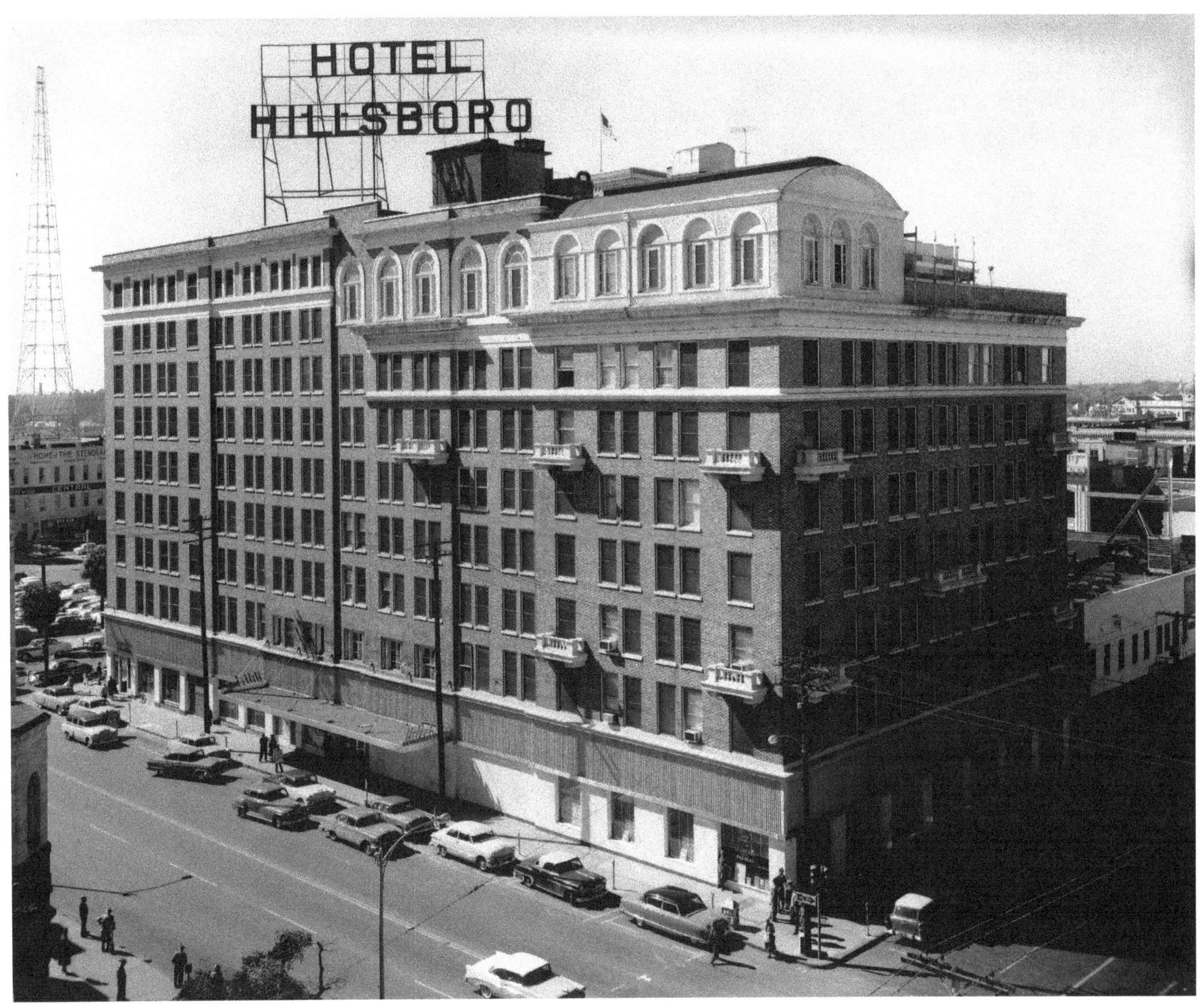

The 320-room Hotel Hillsboro opened at 512 Florida Avenue in 1912, and was expanded with wings on the south side in 1916 and 1920. It is shown here on February 29, 1956, approximately eight years before it was converted into an office building. Inside were the studios of WINQ radio, which had a middle-of-the-road format starting in the early 1960s before it switched to talk radio, then country music, then Christian rock, and then moved out to a studio in Seffner (east of Tampa) in the 1970s. The former hotel building was condemned in 1979. After the station moved to Seffner, it was broadcasting religious shows produced by local churches. In 1981, its call letters were changed to WCBF ("We're Christians by Faith"). In 1988, it switched to country music and changed its call letters to WQYK, under which it broadcasts country today.

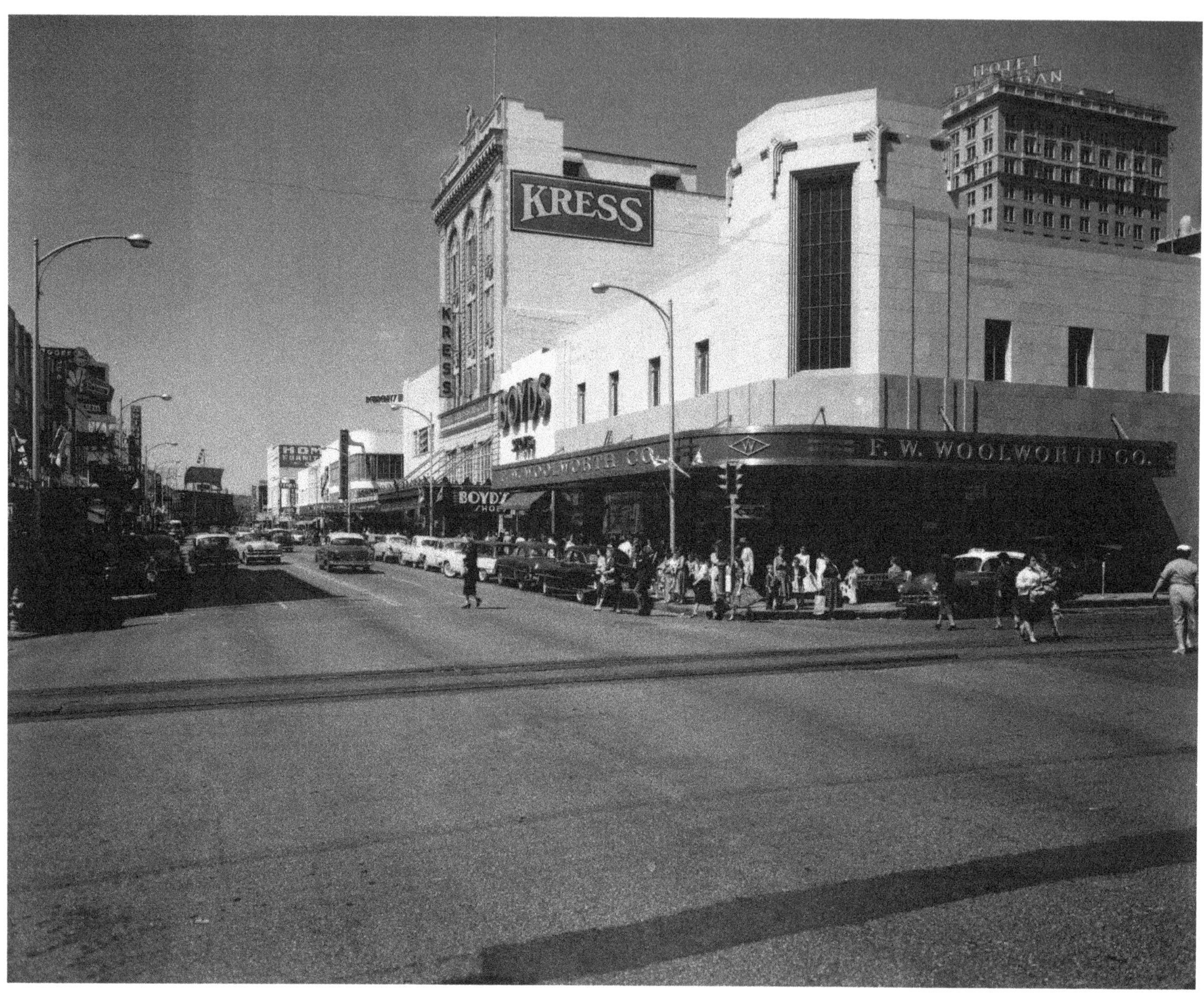

The east side of the 800 block of North Franklin Street had three competing dime stores, J. J. Newberry on the north, F. W. Woolworth on the south, and Kress in the middle. The Kress building was erected in 1929 with the design of New York architect G. E. McKay. Company founder Samuel Kress insisted that his more than 250 stores show artistic details, and the ones from this era focus on the Art Deco style. The store was located on the first floor, and offices were upstairs. There have been proposals to redevelop the block, but preservationists are trying to keep a requirement that the facades of all three abandoned dime stores be restored, rather than demolished.

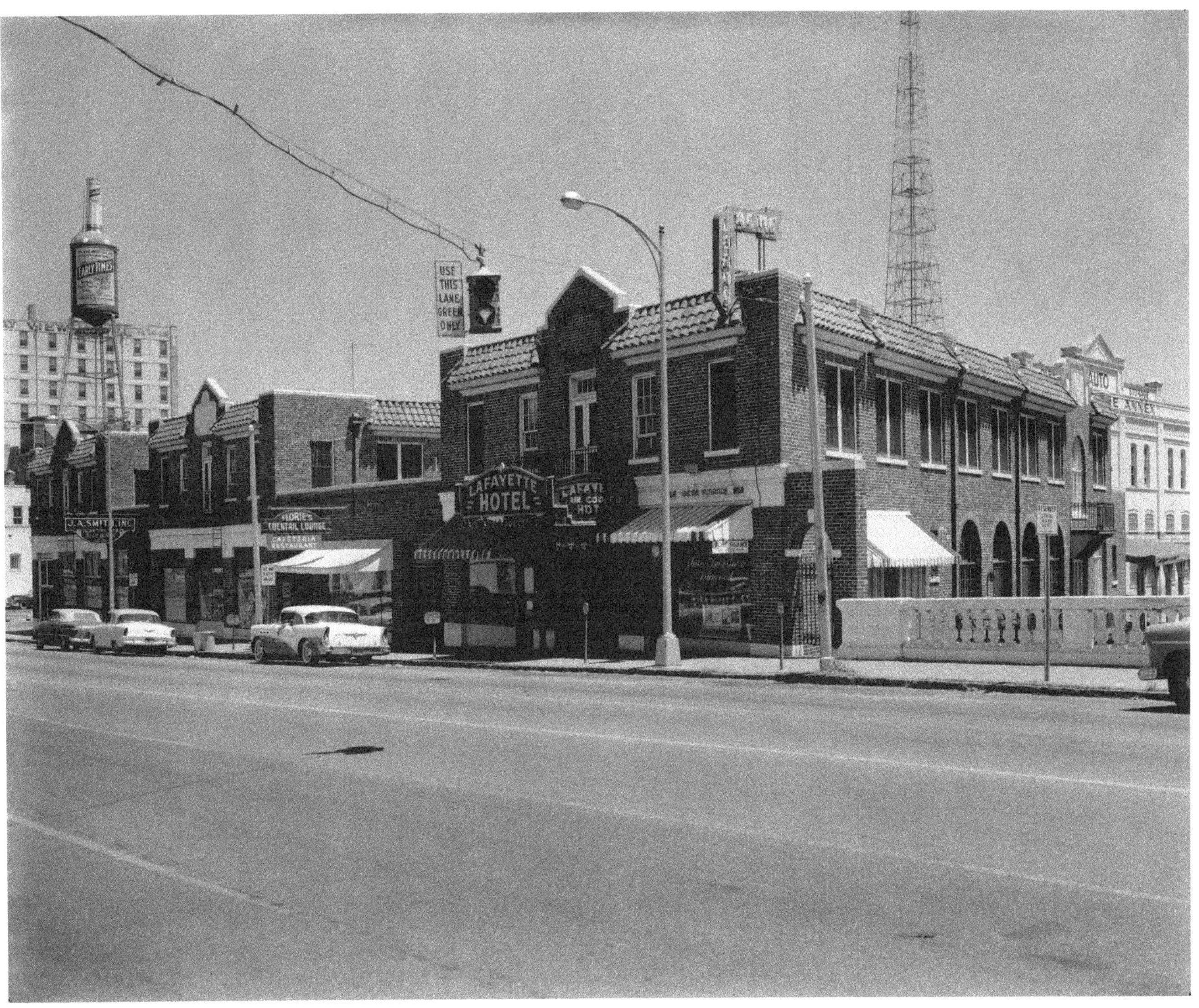

When this photo was taken on April 20, 1956, the address of the Lafayette Hotel was 120 West Lafayette Street. Nearby is a water tank atop a tower, shaped like an Early Times whiskey bottle, and the Bay View Hotel beyond that. The rooms on the west side (the side on the right in this photo) had a good view of the Hillsborough River below. The low white wall leading to the right edge of this scene begins the west end of the Lafayette Street Bridge.

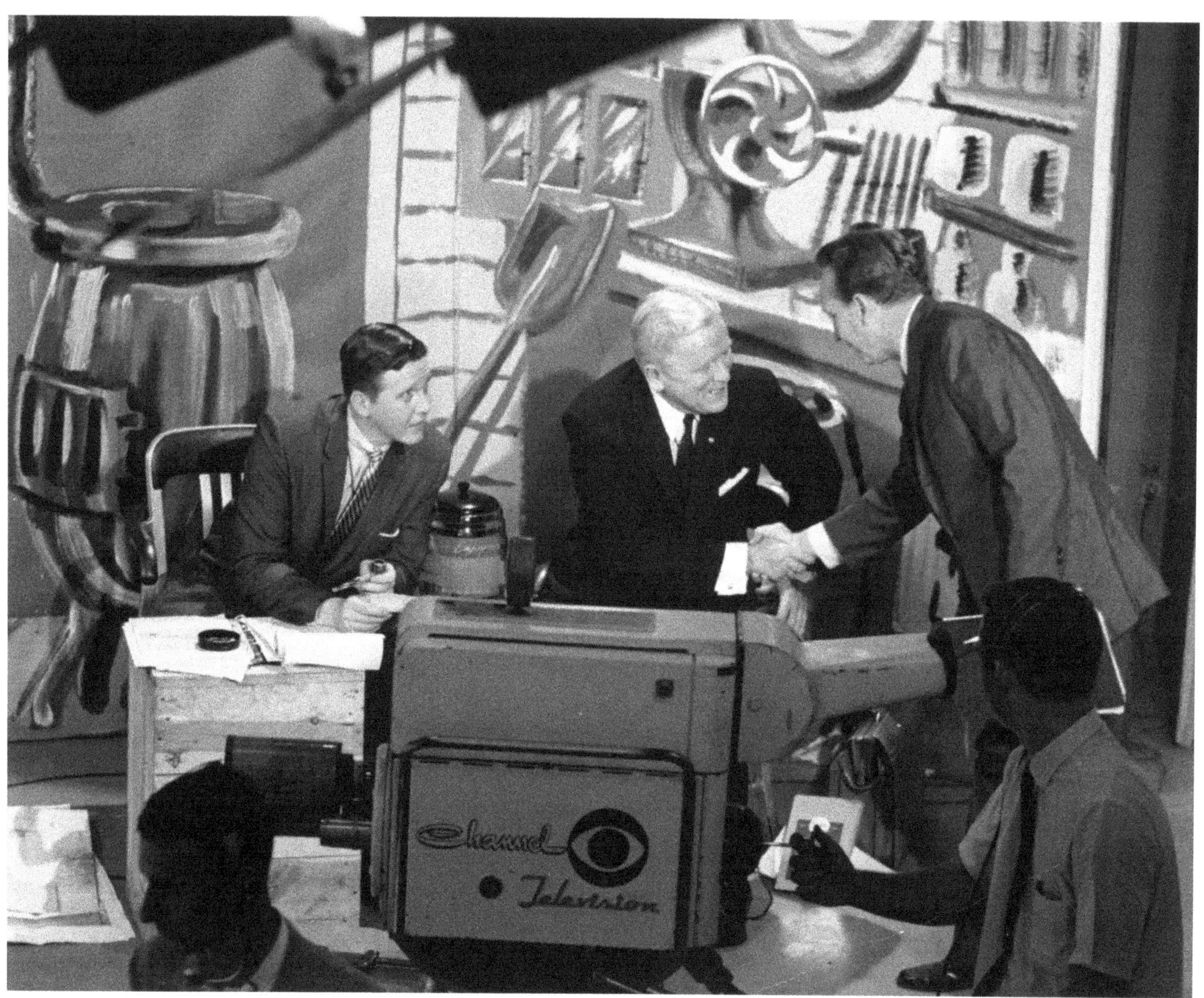

Television host John E. Evans (on the left) watches as gubernatorial hopefuls Thomas LeRoy Collins and Fuller Warren greet each other on the WTVT set. Collins defeated Warren in the 1954 Democratic primary, then beat previous governor Charley Eugene Johns in the general election. Collins served as governor from 1955 to 1961. The station went on the air with its first broadcast on April 1, 1955, and set many Tampa Bay broadcasting "firsts," especially in the areas of news and weather reporting. It was originally affiliated with CBS.

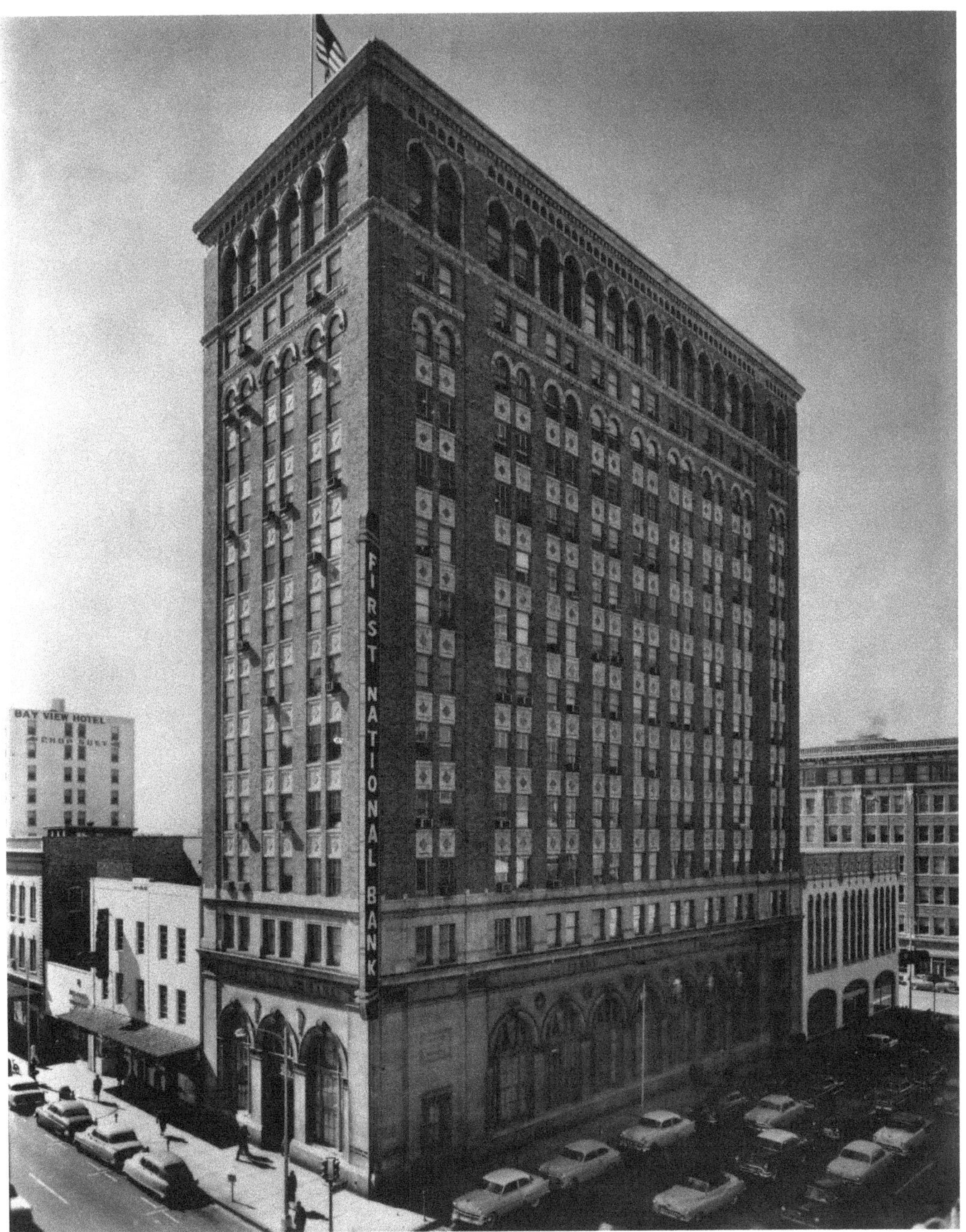

Tampa's first skyscraper was built in the mid-1920s at 414-416 Franklin Street as the home of the First National Bank. This is how it appeared on November 27, 1956. At that time, it was led by Victor H. Northcutt, who succeeded Carson Taliaferro, the son of the bank's founder.

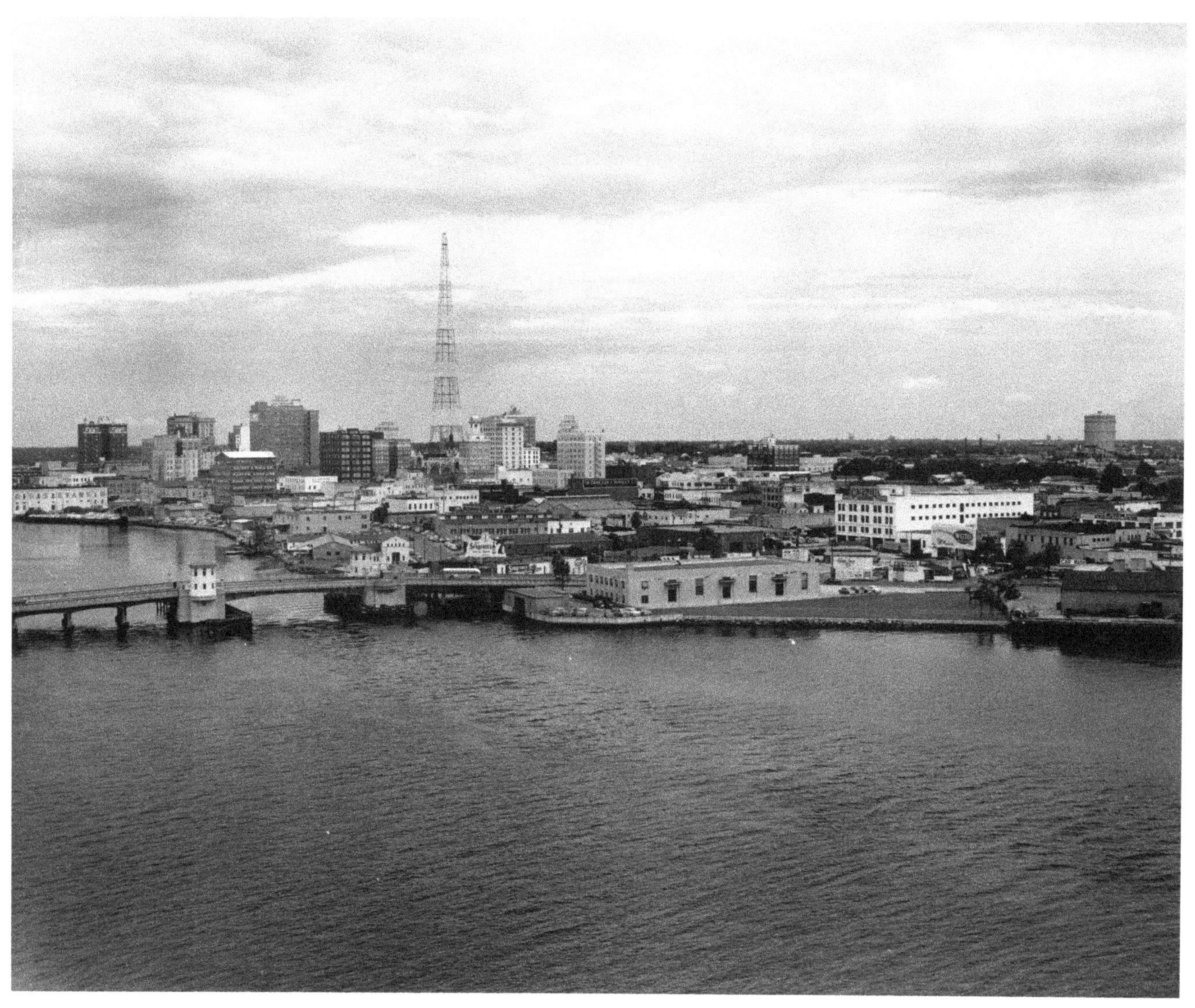

In this 1957 photo can be seen the tender's room on the Platt Street Bridge. It was the tender's job to watch for tall vessels so the center span could be opened to permit passage.

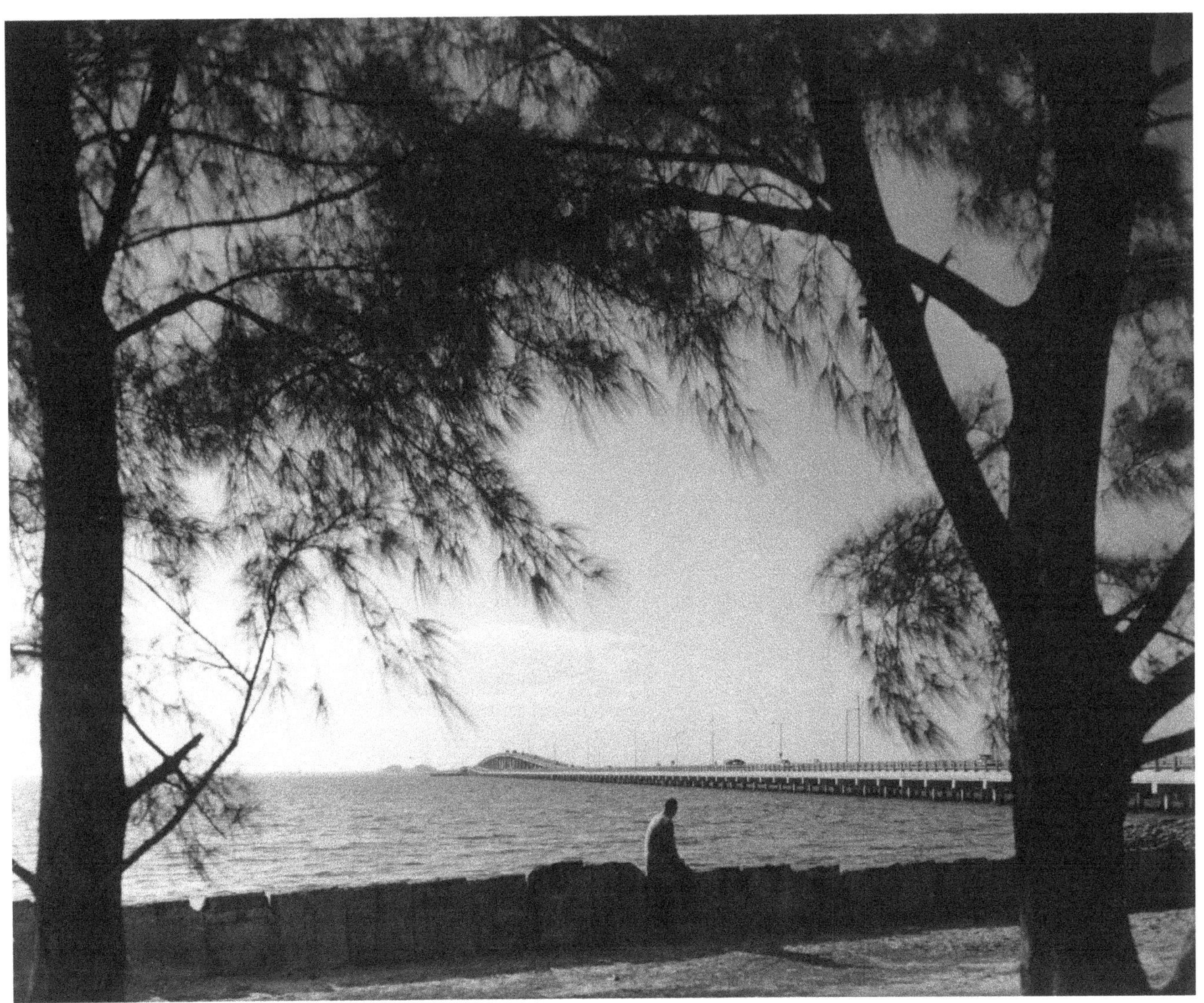

The original Gandy Bridge connecting Tampa with St. Petersburg opened in 1924. It shortened the driving distance between the two cities by 33 miles. The bridge was named for George S. "Dad" Gandy, who built it despite many feeling that it was a crazy idea. The old bridge was replaced in 1956, a year before this photo was taken. In 1997, the bridge was saved from demolition and instead was converted into the Friendship TrailBridge, for use by pedestrians and bicyclists.

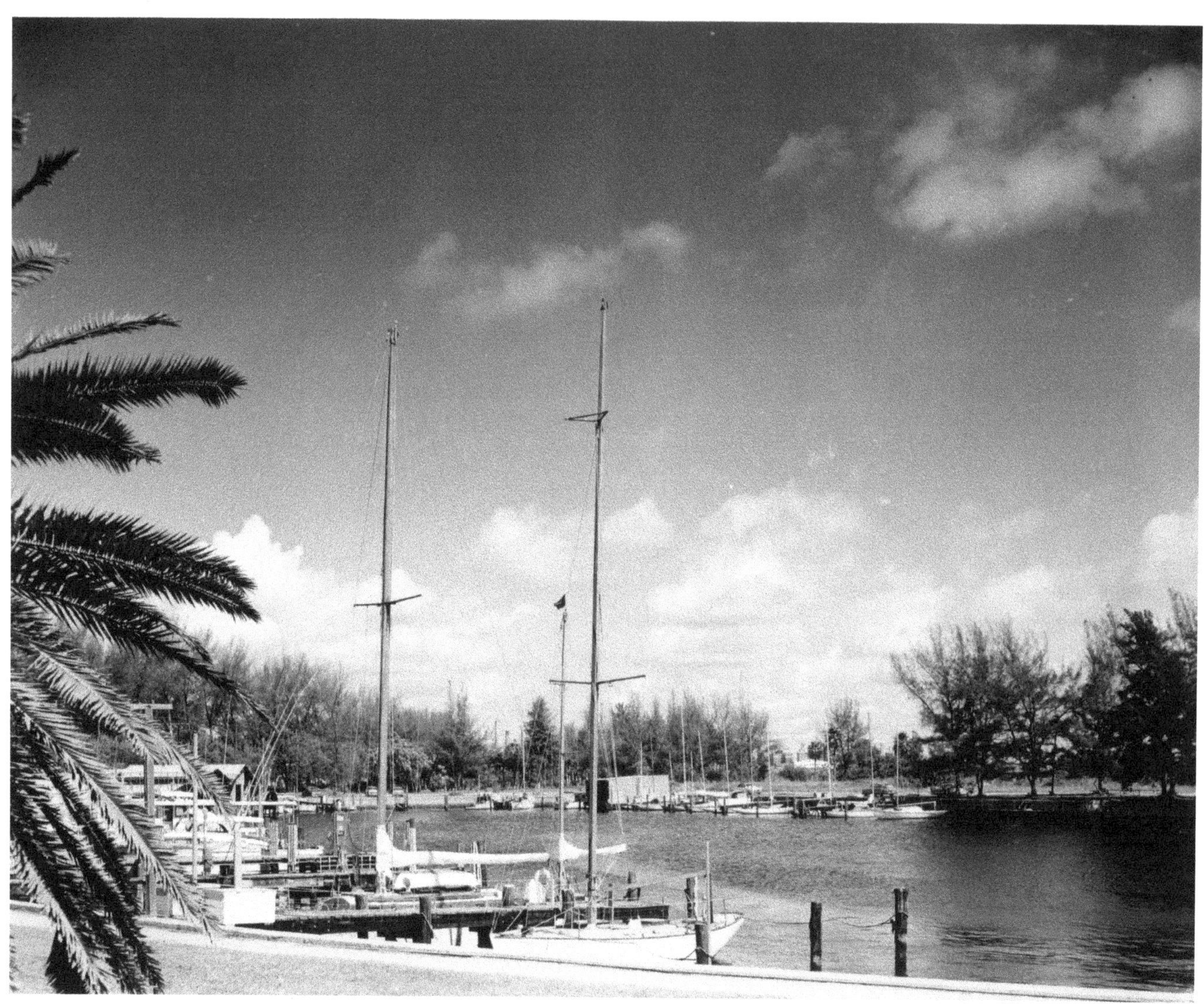

The Tampa Yacht Basin, located near the clubhouse at 5320 Interbay Boulevard, is landscaped with palm and oak trees. It is just south of Ballast Point, an area so named because schooners loaded and dumped their ballast there. It was developed as a waterside pleasure resort and nearby are some of the larger, older Queen Anne-style homes of Tampa.

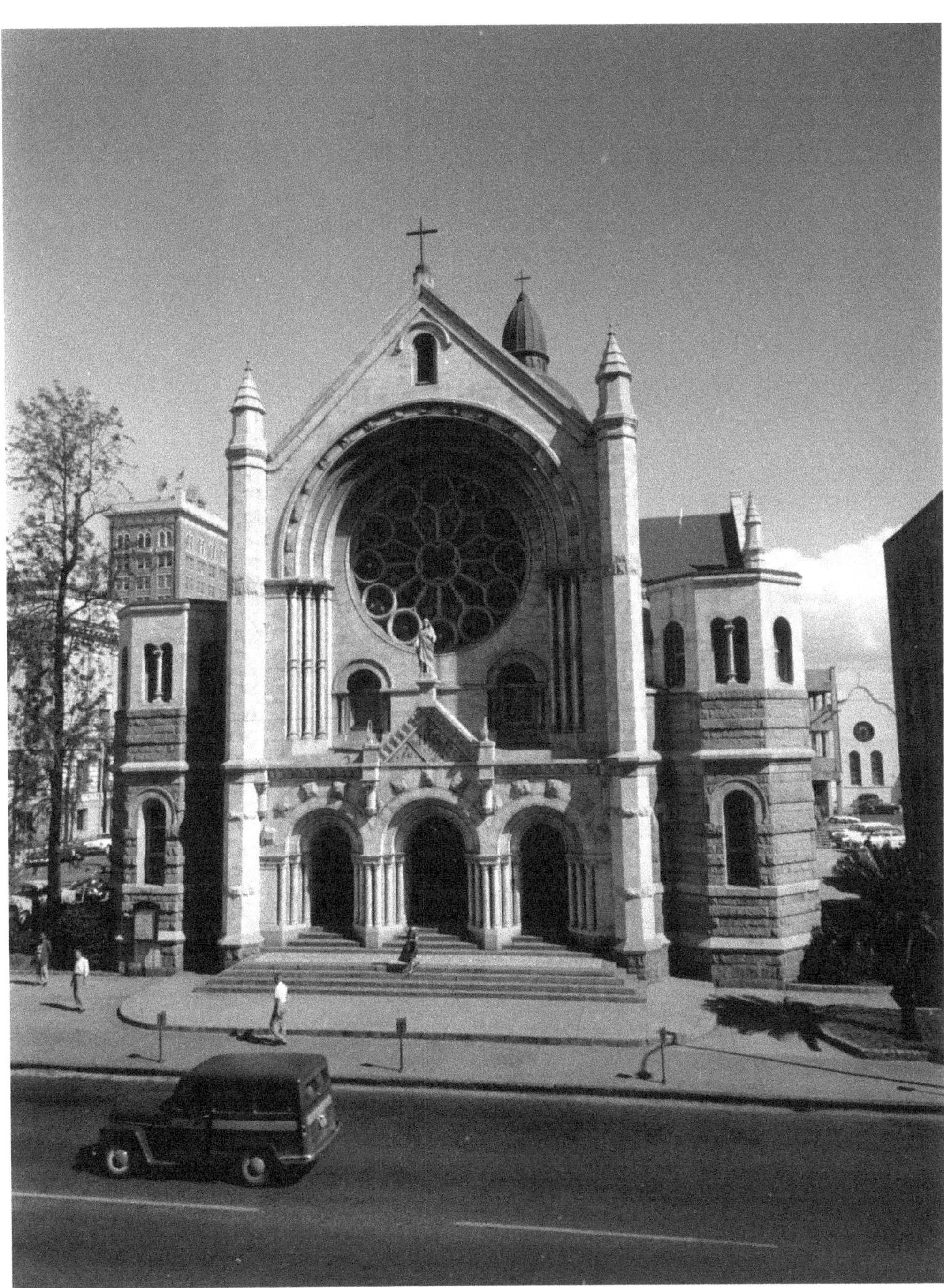

Sacred Heart Catholic Church has a floor plan shaped like a Roman cross, with a large dome at the crossing. Its main altar, built of Italian marble, was donated by the Smith brothers (the same ones on the cough drop box) because, although they were Lutherans, when their mother died while vacationing at the Tampa Bay Hotel in 1903, local Catholics were the ones who provided services for her. This is how the church appeared in 1957. Today its congregation includes about 1,400 families.

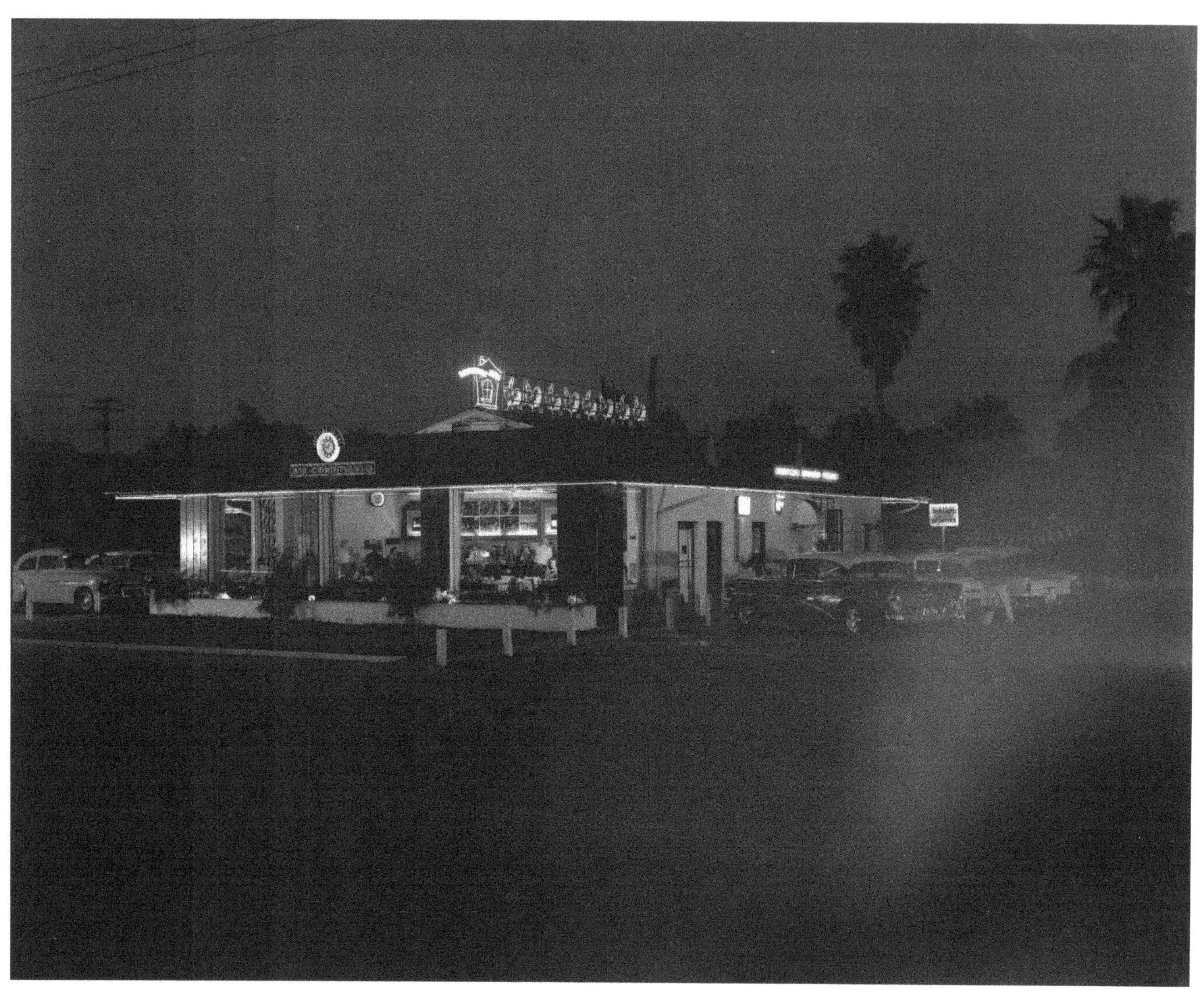

Pictured here on January 10, 1957, is Seeley's Drive-In Restaurant, located at 5021 Florida Avenue in Seminole Heights. During the 1950s and 1960s, drive-in restaurants were popular in Tampa, and patrons could dine on burgers, fries, shakes, and more substantial food without having to enter the restaurant building. The most famous Tampa drive-in was Goody Goody, which lasted from 1925 until 2005. Carhops also served food at the A&W on Kennedy Boulevard, the White Tower on Henderson Boulevard, the Colonnade on Bayshore Boulevard, and Jake Walker's Chicken & Chips on Dale Mabry Highway, to name just a few. In the early 1950s, about 40 different drive-ins were operating in the area.

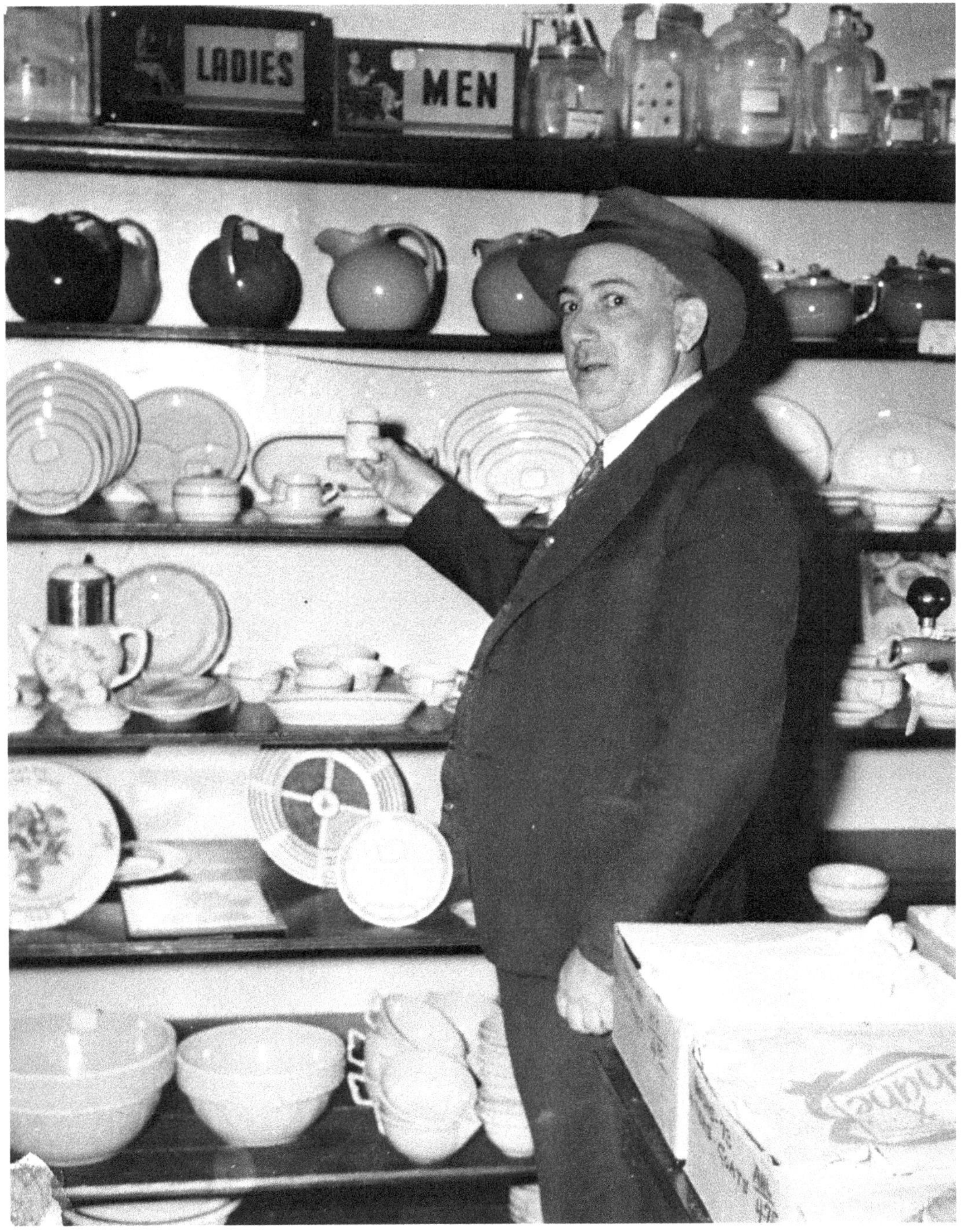

Louis Wohl was a restaurant designer and supplier and owned a city block in Ybor City along 6th Avenue. During the 1920s, his was one of over 30 Jewish-owned businesses in Ybor City. He and his family lived behind their shop, which was located at 1520 7th Avenue. Louis Wohl & Sons, Inc. incorporated in 1957 and is still operating at 11101 N. 46th Street with 15,000-square-foot warehouse. In addition to that and the Ybor City location which opened in 1897, the company opened branches in Jacksonville (1912), Fort Myers (1990), and Orlando (2006). Shown here is one of the sons, Charles Wohl.

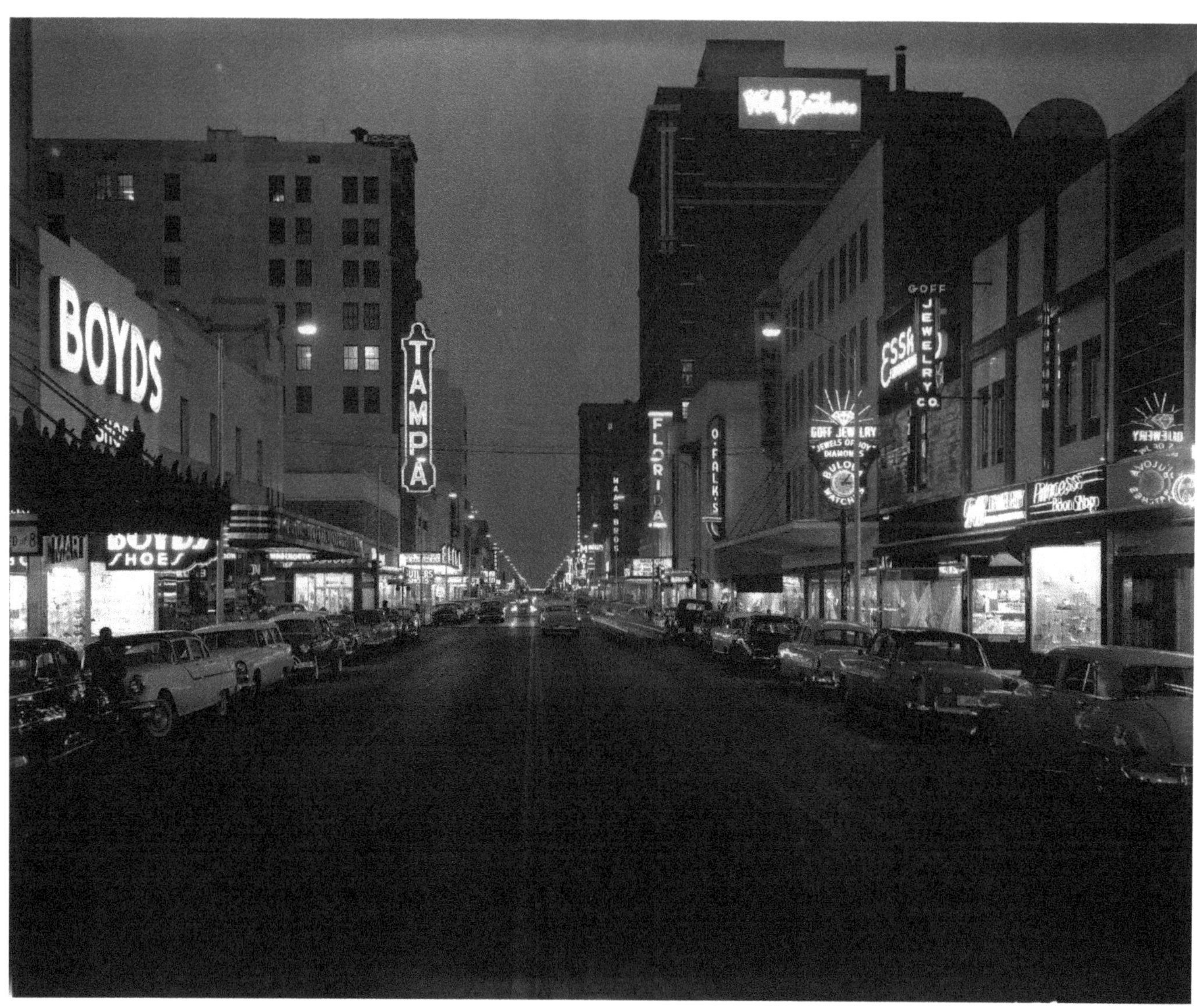

Looking south from Polk Street on June 20, 1957, one of the illuminated signs on the right advertises a business which had already been a fixture in Tampa for more than half a century. It opened as O. Falk and Brother and featured clothing and shoes for men, women, and children. Later, it was known as O. Falk's, and then simply as Falk's. During the 1970s, it went out of business. The skyscraper beyond it is the former home of Citizens Bank and Trust Company.

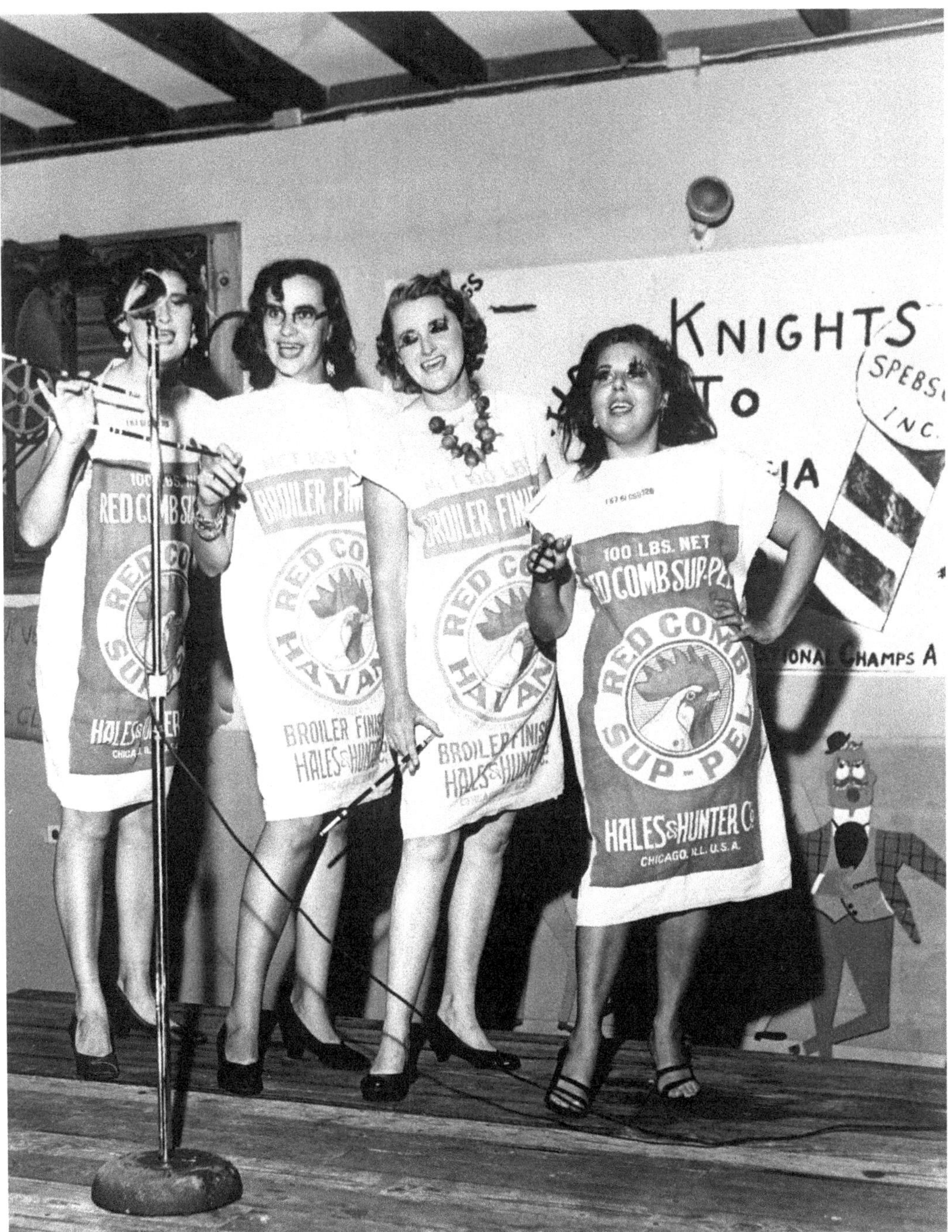

At a gathering of the SPEBSQSA (Society for the Preservation and Encouragement of Barber Shop Quartet Singing in America) in Tampa in 1957, four of its members' wives took the stage to perform a ditty. The group was comprised of Marcie Labie and the wives of Fred Broderson, Wally West, and Keith Sperry.

This June 1957 photo shows employees of an industry which was then relatively new to Florida. They are mixing and blending paint at the Harris Standard Paint plant in Tampa, located at 1022-26 North 19th Street, on land now occupied by the Port of Tampa. The company advertised "Better Paints Since 1904."

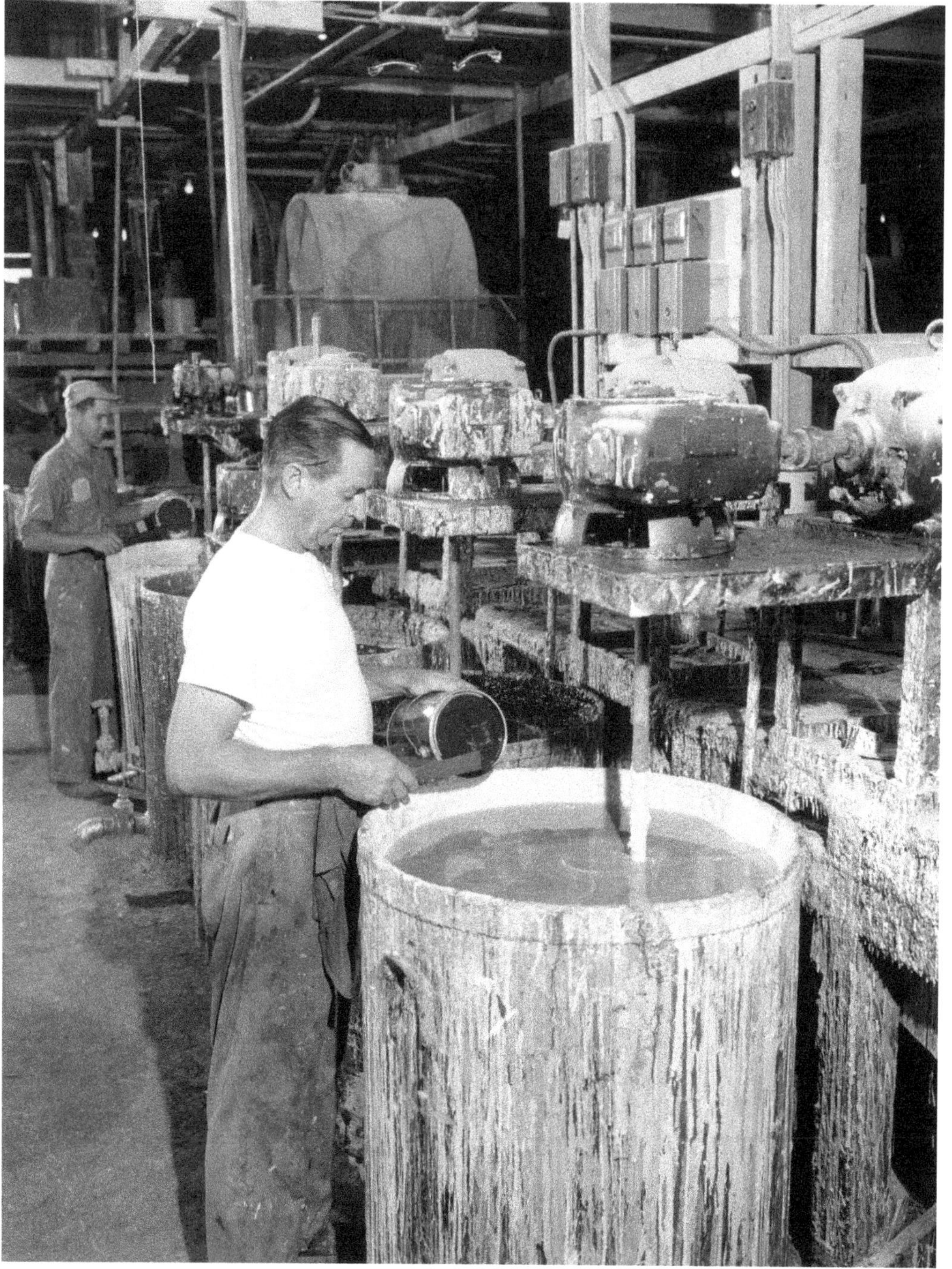

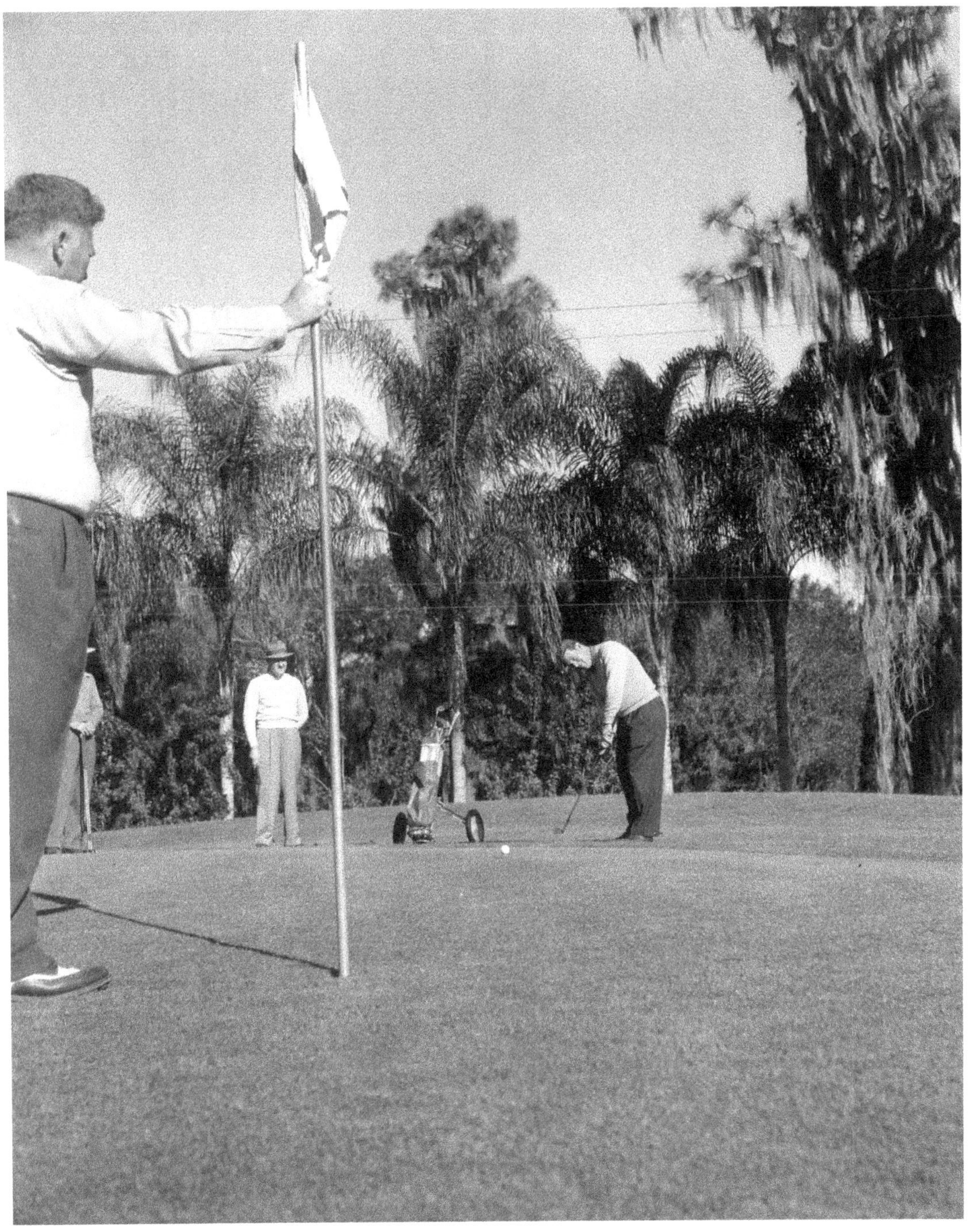

The course at the Temple Terrace Golf Club, located in a suburb of Tampa, was laid out by Tom Bendelow, and the holes were named as well as numbered—called Tower, Road, Live Oak, Out Look, Elbow, Riverview, Swing 'N Hope, Pond, Perfection, Hollow, Hill Top, Grove View, Twin Pines, Pine View, Terrace, Devil's Delight, Happy Hollow, and Hillside. The course was run by the city until 1956, when a long-term lease was entered into with Temple Terrace Outdoors, Inc. A new clubhouse was built in the late 1950s near the tenth hole. These golfers were photographed during play in December 1957.

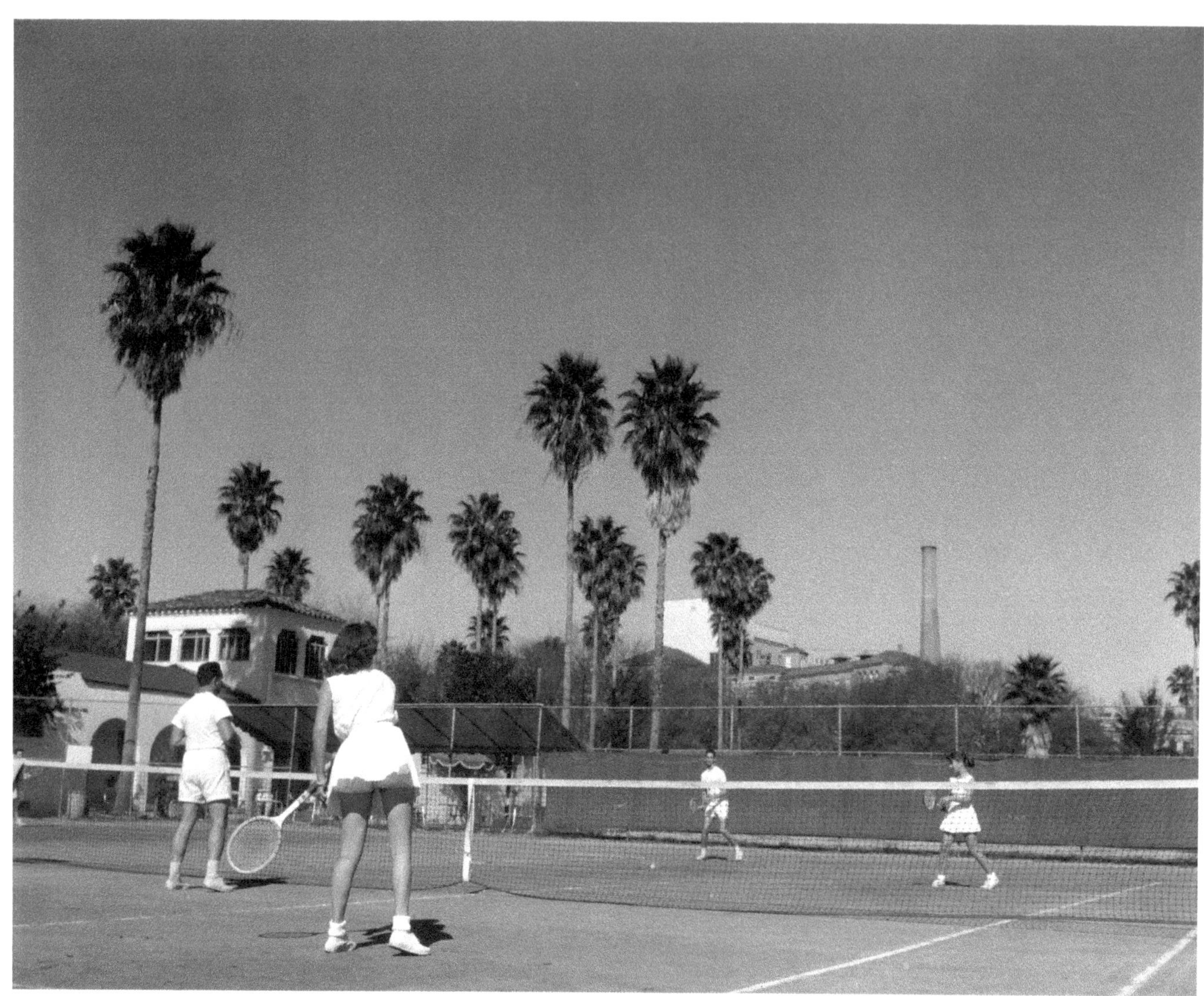

These tennis players enjoy the facilities at the Davis Islands Club (also referred to as Davis Island Club) in December 1957. It was part of the huge project undertaken by D. P. Davis in the 1920s with proceeds from his development of an island near Miami. He brought nearby island Little Grassy Key and Depot Key and connected and enlarged them with fill dredged from the bottom of the bay. Davis committed suicide before the project, including the country club, was completed. It was finished by another developer and consisted of about 4,600 lots. It closed in 1970.

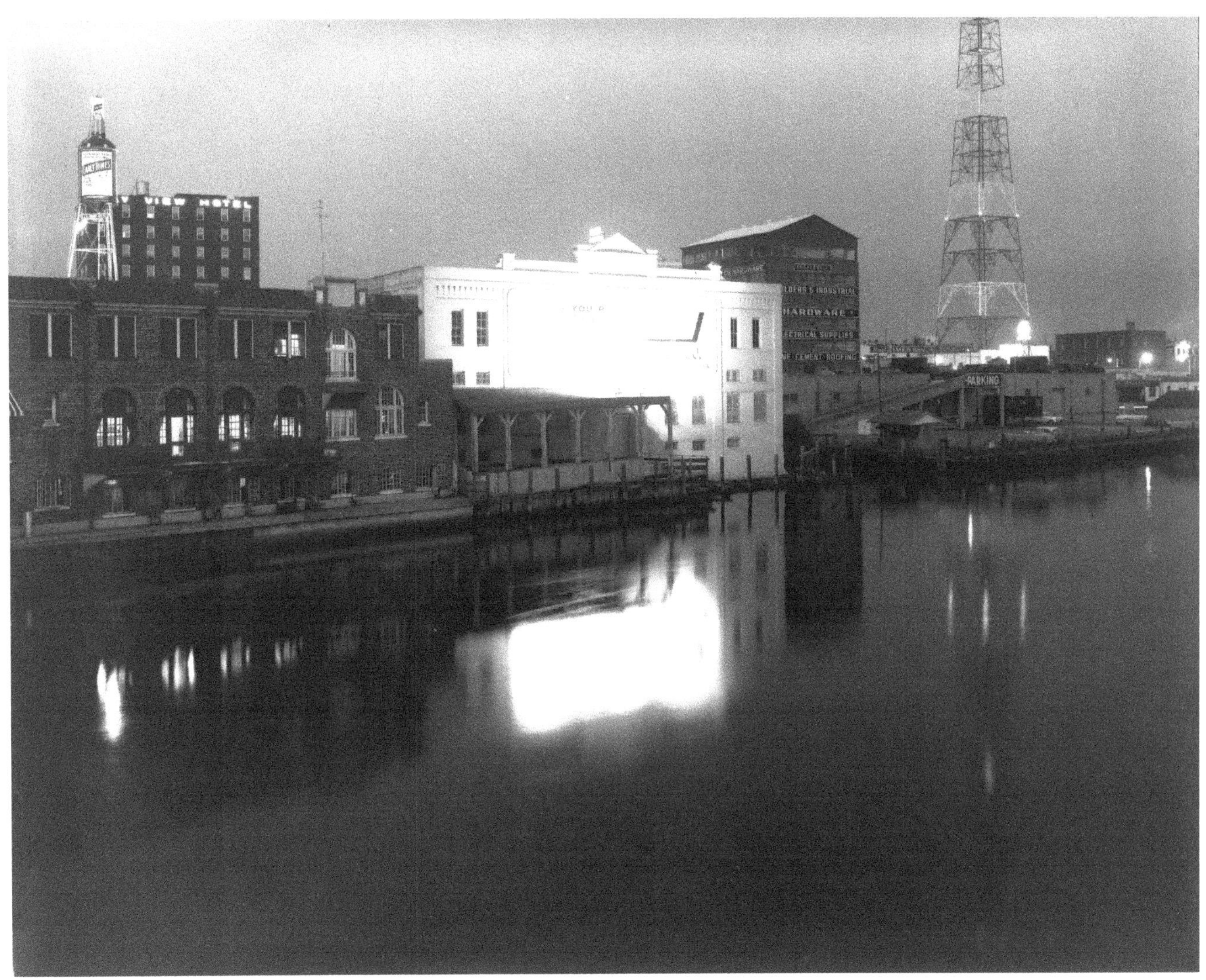

This was the scene in August 1957, looking southeast from the Lafayette Street Bridge. The area was packed with industrial buildings, including warehouses. Behind the whiskey bottle-shaped elevated water tank is a building which has connections to both. In 1912, the building was designed by Robert Mugge to be a warehouse for his liquor business. However, while it was being built Mugge decided that it would instead be a hotel, and it served as such for several decades. The Bay View was imploded on February 24, 1980, and the land was cleared for redevelopment.

At 5125 South Dale Mabry Highway was the Tampa Jai-Alai Fronton, a large indoor court where jai-alai was played, beginning in 1953. The sport was imported from Andorra and featured two or four men who used wicker baskets strapped to their right arms to catch a hard ball, then fling it against a wall in an attempt to sail it past the opponent. Spectators bet on the outcomes of games until the facility closed in 1998, and the structure was turned into a Home Depot, Sam's Club, and a bank.

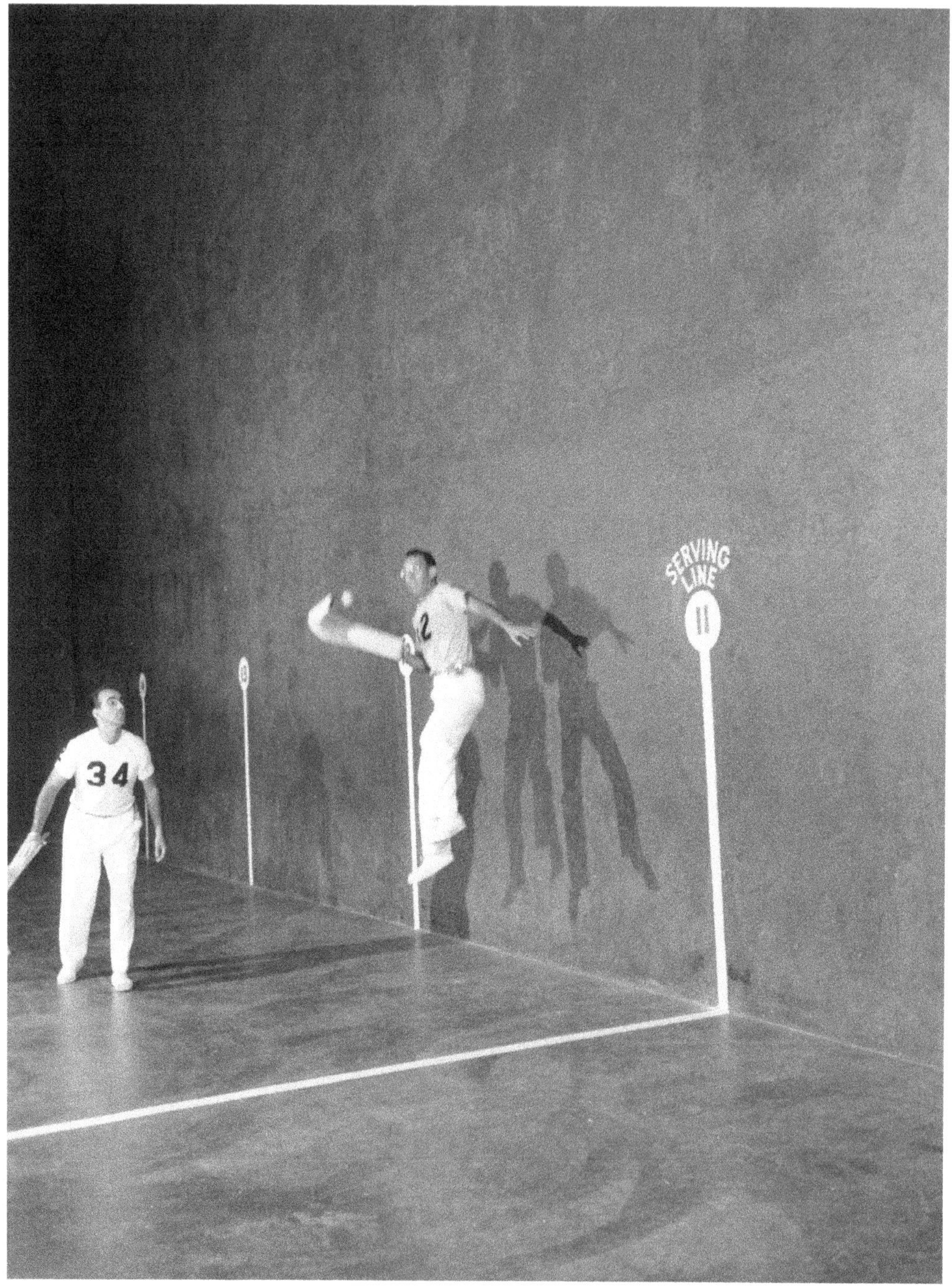

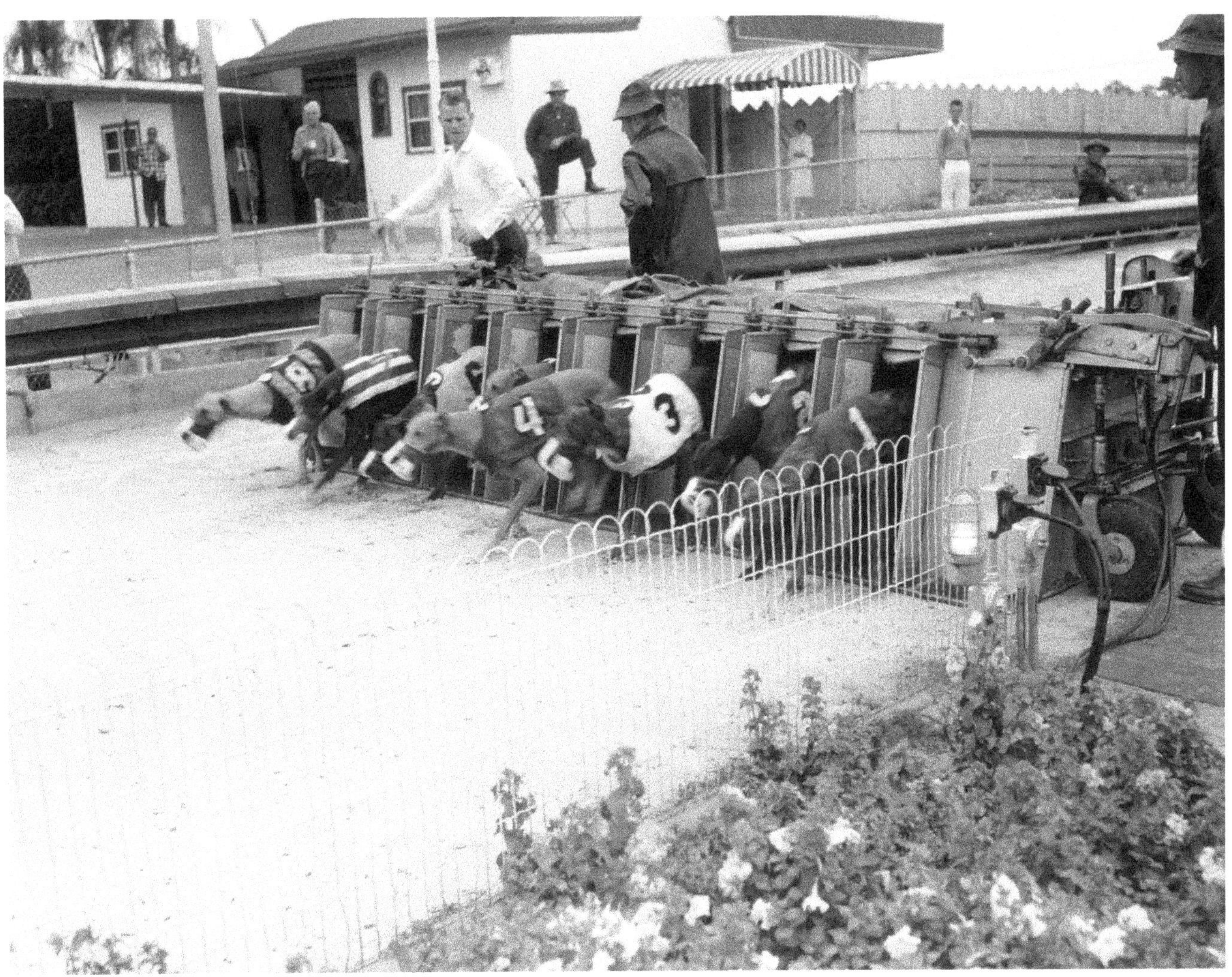

The Tampa Greyhound Track opened in 1933, making it one of the oldest in the country. It is located at 8300 Nebraska Avenue, and from 1933 to 2007 it hosted about 3,000 races annually for the entertainment of betting and non-betting spectators. Shown here is the start of one of those races held in December 1957. In 2007, its management decided to cease having live races and instead shifted its focus to poker and betting on televised races from other venues.

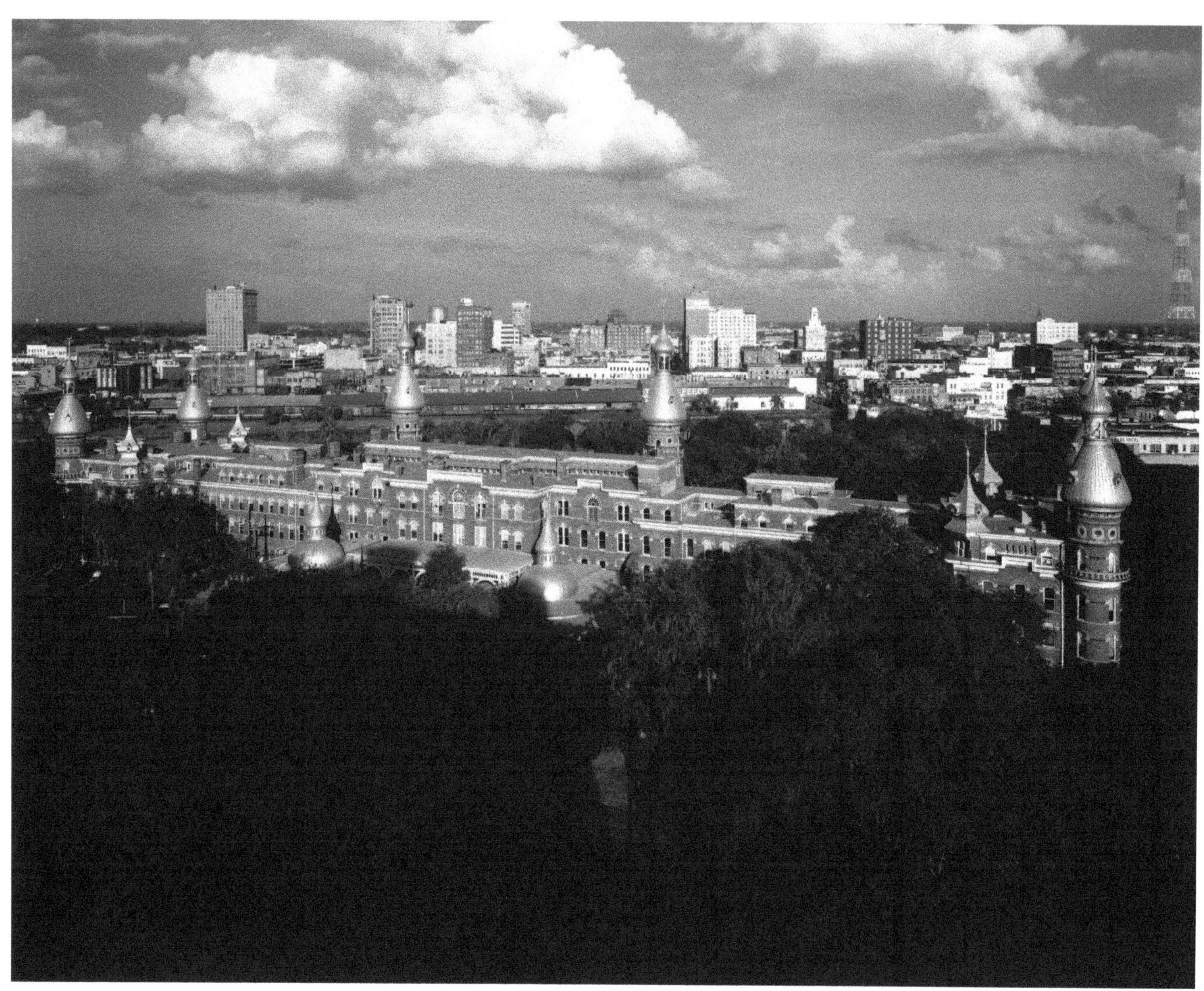

During the 1880s, Henry B. Plant bought 60 acres on the west side of the Hillsborough River, and there built the Tampa Bay Hotel as a destination for his railroad passengers. The glass for its 511 windows was imported from France, the bricks were manufactured in Cincinnati, and it was modeled after the Alhambra palace in Spain. The hotel, with its twelve towers with onion-shaped domes, closed in 1932, and the following year became the home of the University of Tampa. This is how it appeared in 1958.

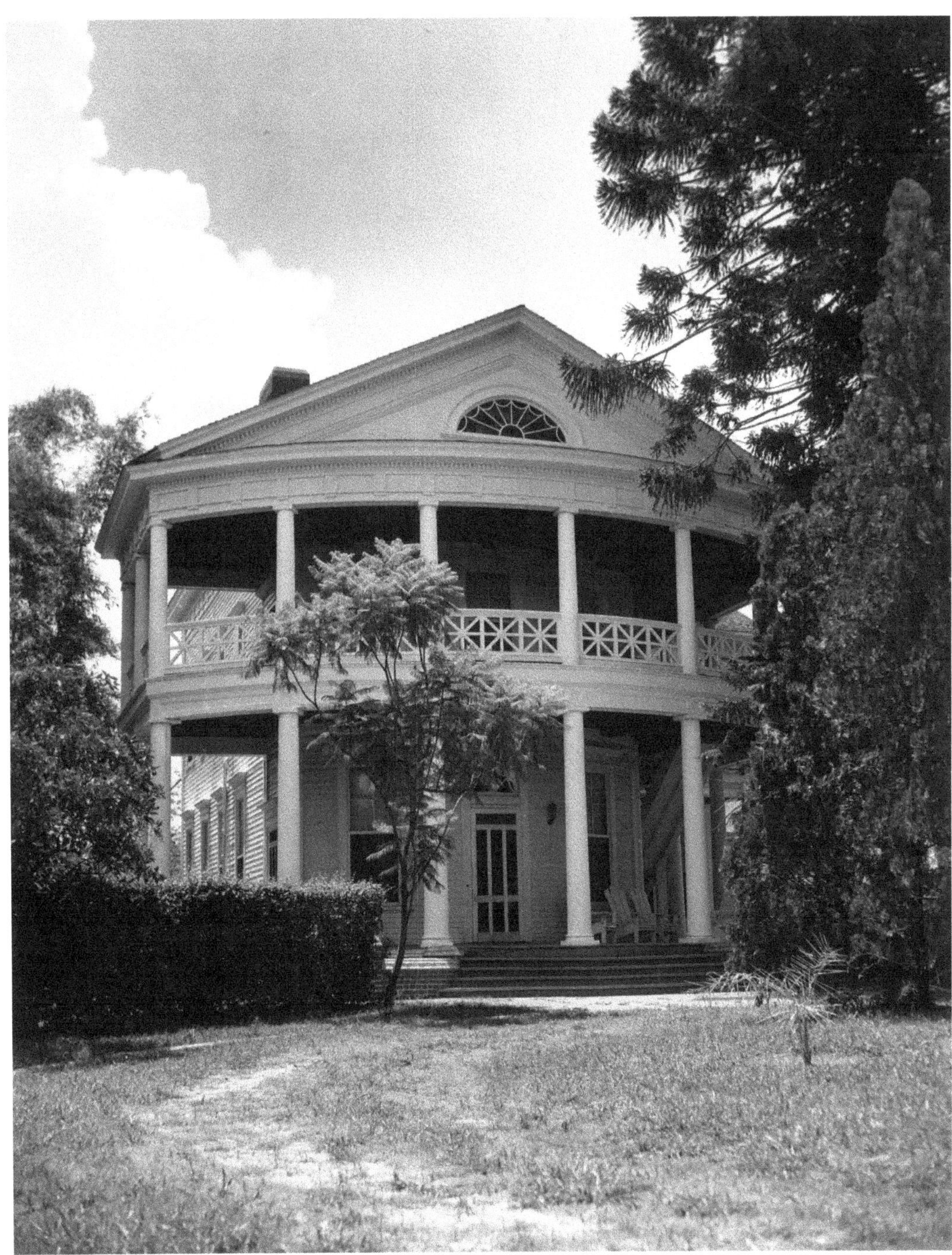

In 1892, this home was built for Chester W. Chapin, who owned the Tampa Electric Company and the first streetcar line in the city. Its tracks ended at the back door of the house at 4607 Bayshore Boulevard. Until the 1930s, the upstairs rooms were accessed only by outdoor stairways. The then owner added an indoor stairway and attached to the main house a small separate kitchen and servants' quarters. This is how it appeared in 1958. During the 1980s, it was replaced by modern construction.

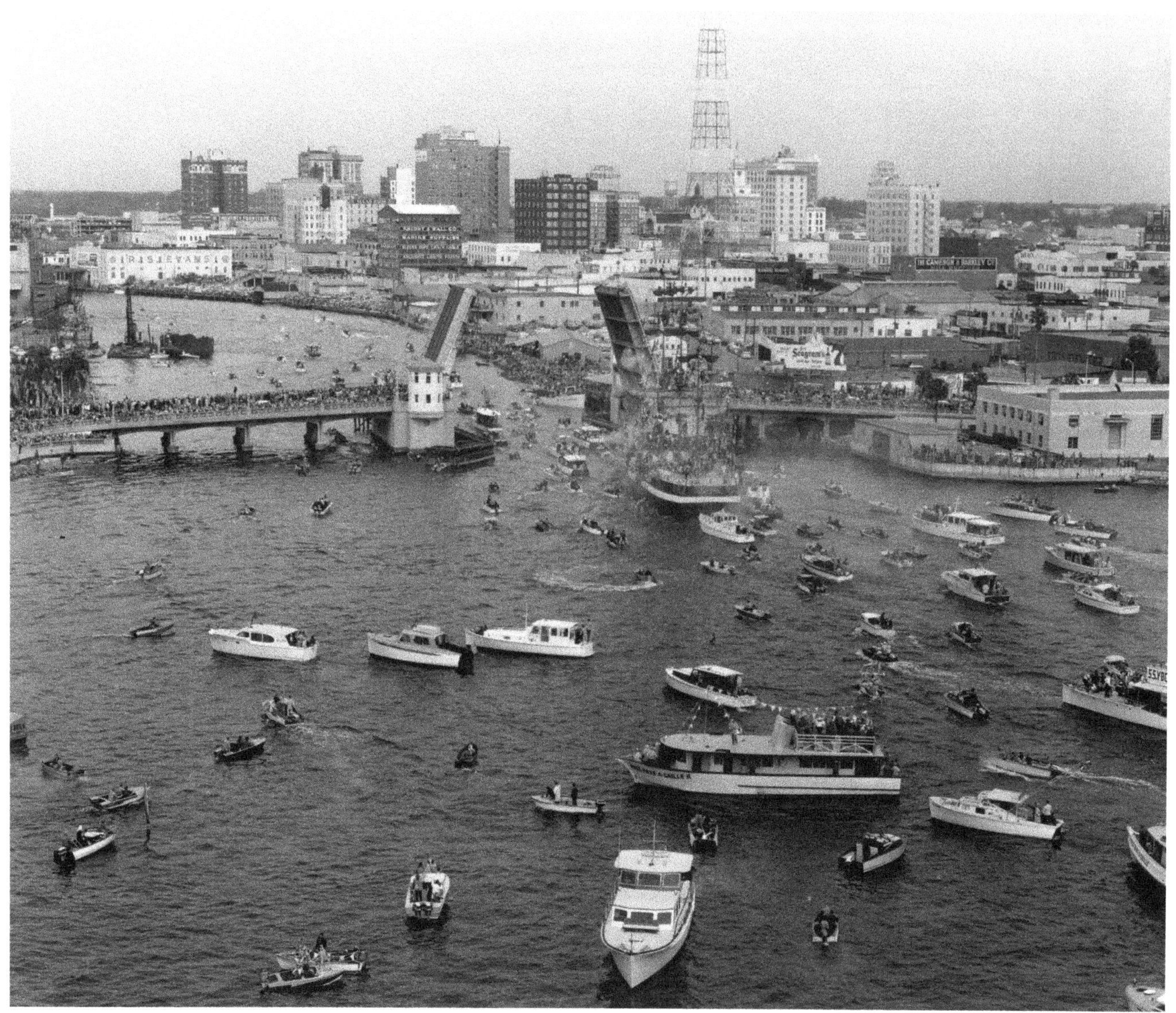

The drawbridge portion of the Platt Street Bridge is raised to allow the *Jose Gaspar* to pass through as part of the 1958 Gasparilla Festival. The ship is a replica of an eighteenth-century pirate ship, and was built earlier in the decade. When not sailing up the Hillsborough River to "attack" Tampa, it is permanently moored at the Tarpoon Weigh Station on Bayshore Boulevard.

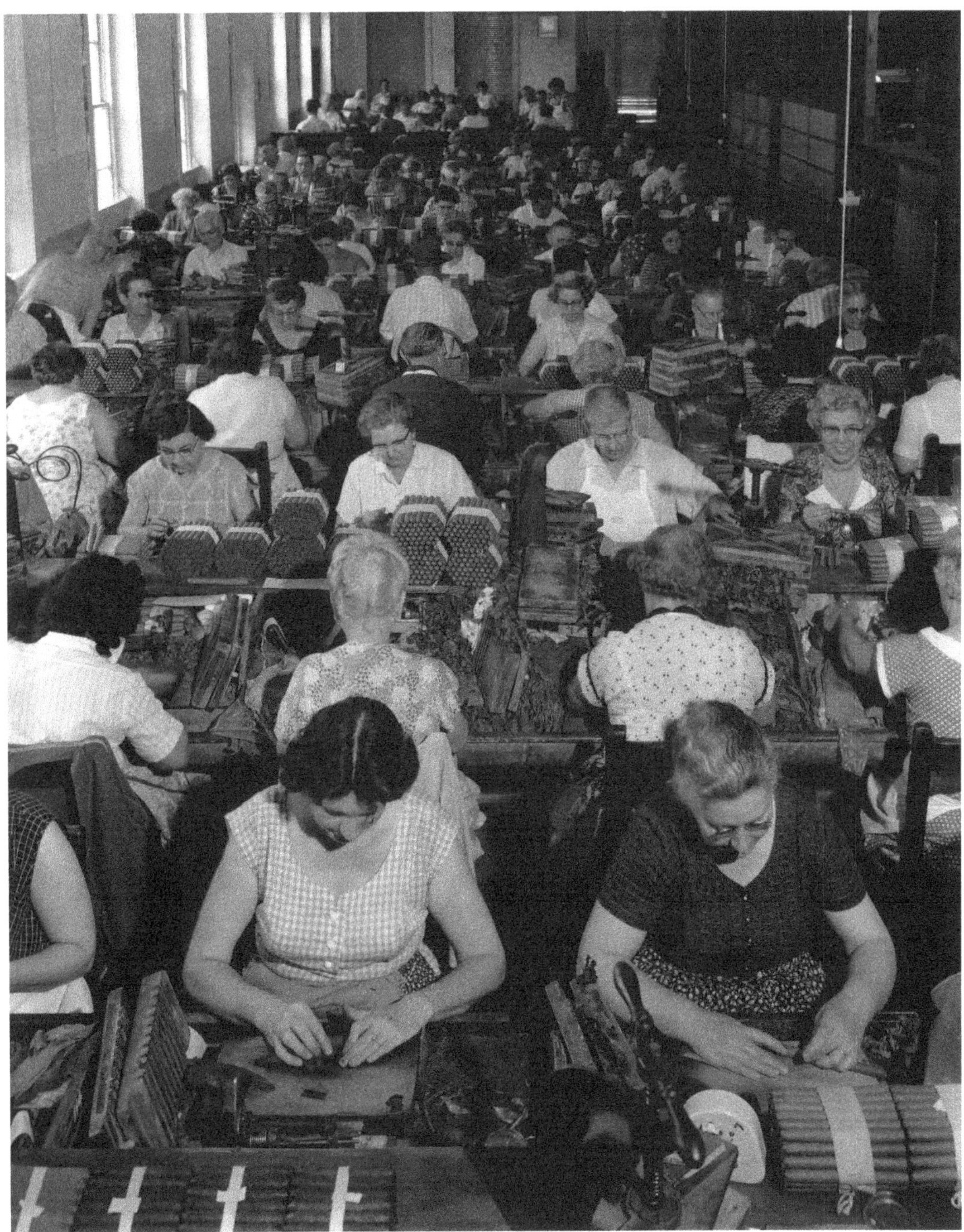

In West Tampa at 3102-04 North America Avenue is a cigar factory with the date of 1882 on its front wall, and it may have been occupied by the Bonded Havana Cigar Company that year (which would predate the first companies in Ybor City). In 1907, it became the home of Gracia y Veya, a company founded by Alvaro Garcia and Jose Vega. Workers such as these shown in the late 1950s produced brands which included El Mas Noble, Flor de Garcia y Vega, Austino, La Perla Espanola, and Duguestia.

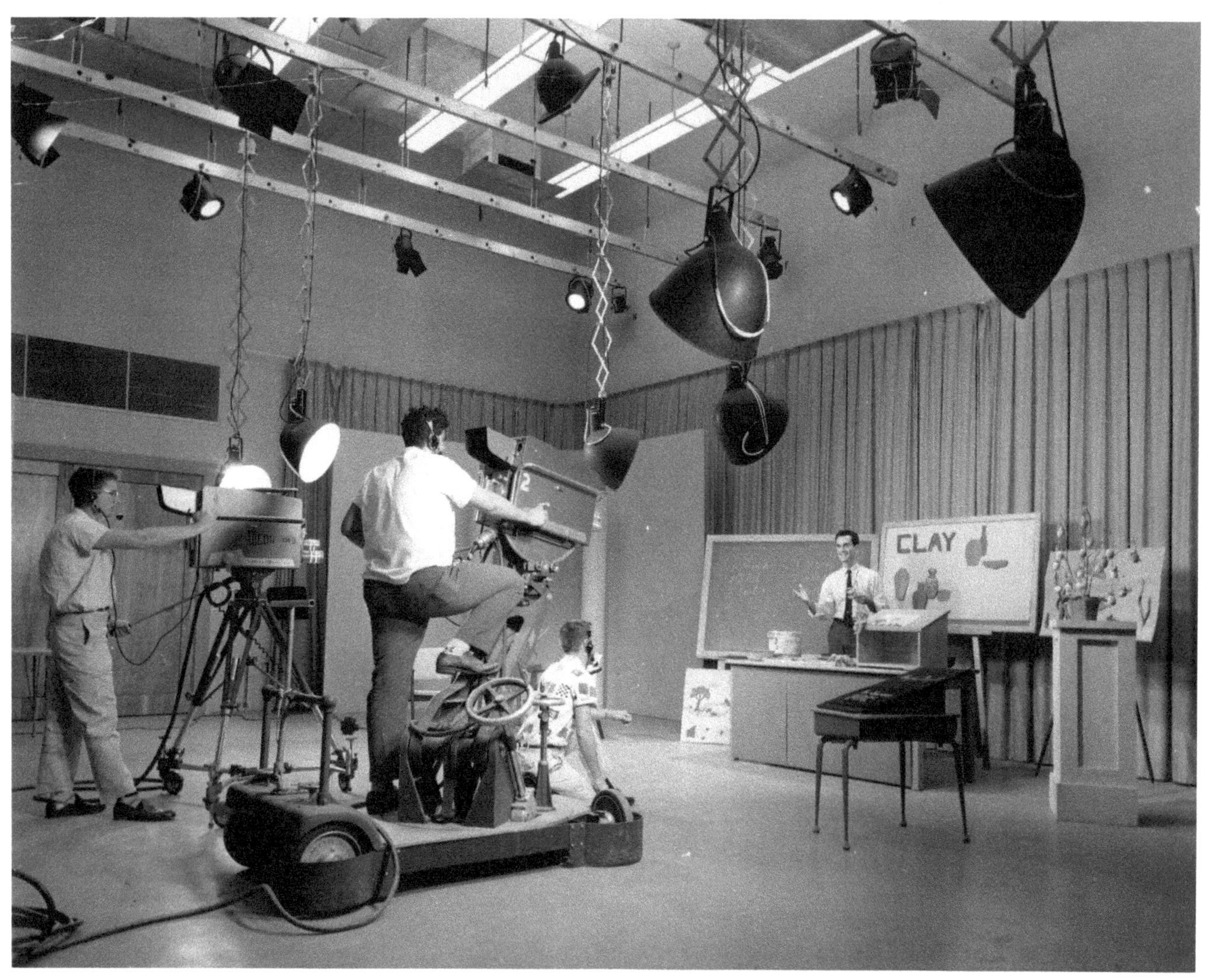

WEDU Channel 3 signed on for broadcasting for the first time on October 17, 1958, as an affiliate of National Educational Television. It remains on the air as the area's primary PBS affiliate.

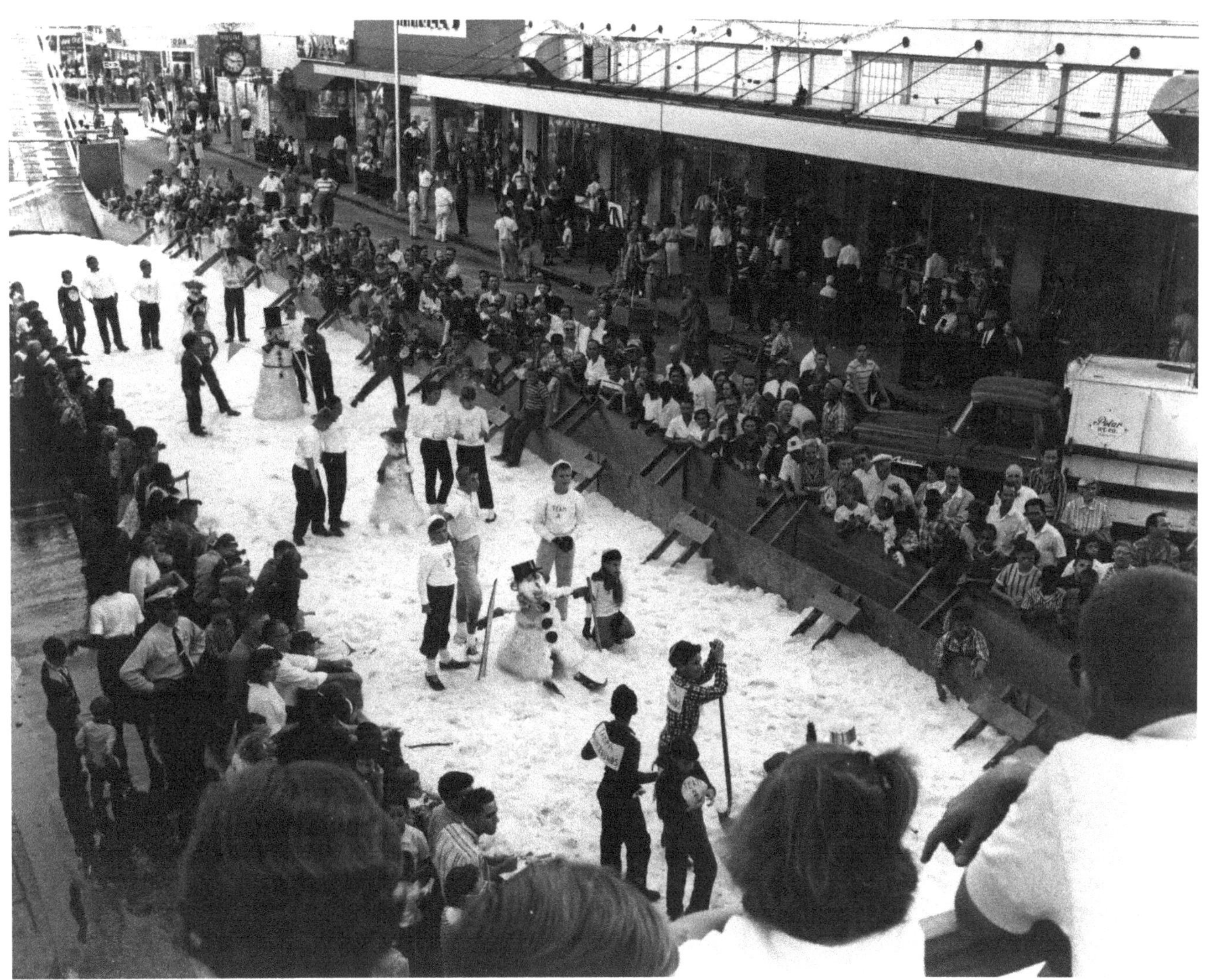

At Christmastime in 1958, this expanse of snow was set up for children to play in on Franklin Street in front of the Maas Brothers Department Store. The Maas building was one of the first air-conditioned stores in Tampa, and had the city's first escalator. The popular store closed for good in February 1991, and stood vacant for several years. It was torn down in 2006 to make room for a 500-unit residential condominium project.

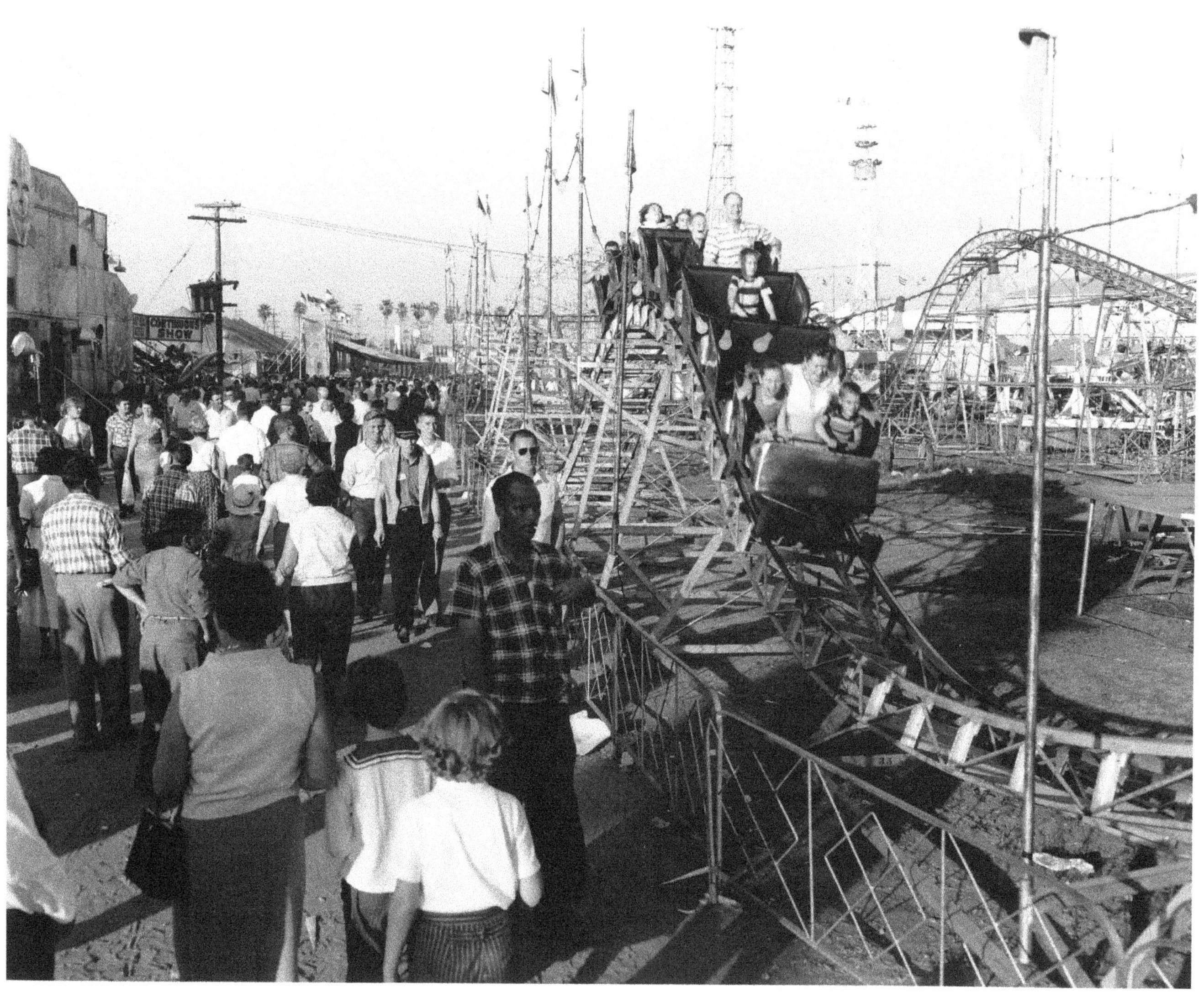

Henry B. Plant started holding fairs in Tampa in 1890 to entertain the guests at his Tampa Bay Hotel and promote interest in South Florida. In additional to other activities, horse races were held on a track northwest of the hotel. The fairs ceased after Plant's death in 1899, but were resume for 1905 and 1906, and then again in 1910. Shown here is a small roller coaster at the 1959 Florida State Fair, held at the 50-acre fairground near the hotel.

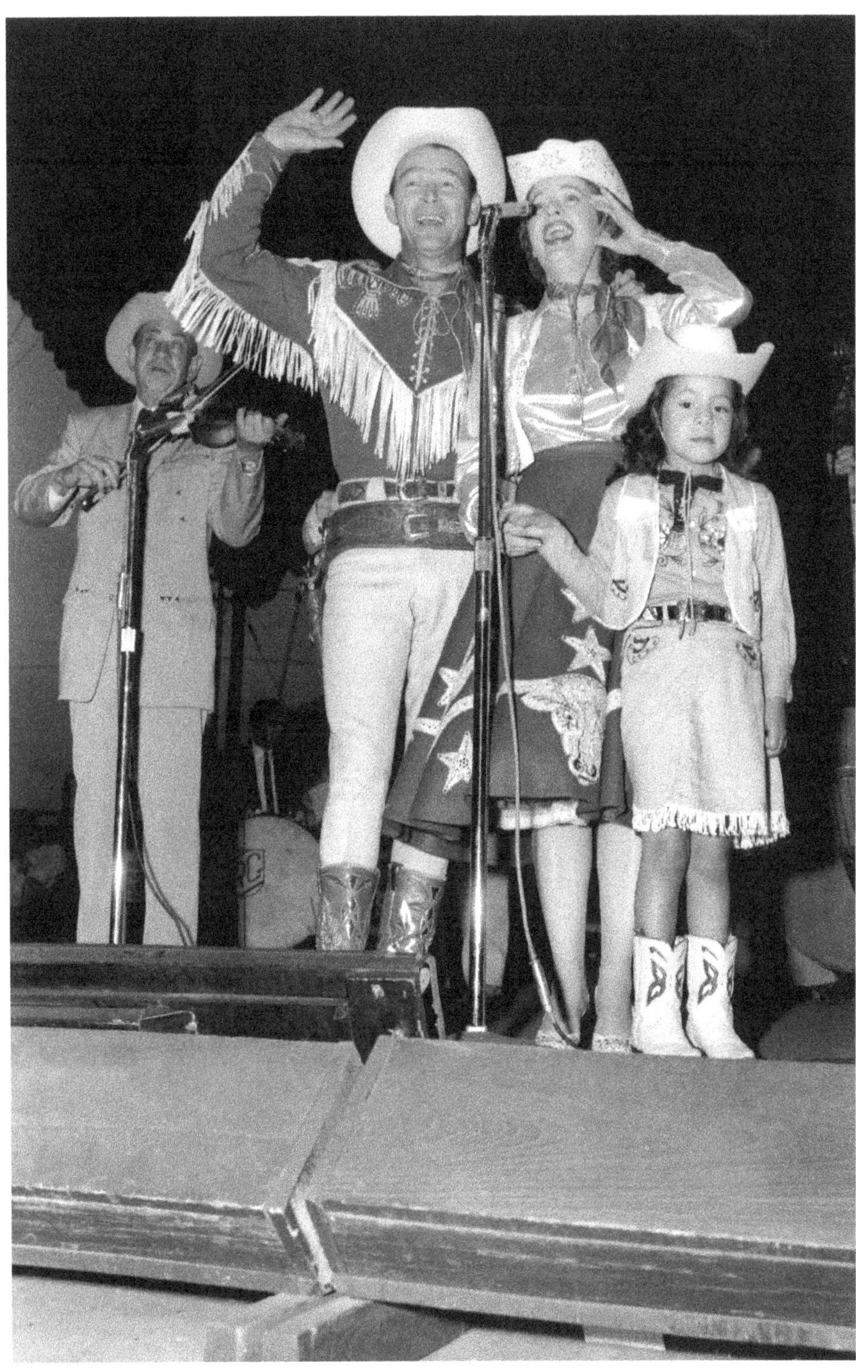

Roy Rogers and Dale Evans performed at the 1959 Florida State Fair while their daughter stood by. Born Leonard Franklin Slye, he was a singer and cowboy actor who performed in over a hundred movies and who starred in *The Roy Rogers Show* on television from 1951 until 1957. He was known as "King of the Cowboys" and married Dale "Queen of the West" Evans, his third wife, in 1947.

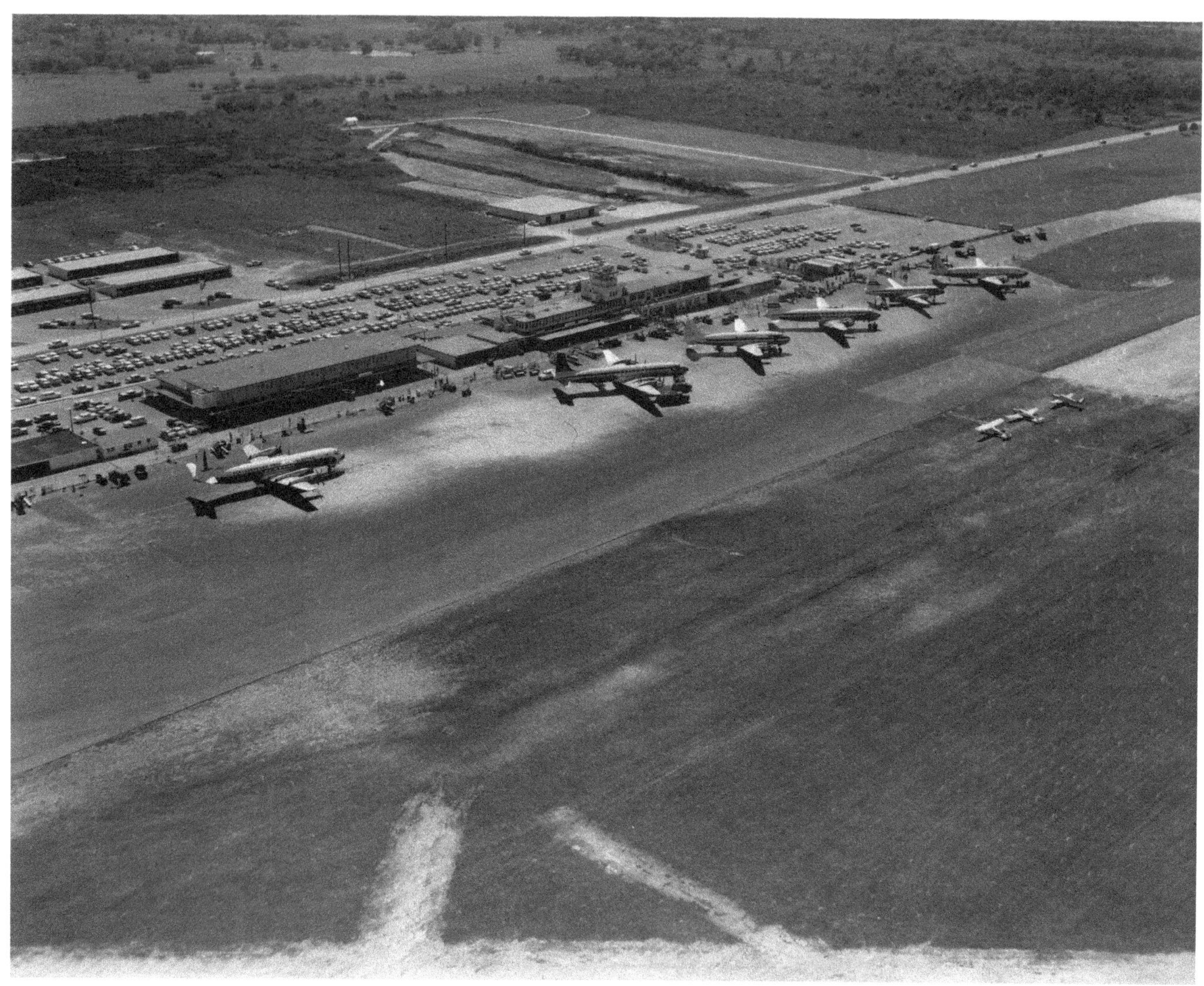

This is a view of the Tampa International Airport in 1959, the year it increased the number of airlines served from four to ten. It also received federal recognition that year as an intercontinental airport. At about the same time, its single north-south runway was lengthened to 8,300 feet to accommodate jet airliners.

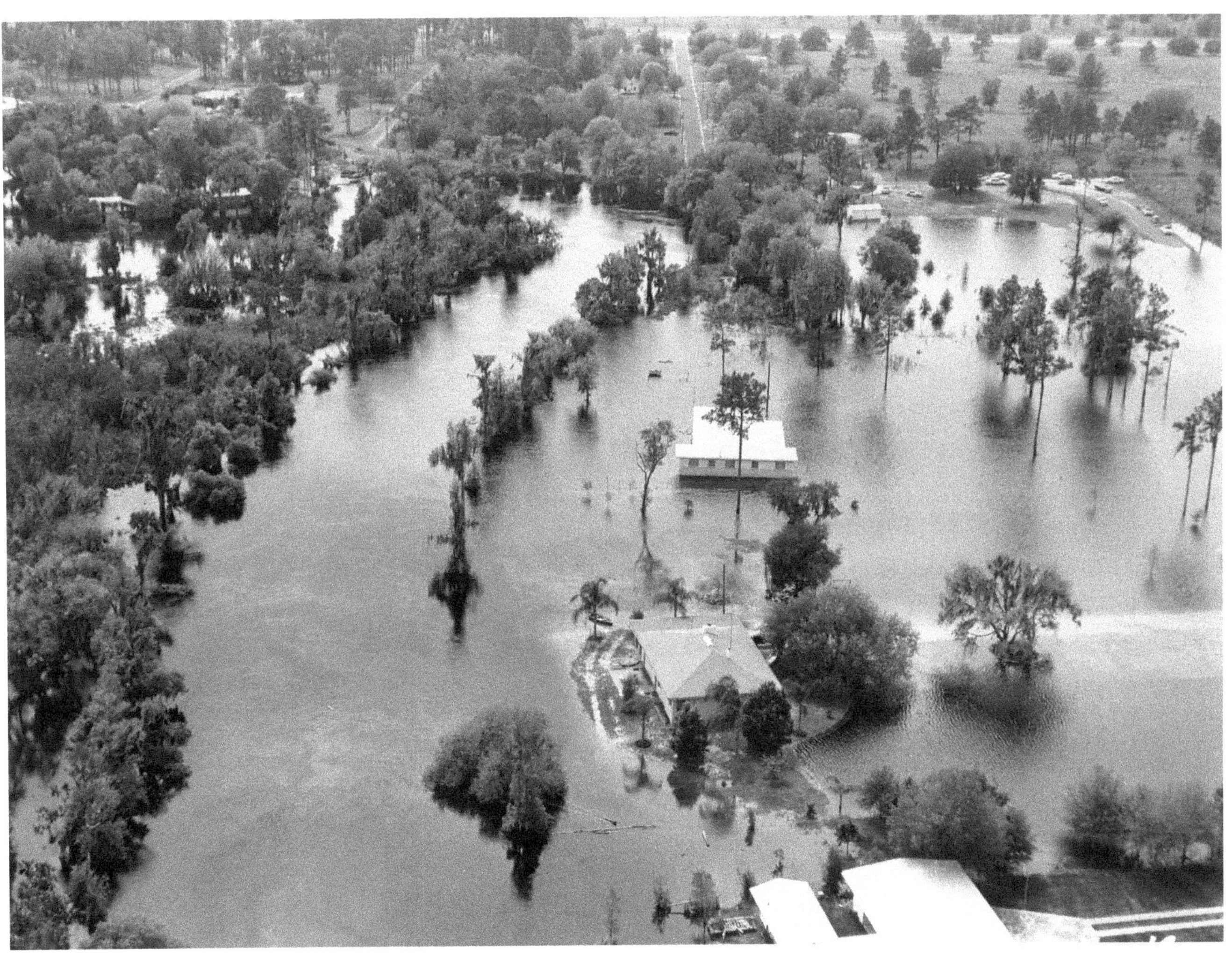

Today, there are ten county parks between downtown Tampa and the northern boundary of Hillsborough County. They are designed to flood during periods of too much rain—and could become covered by as much as ten feet of floodwaters. That is intentional, to prevent floodwaters from reaching metropolitan Tampa. In March 1959 when this photo was taken, and in 1960 when Hurricane Donna struck the area, the Hillsborough River had two of history's three heaviest rainfalls to carry to Tampa Bay—and along the way flooded Tampa, washing many homes away. As a result of those floods, measures were taken to acquire land and establish parks which would take the brunt of floodwaters rather than risk residential and commercial areas.

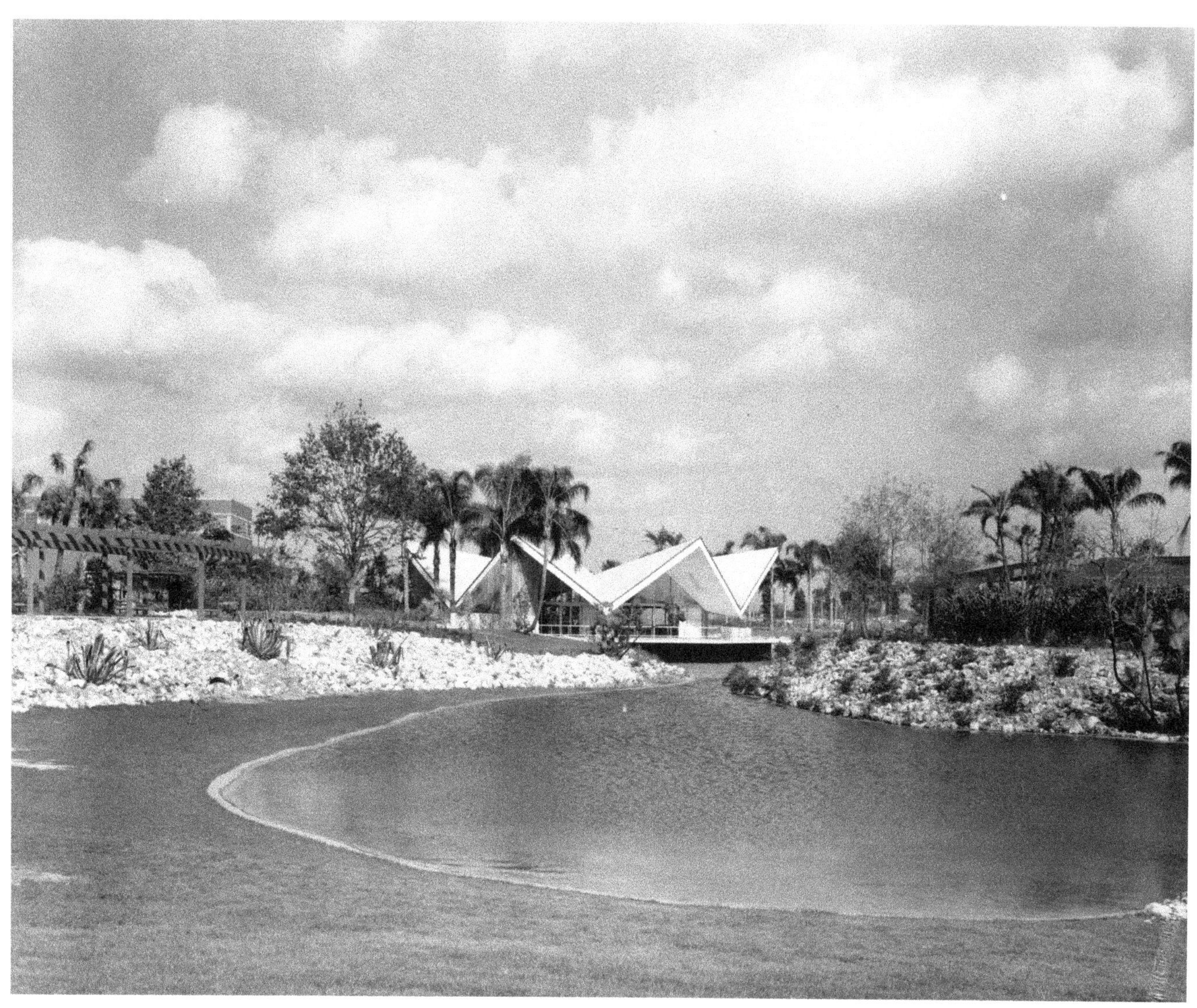

After Henderson Field ceased to be an airport in the early in 1950s, it was redeveloped as the Tampa Industrial Park. Later, the World War II cantonment area on the park's south end was made into a small amusement park known as Busch Gardens, developed around the Anheuser-Busch brewery. Shown here in April 1959 is its Hospitality House, in which adult visitors could try free samples of Busch beer.

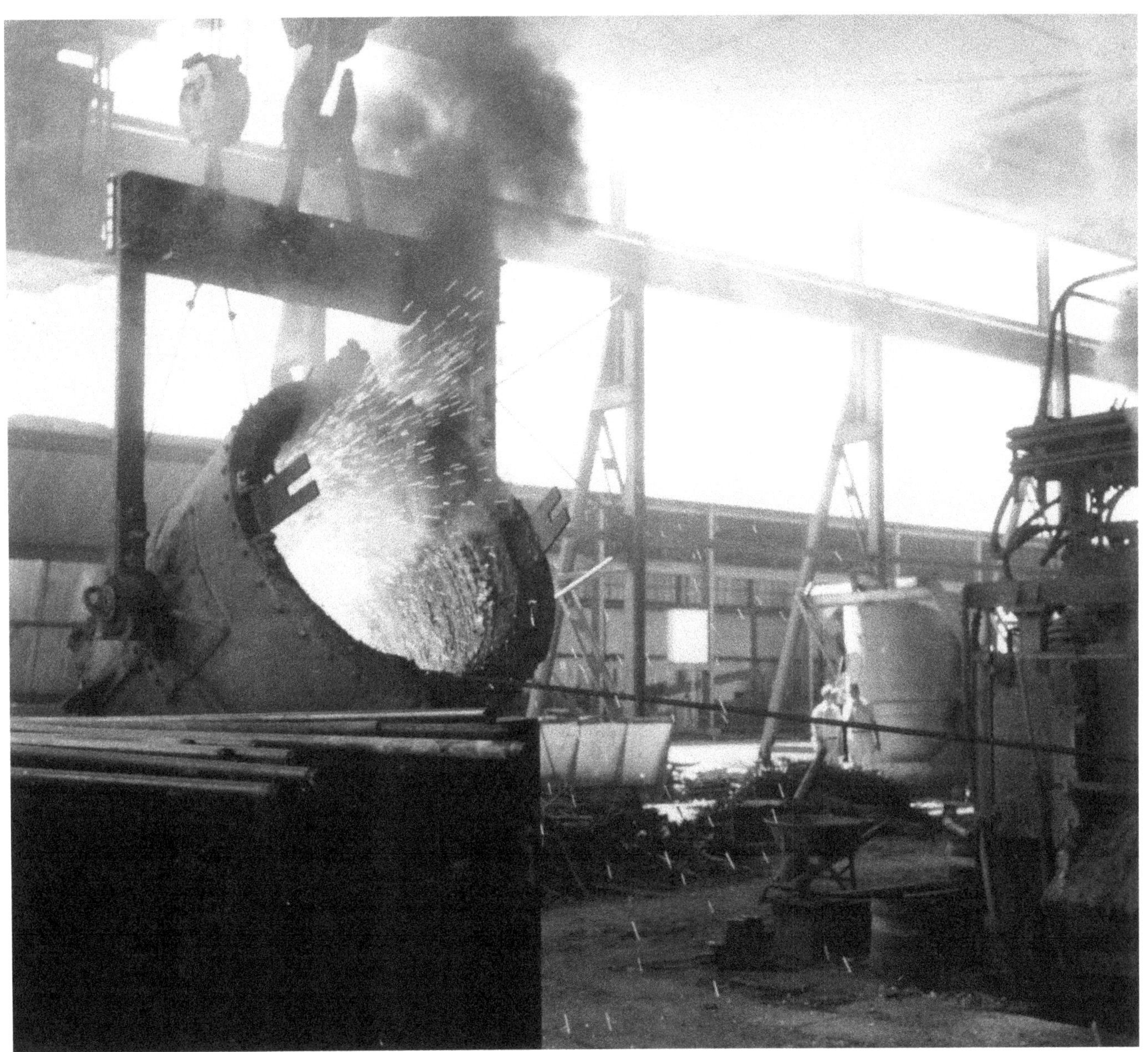

Florida Steel Products was founded in Tampa in 1937, and in 1956 was enlarged by a merger of several companies. Later, it became owned by the company known as Gerdau Ameristeel. Shown here is the Tampa foundry in June 1959. The facility was operated from 1956 until 1995, and now the only major steel mill in Florida is located in Jacksonville.

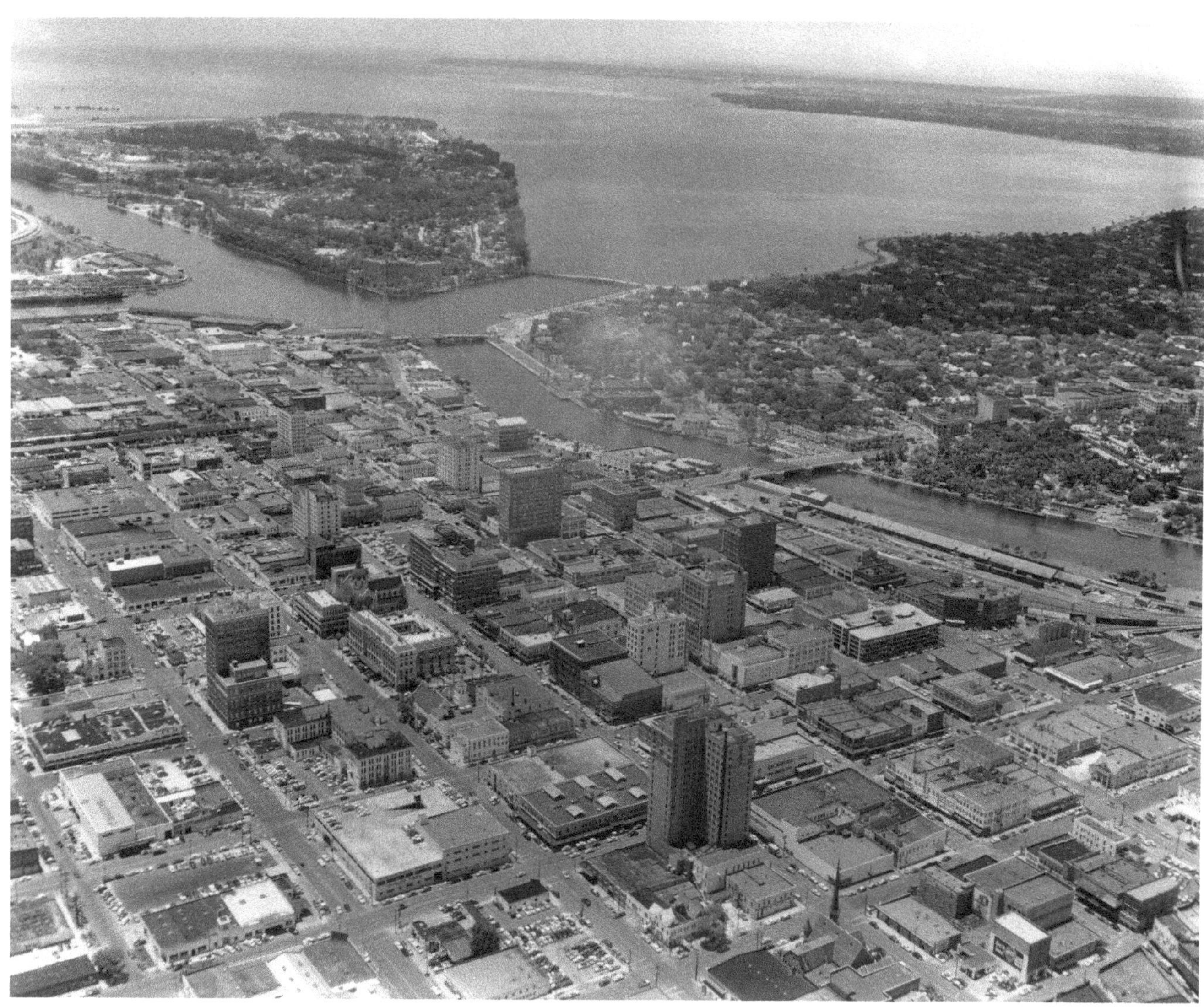

Looking south over downtown Tampa on July 20, 1959, many buildings are recognizable. The tallest one, the dark tower in the center foreground, is the Floridian Hotel. Designed by F. J. Kennard and Son and owned by developer A. J. Simms, it was built in 1925–27, and it remained the tallest building in the city until 1966. It was a luxury hotel that operated into the 1950s, then catered to a less affluent clientele until it closed in 1987. Restoration work began in 2005.

Rebuilding the City

(1960–1969)

The 1960s ushered in a period of building for the entertainment of residents and visitors. The expanding Busch Gardens was attracting people to the area, and they needed more to keep them occupied. The small zoo located near the Tampa Bay Hotel was moved to Lowry Park where it had room to grow. Its first elephant, which was its first major non-indigenous specimen, was donated by General Sumter L. Lowry, Jr., and the Lowry Park Zoo was on its way to becoming a major attraction. A youth museum was established in 1962, and it expanded to become the Hillsborough County Museum in 1967. Today, it is known was the Museum of Science and Industry and its large facility across the street from the University of South Florida attracts visitors of all ages.

To provide a venue for performances and indoor athletic events, Curtis Hixon Hall opened in 1964. It was named for the man who served as Tampa's mayor from 1943 until his death in 1956, and had a seating capacity of 6,000. Concerts, college and professional basketball games, and many other events were held there until it was torn down during the 1990s.

For even larger events, the late 1960s saw the construction of the 47,000-seat Tampa Stadium along North Dale Mabry Highway on land that had formerly been a hog farm. Nicknamed "The Big Sombrero" because of its shape, it hosted its first National Football League game on August 10, 1968. Having the stadium helped Tampa to obtain an NFL team of its own during the following decade. To accommodate the crowds who wanted to see the Buccaneers play, the areas behind the end zones were filled in to increase the seating capacity to 72,000.

The building boom in those parts of Tampa, however, did not initially extend to the old neighborhood of Ybor City. At the beginning of the decade, local politicians referred to it as an example of a modern slum, abandoned by the younger generation. The city, desiring to bring it back to the status of a top-rank tourist attraction, set aside $9.6 million to rehabilitate, clear, and redevelop the cigar-producing area. Part of the project included the construction of Interstate 4 through the neighborhood, and the resulting relocation of 1,200 families. The revitalization of Ybor City, while retaining as much of its historical architecture and character as possible, was a long-term project which took several decades. The work begun in the 1960s is now reaping rewards, with visitors returning and putting their dollars back into the local economy.

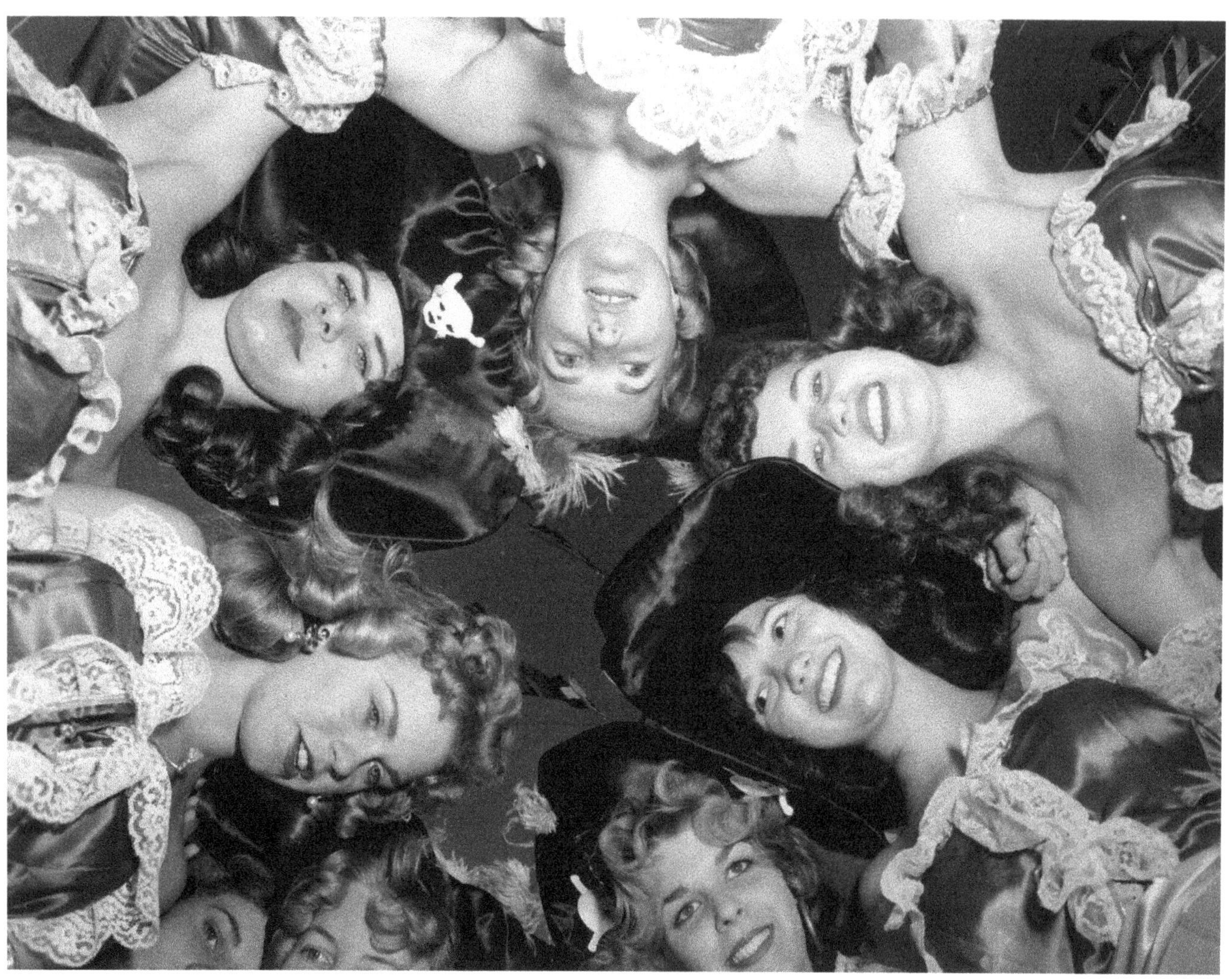

This is a group of young women huddled together during the 1960 Gasparilla Festival. Since 1904, it has been staged by Ye Mystic Krewe of Gasparilla, a group of residents who, in full costume and masks, "capture" the city during the festival in January. There are activities for all ages and interests, all centering around the theme of pirates who terrorized the region centuries ago.

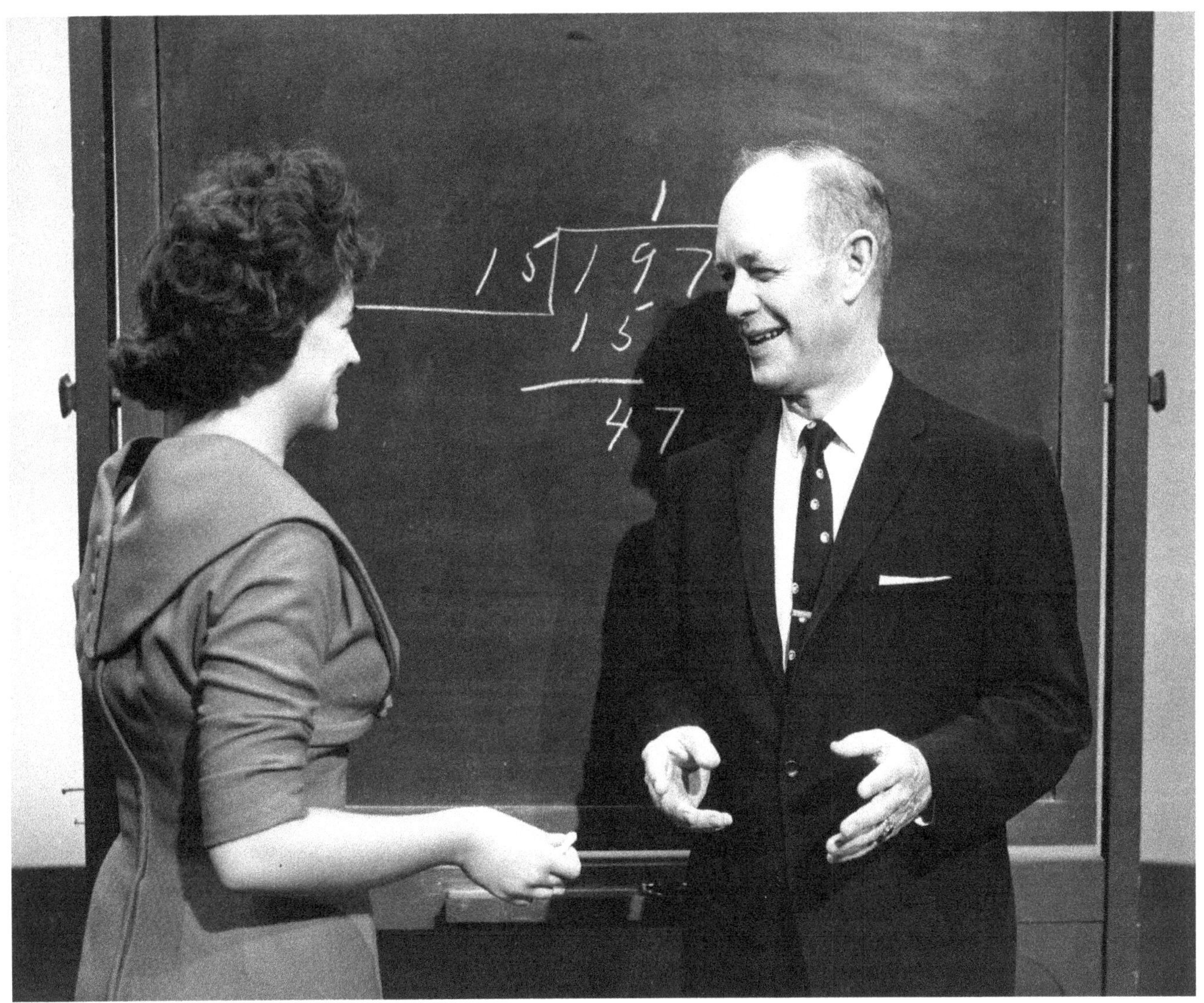

In 1960, Cecil Farris Bryant of Ocala was running for governor, and during the campaign was photographed in Tampa speaking with this elementary school teacher. He won the election and focused heavily on education issues. During his four years in office, funders were obtained for 28 junior colleges and additional state universities were established.

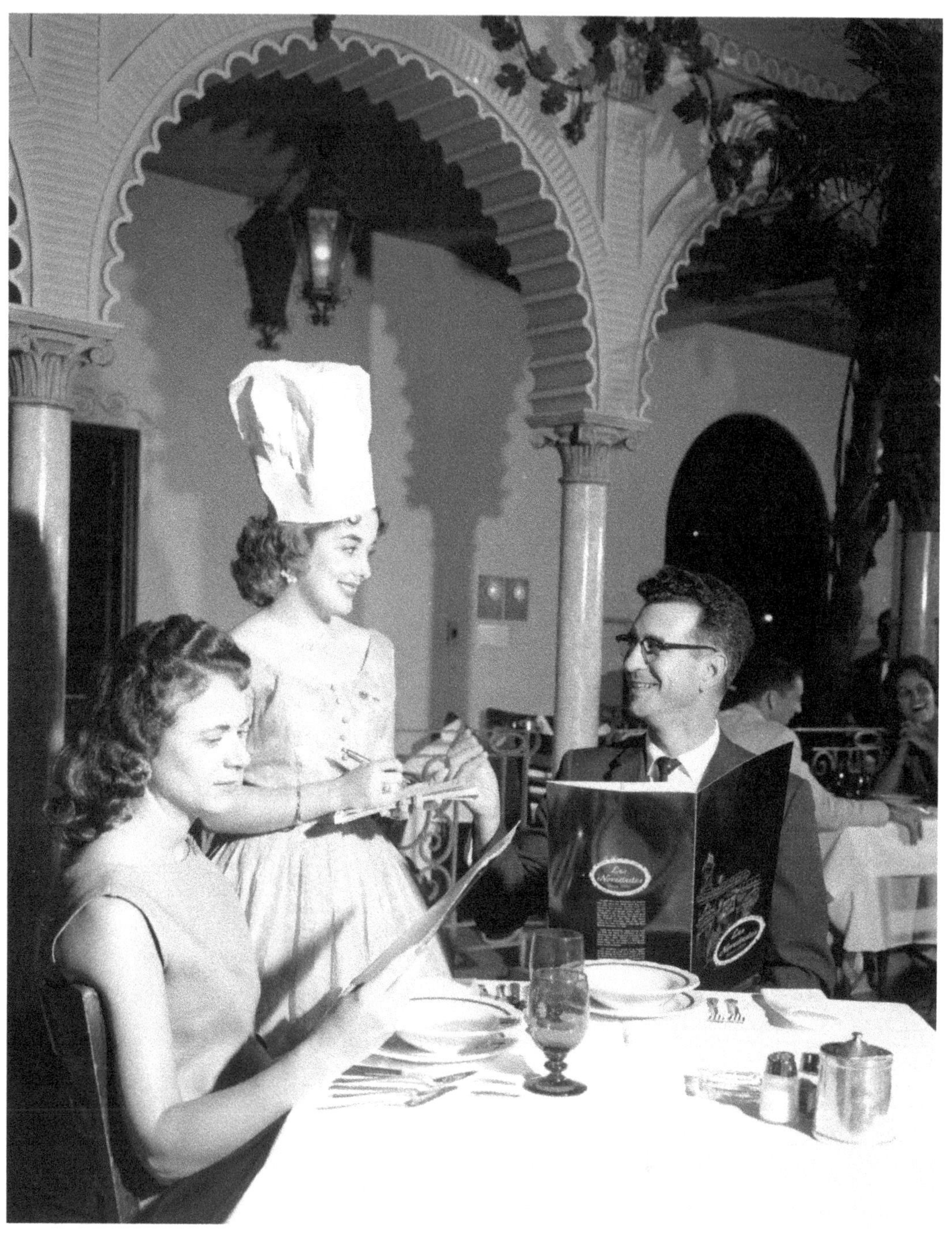

The server in this May 1960 photo is Helen Diaz, who was named Miss Cigar Queen in 1960. Her customers were having dinner at Las Novedades Restaurant during the Tri-City Suncoast Festival.

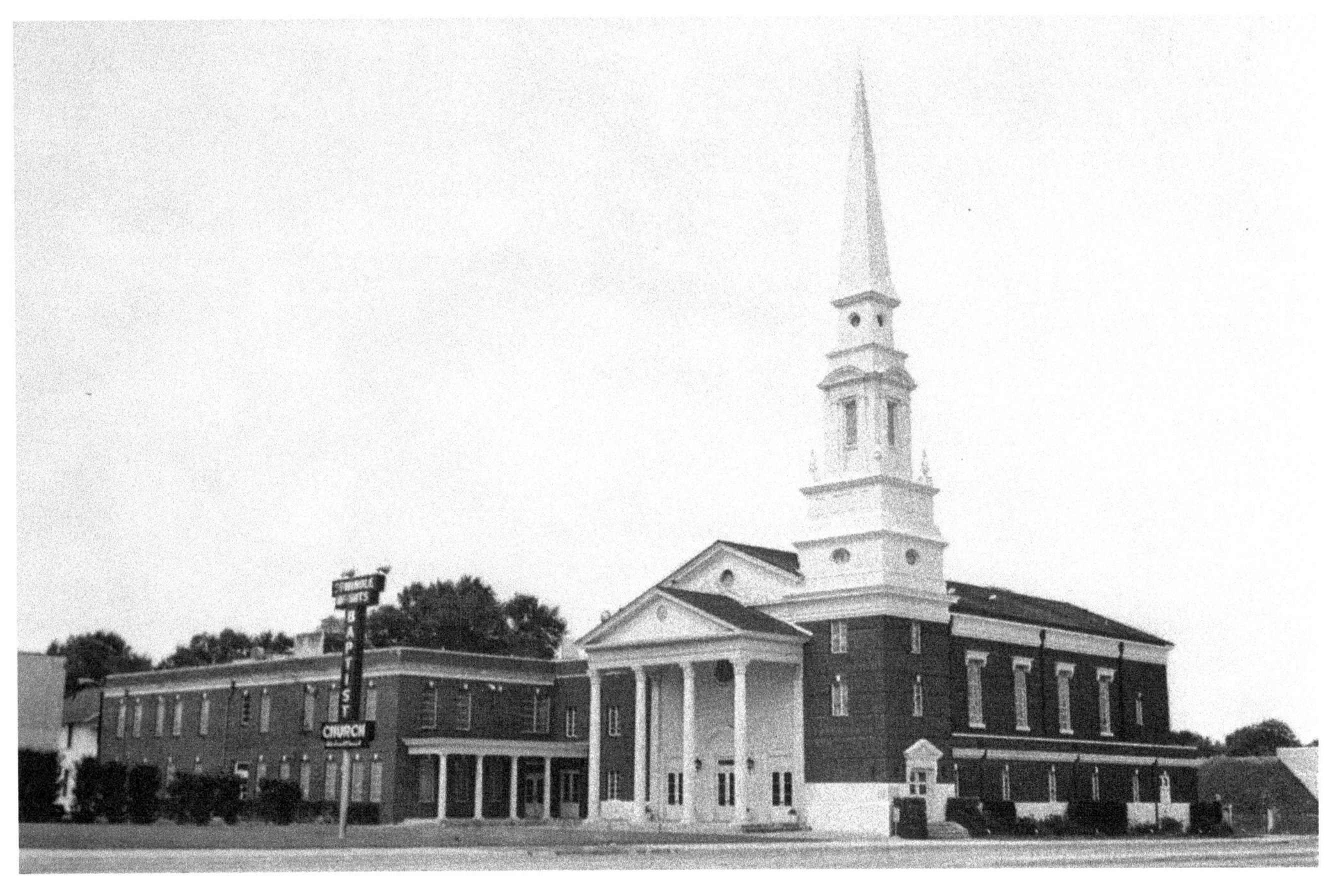

The Seminole Heights Baptist Church, with its tall white steeple, is located in the center of the Seminole Heights National Historic District, and is easily the most recognizable structure in the district. It stands at the junction of the heavily trafficked Interstate 75 and Hillsborough Avenue.

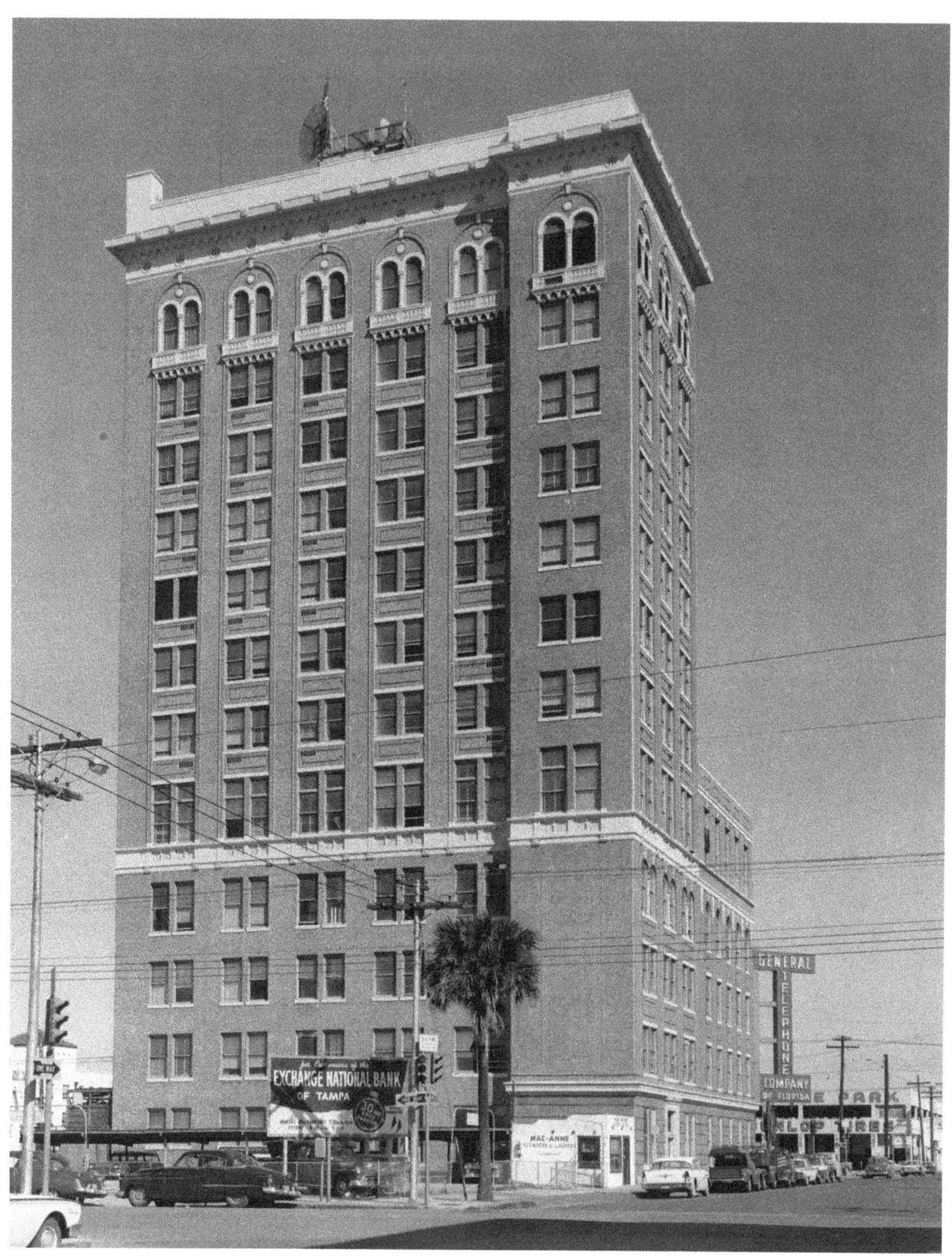

The white band encircling this building indicates its roofline when it opened in 1915. Located at the corner of Zack and Morgan Streets, it was increased to 12 stories in 1926. When photographed in April 1960, it was the headquarters of the General Telephone Company of Florida, its new name as of 1957.

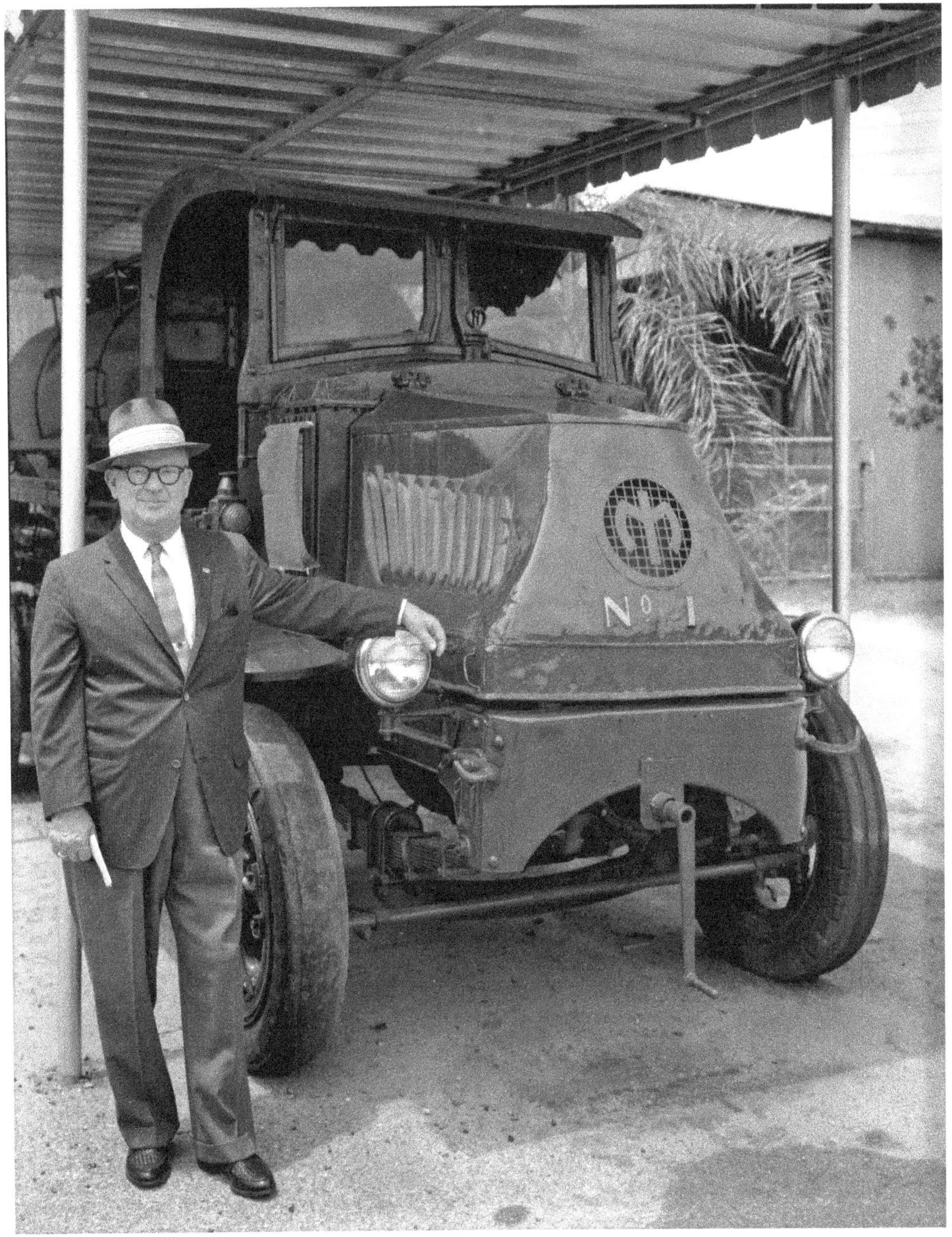

W. L. Cobb posed in April 1960 next to one of the old Mack trucks used by his W. L. Cobb Construction Company. Its headquarters was located at 1102 North 22nd Street at the western edge of Gary, a small town not far from Ybor City and Palmetto Beach, which has now essentially been absorbed into Tampa.

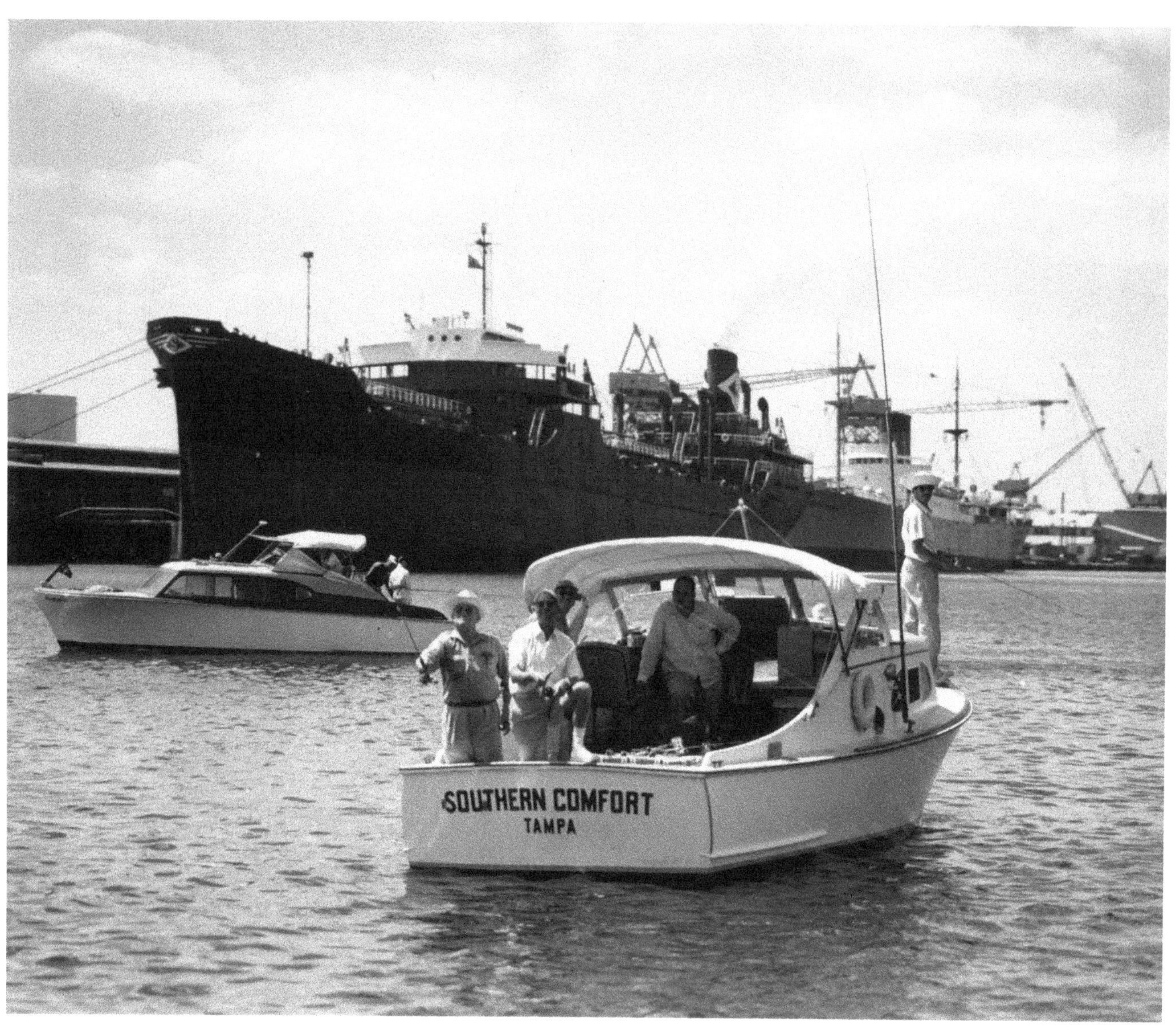

In Tampa's harbor in June 1960, fishermen aboard the *Southern Comfort* and the *Mil Gil* are shown during their participation in a fishing tournament. It was part of the World Series of Sport Fishing and many of the participants were trying their best to land the largest tarpon.

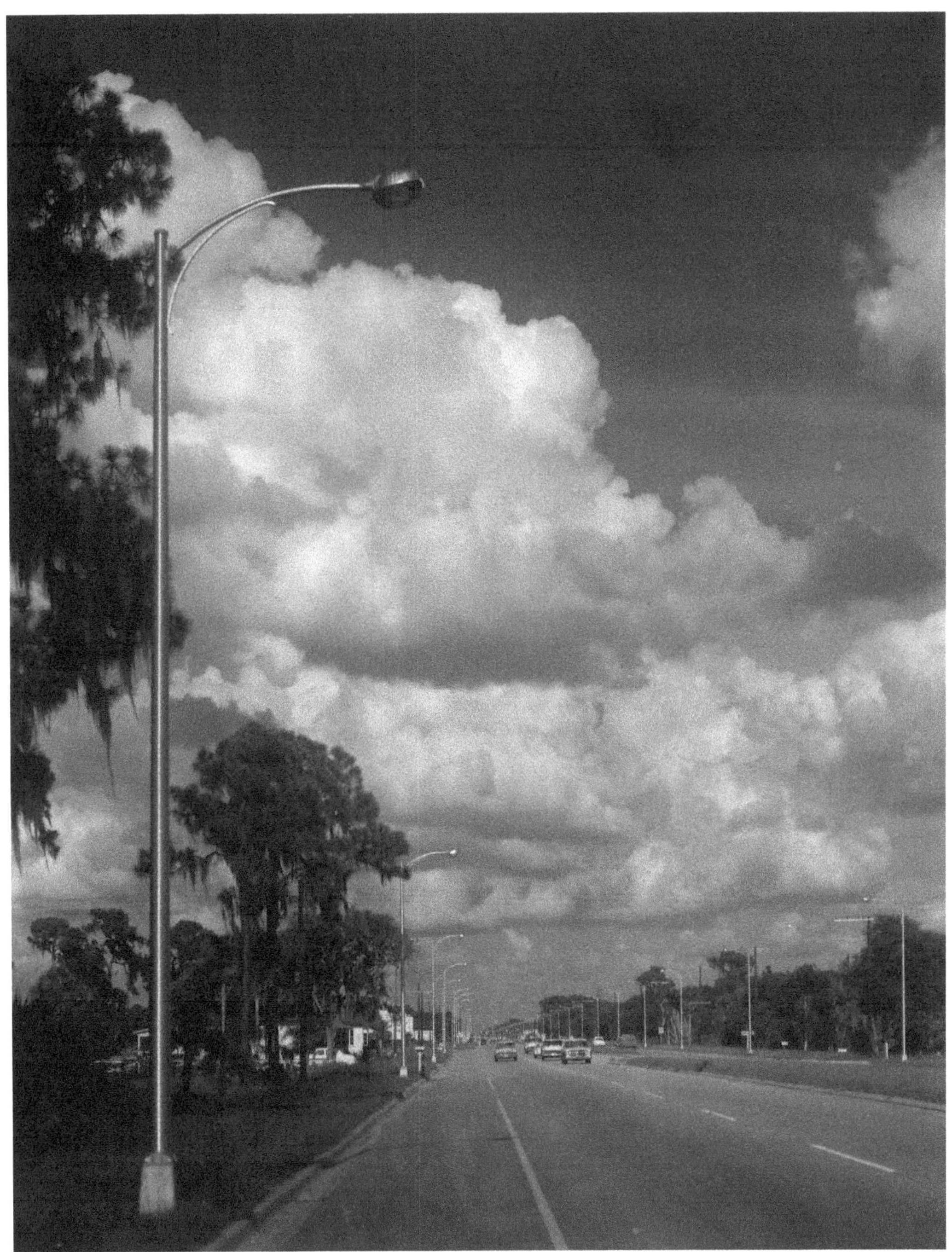

On January 1, 1921, this road was dedicated as Memorial Highway to remember the Tampa residents who died in World War I, plus 23 who went down on the Coast Guard cutter USS *Tampa* in 1918. The road ran westward from Plant Park to the Pinellas County line. Its cost was $870,000, and the Rotary Club of Tampa planted decorative trees along it. Later, after it was renamed as Grand Central Avenue, it looked like this in the vicinity of Westshore Boulevard on August 6, 1960.

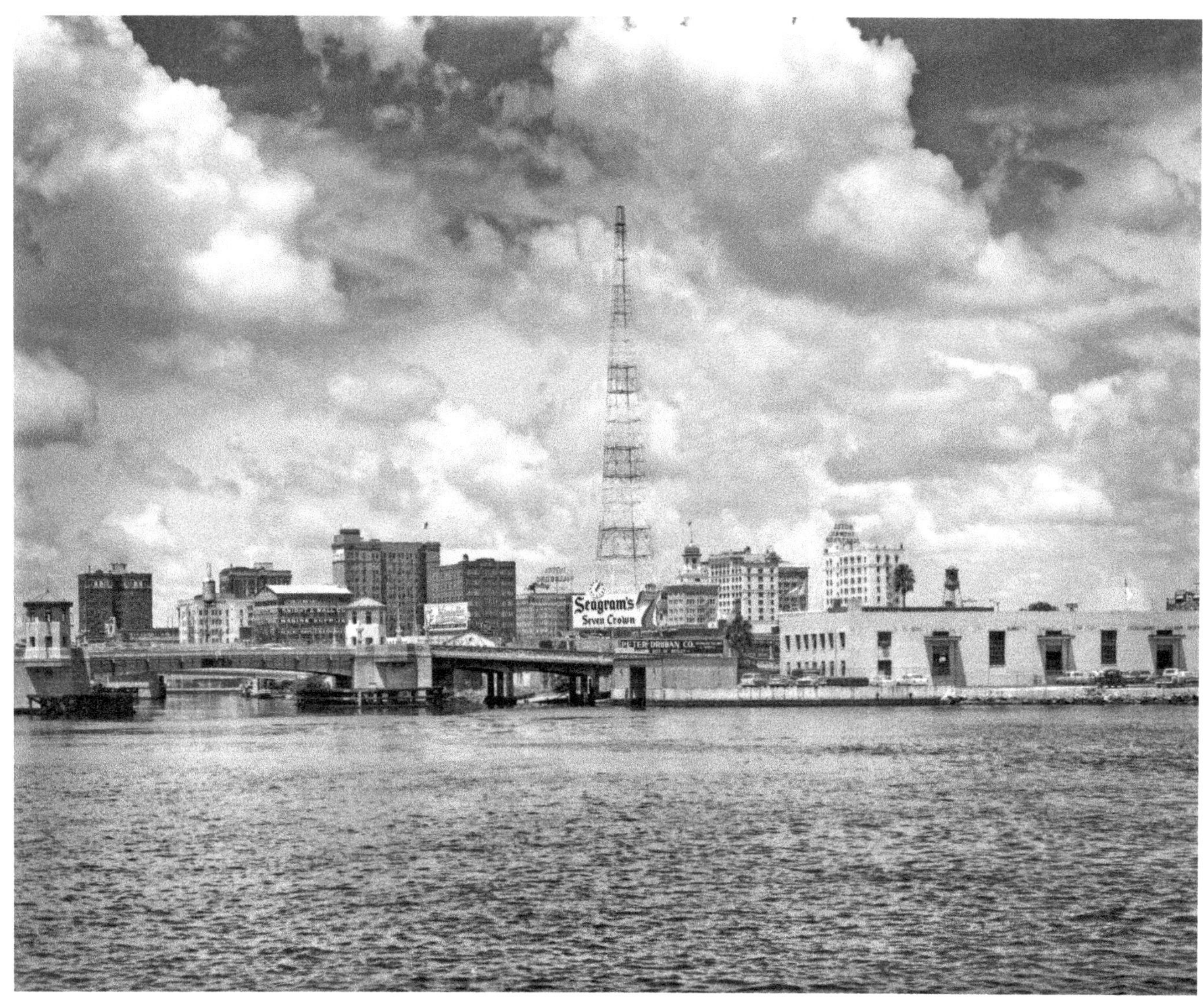

Beyond the east end of the Platt Street Bridge stands the tallest structure in 1960s Tampa. Unlike modern broadcasting, which transmits signals from urban studios to tall towers in remote areas, for retransmission to a region, this radio tower was fastened to the top of the radio station's downtown building.

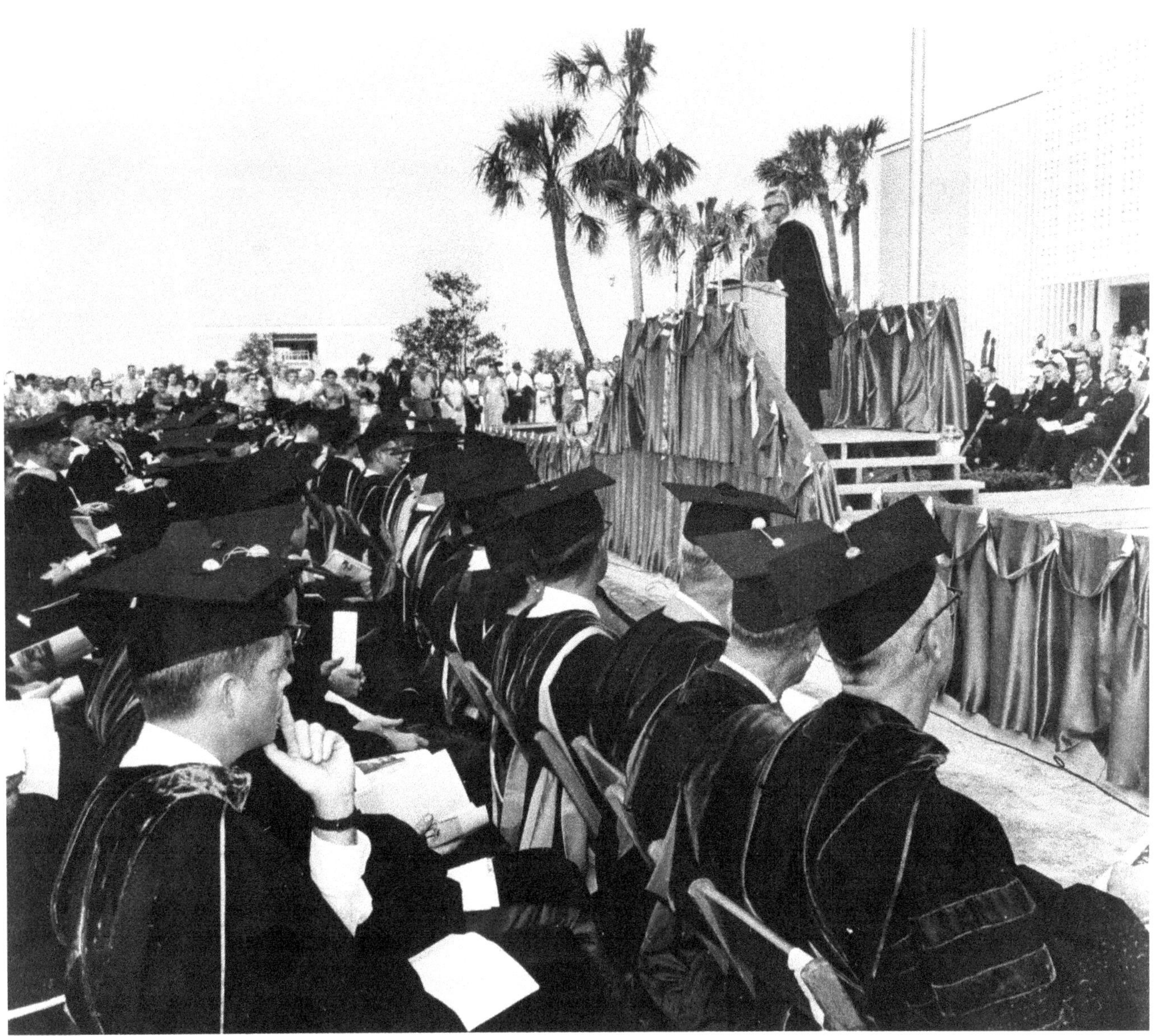

On September 26, 1960, the keynote speaker at the University of South Florida convocation was Governor Thomas LeRoy Collins. The school was officially founded on December 18, 1956, and when it opened almost four years later, it was the country's first major state university planned and built entirely during the twentieth century.

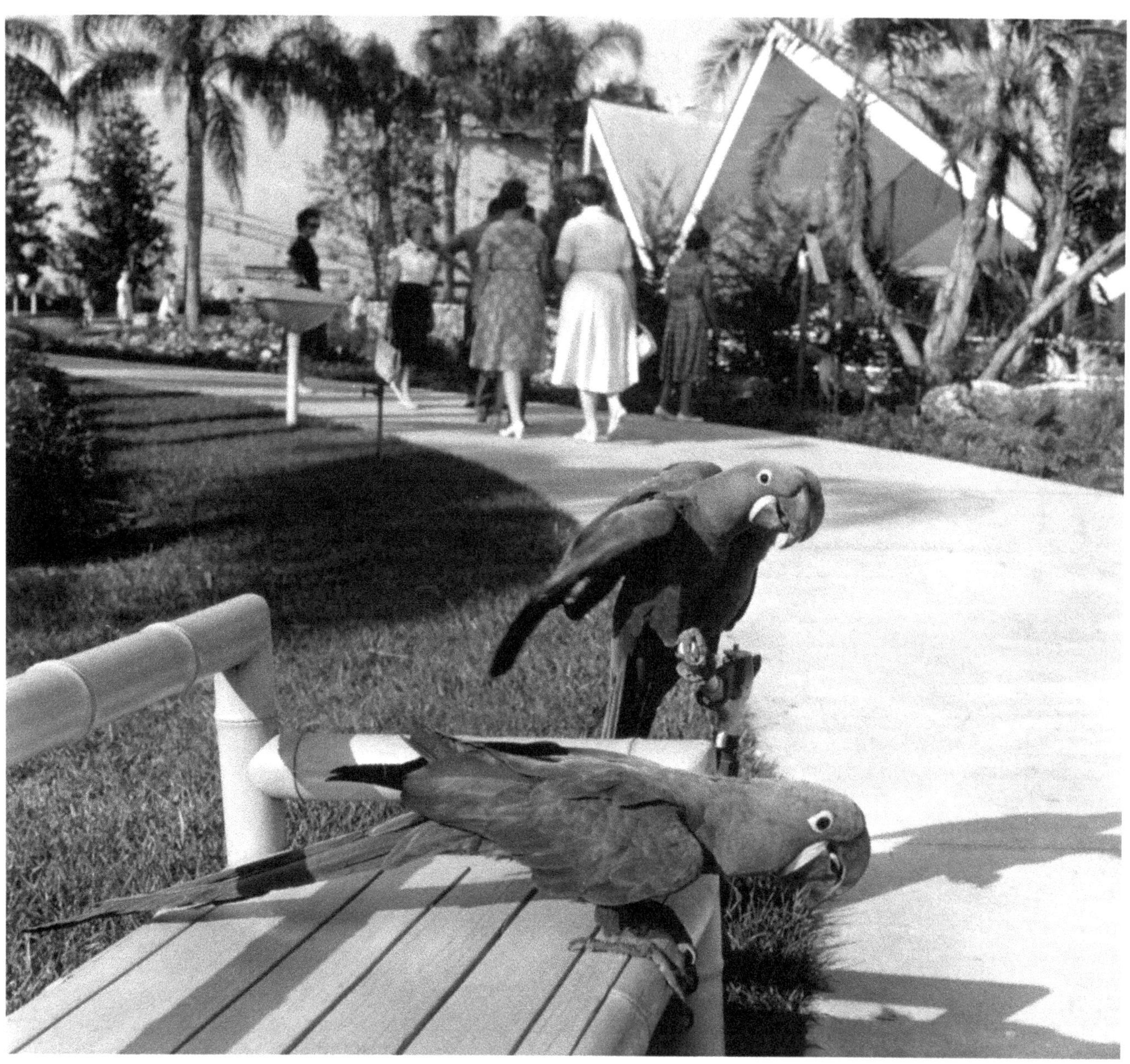

Busch Gardens opened in 1959 with four parrots and four human employees, and the two parrots here were photographed in October 1960. They roamed free and visitors were allowed to pet them. The original section of the greatly enlarged theme park is still used mainly for gardens and animals, including an educational bird show.

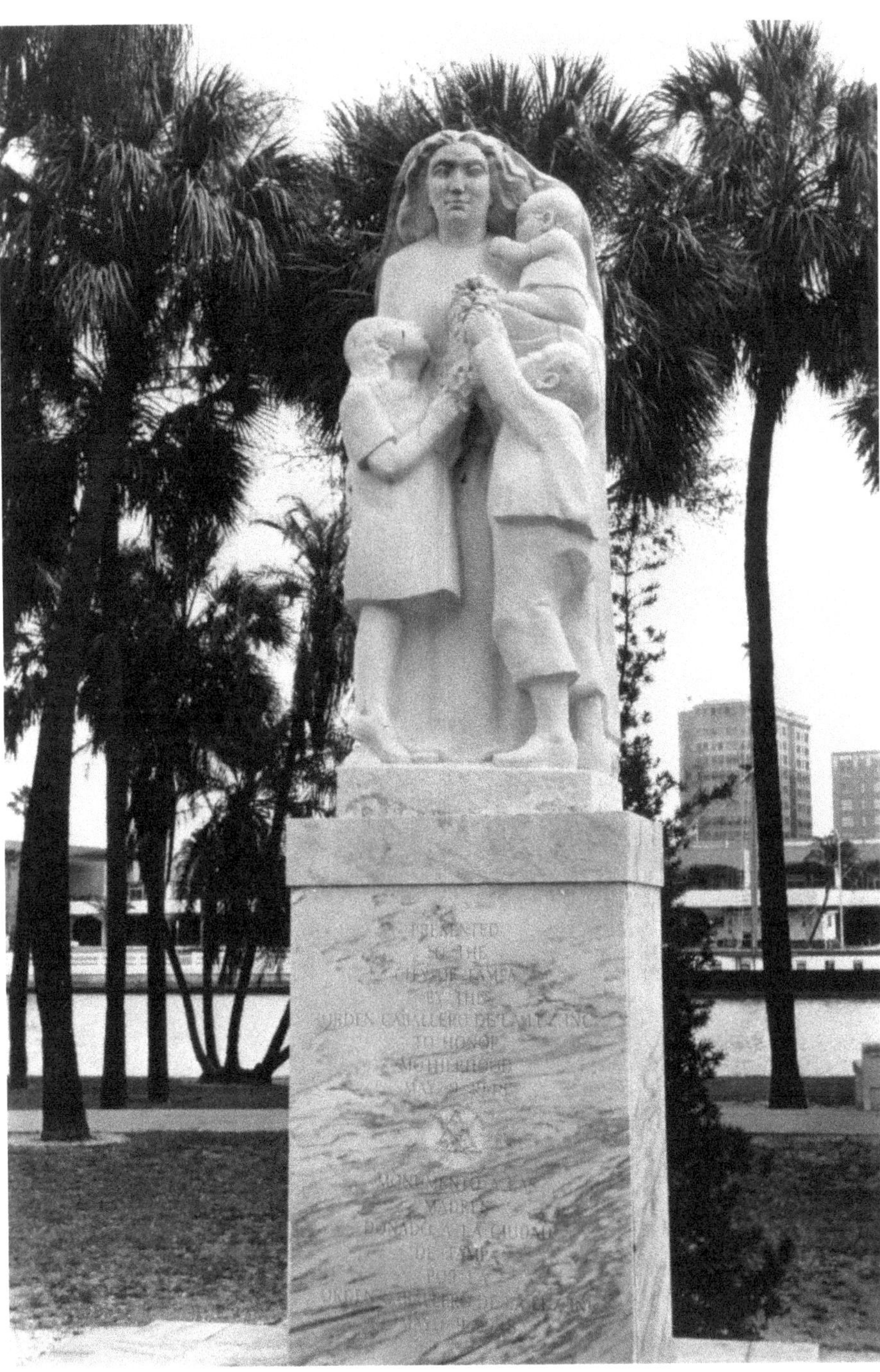

The monument photographed during the 1960s was presented by the Orden Caballero de la Luz on May 9, 1948. It was a gift to Tampa and entitled "Honor to Mothers of the World." T. Ramos Blanco sculpted the mother and her three children out of concrete, and this originally stood in Plant Park near the Tampa Bay Hotel. It was later moved to Plaza Expañol along 7th Avenue in Ybor City.

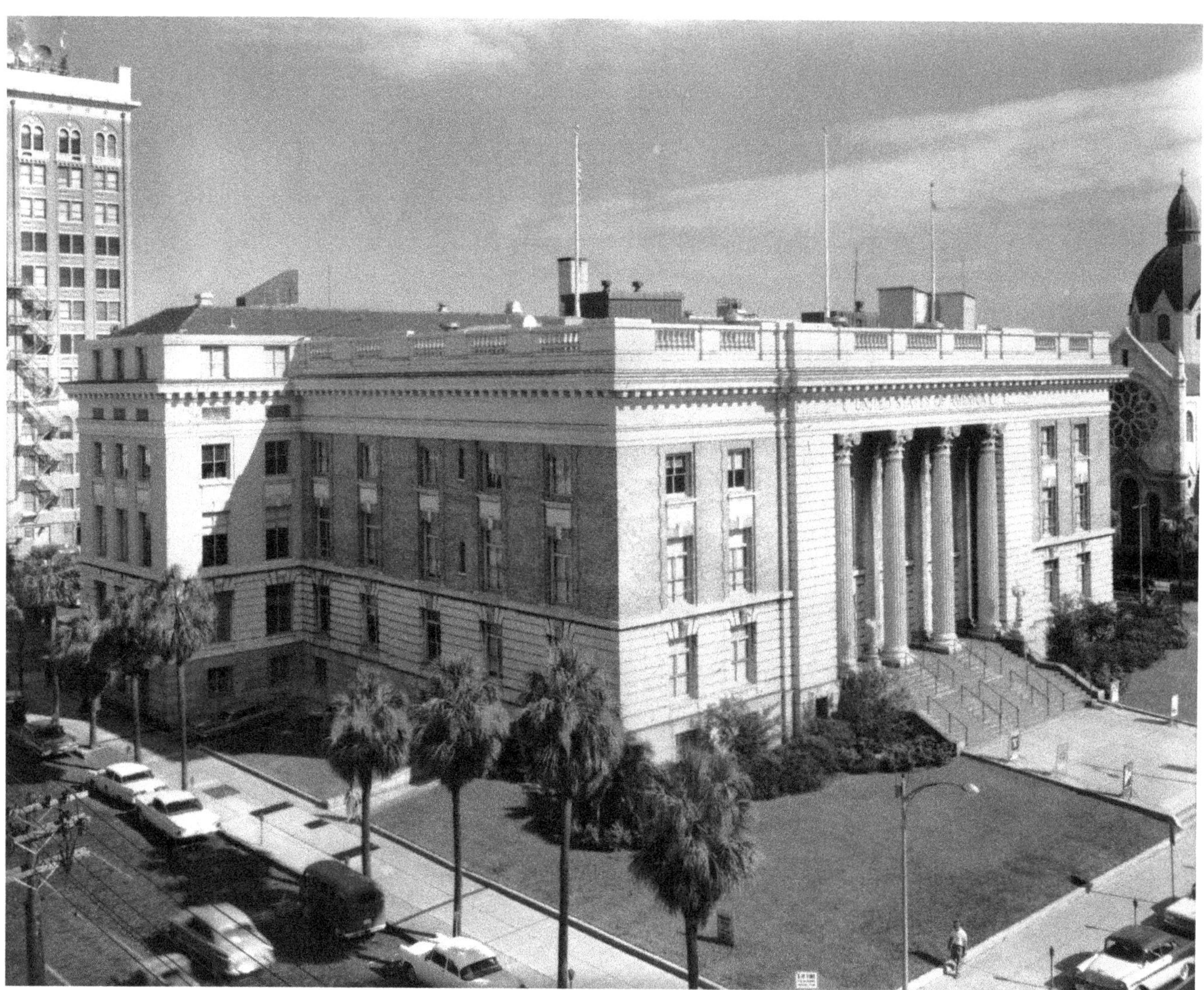

At the corner of Zack Street and Florida Avenue is the Federal Building, which included Tampa's main post office, customhouse, and federal courthouse. It was designed by James K. Taylor and was built in 1902–05. It is the oldest significant remaining building in Tampa originally designed for government use. It was added to the National Register of Historic Places in 1974, nine years after it was superseded by a more modern Federal Building at another location.

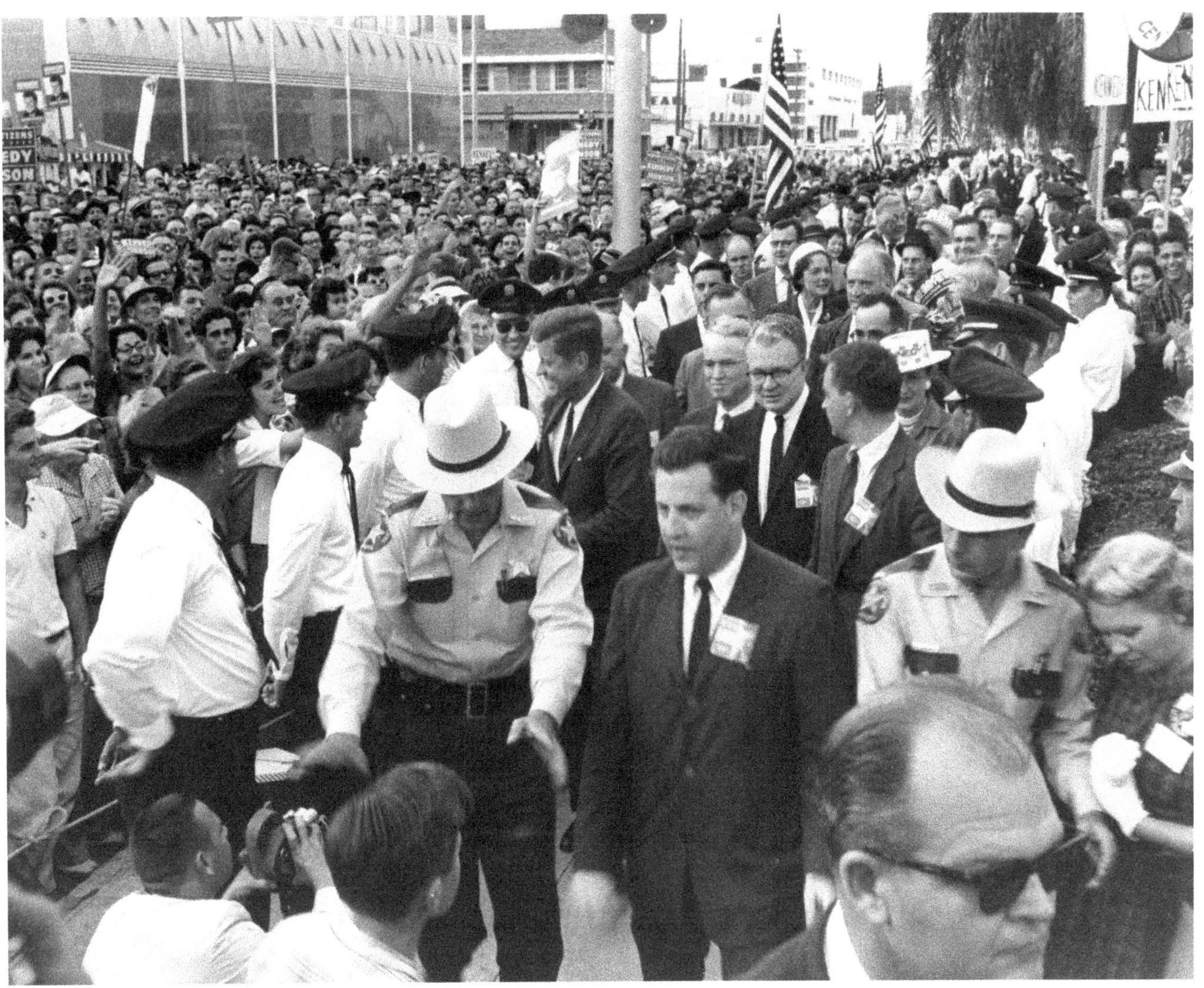

Shown here on October 18, 1960, is Senator John F. Kennedy campaigning for president in Tampa. Florida had voted its 30 delegates at the Democratic National Convention for "favorite son" candidate George A. Smathers. In November, Hillsborough County and the 10 state electoral votes went to Richard M. Nixon, who lost the national election to Kennedy.

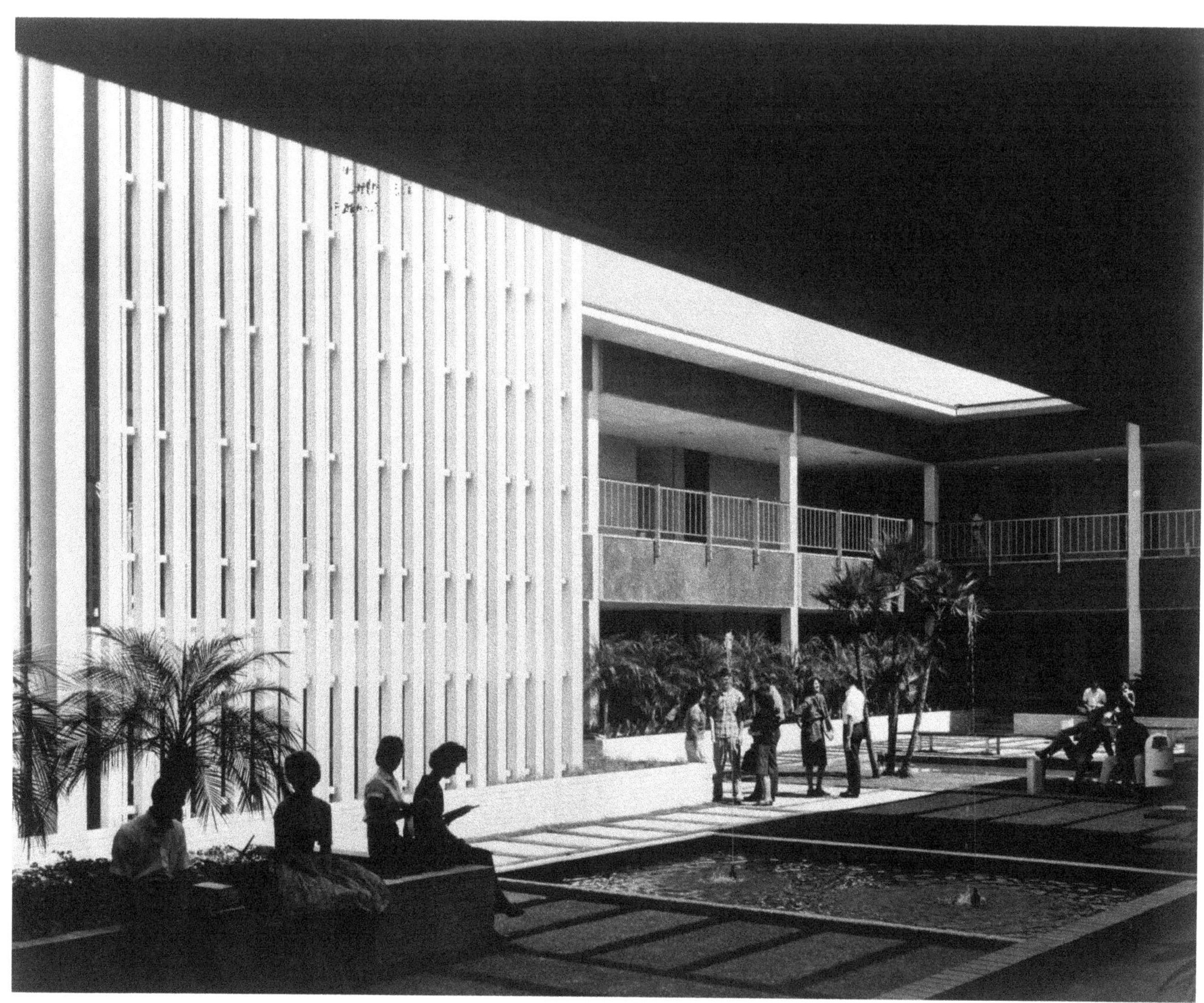

This was the scene in 1960 in the central court of the Administration Building at the University of South Florida. Officially known as the John and Grace Allen Administration Building, it was named for the school's founding president and his wife. Dr. Allen designed the university's first curriculum and the original layout of the campus Allen described USF as "a campus on which the concrete never sets."

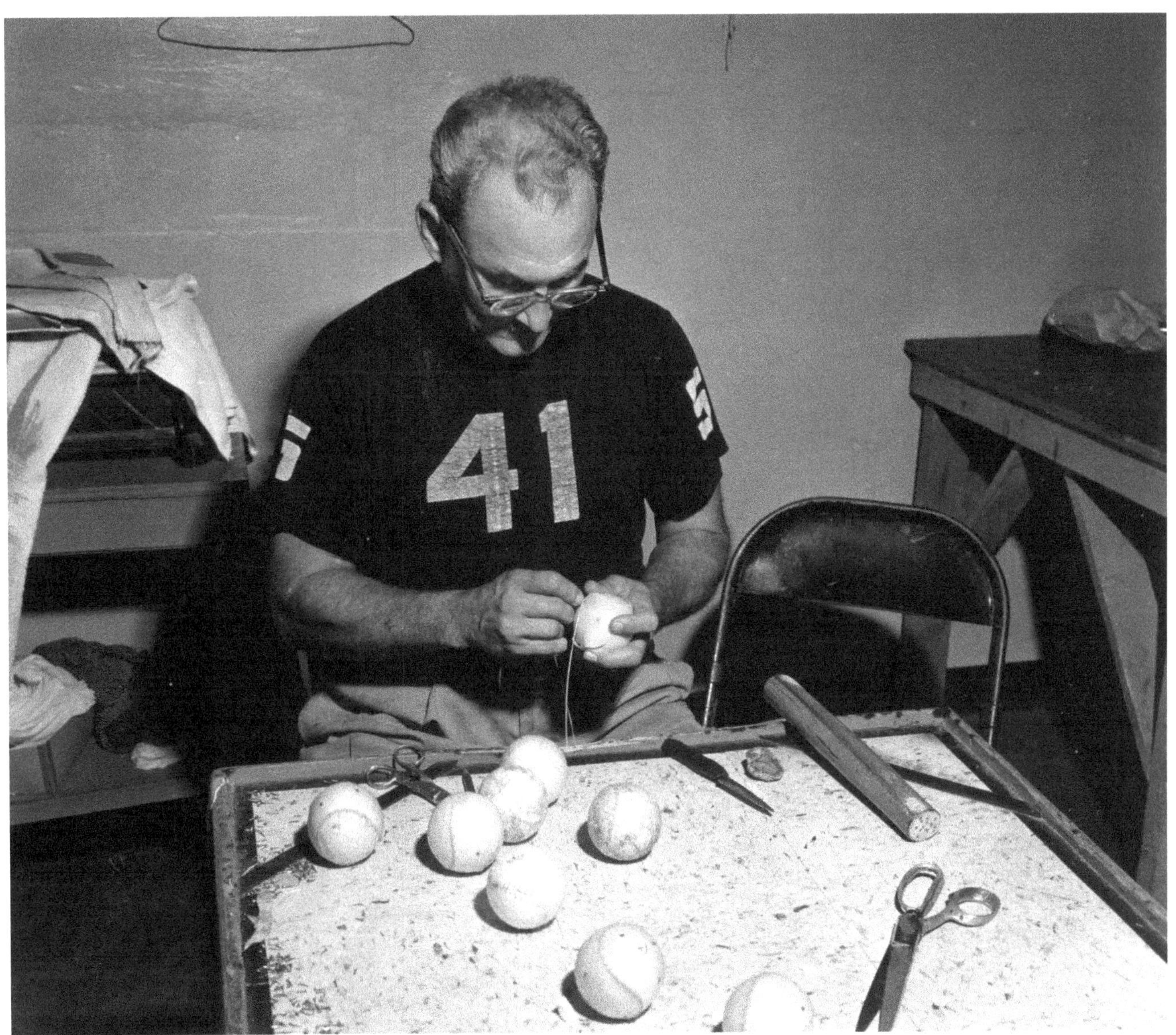

Shown here in February 1961 is Anibal Vélez, who played jai-alai competitively for 23 years. A native of Cuba, he manufactures balls for the sport, known as pelotas. They are always made by hand rather than machine, and consist of hand-wound Brazilian rubber with two goatskin covers sewn together. Each pelota costs about $150 and the covers must be replaced after being used for only 15 minutes.

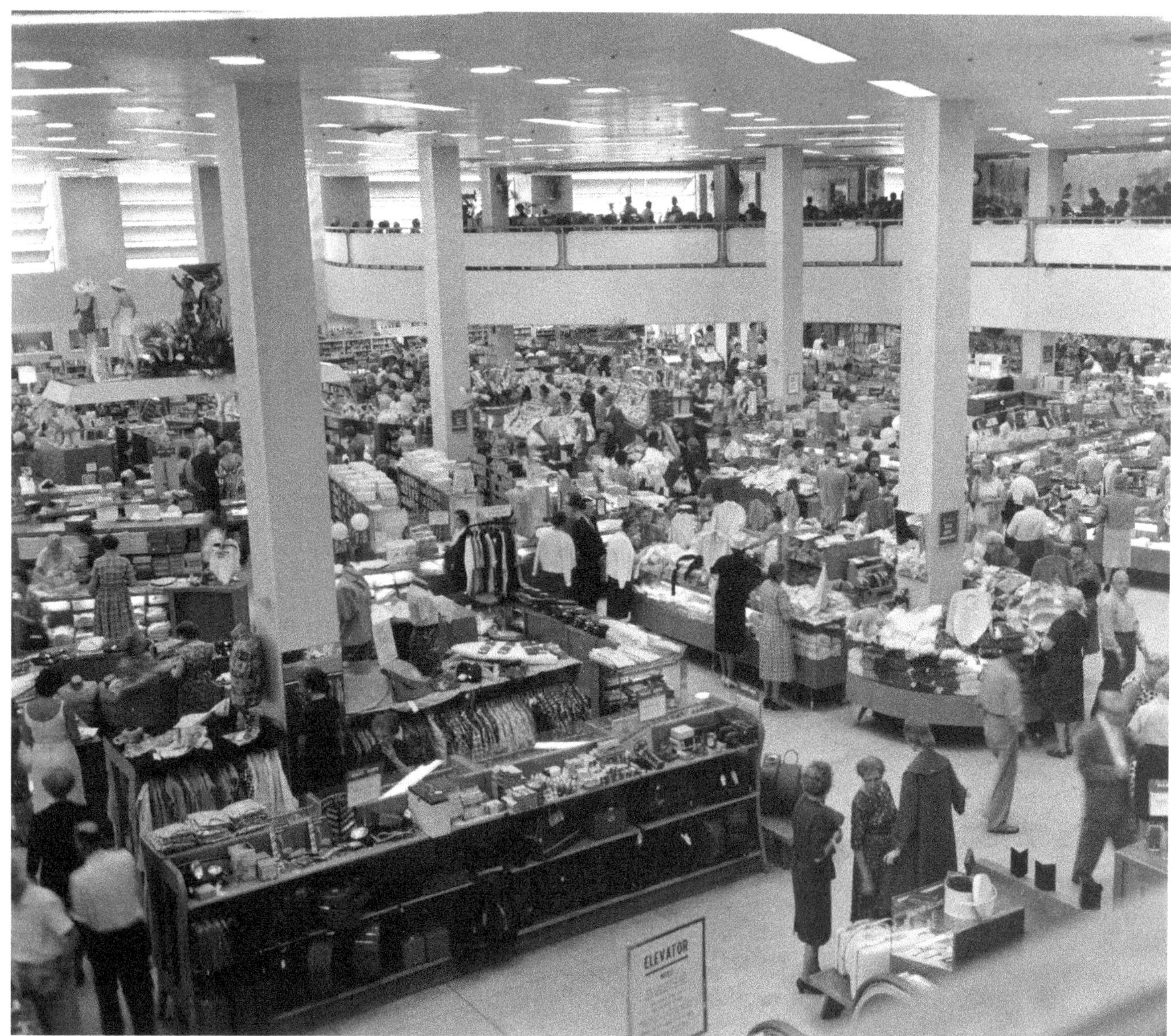

This scene of the interior of the Maas Brothers Department Store in February 1961 is very different from those which predated World War I. Then, all of the store's salespersons were men, but with the shortage of male labor caused by the need for soldiers, management allowed women to take their place and they remained in later decades. By the mid-1930s, the store affiliated with the Hahn Department Stores (later known as the Allied Stores Corporation), but it continued to be operated with a local touch by the Maas family.

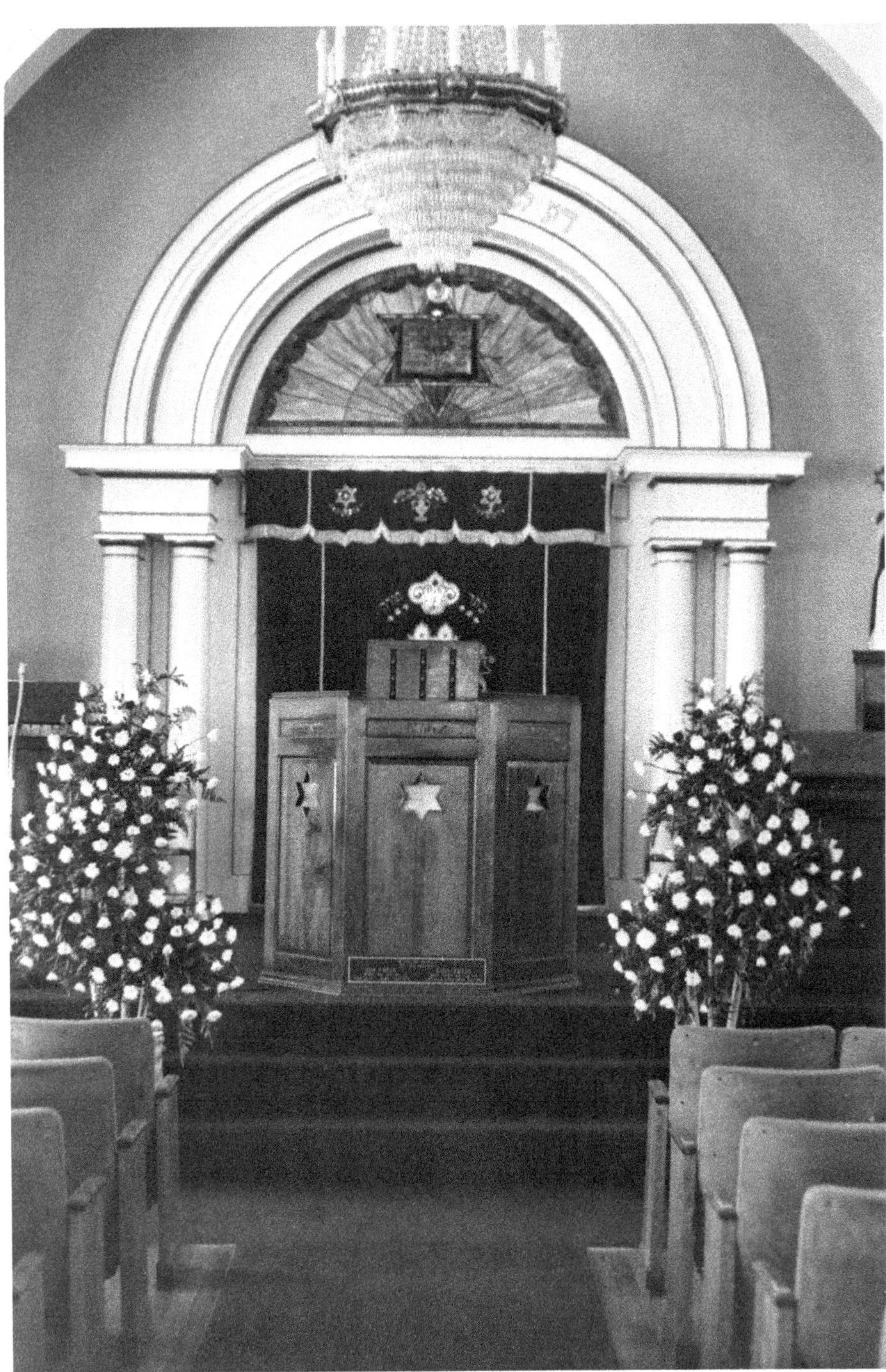

Tampa's Rodeph Sholom Synagogue was established in 1903 when a group of members split from the older congregation Schaarai Zedek. Six years later, the new congregation dedicated its first building. Another opened in 1925 at 309 E. Palm Avenue in Tampa Heights. This is how its interior appeared in 1961.

At the Corral, Wodiska and Company cigar factory in the 1960s, these employees were involved in selecting the best tobacco leaves to use in the cigars. The selectors were positioned close to windows so they could have natural light and make their selections on the basis of color, texture, and maturity.

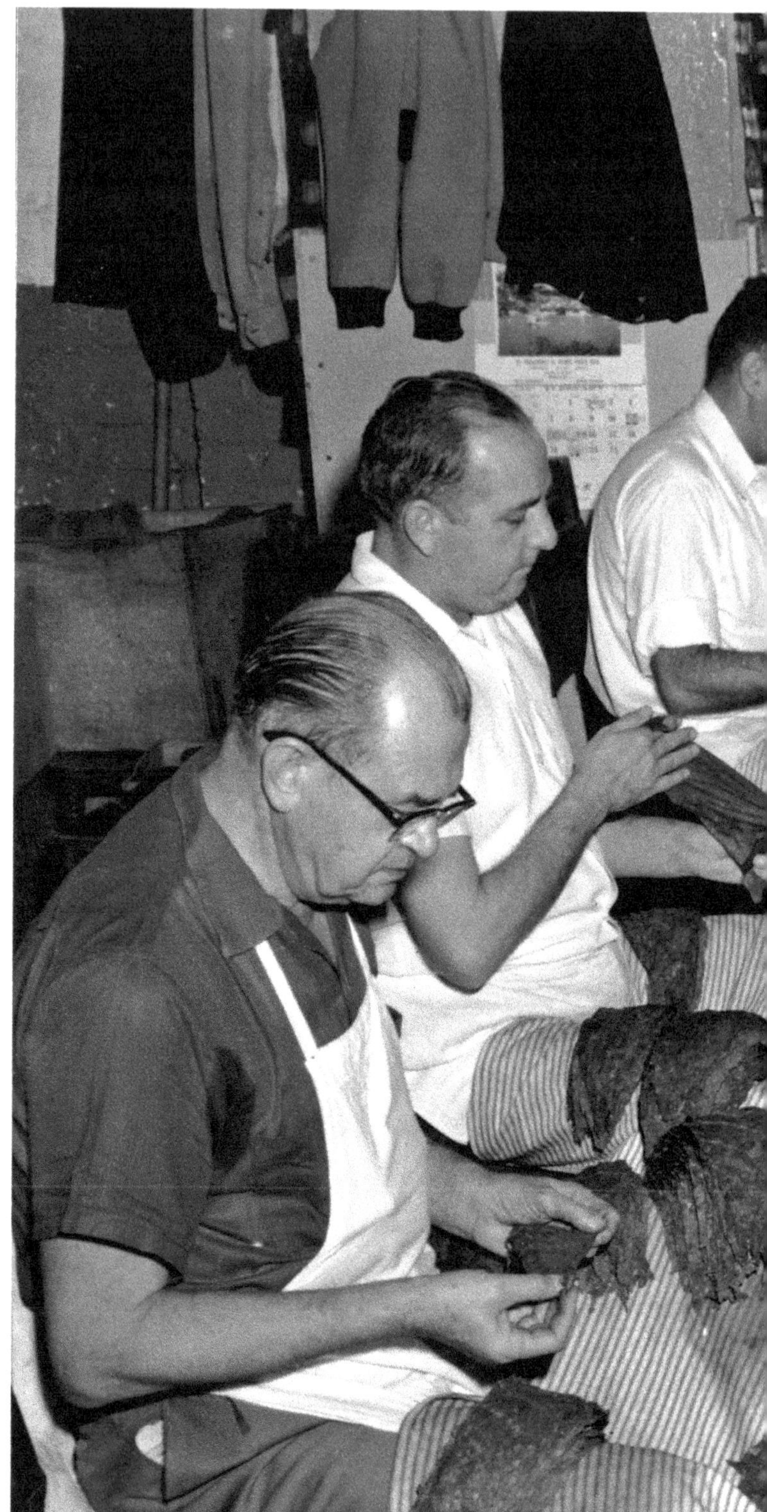

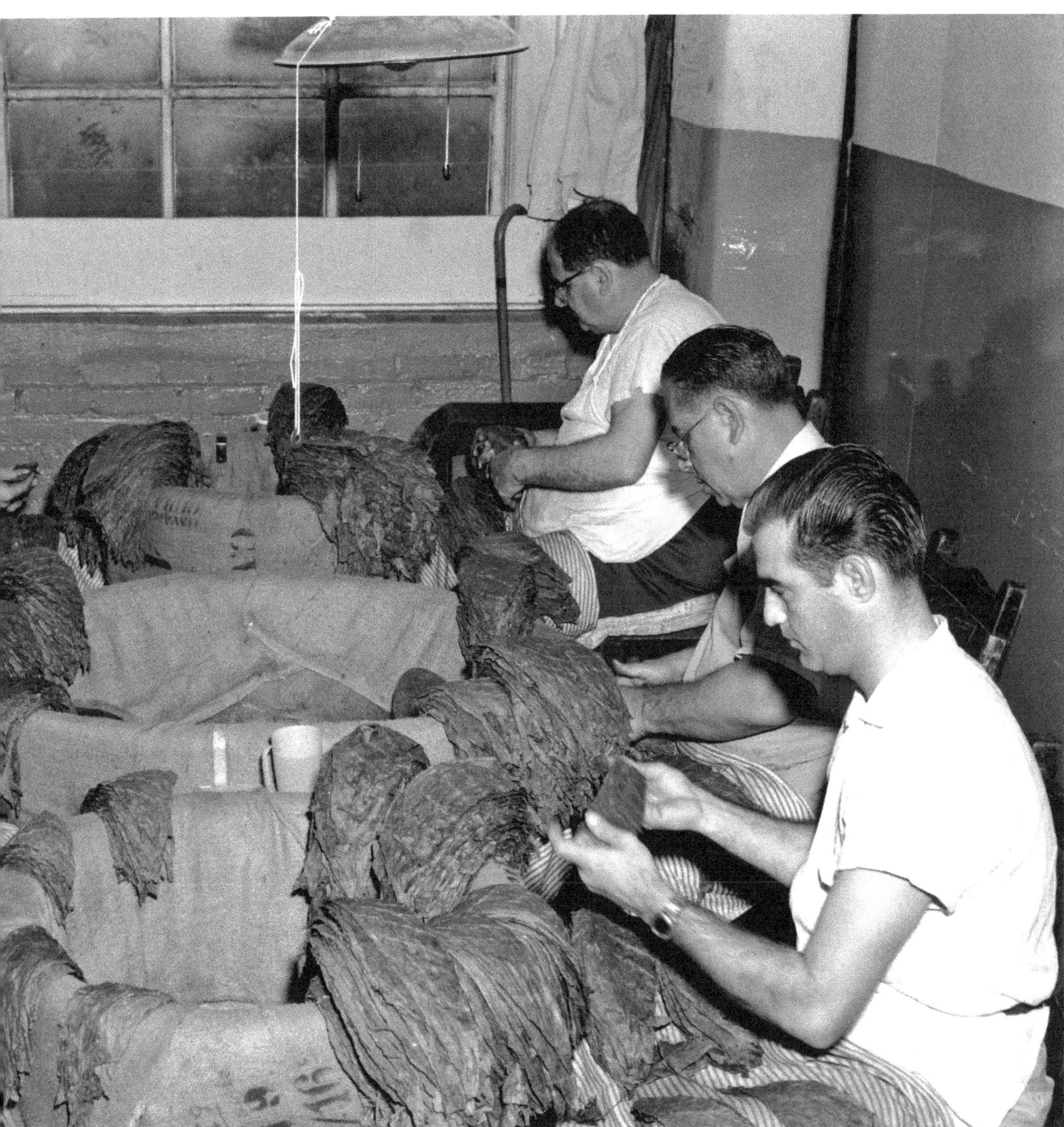

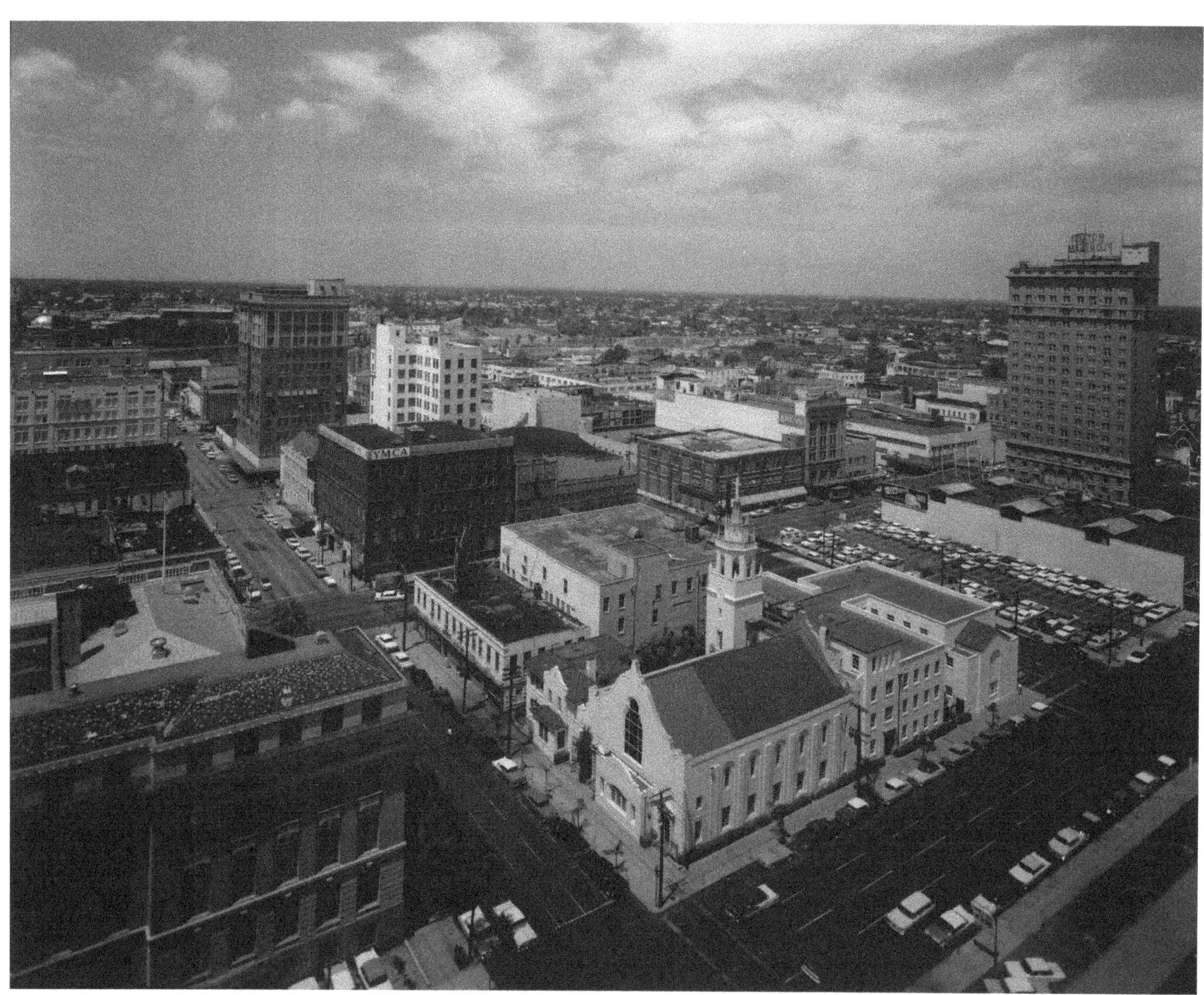

In the foreground is the First Presbyterian Church, founded in 1884. Since 1900, its sanctuary has been located at the northwest corner of Zack and Marion Streets. The one shown in this 1961 view was constructed in 1922 with a 70-foot corner tower. The complex was enlarged by the addition of a manse along Zack Street in 1924, and the 1949 completion of the John Chapel Tims Educational Building and the Memorial Building, both on Marion Street.

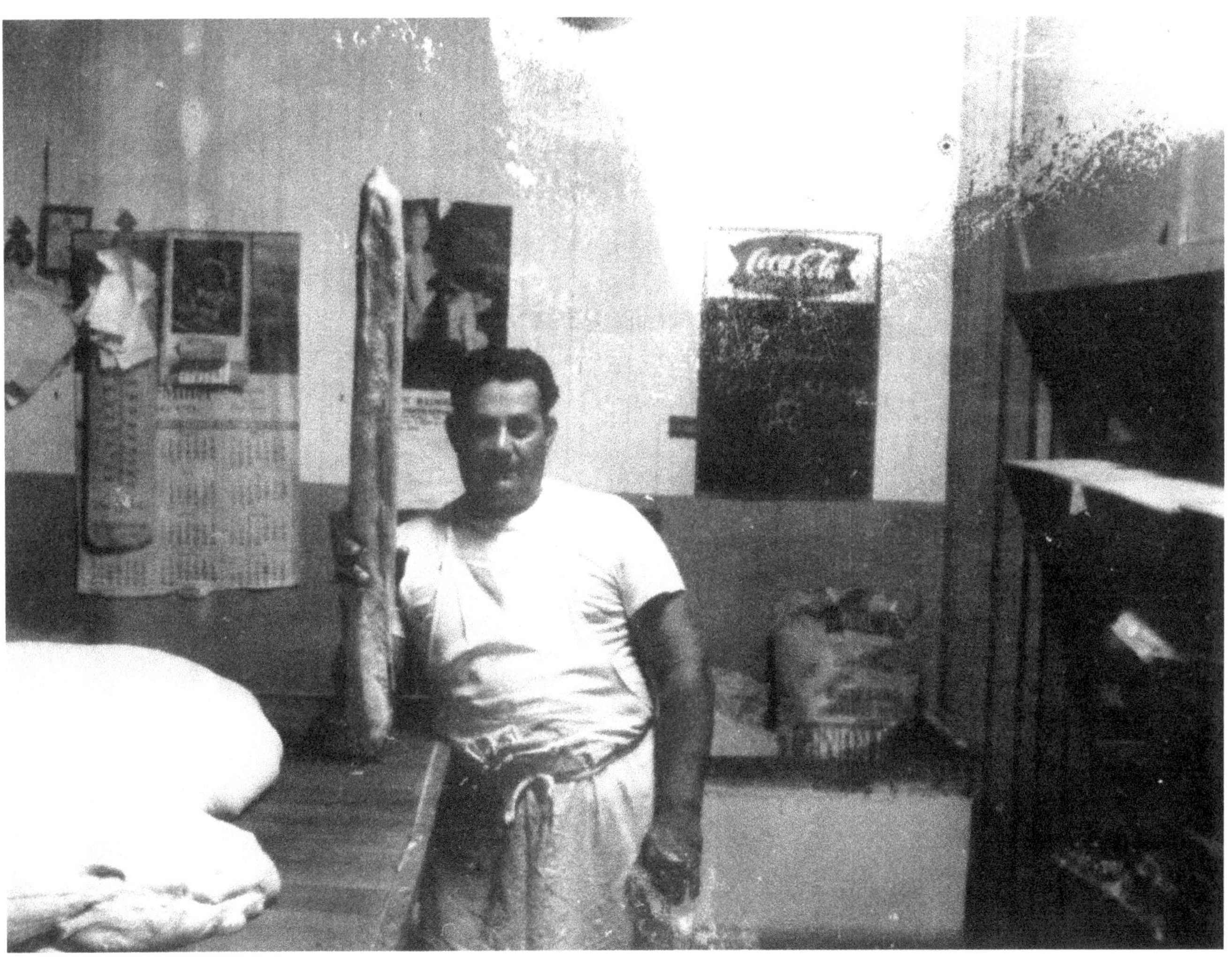

Francisco Ferlita moved to the United States from Santo Stefano, Sicily, and founded the Ferlita Bakery. It was initially located in a wood frame building, and in it he baked bread which he sold for three and five cents a loaf. Francisco died in 1931 and the business was continued by other members of his family. When the bakery was operating at its peak, the family was baking 35,000 loaves per week. Pictured here, in the early 1960s, is John Ferlita posing with some of the bread he had baked.

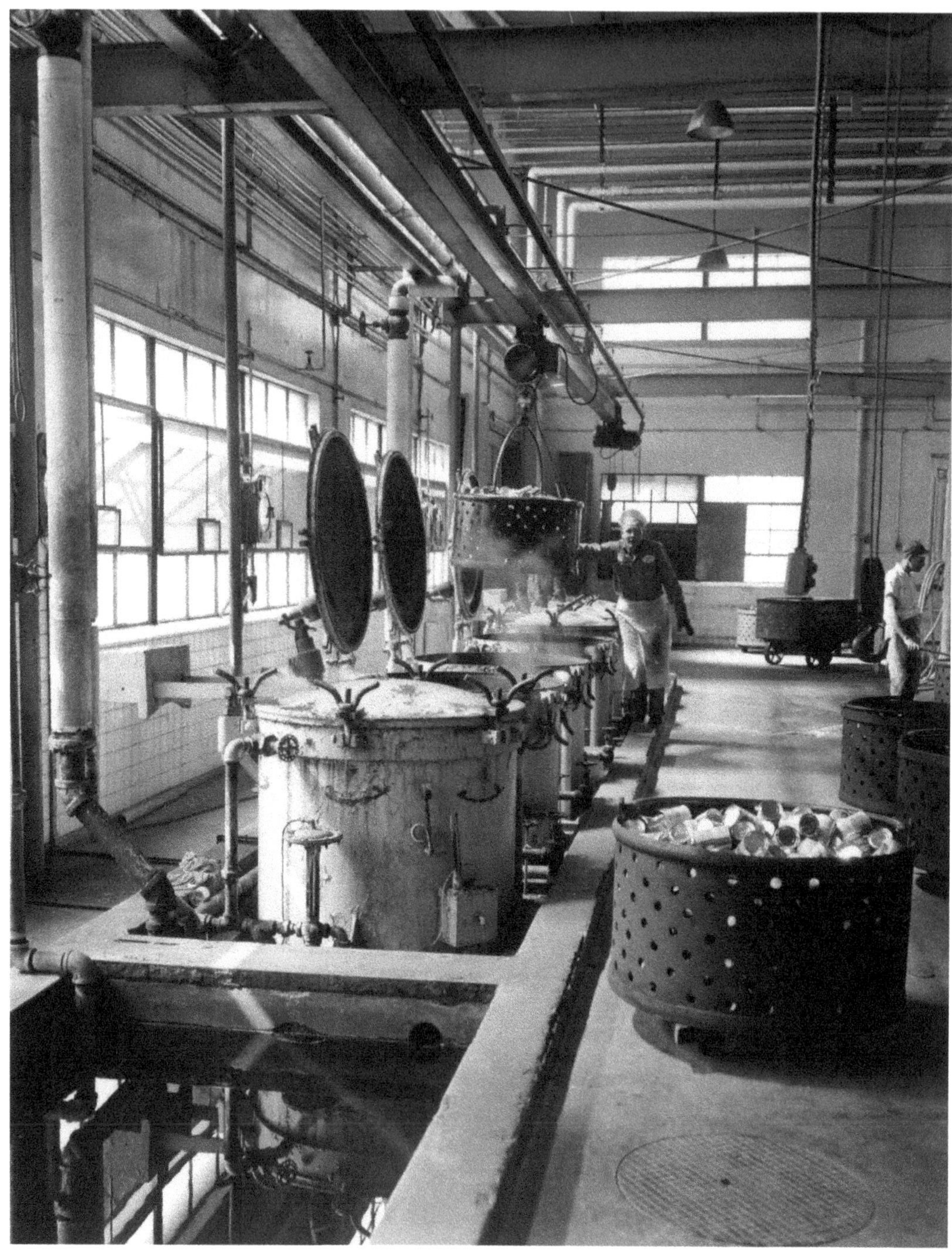

Dr. Howell T. Lykes shipped cattle from Tampa to Cuba during the 1880s, and his seven sons joined him in the business. The sons incorporated the business in 1910, and by the 1940s they expanded into planting and citrus groves. Shown here in 1962 is the Lykes Brothers meat canning plant located on Tampa's 50th Street. It was superseded three years later by another in Plant City.

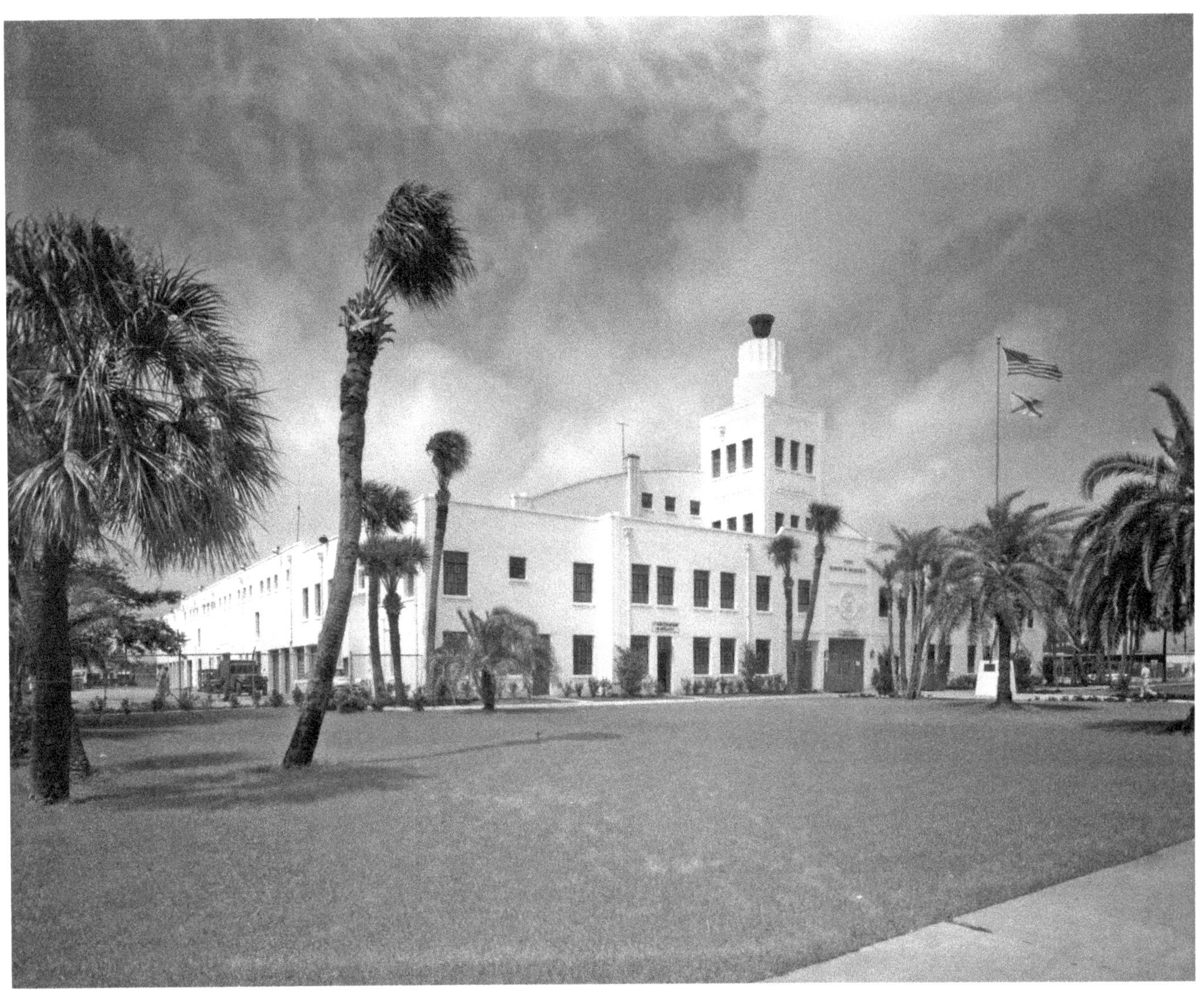

Fort Homer W. Hesterly Armory at 500 North Howard Avenue was built in 1938–41 as a Works Projects Administration job on land donated by George N. Benjamin. It was dedicated on the day following the Japanese attack on Pearl Harbor. The armory was named for Homer W. Hesterly, who lived in Tampa at the time he enlisted to serve in the army during World War I. In the 1920s, while back in Tampa, he was active in the organization of the National Guard.

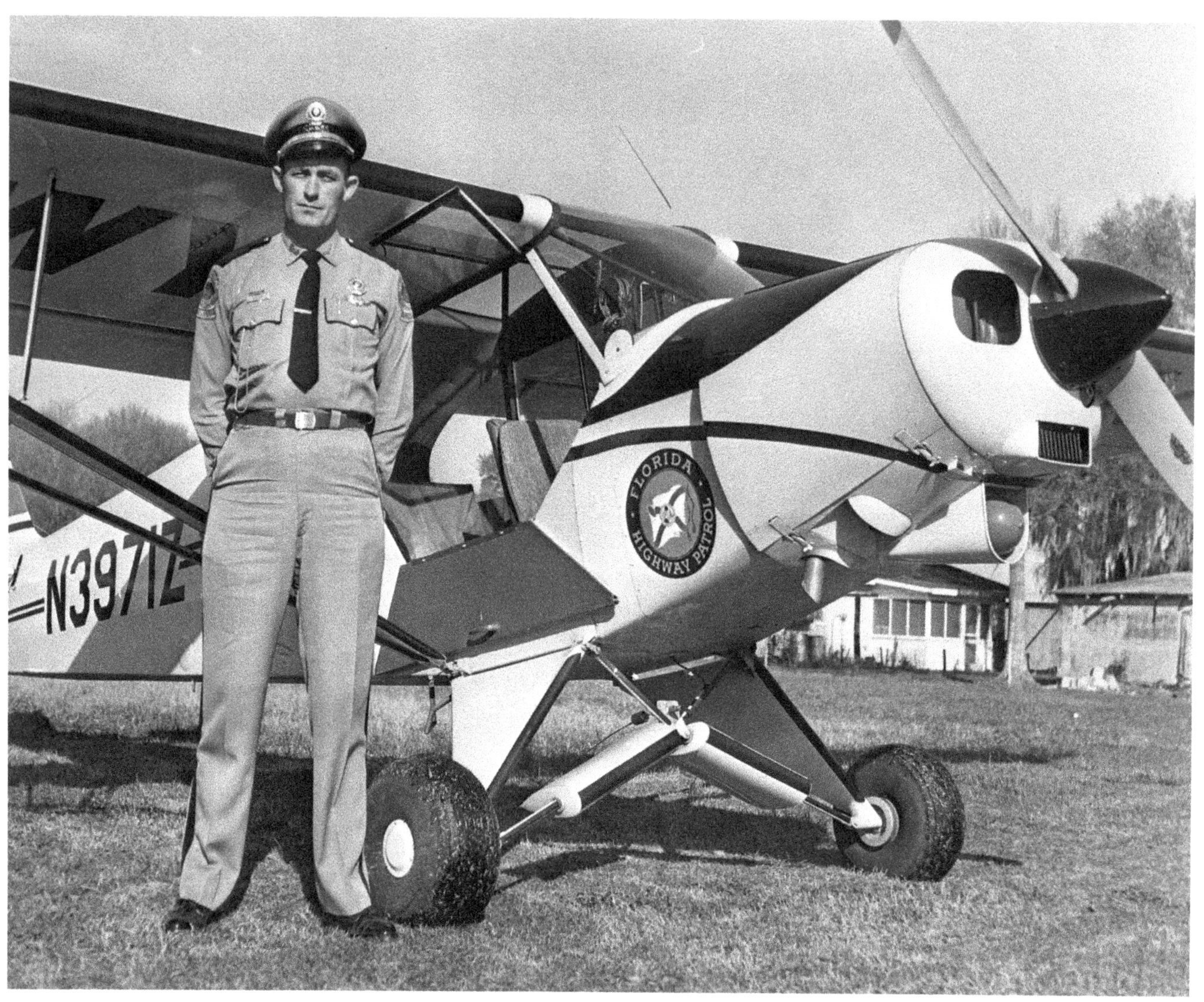

Pilot Ralph Moore of the Florida Highway Patrol poses beside his plane. It was the Patrol's second traffic plane and was based in Tampa in 1963. The use of airplanes, which began in 1962, was necessitated by the opening of the Florida Turnpike and numerous expressways.

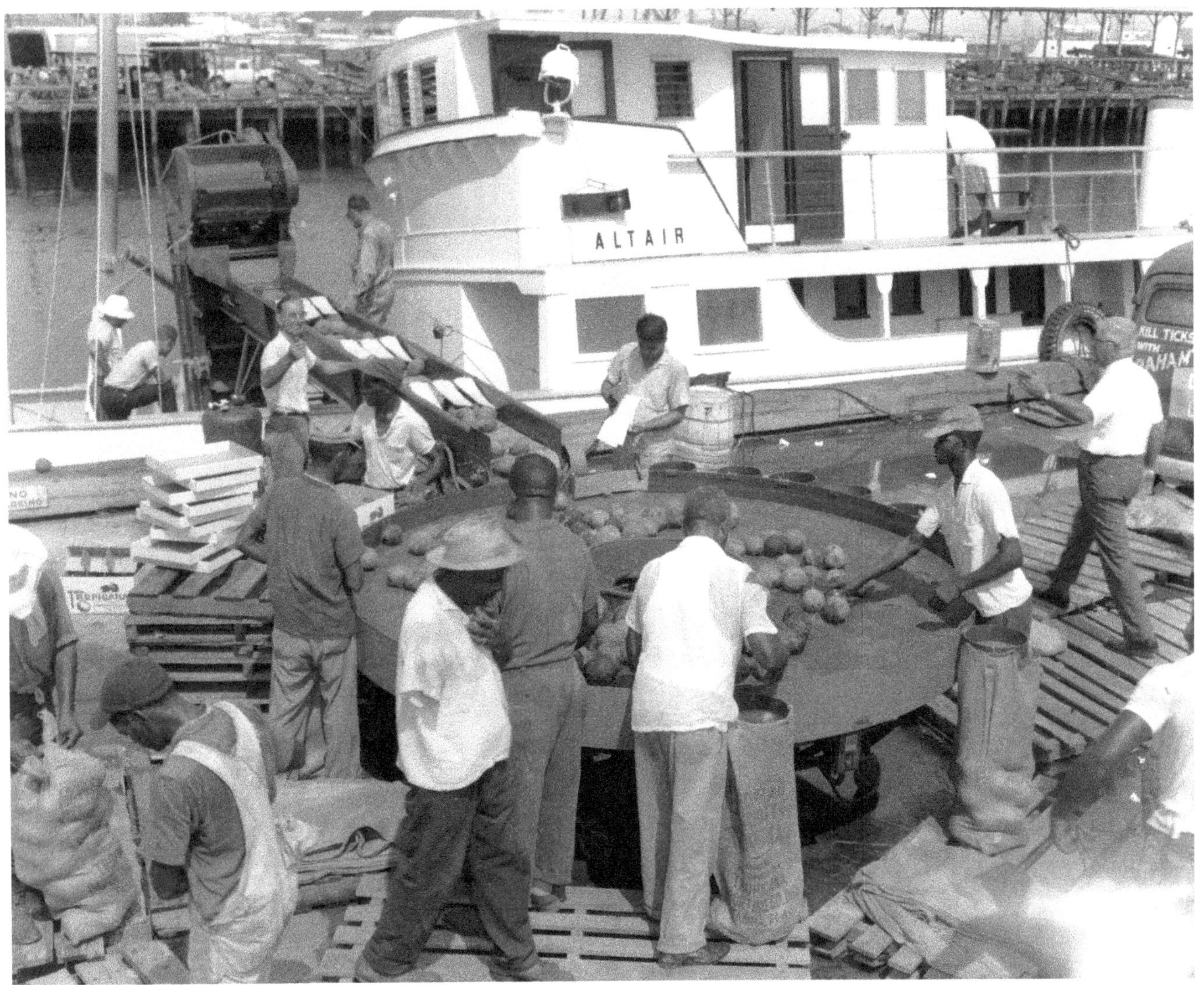

These men at the Tampa harbor are unloading coconuts, probably arriving from areas further south in Florida. After they rolled down to the circular table, they were sorted by size and other characteristics for shipment and processing.

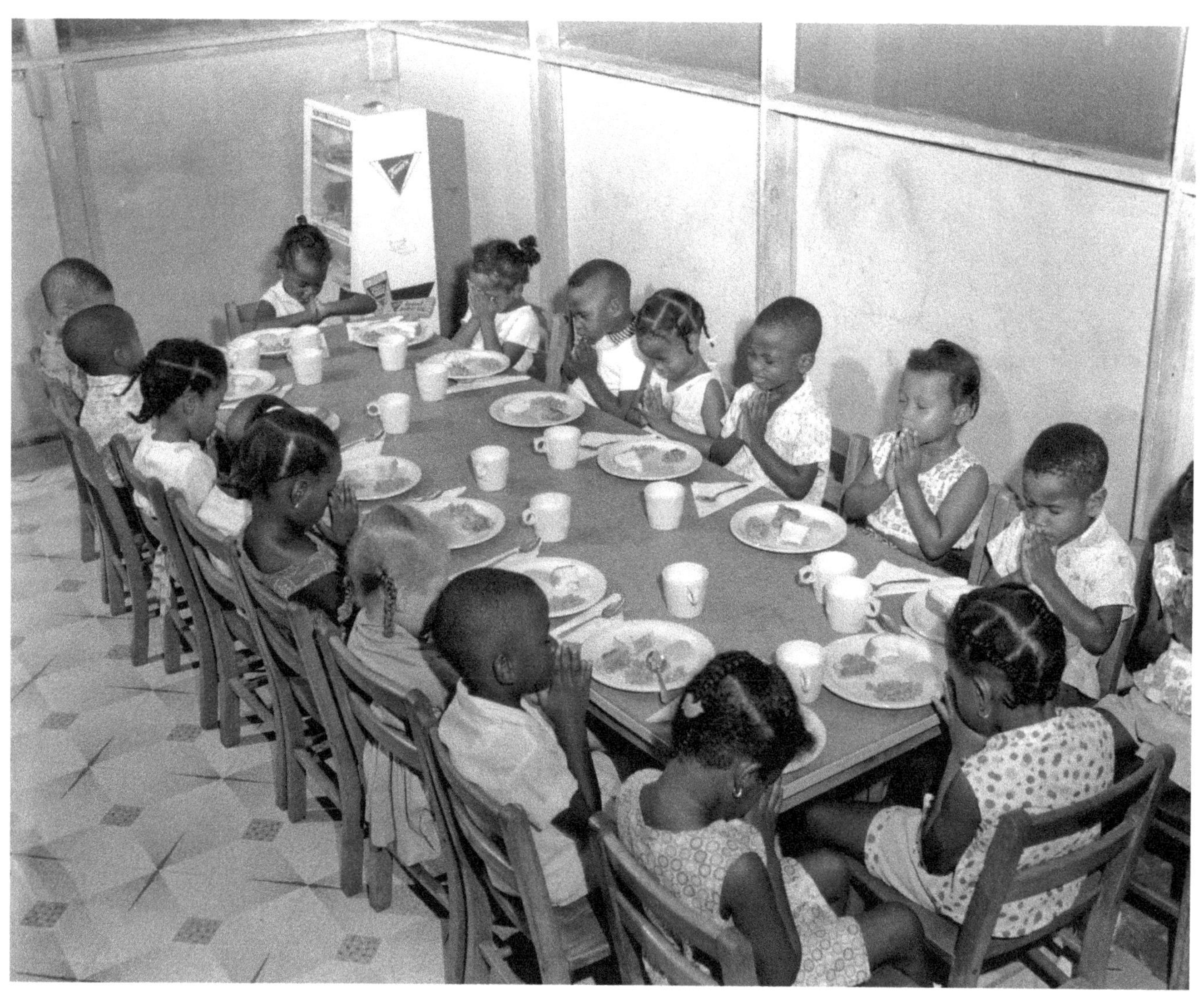

Pictured here, on September 18, 1963, children pause for mealtime at the Helping Hand Day Nursery and Kindergarten. Helping Hand was established by a Mrs. Von Charlton in 1924 and now has locations in Ybor City, Temple Terrace, and two near the University of South Florida.

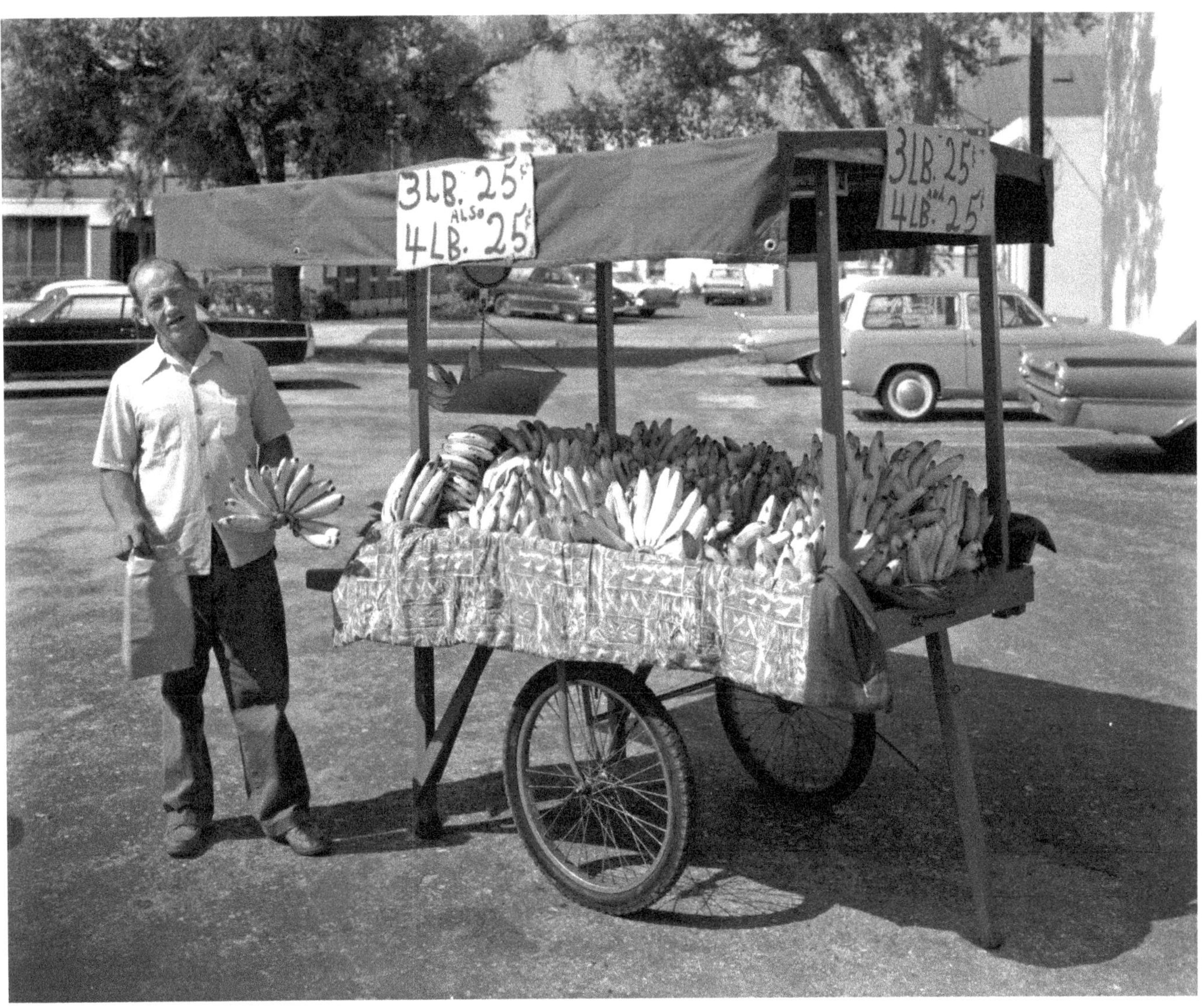

On October 23, 1963, this man was selling bananas from his cart on a street in Tampa. It's quite likely that they were imported from far away because, although banana plants are used in Florida landscaping, nearly all grown in the United States for human consumption come from Hawaii, with a little in California and the bulk of the world's production from countries further south.

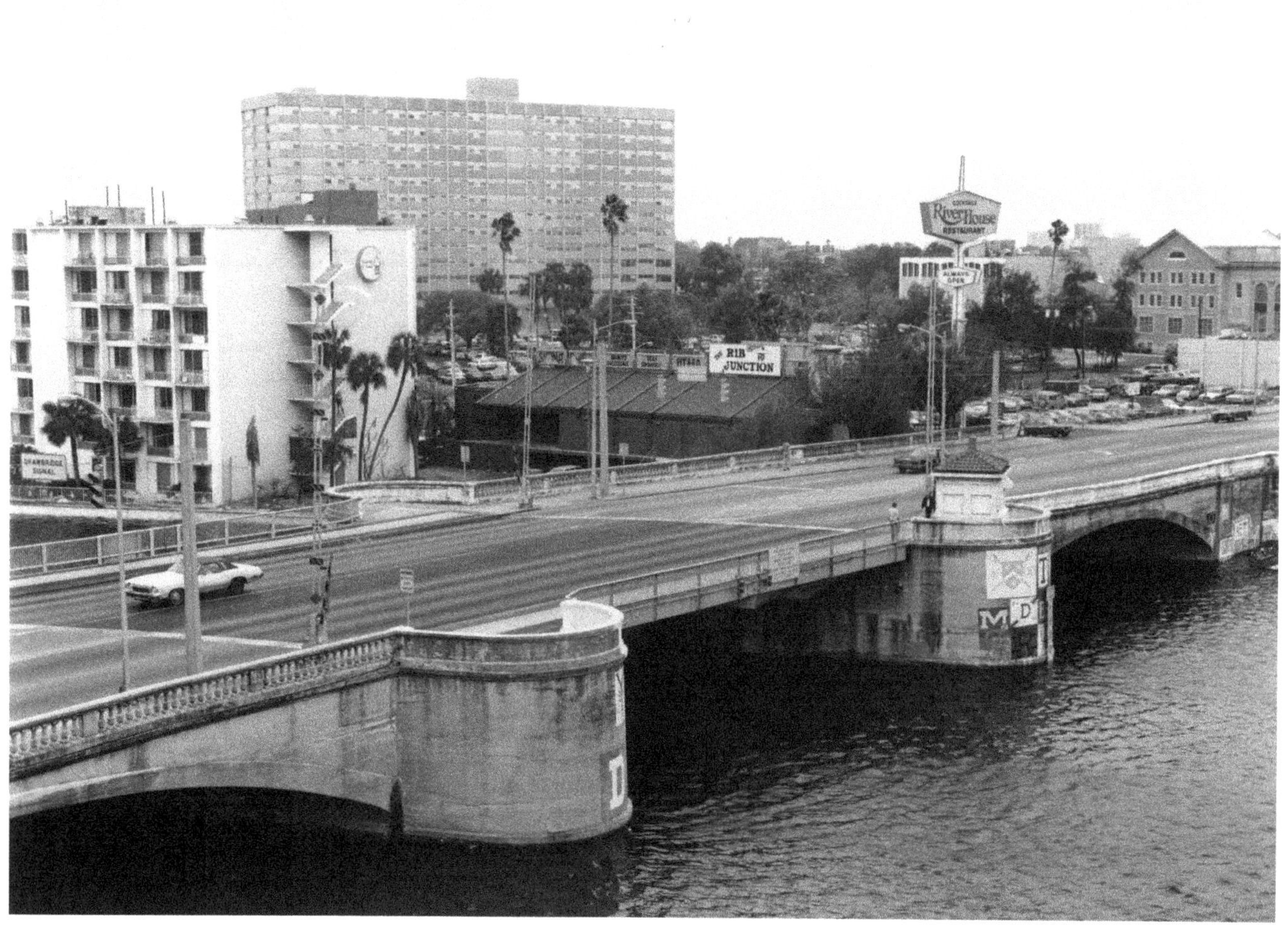

This bridge crossing the Hillsborough River, and its predecessor spans, were originally known as the Lafayette Street Bridge, named for the French general who fought for the colonists during the Revolutionary War. It and the road which it carries were renamed Kennedy Boulevard for President John F. Kennedy.

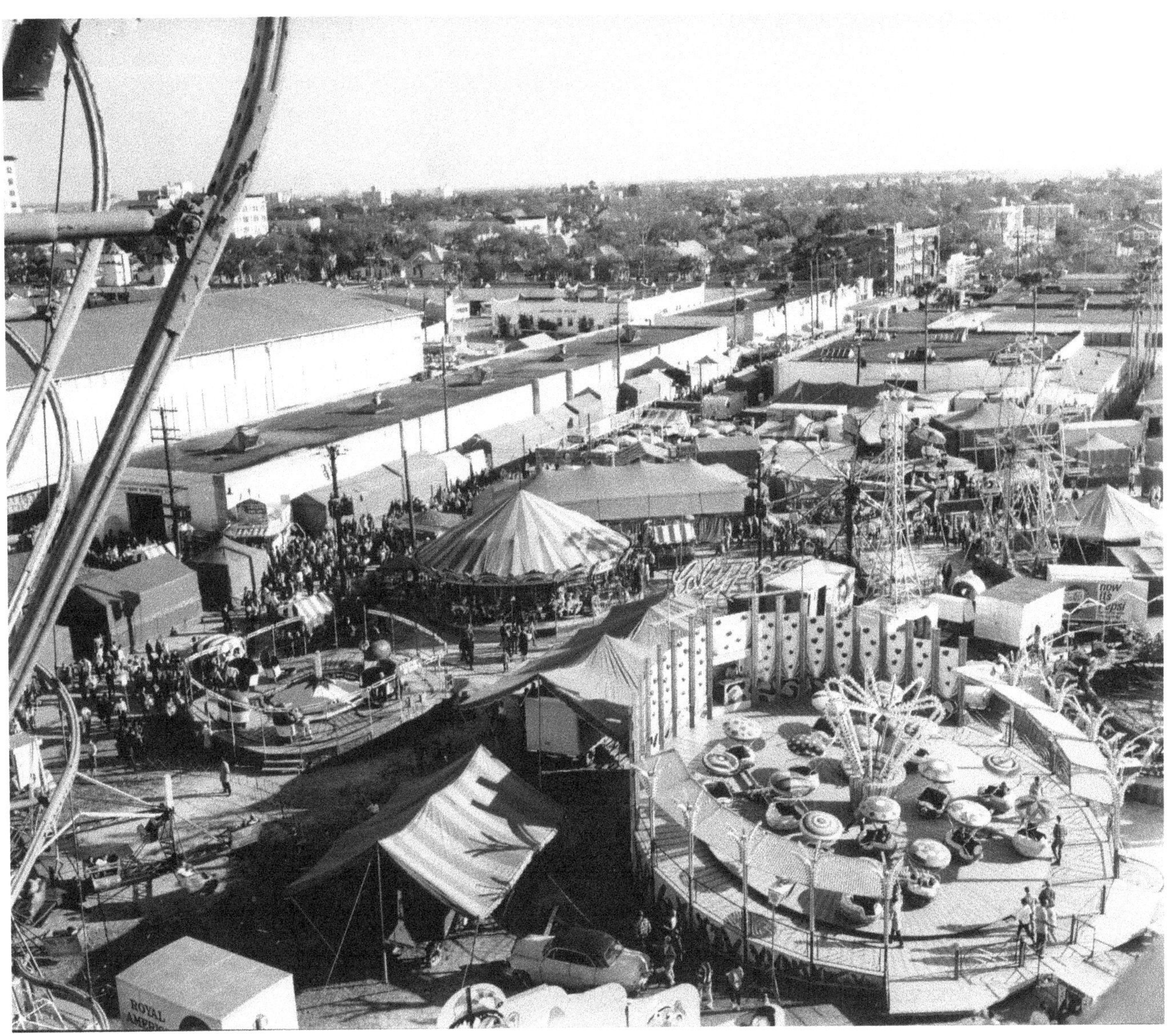

A major draw of each annual Florida State Fair was the collection of rides—the same ones which could be found at most traveling carnivals. Where the fairground was located in 1964 when this picture was taken, there was very little room between the rides, games of luck and skill, and food vendors because of the lack of land. Since the late 1970s, the rides and other features of the fair have been able to spread out at a much larger venue and better accommodate large crowds.

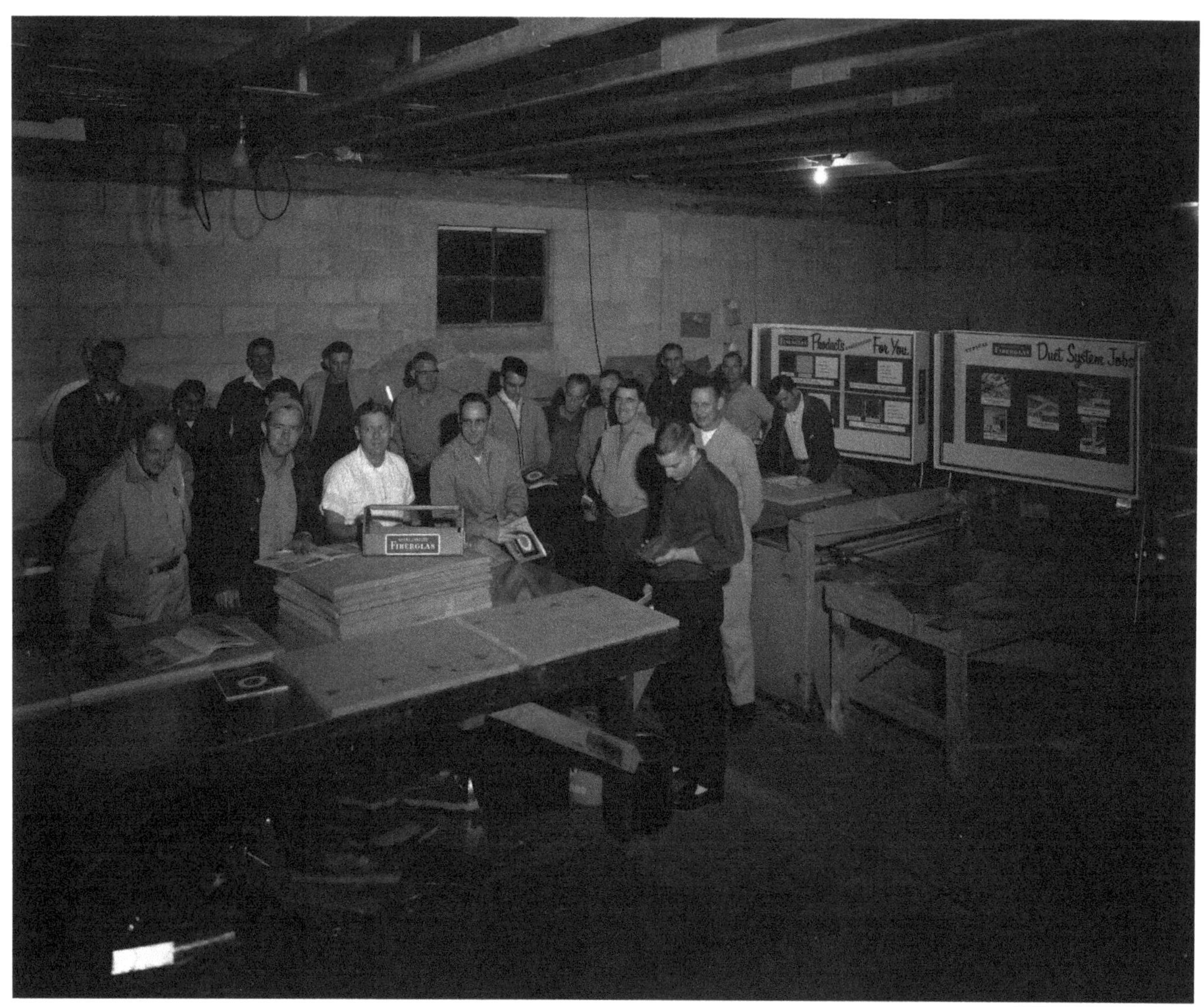

This was the scene in the dark, concrete block building located at 4713 North Clark Avenue near the Tampa International Airport. When this photo was taken in February 1964, these were the employees of JW Metals, Inc., which was incorporated from 1963 until 1974. Today, the building, constructed in 1958, is the home of the Rigo Cabinet Shop.

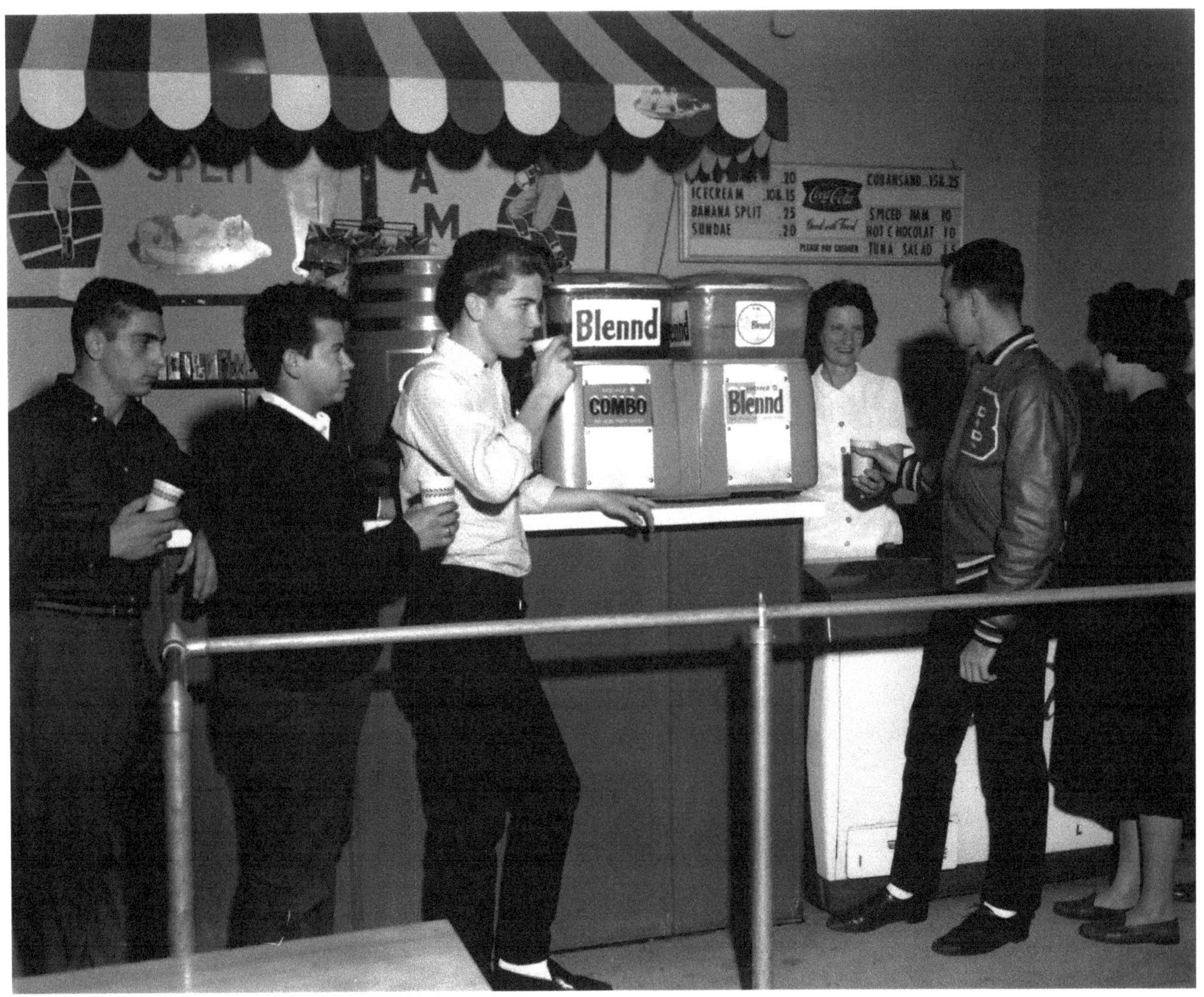

Pictured here, on February 12, 1964, is the scene at the snack bar at Brewster Vocational School. In addition to classes to prepare students for jobs in various trades, during World War II the curriculum included subjects designed to help the war effort, such as aircraft upholstery. Now known as the Henry W. Brewster Technical Center, it is located at 2222 North Tampa Street in Tampa Heights. It is named for a man whose widow donated the land on which the school was built in 1925.

On the left in this 1965 photo is Mayor Nick C. Nuccio, hand-trucking a load to the new Celotex headquarters at the corner of Florida Avenue and Washington Street. With him is Celotex Vice President Marvin Greenwood. In 1929, Nuccio entered the Tampa government and became the first Latin (specifically Italian) individual to take some of the power from the predominantly Anglo establishment. After a year as a city alderman and two decades as a county commissioner, he became the mayor in 1956 and served until 1959, then again from 1963 until 1967.

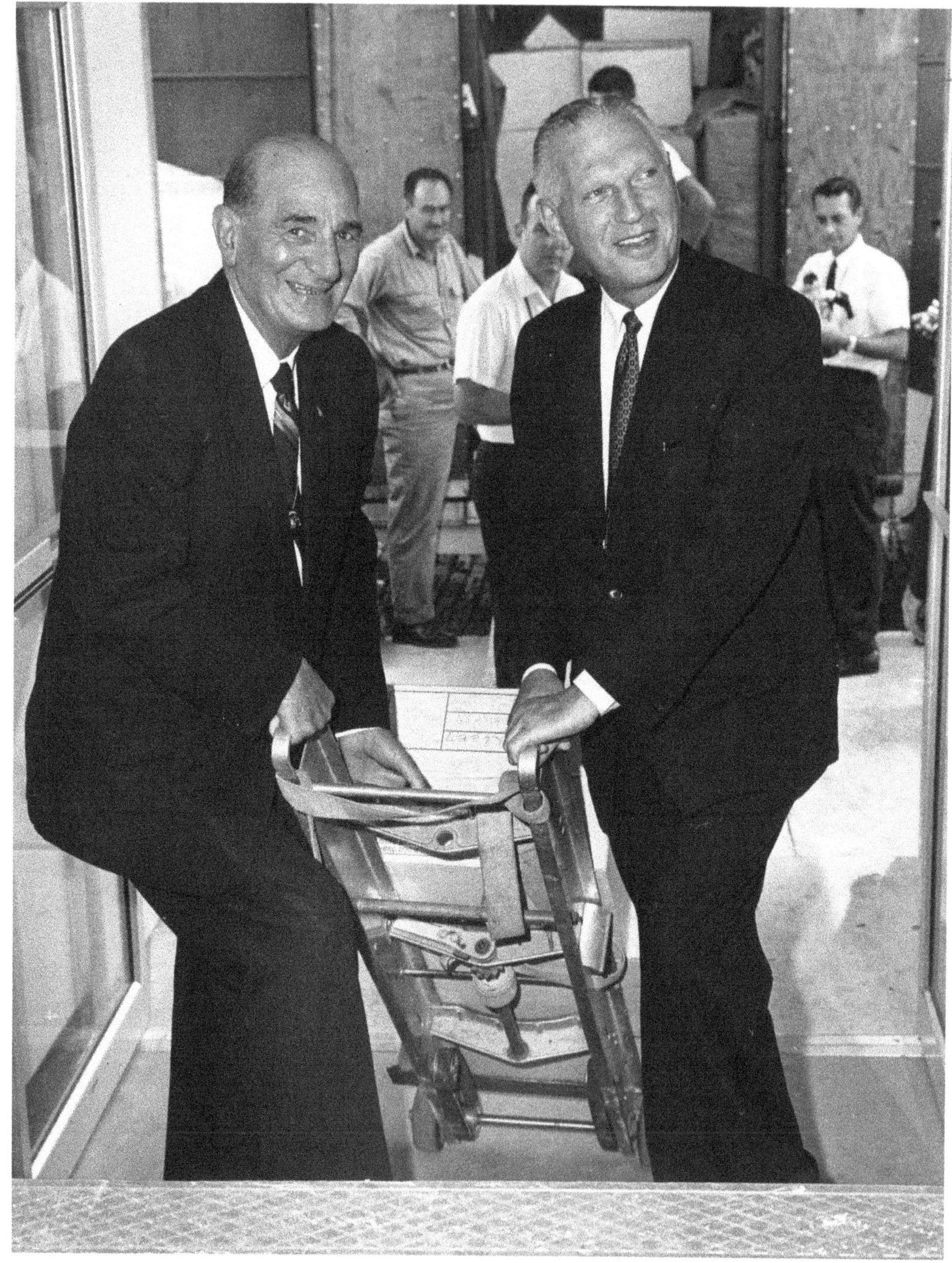

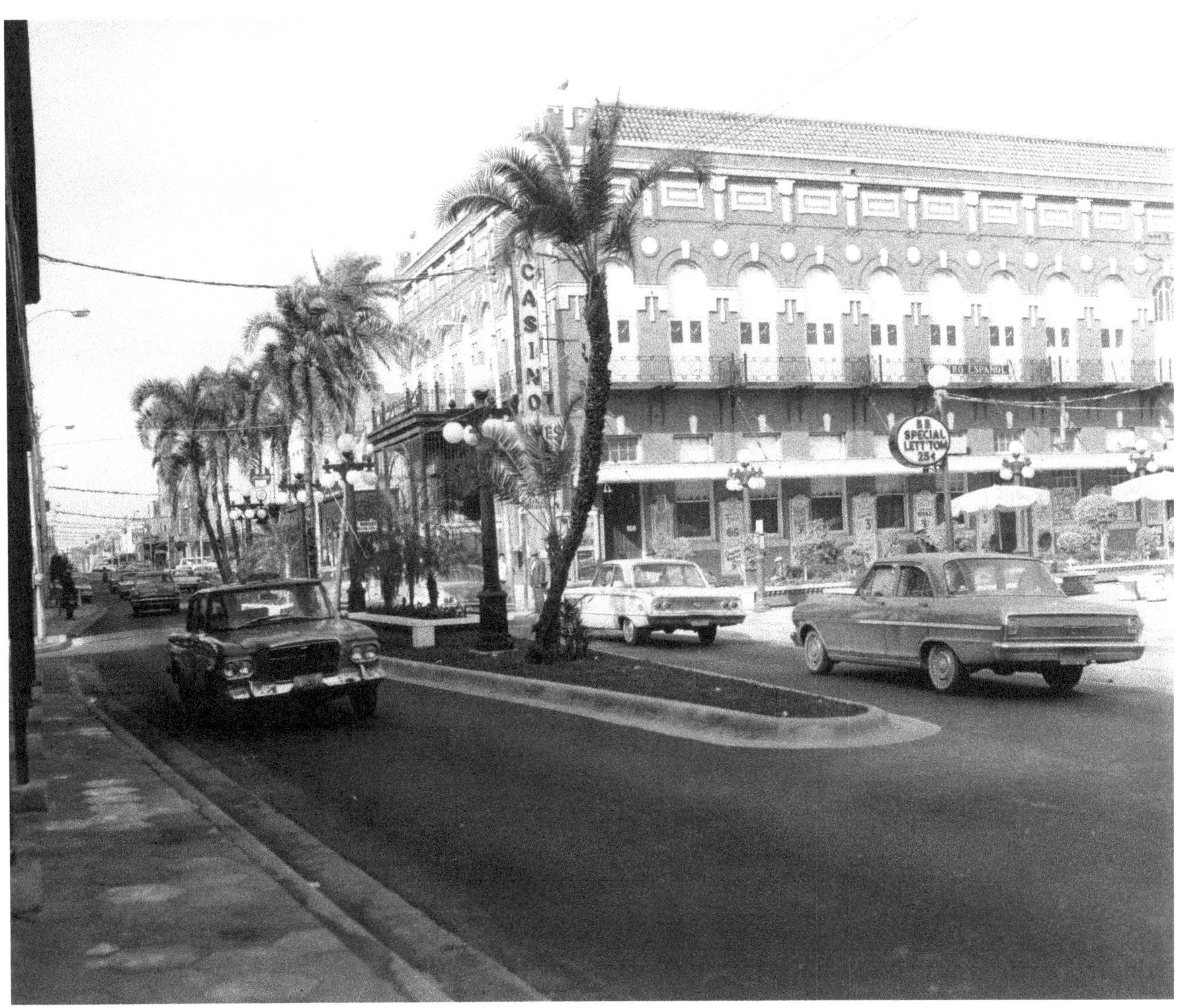

Centro Español, a club headquartered in Ybor City for those of Spanish descent, was chartered in 1891. Unlike some of the other ethnic societies in Tampa, its members did not have to be born in the country of their ancestors—only the president and vice president had to be born in Spain. After its first wooden clubhouse burned down, this one, pictured here in 1965, was dedicated in 1912. Centro Español offered the country's first socialized medical care plan and operated its own hospital from 1906 until the mid-1960s.

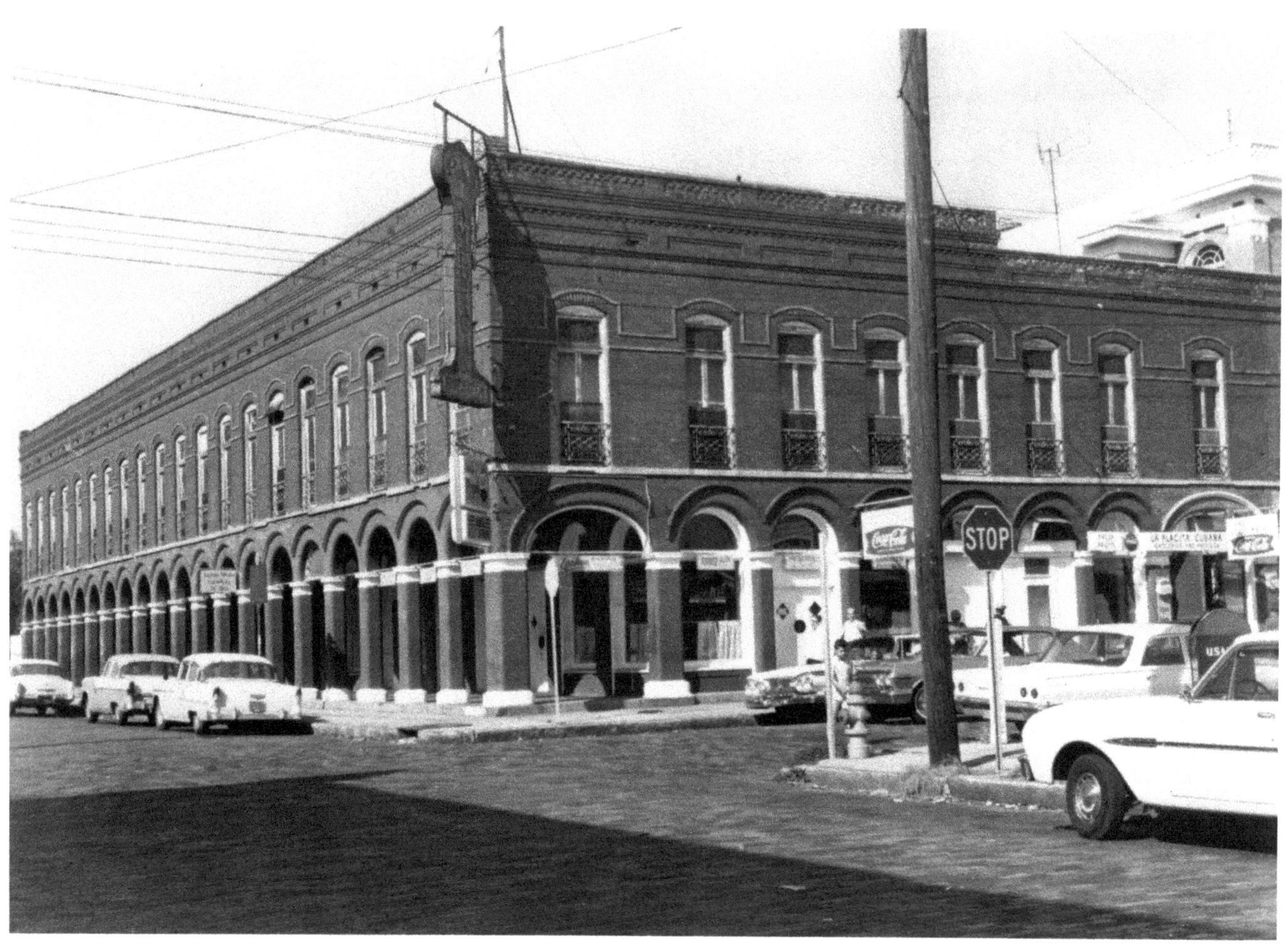

The Cherokee Club was founded in 1895 in this, the second brick building erected in Ybor City (in 1886–88) at the northwest corner of 9th Avenue and 14th Street. On his first visit to Tampa on November 25, 1891, Cuban patriot Jose Marti slept here. While American soldiers were encamped in the Tampa area in 1898 awaiting orders to go to Cuba and fight in the Spanish-American War, the club hosted some of the officers including Gen. Leonard Wood and Col. Theodore Roosevelt. This is how it appeared in 1965.

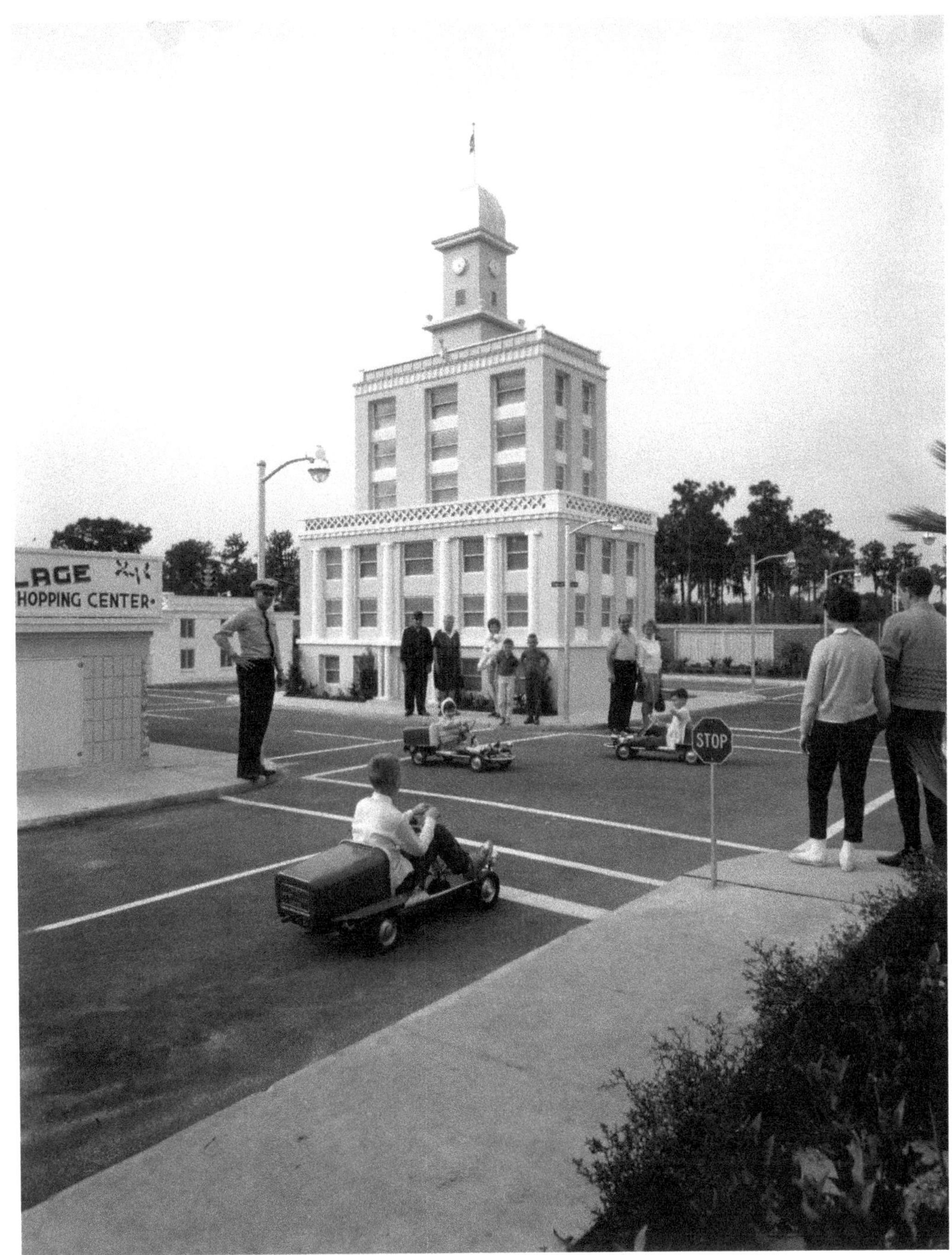

Children ride coaster cars past a small-scale replica of the Tampa City Hall at Safety Village in 1966. It was established during that decade to teach children the rules of the road and how to be safer pedestrians, by giving them a chance to experience situations as "drivers." Later, with the name of Kid City, it also helped to teach them about the various careers represented by the small-scale buildings. The facility continued to be a teaching tool through the end of the century, and then closed.

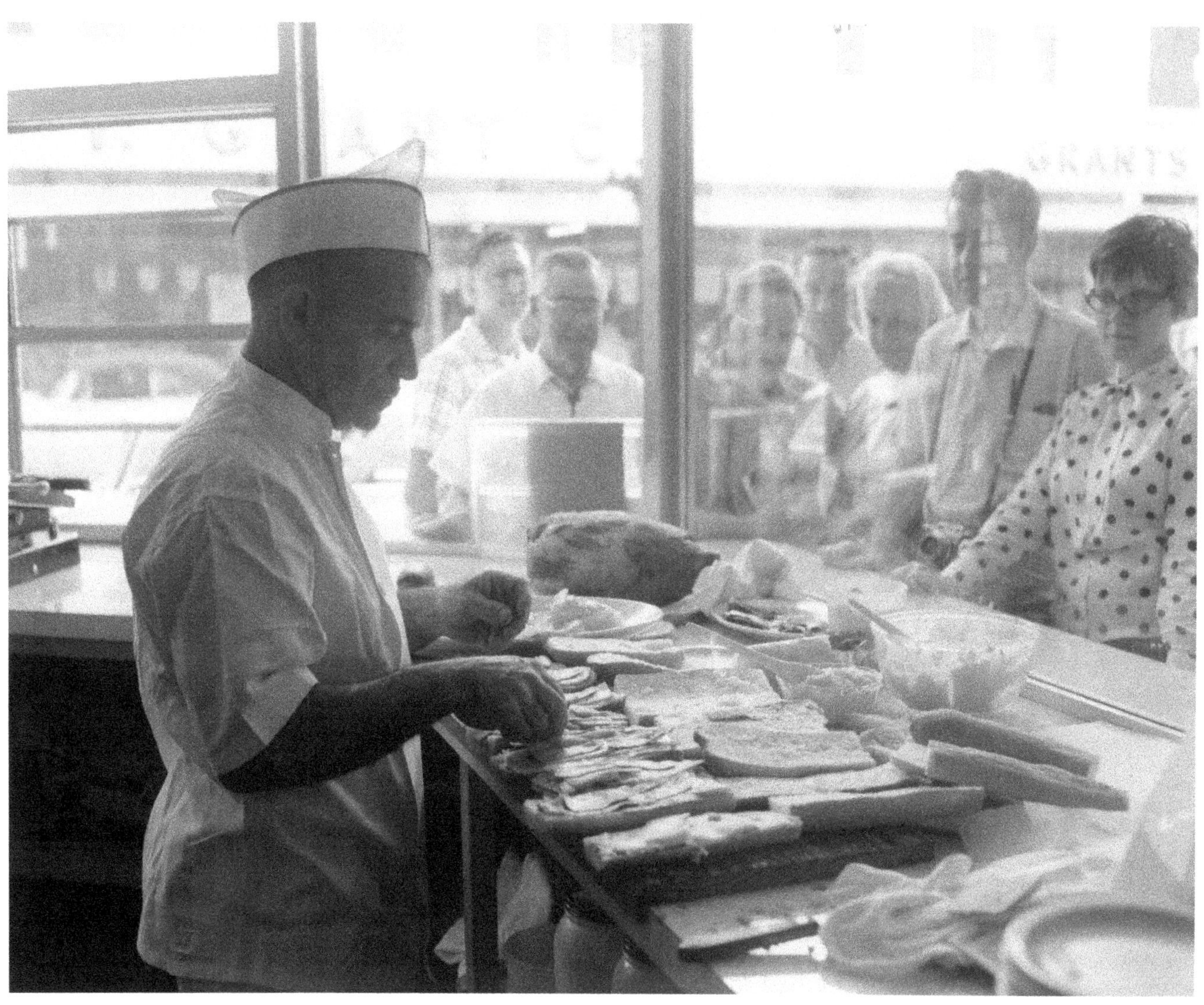

This photo of a man in 1966 making Cuban sandwiches in Ybor City was used by the Florida Department of Commerce to promote the area as a destination for families and other visitors. What is not shown in this view is the deterioration and debris that was evident along its streets. A few years after this, the area did finally live up to what had been promoted.

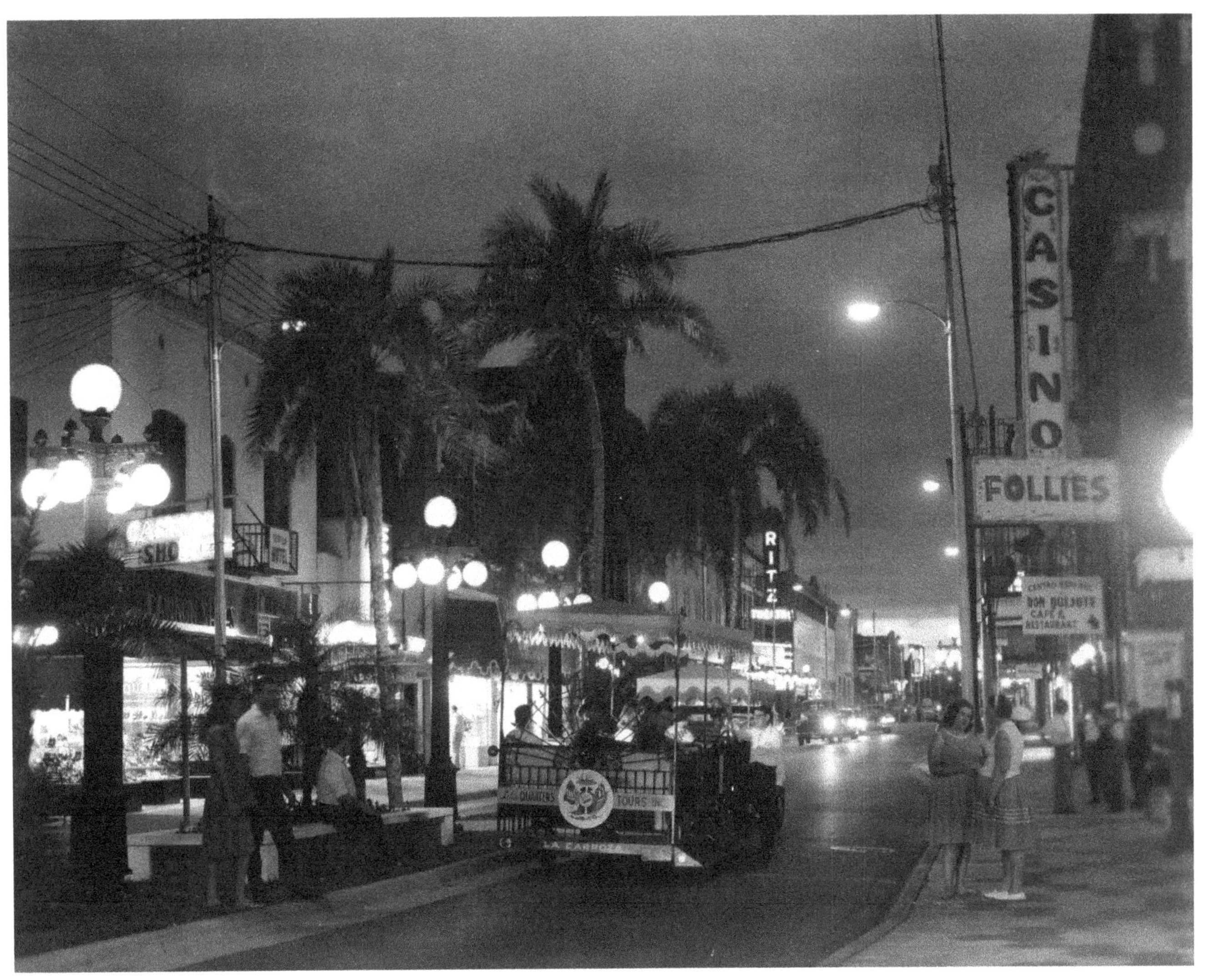

This February 1966 picture of nighttime in Ybor City was used by the Florida Department of Commerce to attract tourists to the area. In reality, it was not yet the clean, safe place that is depicted here and that would normally attract visitors, but it is today.

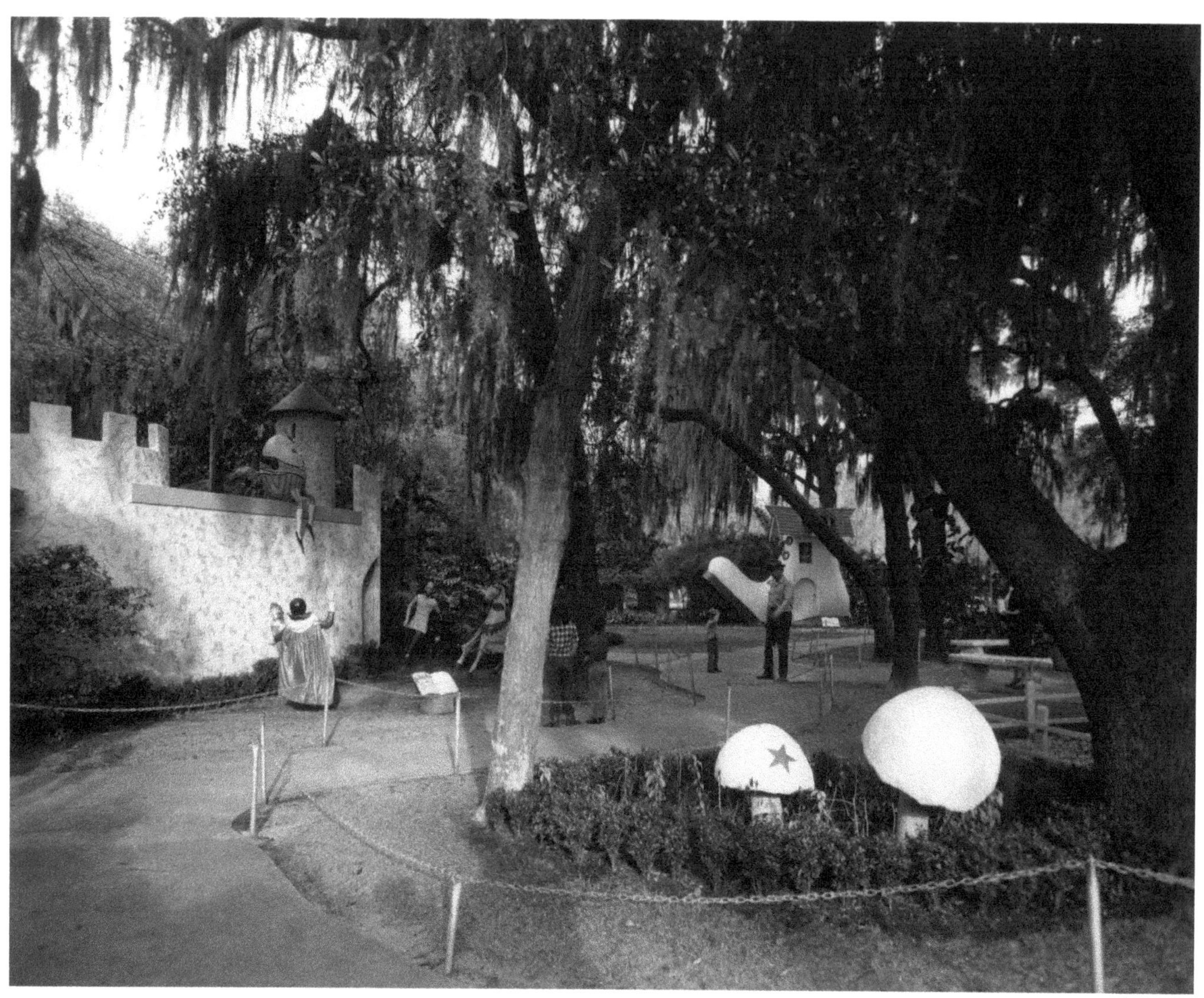

Adjacent to the Lowry Park Zoo was a miniature fantasy village known as Fairyland. It included Rapunzel's Castle Tower and the Rainbow Bridge, as well as structures reminiscent of nursery rhymes. Because of safety concerns, Fairyland was later removed and today the site is occupied by the Florida Environmental Education Center.

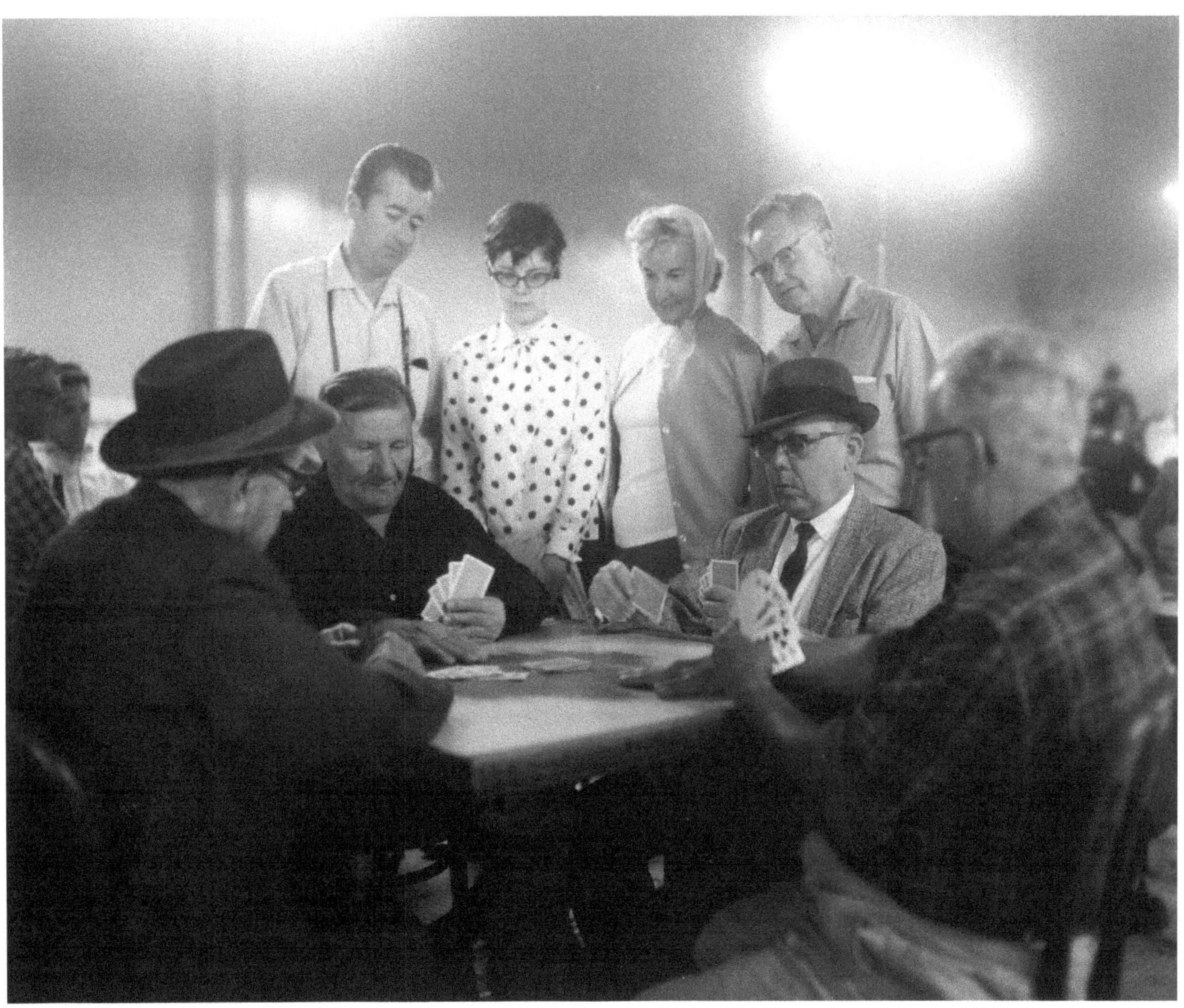

Most immigrants who moved to Tampa beginning in the mid-1880s to manufacture cigars joined one of several mutual aid societies. Each ethnic group started its own, and helped its members adapt to their new surroundings. More than just social clubs, the organizations had connections with hospitals, pharmacies, and doctors, so that medical care was made available to club members. The social activities included dances, dominoes, and cards, as shown here.

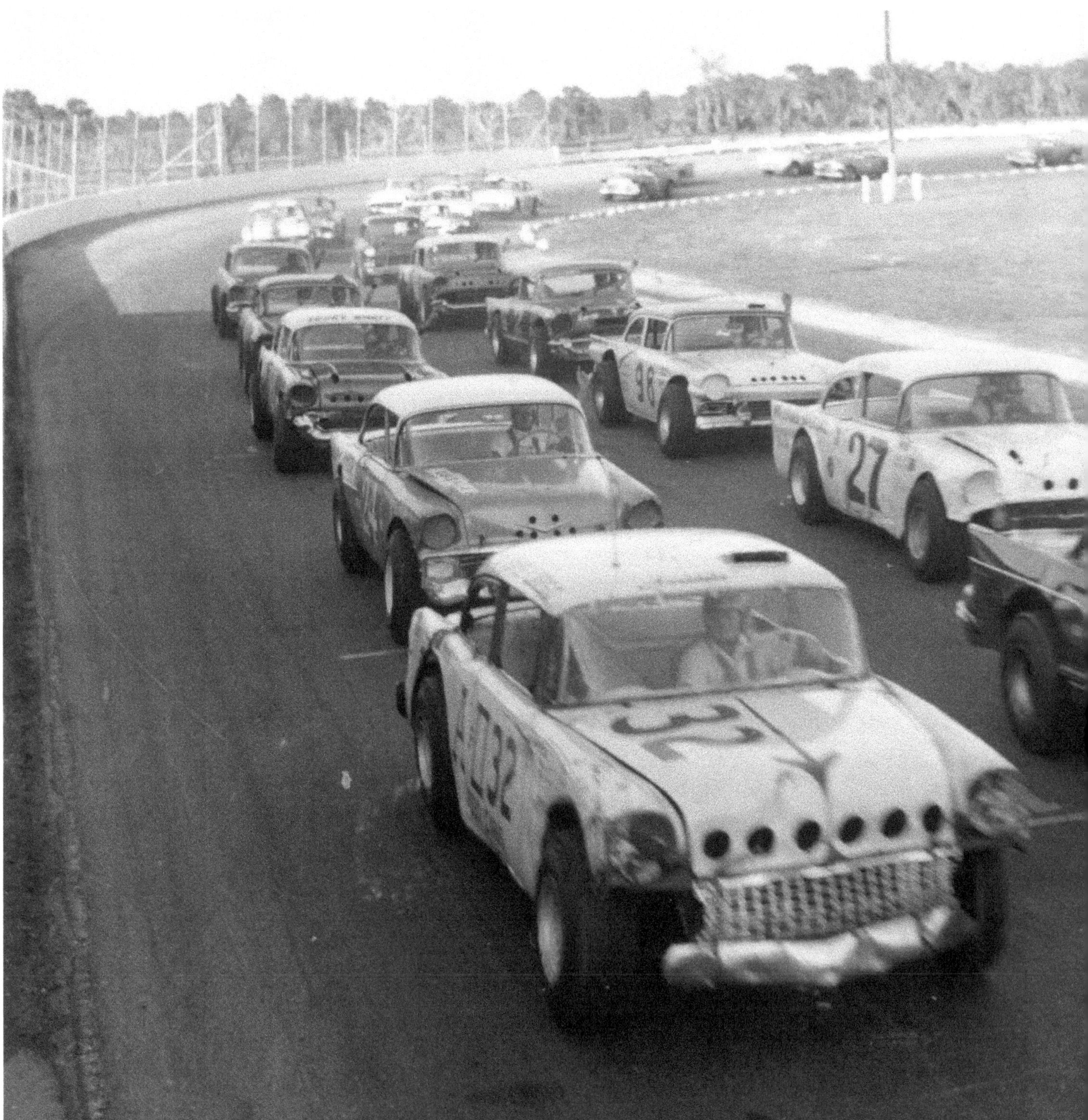
32
27

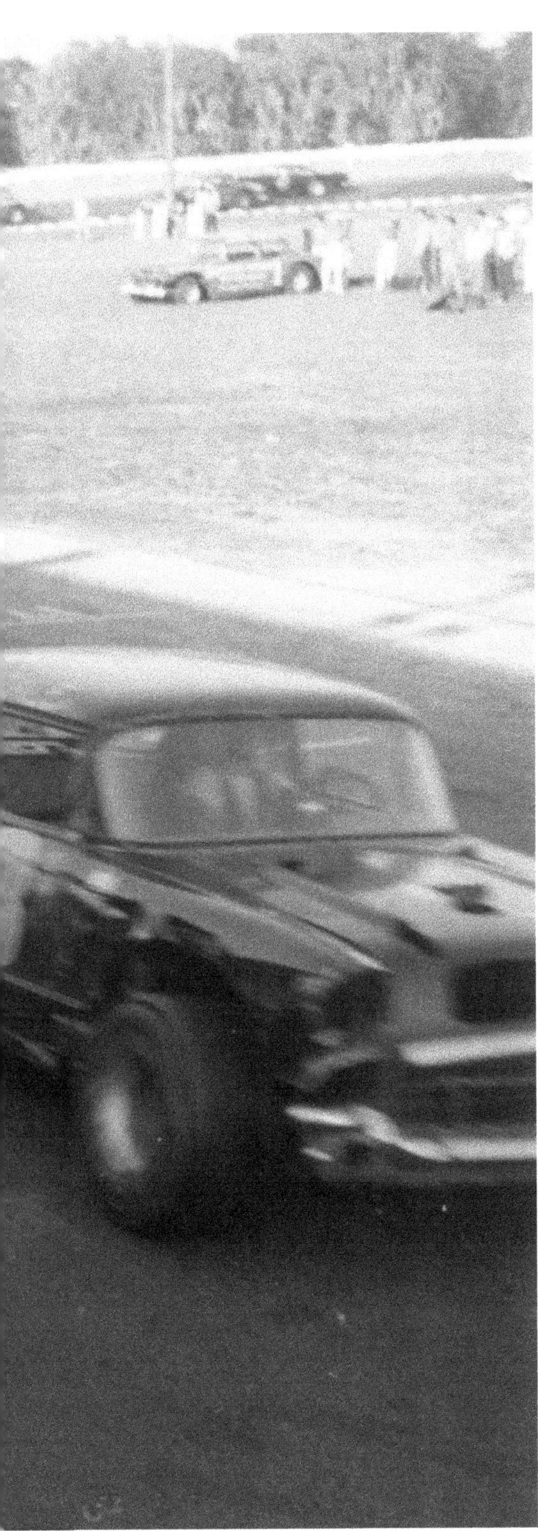

Modified stock cars are shown on the track of Golden Gate Speedway in May 1966. The track, which opened in 1962, was located on East Fowler Avenue, and a sign on a tall golden arch greeted arriving spectators. Noise complaints from residents of a trailer park across the street resulted in the closing of the racetrack. Later, the racetrack's land became the site of the Big Top Flea Market.

Perhaps the most popular activity of the annual Gasparilla Festival, following the parade through the streets of Tampa, is the boat parade. The *Jose Gaspar* pirate ship, accompanied by numerous craft of various sizes, sails up the Hillsborough River to attack and capture the city. Shown here in 1967 are Tampa businessmen turned pirates about to launch their attack.

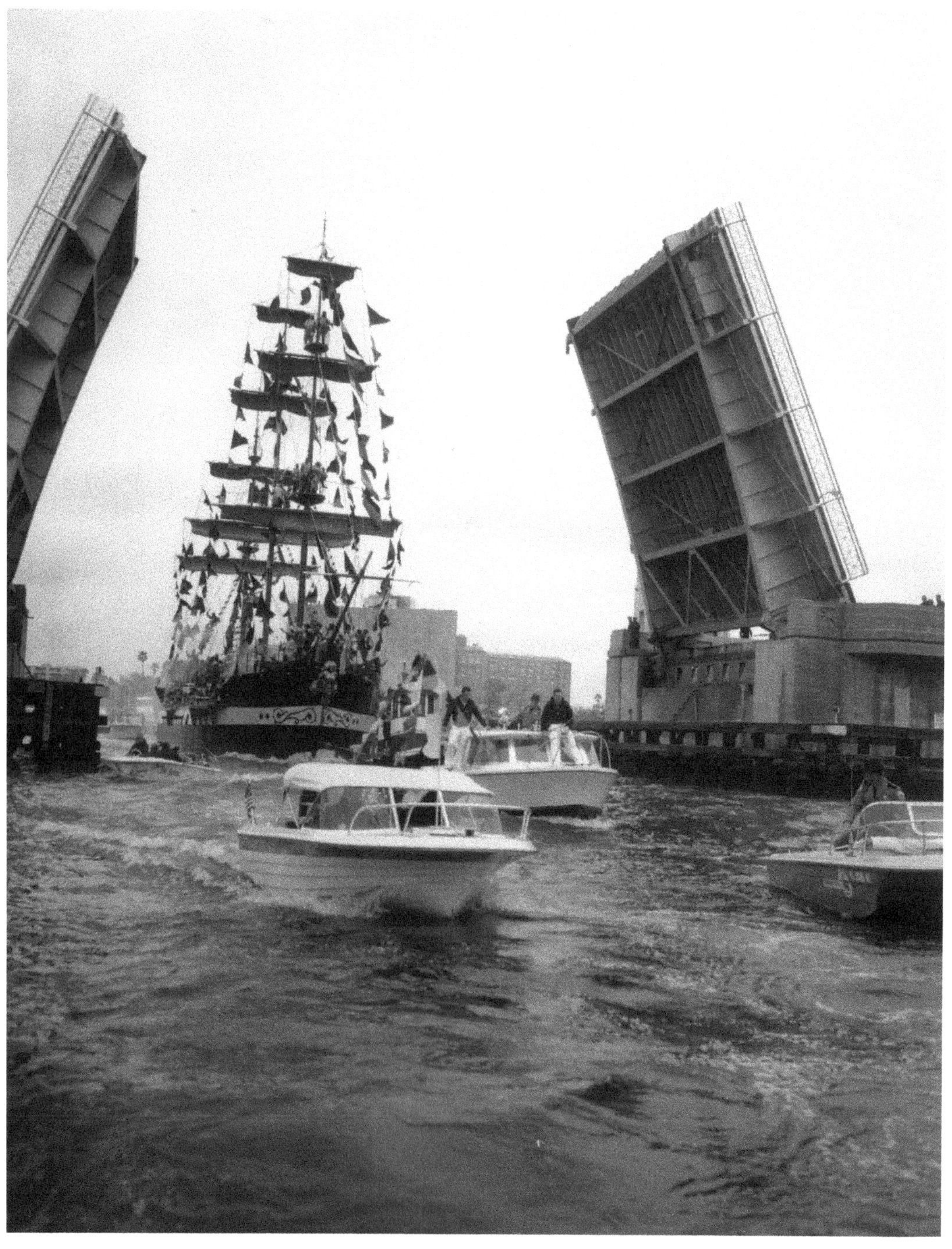

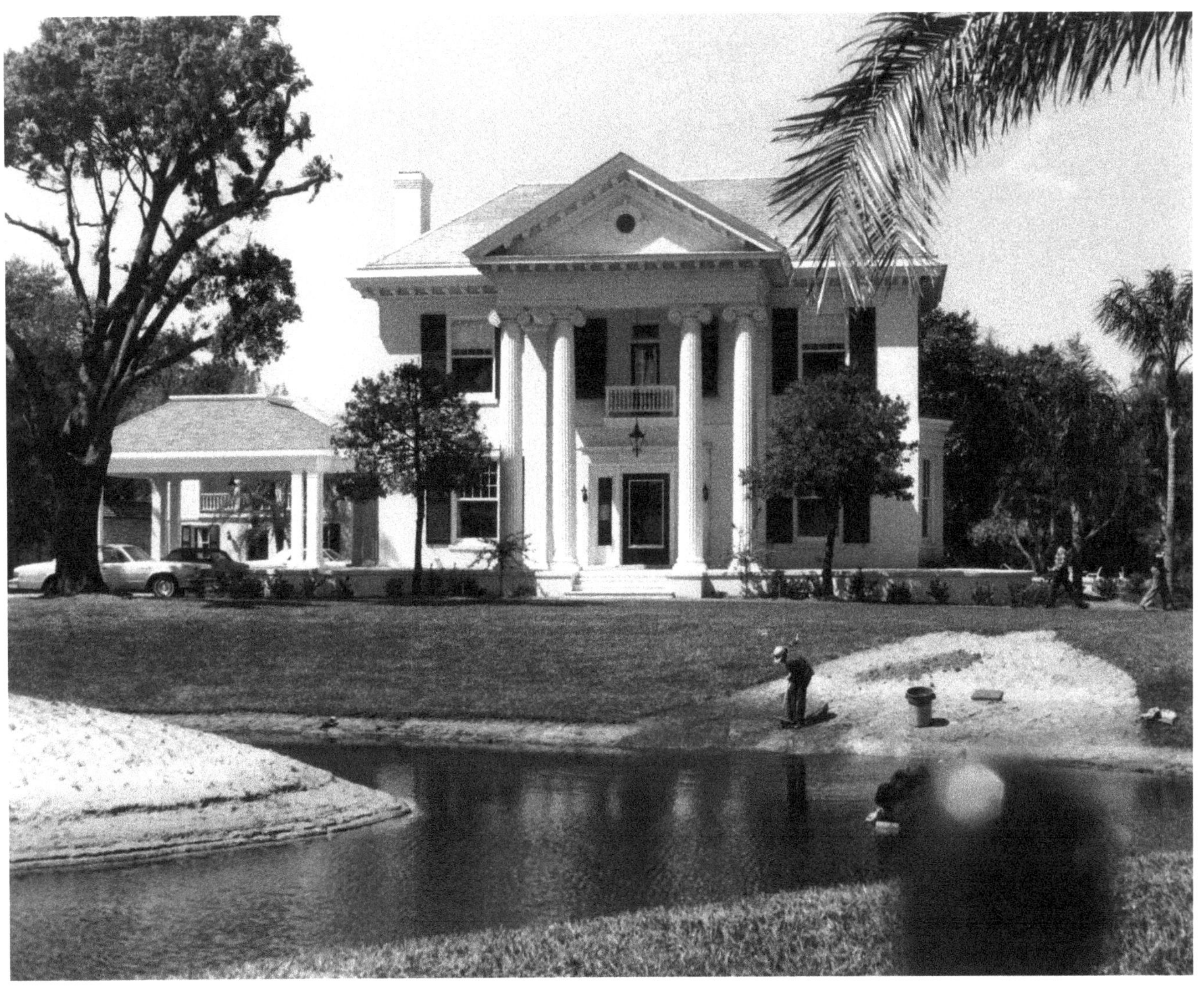

This was the home of Wallace Stovall, publisher of the *Tampa Tribune* newspaper beginning in 1893. Located at 4621 Bayshore Boulevard, it was built in 1909 in a Neoclassical Revival style. It was later the home of L. T. Tousdale, the general manager of the Florida Brewing Company, and was placed on the national Register of Historic Sites in 1974.

On August 19, 1967, library officials visited the new downtown library building while it was still under construction. From left to right on the landing in the foreground are state library consultant Mary Jane Anderson, library board member Mrs. Haven Poe, library director Cecil Beach, and library board member Charles Fendig. Above them, with a jacket over his shoulder, is library board member Bob Connolly.

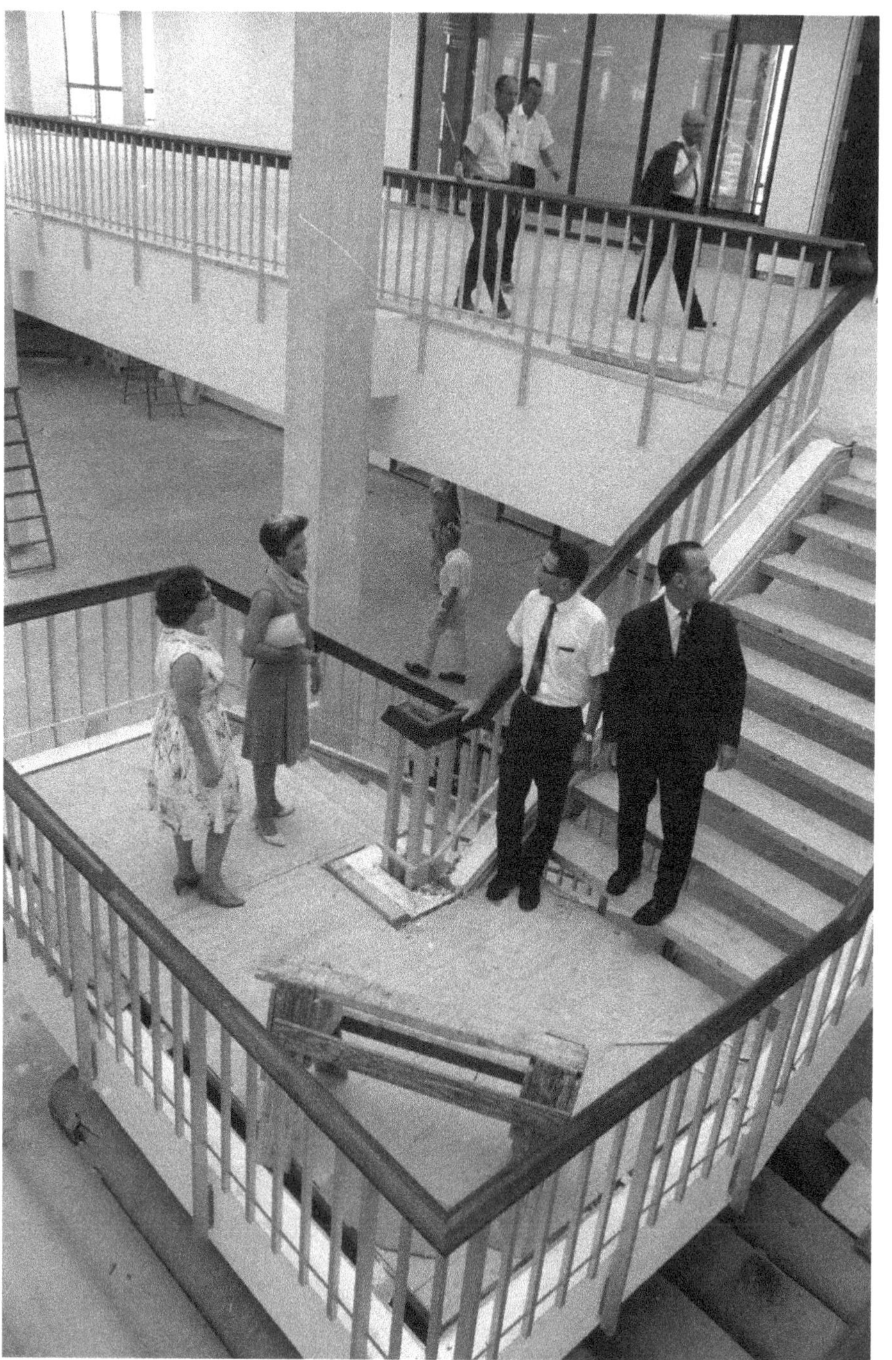

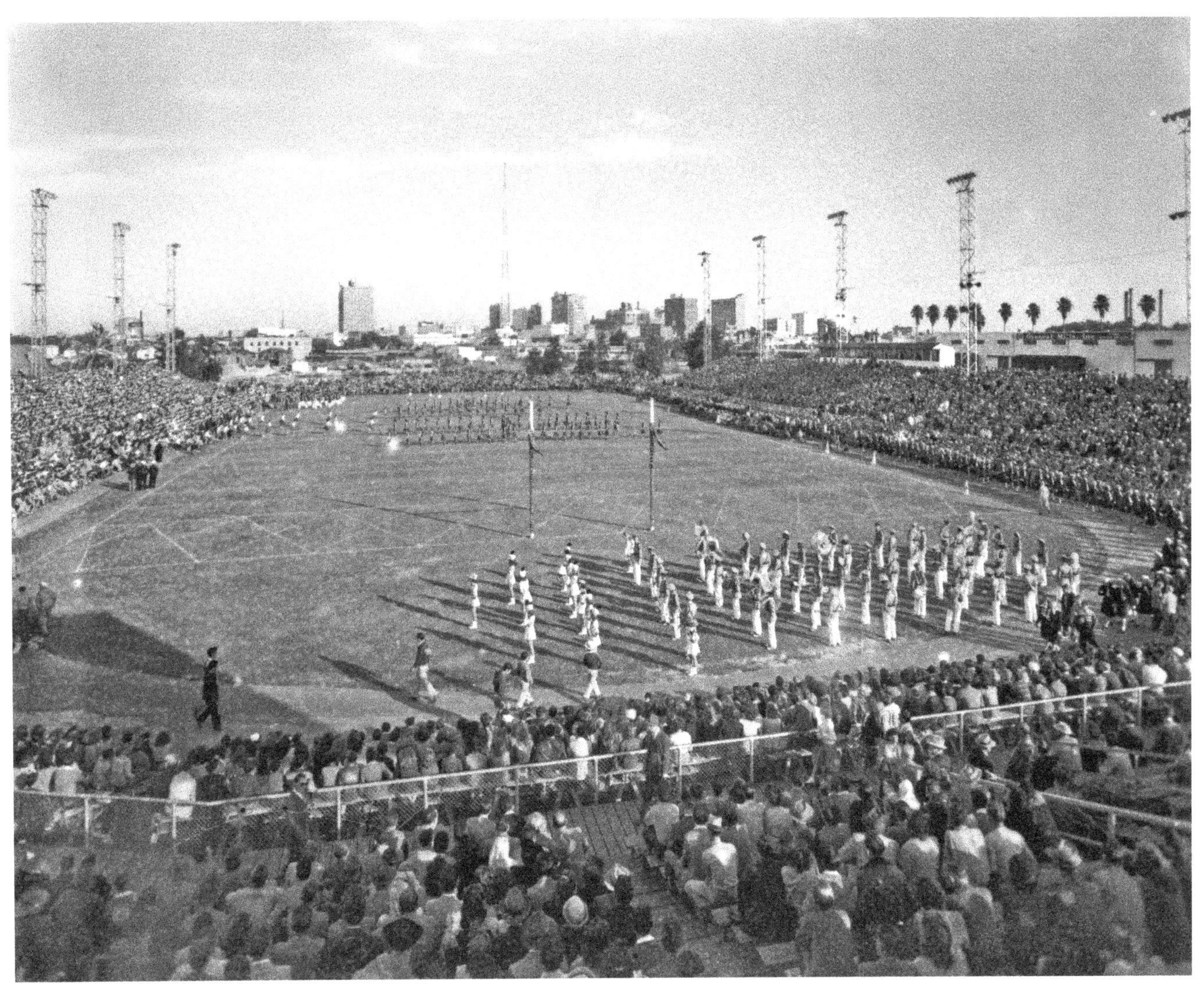

This is halftime of the football game held on November 27, 1967, one of the last at Phillips Field. It was constructed in the late 1930s for the football games of the University of Tampa Spartans, and was eliminated when Tampa Stadium was built. The schools involved in this game are Henry B. Plant High School and Hillsborough High School.

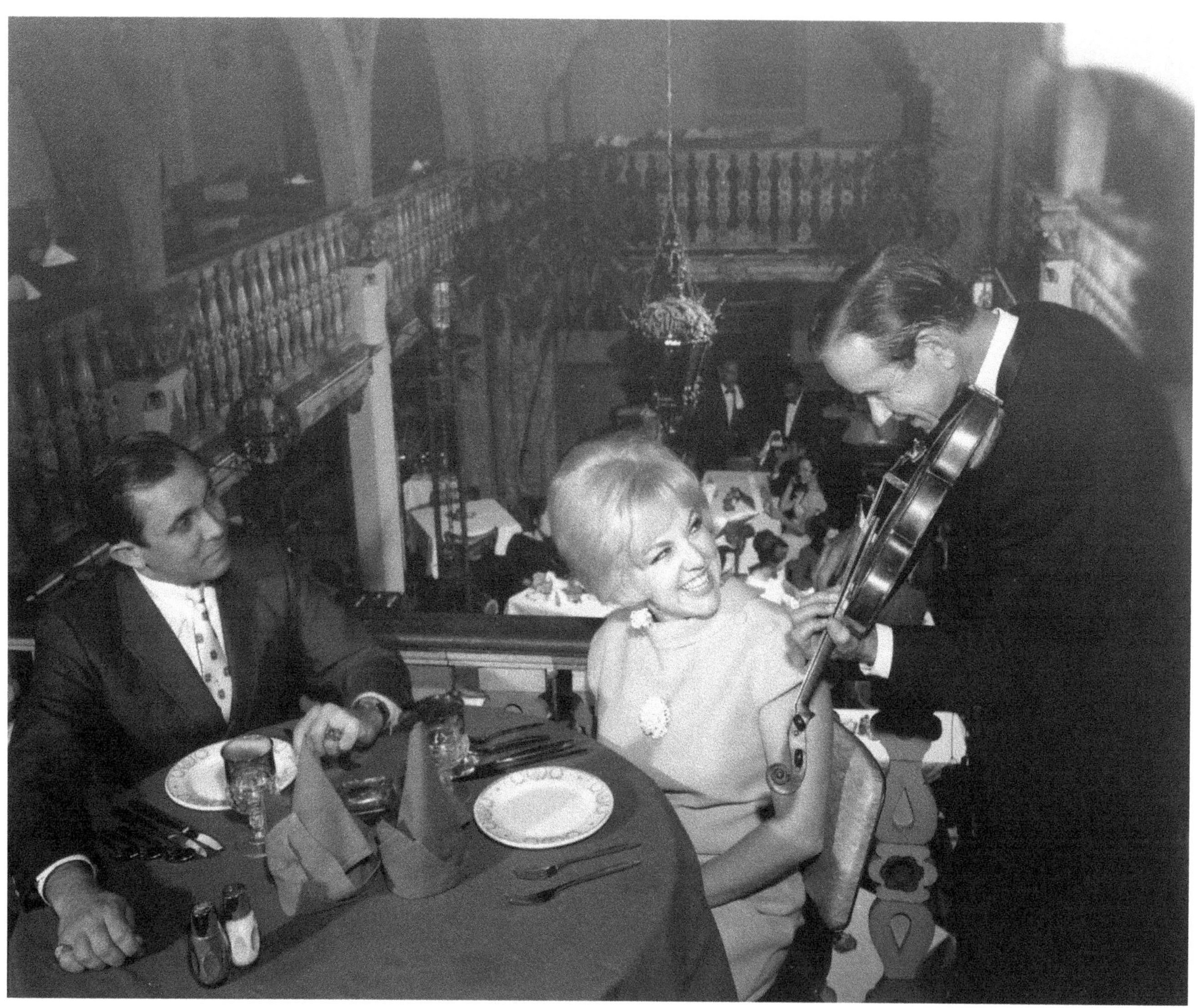

The Columbia Restaurant, with its Spanish and Moorish architecture, has 11 dining rooms. The first air-conditioned dining room in Tampa was the Don Quixote Room, which opened at the Columbia in 1935. Pictured here is some of the entertainment provided in 1968.

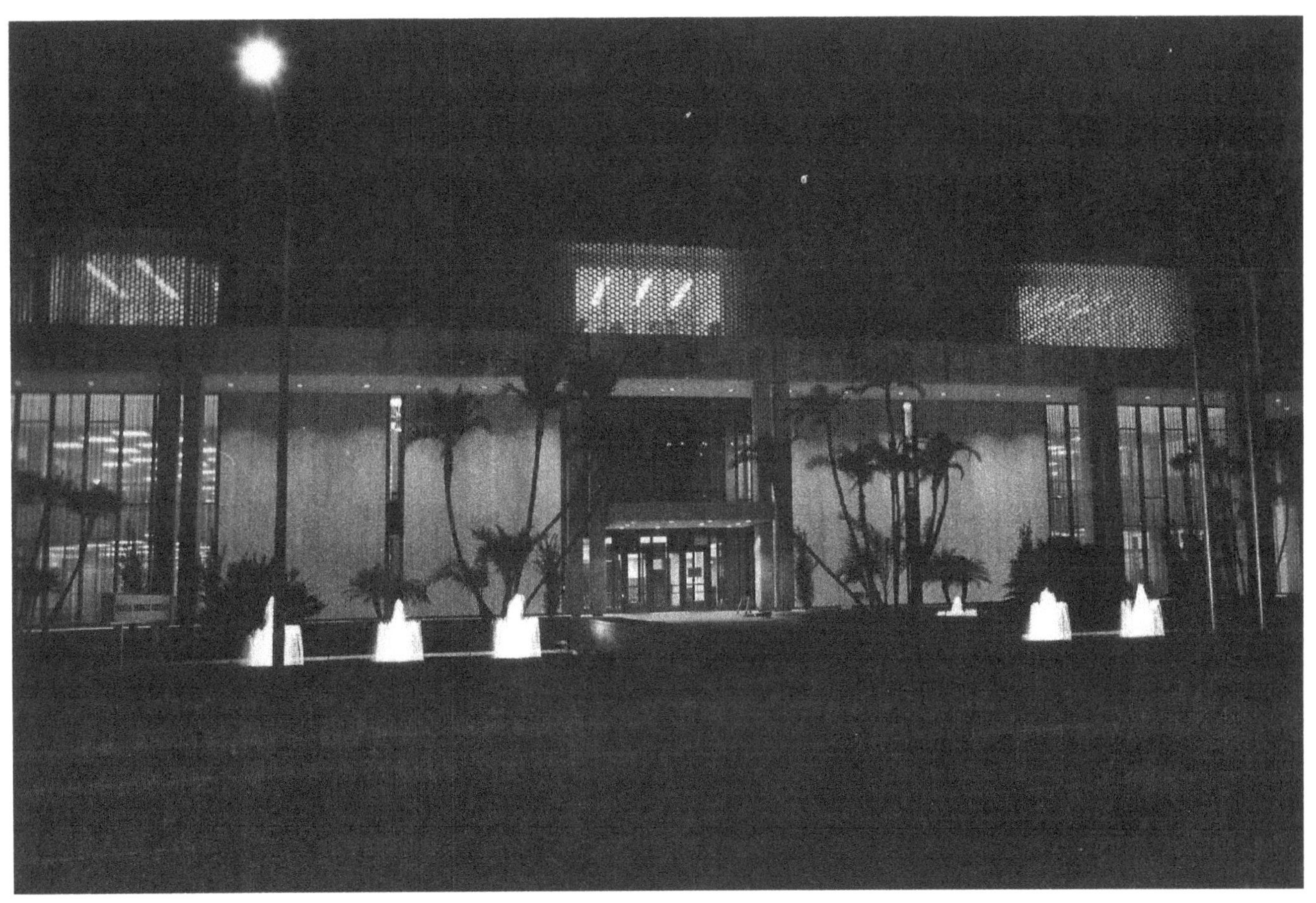

On March 26, 1968, the Tampa Public Library was photographed at night. Located at 900 North Ashley Drive, it still serves the library needs of the downtown area. In 1999, it was renamed as the John F. Germany Public Library to honor the local judge who, beginning in 1961, headed the Friends of the Library and the effort to fund and build the library.

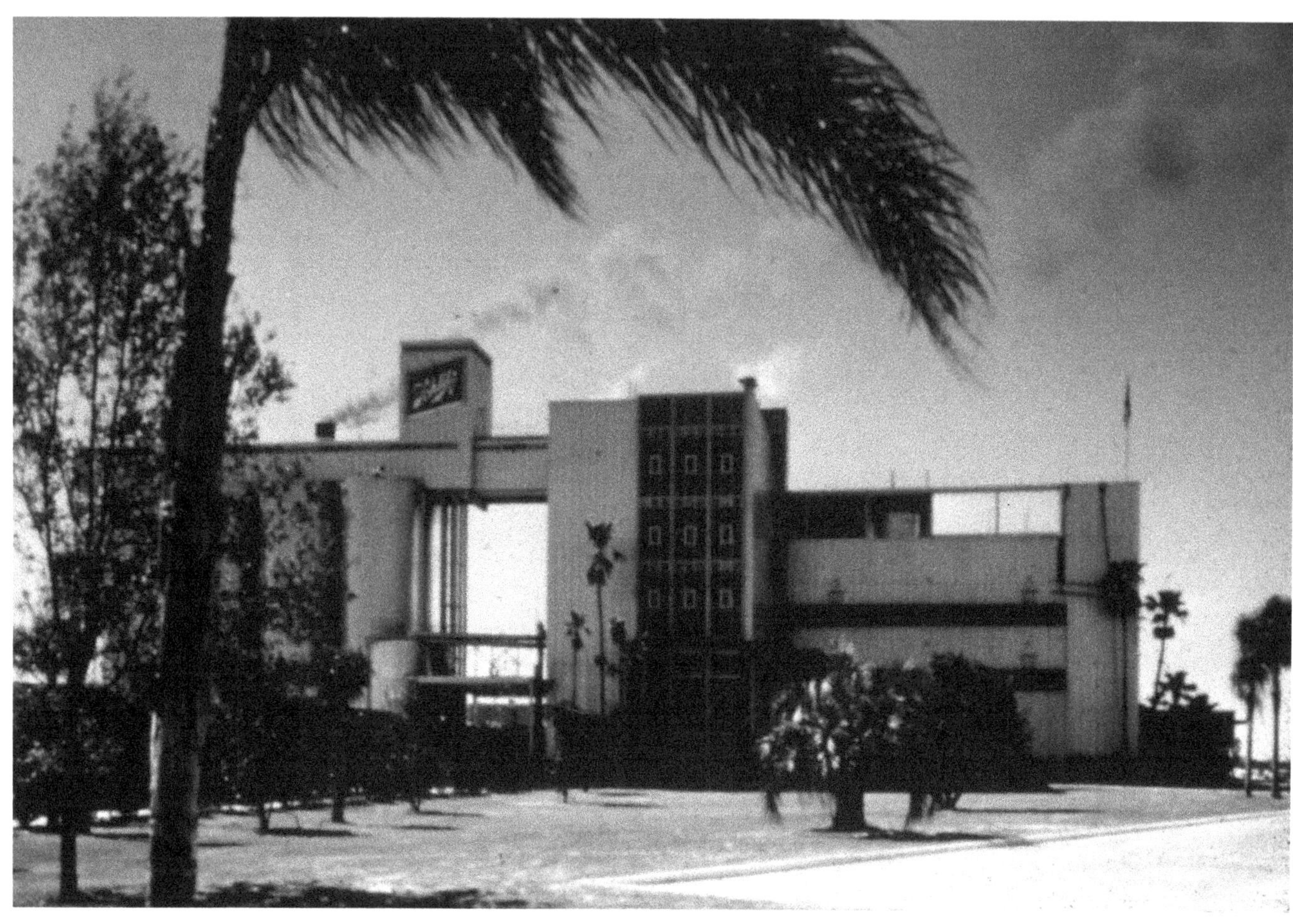

Hillsborough Army Airfield, later known as Henderson Field, served as an auxiliary airfield for Drew and MacDill fields during World War II. It had three 5,200-foot paved runways and served as a physical fitness center. Henderson closed in 1945 and served as a civilian airport until the early 1950s. It was then turned into Tampa Industrial Park, which included two breweries, Anheuser-Busch and Schlitz, the second of which is shown here in 1969. In April 2000, this building was purchased by Yuengling Brewery of Pennsylvania.

Continued Modernization

(1970–1979)

Tampa was becoming a sports town with the addition of three professional teams. In 1968, the Muskies of the American Basketball Association had moved from Minnesota to Miami and changed their name to the Miami Floridians. Two years later, they dropped the "Miami" from their name and for the last two years of their existence the Floridians played several of their "home" games in Tampa's Curtis Hixton Hall.

The 1970s saw a nationwide attempt to bring soccer to American audiences. The North American Soccer League established franchises in several major cities, and Tampa was the 16th to receive a team. The Rowdies did well, and in their first season won the Soccer Bowl, the league's championship game. Before the league went under in 1984, the Rowdies accumulated five Eastern Division championships.

They also had success in the NASL indoor league, winning two championships there. Despite the demise of the league, the Rowdies continued to play as an independent team and then in two other leagues until the move to make soccer a major U.S. spectator sport diminished in the 1990s.

Football, however, was already hugely popular and Florida wanted a second national Football League team. The Buccaneers began play in 1976 and set a record for futility that still stands. Losing their first 26 games was frustrating, but by 1979 they learned how to win and made it to the playoffs. Even with the early string of losses, loyal Tampa fans filled Tampa Stadium and the Bucs still occasionally draw well today.

Much of Tampa saw a building boom, with tall glass and metal office buildings changing the skyline dramatically. However, other parts of the city were suffering. Ybor City, for example, had developed a reputation as a dangerous area. High crime and dilapidated buildings discouraged visitors and became an embarrassment for the city. This decade saw the continuation of a major push to fix the neighborhood's problems and make it a place were people could safely have fun.

In 1974, the Ybor City Historic District was established to preserve the structures which exemplified the early cigar industry and the various businesses and cultures which existed there. A crackdown on crime and several rebuilding projects resulted in a popular place to shop, have fun in a nightclub, experience history, or enjoy a wonderful meal, all in attractive and safe surroundings.

Downtown Tampa was not as fortunate. In an attempt to revitalize a deteriorating city core, in 1973 a five-block section of the major North Franklin Street was closed to vehicular traffic. The plan was to bring foot traffic which would increase the number of people visiting the shops and restaurants. Instead of bringing them back from the large enclosed malls, the plan actually sent them the other way. After about a decade, many of the buildings in that section of town were abandoned. Many were still boarded up after the passage into the twenty-first century, but urban renewal is still happening in Tampa and should continue for many years to come.

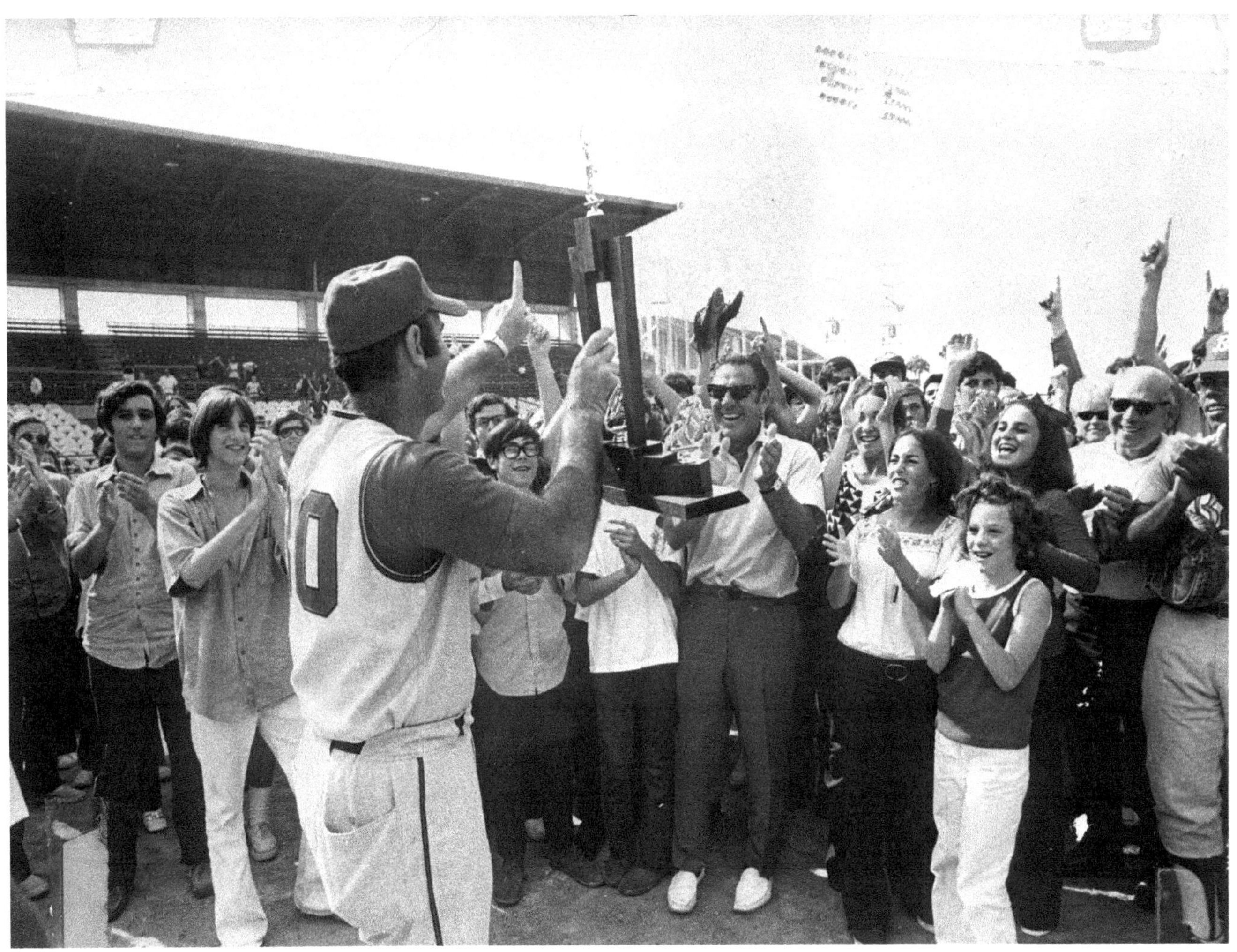

In 1970, this crowd at Tampa's Al Lopez field cheered Coach Skip Bertman. He had just led his team from Miami Beach High School to its first state championship. Bertman was born in Detroit, moved to Miami Beach in 1942 and was an accomplished athlete, then in 1964 became an assistant baseball coach at his old high school. In addition to the 1970 title, he also coached the high school to a year where it was the runner-up, plus he was a coach for Louisiana State University, the University of Miami, and the 1988 and 1996 Olympic teams.

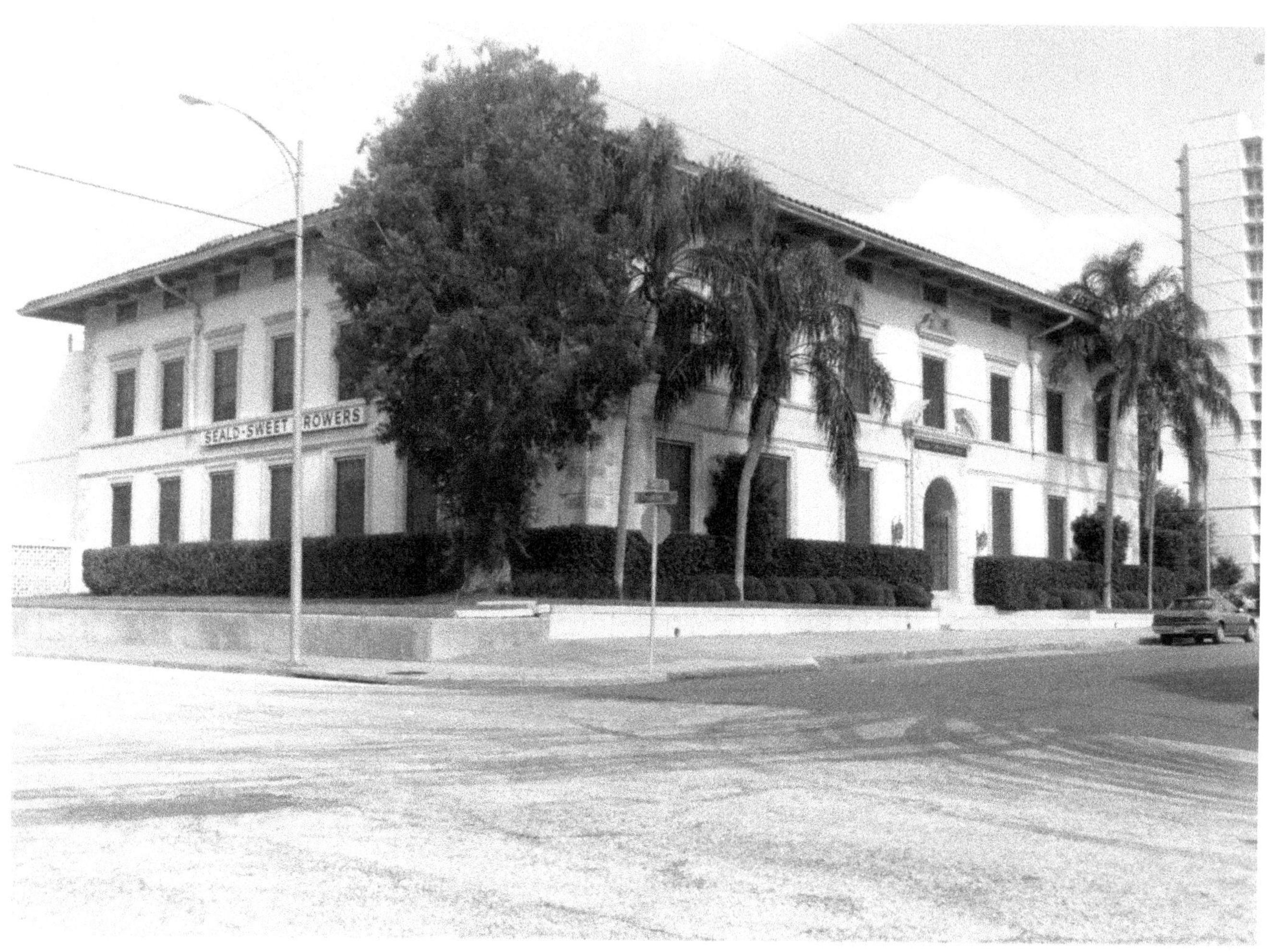

In 1909, citrus businessmen formed the Florida Citrus Exchange in Tampa, an effort to standardize grading of fruit and disseminate information about how best to grow and ship citrus. The result was an improvement industry-wide throughout the state. On April 8, 1969, the Florida Citrus Exchange became the Seald-Sweet Growers. This was its headquarters at the corner of Franklin Street and Oak Avenue.

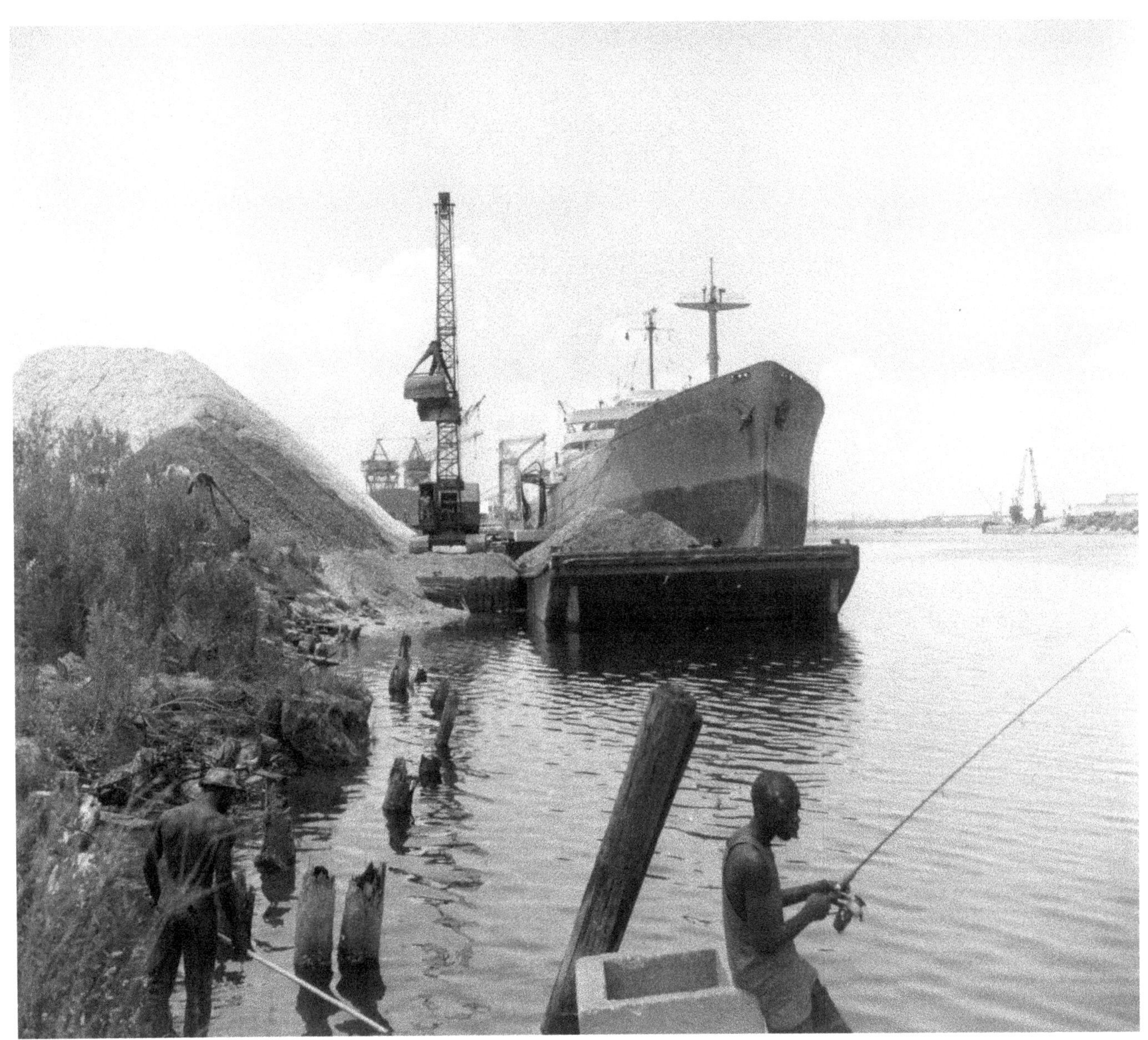

One of the major exports from Florida in 1970 was phosphate, with the state supplying a third of all phosphate being produced worldwide. The mineral is shown being loaded onto a ship in Tampa Harbor, likely to ultimately be turned into fertilizer. The Atlantic Coast Line Railroad had a large phosphate elevator at Port Tampa to facilitate the loading, beginning in 1922. It was removed in the early 1970s.

This game in about 1970 involved the Cincinnati Reds, who held their spring training in Tampa in 1931–42 and 1946–87. Pete Rose, Major League Baseball's all-time hits leader, is shown leading off third base. The field is named for Tampa's first hometown major league star, Alfonso Raymond Lopez. He was inducted into the Baseball Hall of Fame in 1977 after a 36-year career as a catcher and manager. As manager, he led the Cleveland Indians (1954) and the Chicago White Sox (1959) to American League penants.

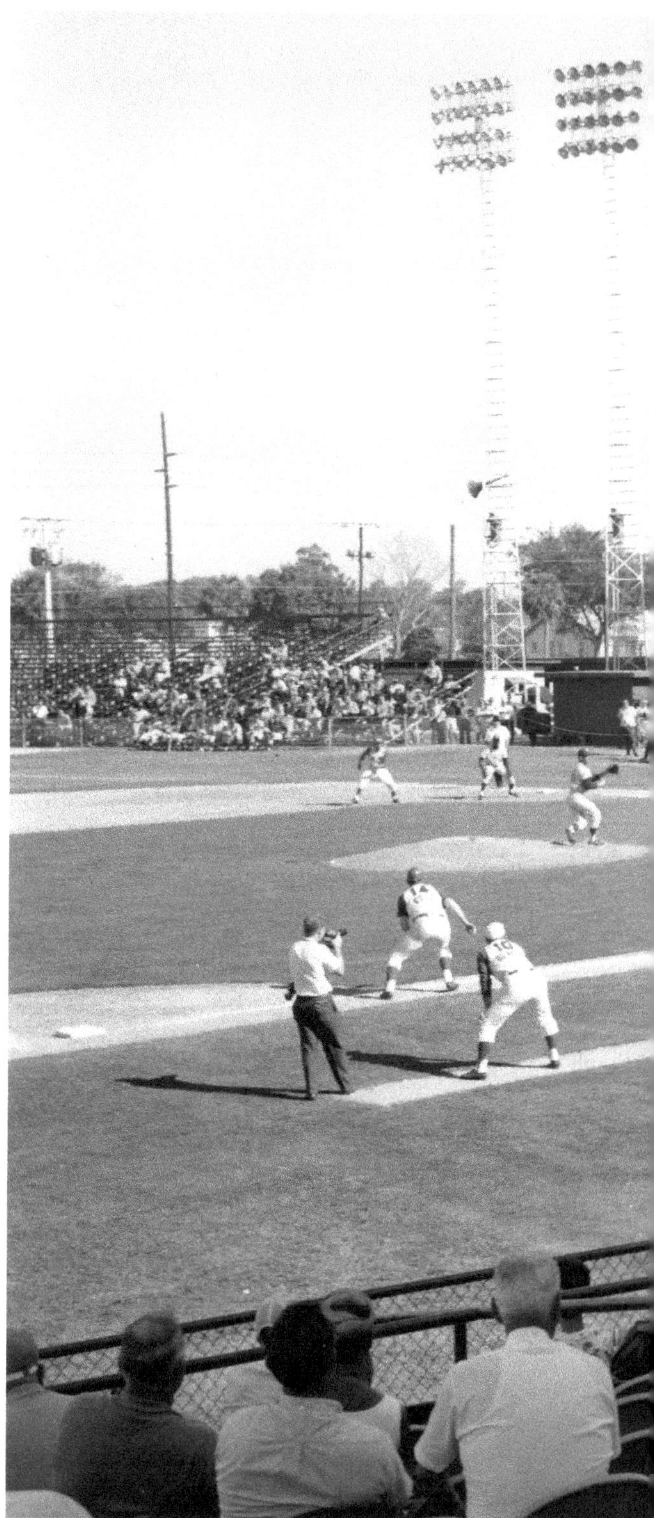

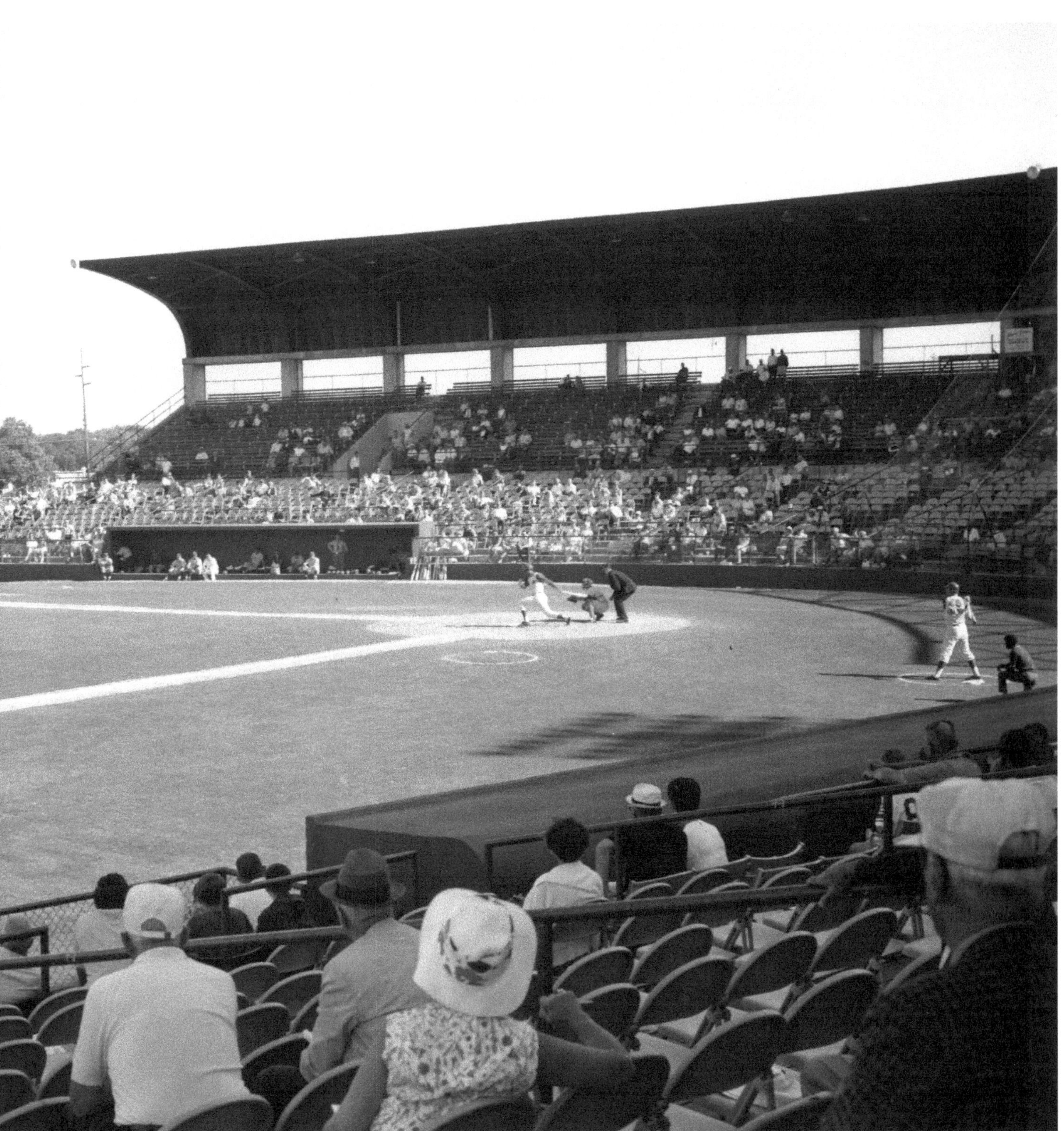

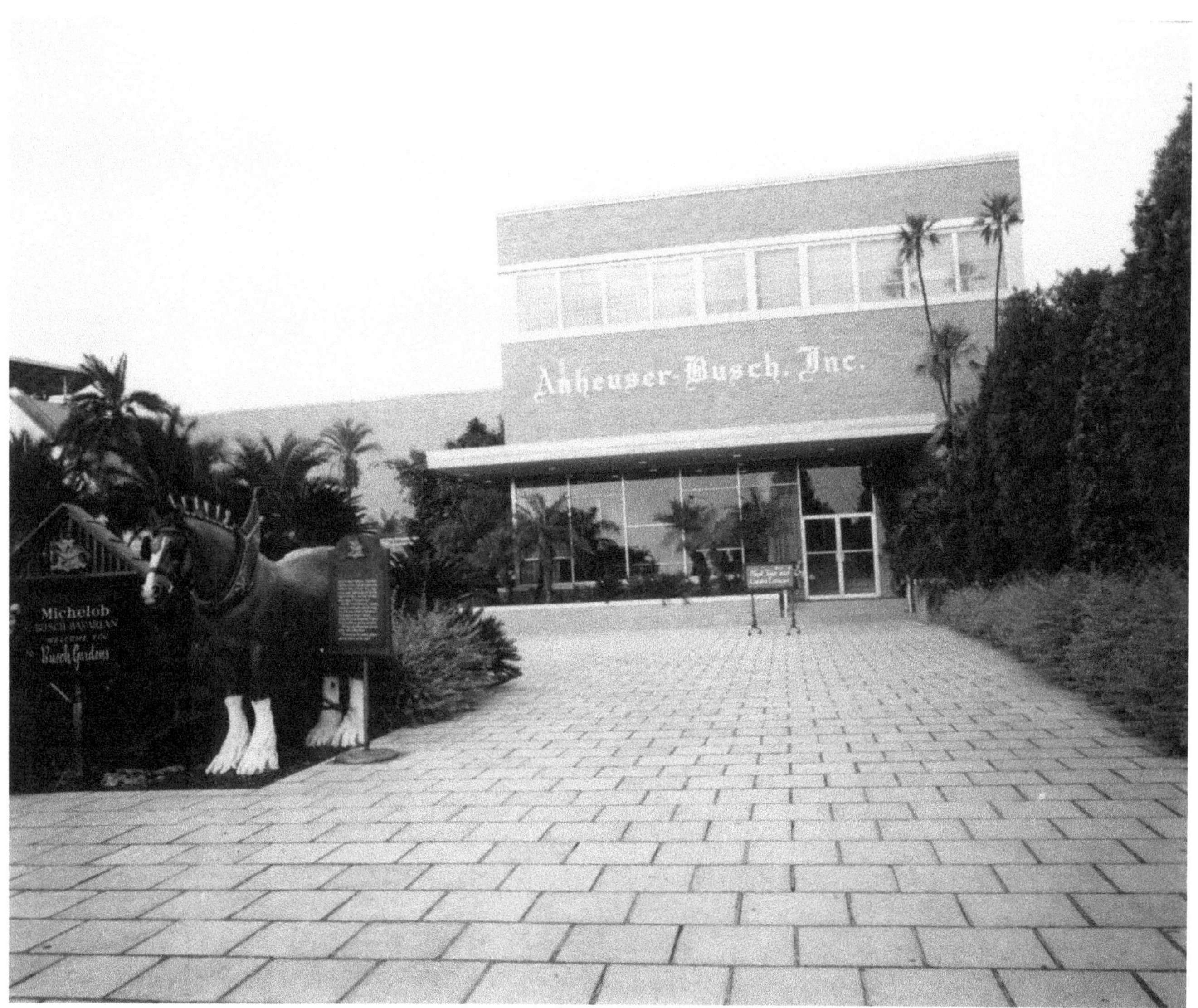

The first attraction at Busch Gardens was the tour of the Anheuser-Busch Brewery, shown here in 1970. It began with a long ride up on "the stairway to the stars," an outdoor escalator which carried visitors to the top of the building. The free tour then went indoors to view the brewing and packaging process, heading downstairs and ending with a walk through the Hospitality House where free samples were available. The brewery closed in 1995, the building was torn down, and in its place the wooden Gwazi roller coaster now stands.

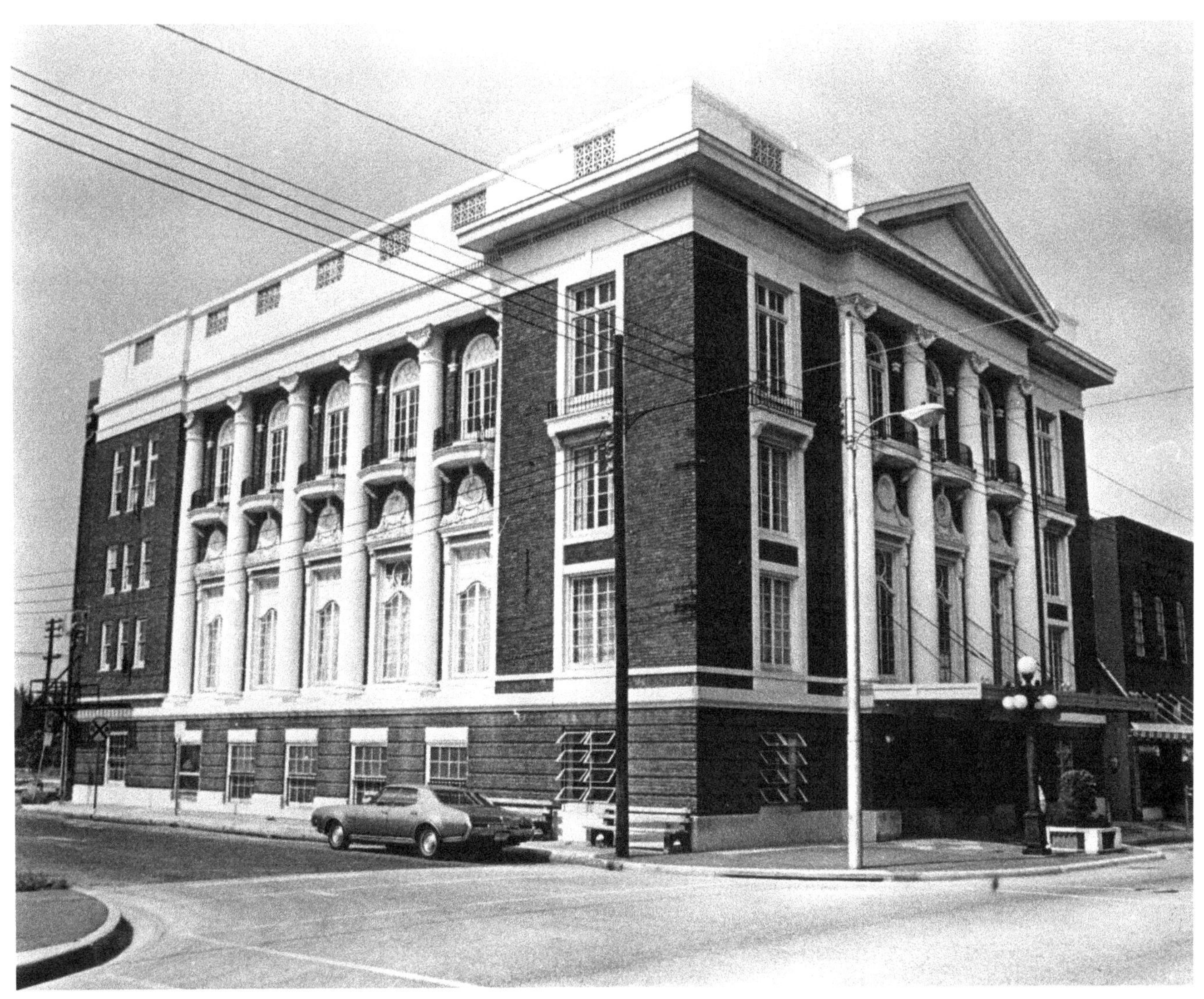

In 1894, Bartolomeo A. Filogamo was elected as the first president of La Societa Italian di Mutuo Soccorso, later called L'Unione Italiana and the Italian Club. Most of its 124 members were from four towns in western Sicily. This building was erected in 1918 to replace one across the street which had been built in 1912, but burned down in 1915. It was intended that this Italian Renaissance-style structure in Ybor City would serve as a cathedral for the working man.

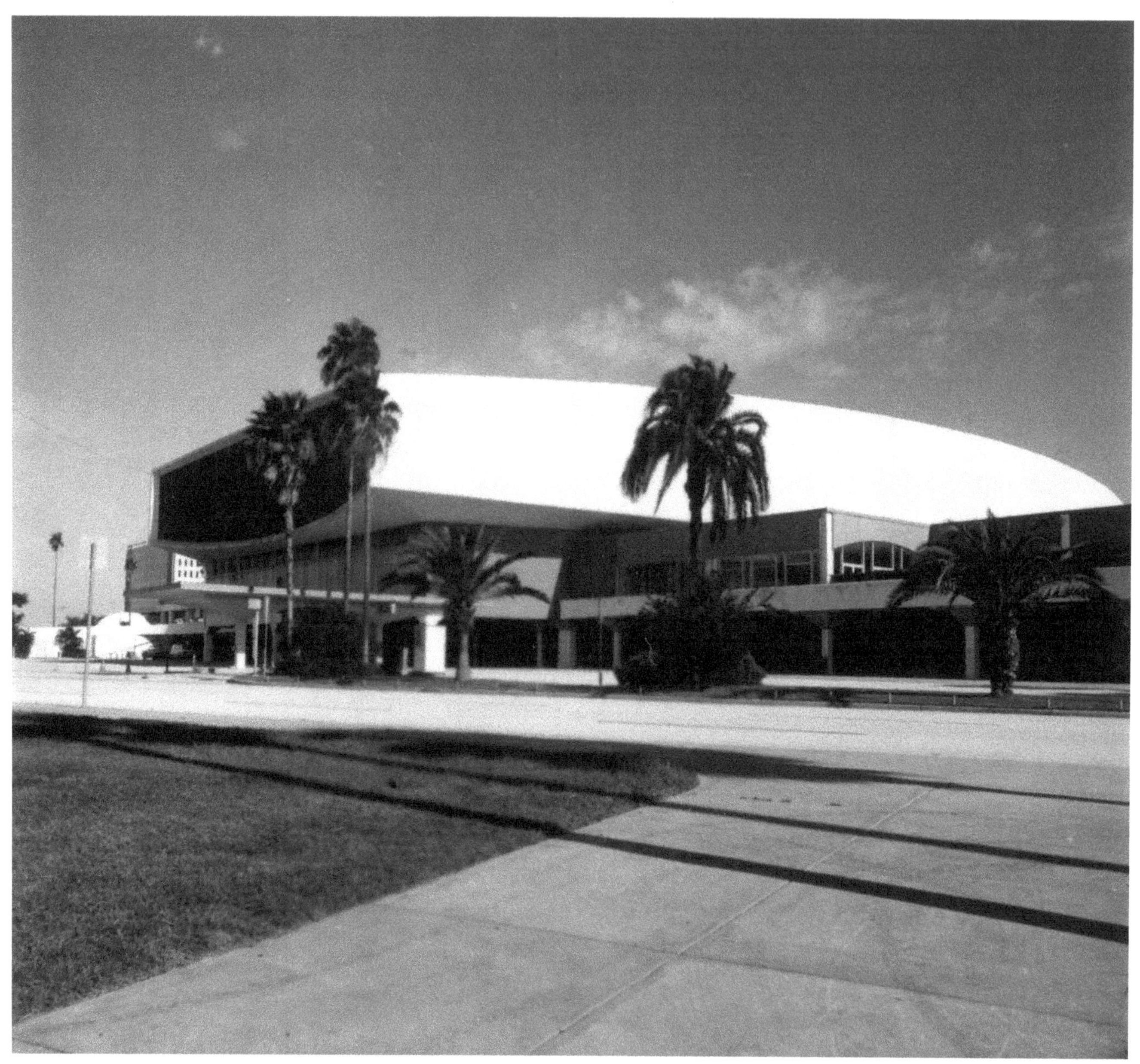

During the 1880s, on the land along the eastern bank of the Hillsborough River, near the foot of Madison Street, stood the lumber mill owned by Captain Nicholas Dixon. In 1964, Curtis Hixon Hall, photographed here in 1971, was built at that site. It was a popular venue for rock concerts and basketball games, including some of the home games of the ABA's Floridians.

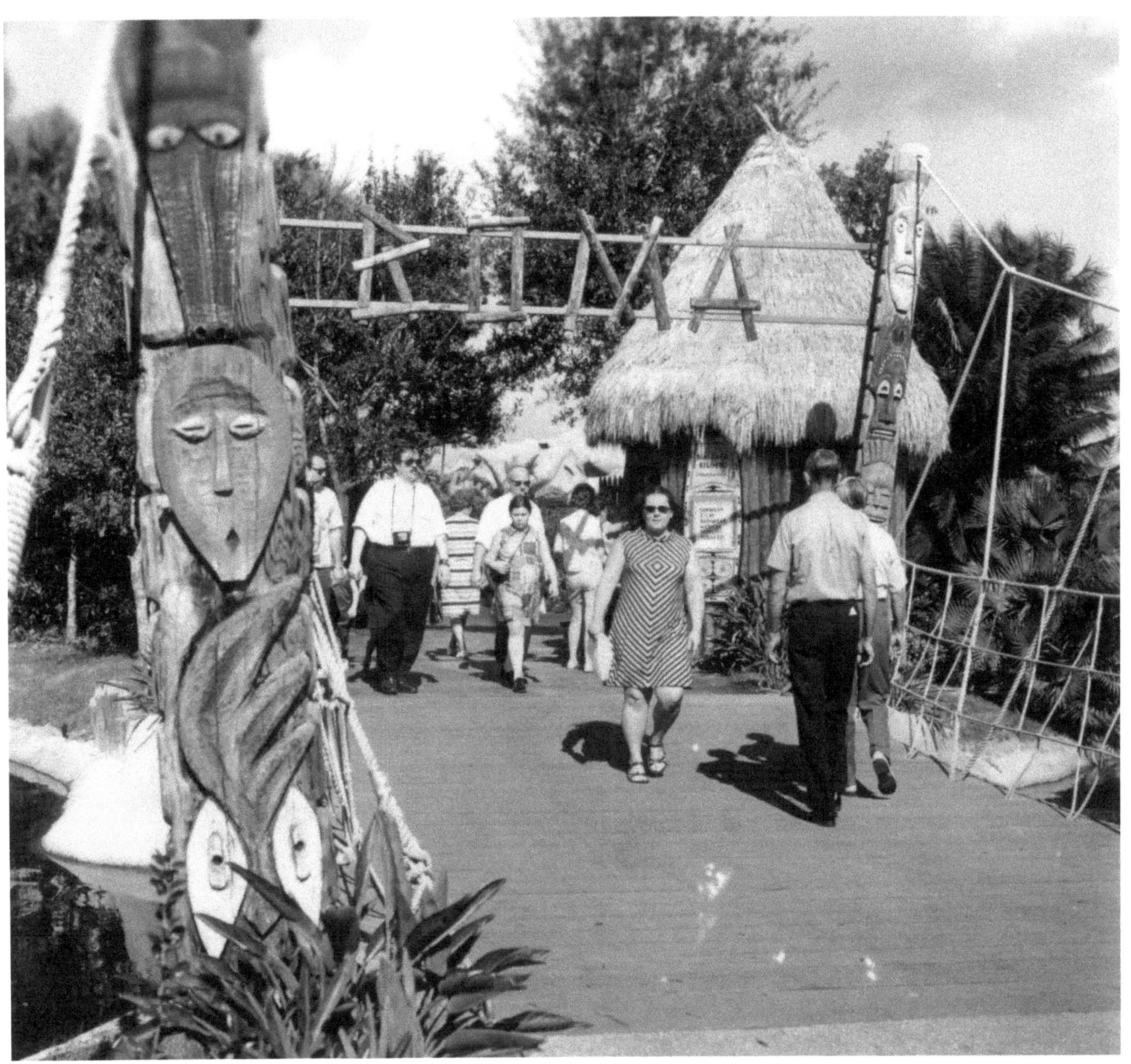

One of Busch Gardens' earliest sections, Boma had exotic plants and animals. It was essentially a small zoo and many of the animals (or their descendants) are still there today, in the area remodeled as Nairobi. Its inhabitants include gorillas, chimpanzees, and Asian elephants.

While attending a campaign barbecue in Tampa on March 12, 1972, candidate Edmund Muskie was visited by supporters of another Democrat, George McGovern. The leader of the group, the woman to the left wearing a hat, is actress Shirley MacLaine. Muskie's 10,216 votes in Hillsborough county placed him fourth statewide behind George Wallace, Hubert Humphrey and Henry "Scoop" Jackson, and the Democratic nomination went to George McGovern, who lost in November to Richard Nixon.

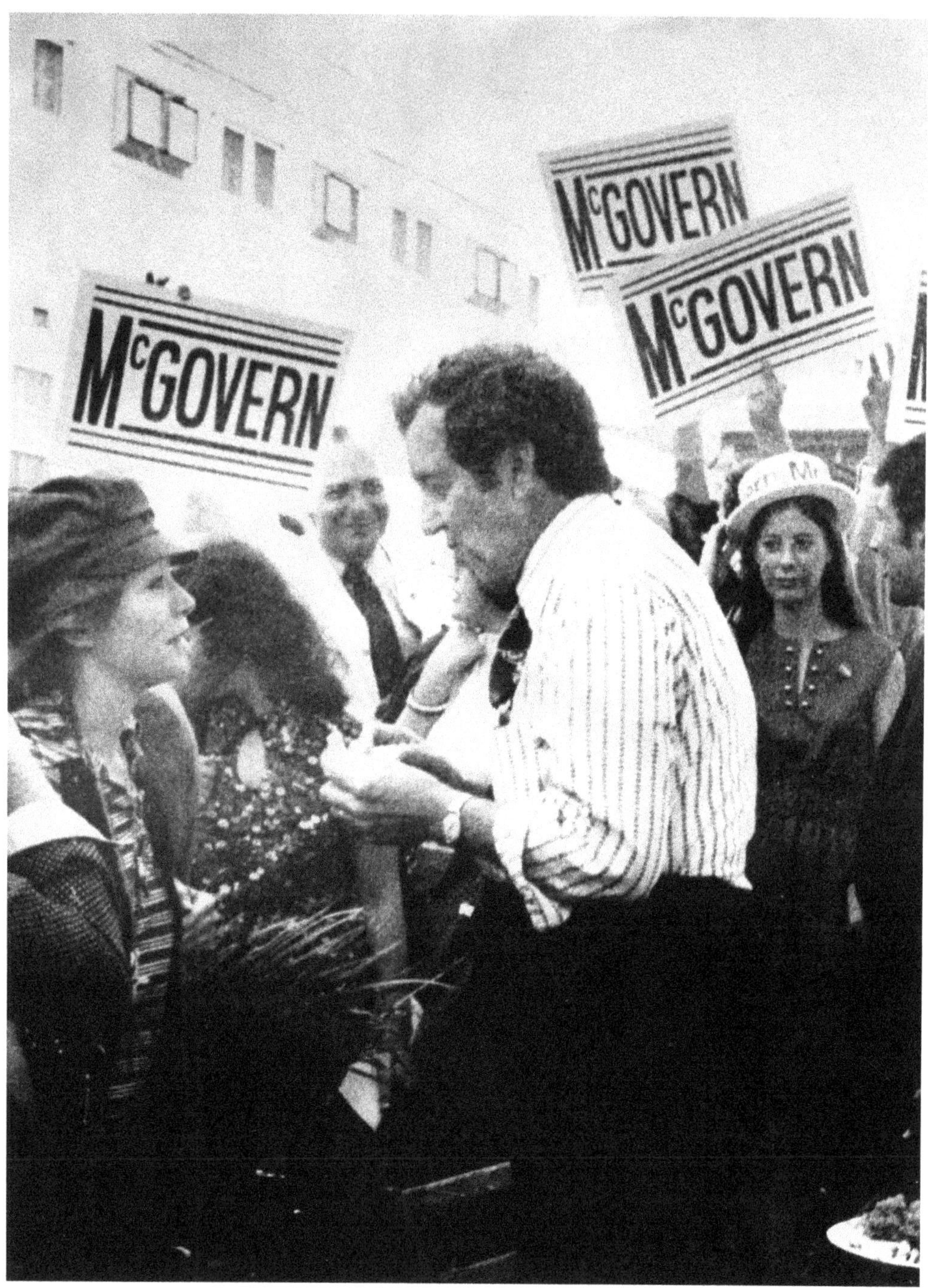

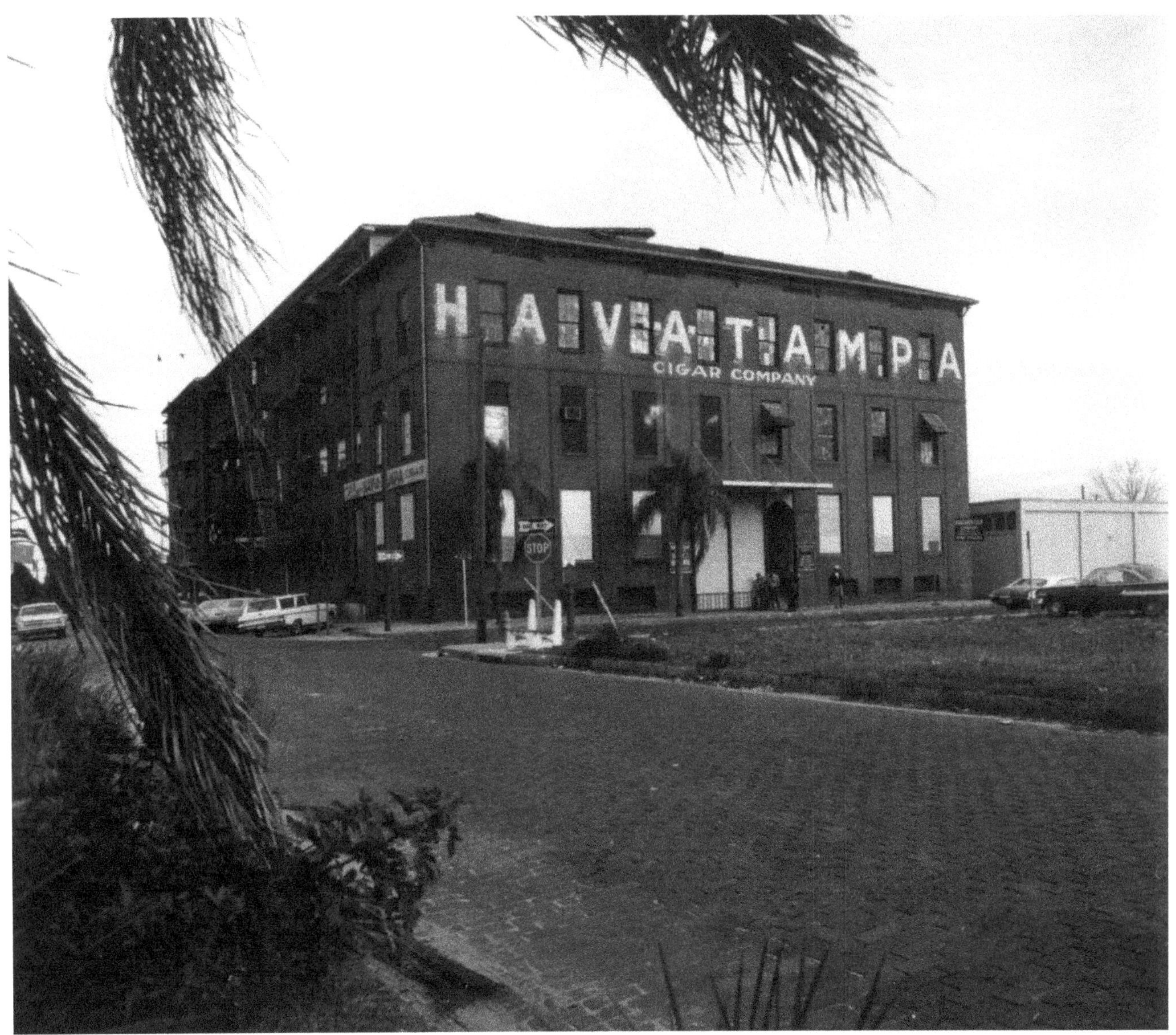

Hav-A-Tampa Cigars opened for business in Tampa in 1902, with one of its popular brands being the birchwood-tipped Tampa Jewel. Shown here is its factory in 1972. In later years, it moved its operations to Seffner, not far from Tampa, and partially because of its name was still considered a Tampa operation. The brand was acquired by the Eli Witt Cigar Company, and it was one of the early companies to switch from hand rolling to machines. In 2009, the owner moved its operation away from the area and, although the Hav-A-Tampa brand is still being produced, they are now made in Puerto Rico.

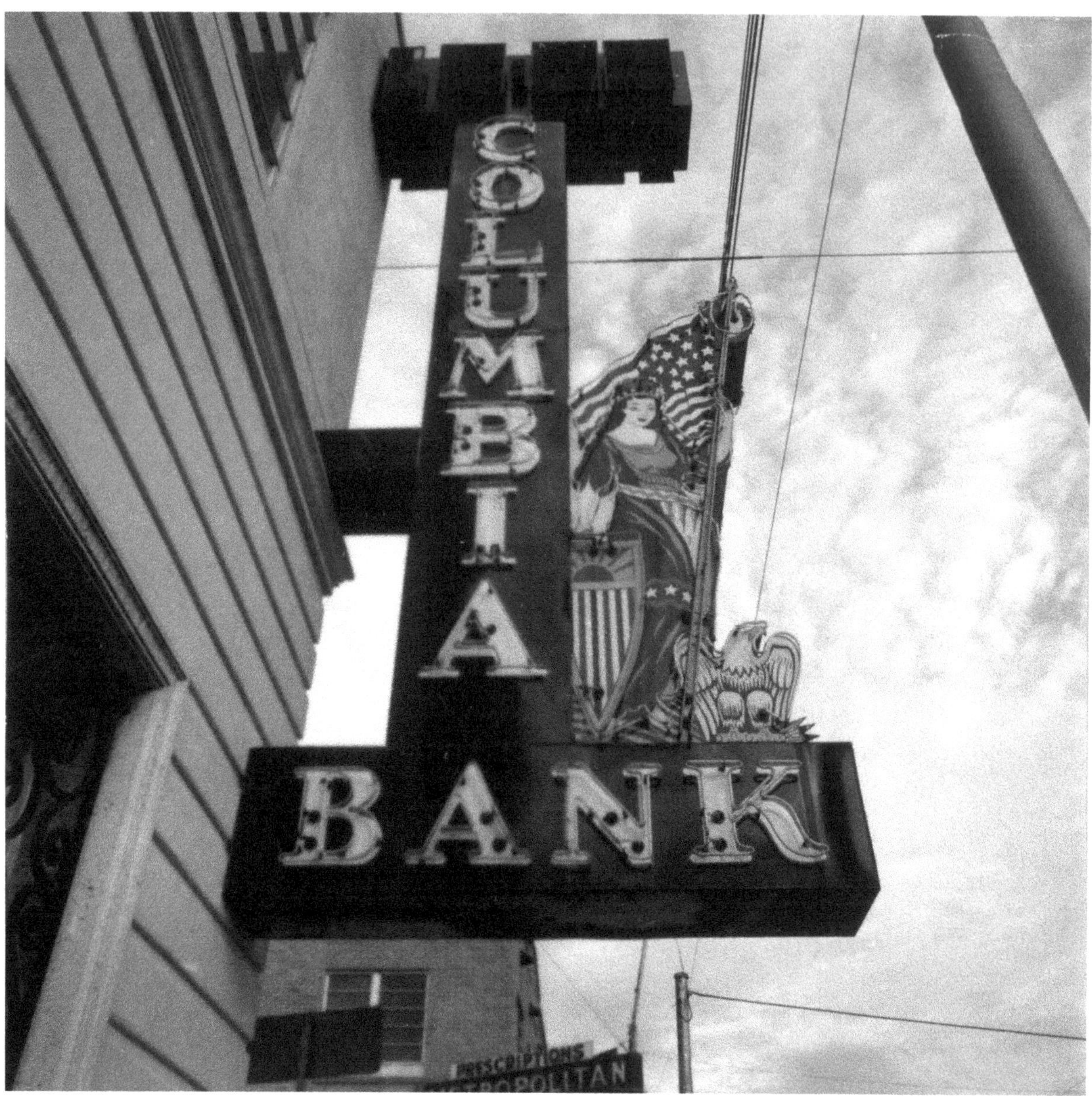

The Columbia Bank was founded by Simon A. Grimaldi in 1923, and was the only bank in Ybor City to survive the 1929 stock market crash. It moved into the Scozzari Building at 1901 7th Avenue in 1934. This is a picture of its sign from 1972, when it was housed in the 1918 building standing at 2028–32 7th Avenue. In 2000, it merged with Southern Exchange Bank.

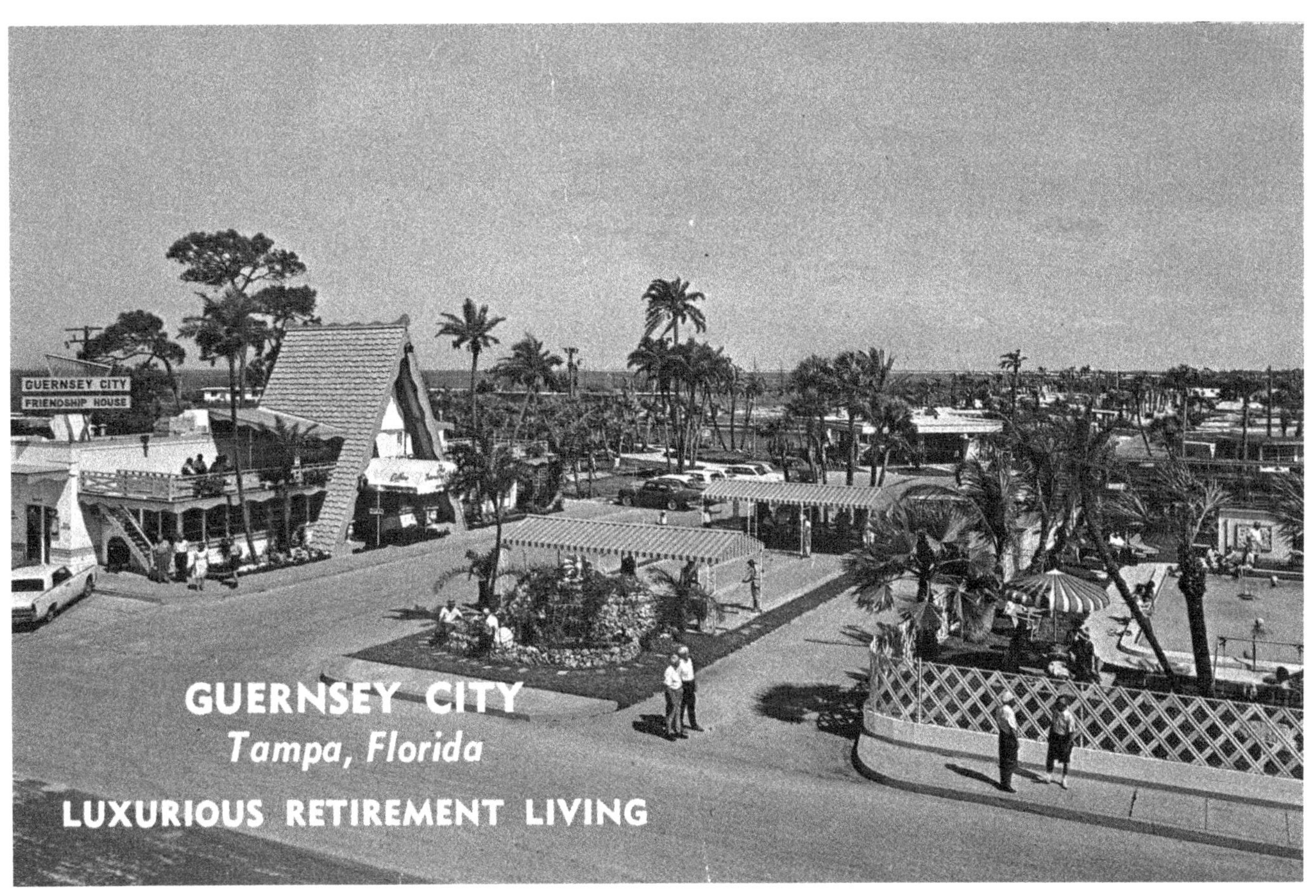

This image of Guernsey City was meant to entice seniors to move to a comfortable retirement community during the early 1970s. It was built on land located near the Gandy Bridge by Welburn Guernsey of Indianapolis, who named the development after himself. He didn't finish the projected $5 million housing project or the $3 million shopping center, but he did create a waterfront mobile home park, which was renamed as Regency Cove in 1974. Its residents bought the park for $12 million in 1992 to prevent in from being acquired by an outsider and torn down for redevelopment.

Between Bird Street and the Hillsborough River, a little north of downtown, is Sulphur Springs, a place believed by some to have healing waters. Around the area, the Sulphur Springs neighborhood grew up, and near the water was built a dance hall, Ferris wheel, and swimming pool shortly after 1900. In the 1920s, Josiah Richardson expanded the area into a tourist resort and constructed this 210-foot-tall water tower with an observation platform reached by an elevator. Richardson went broke in the 1930s and his grandiose plans were scrapped. The tower now overlooks the public River Tower Park.

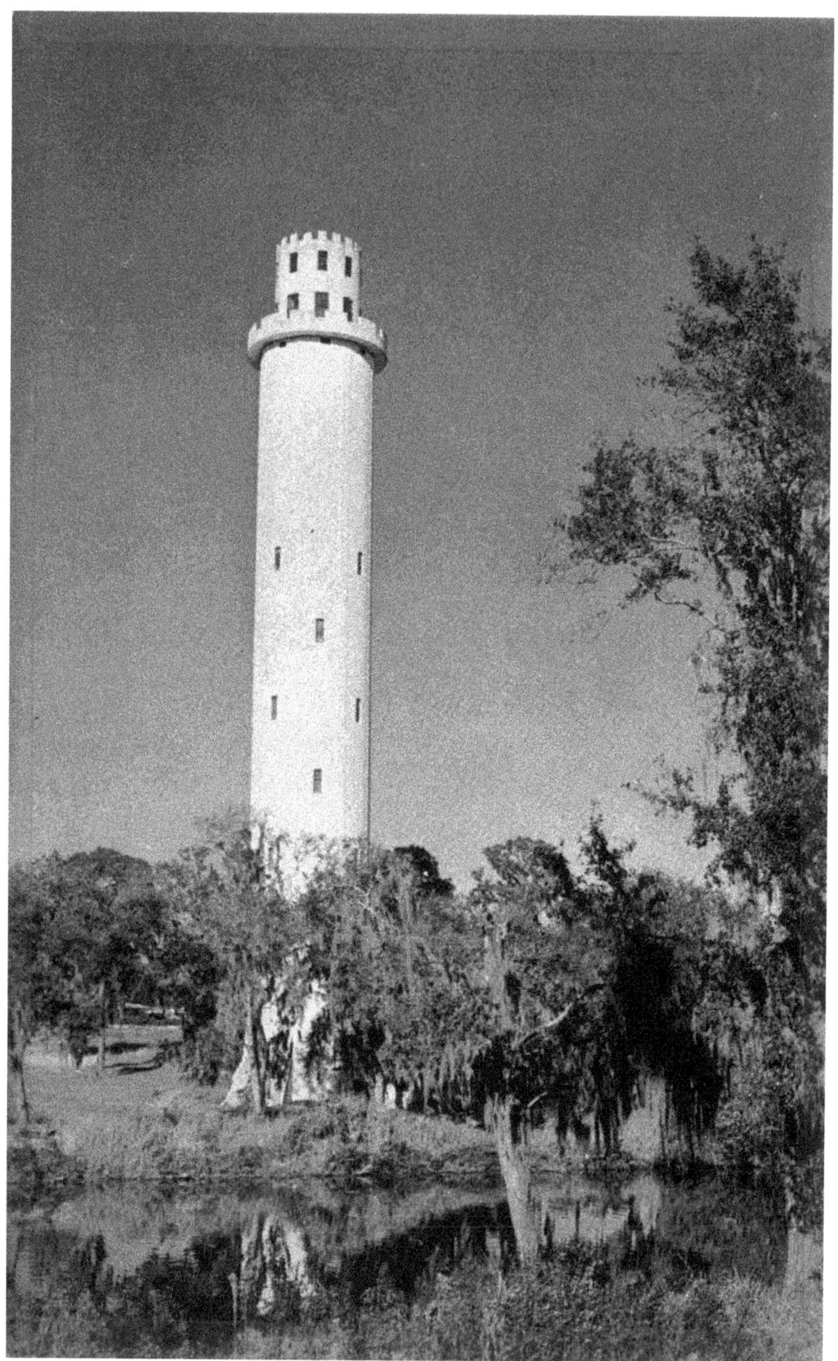

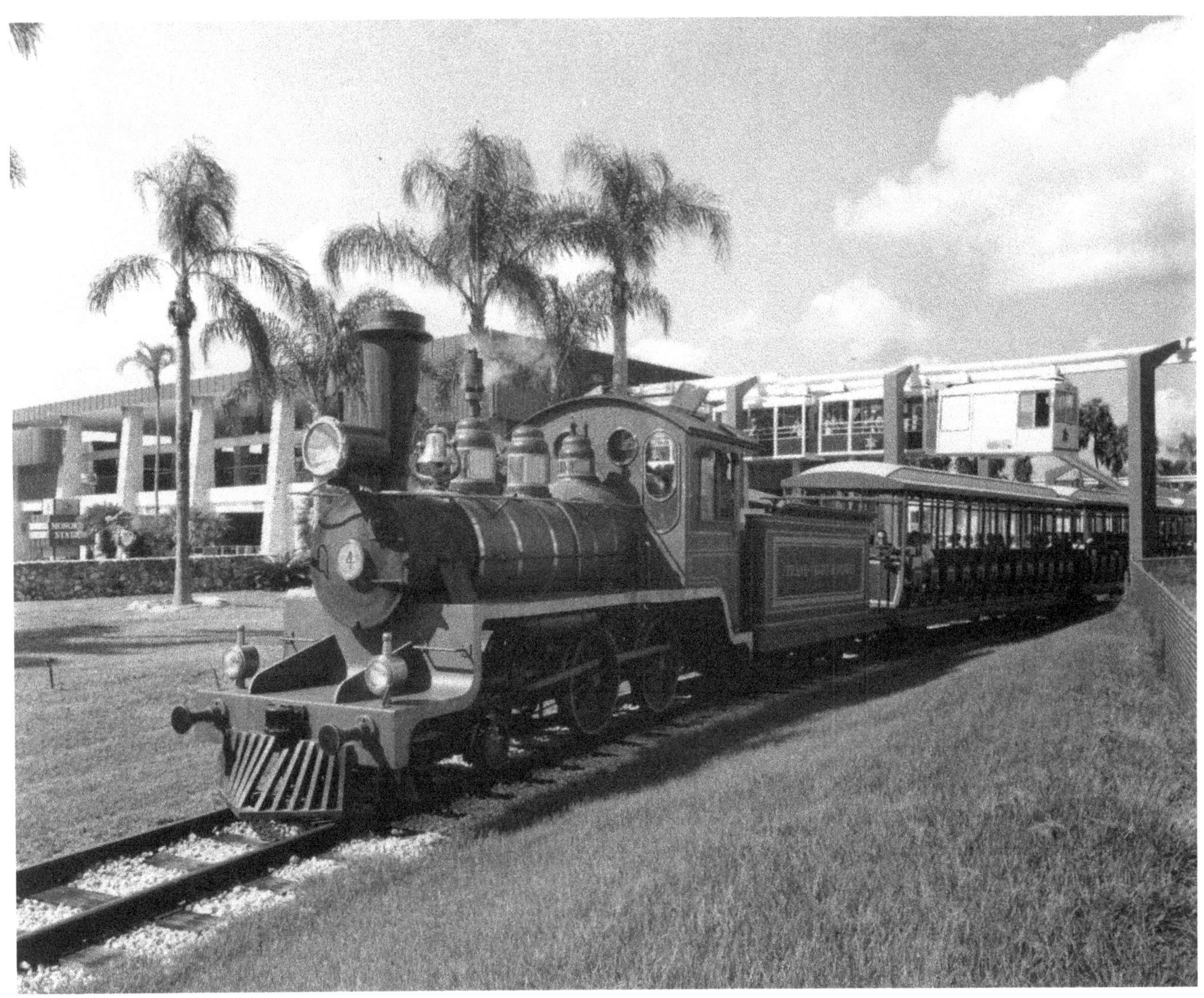

The 335-acre Busch Gardens was initially a free attraction with an emphasis on animals and simple rides, such as the Serengeti Express steam train, photographed here in 1973. It runs on two miles of track along the back end of the park and has stops at Nairobi, Congo, and Stanleyville. It was the first substantial ride constructed following the completion of the monorail.

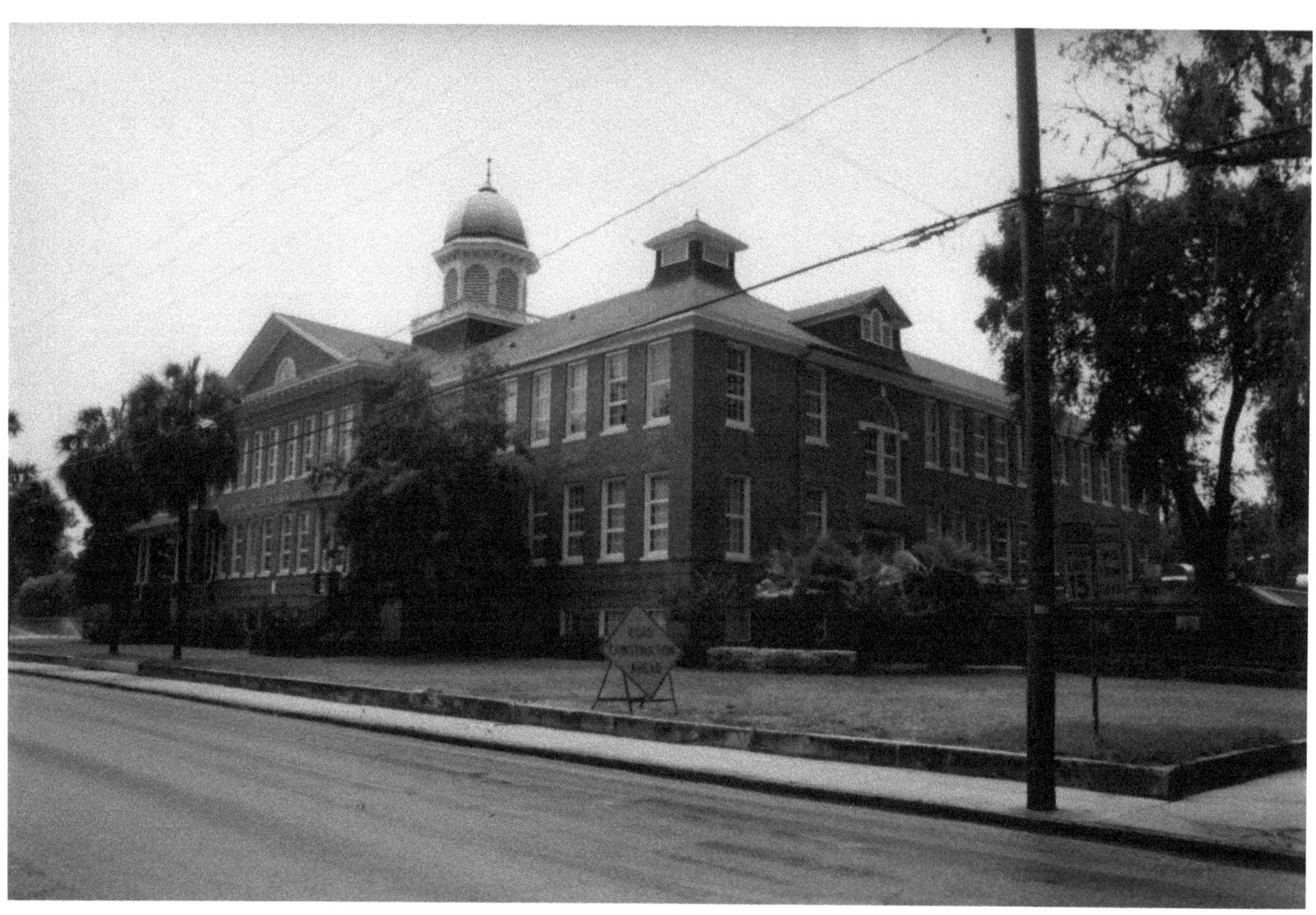

This school was built with a distinctive copper dome in about 1906, making it Hillsborough County's oldest remaining school building. It is located at 305 East Columbus Drive and was built with brick walls, wood floors, and hand-glazed windows by volunteers who lived nearby. While it was still under construction, it opened as the Michigan Avenue Grammar School and offered classes to a largely Hispanic student body. In 1943, when Michigan Avenue was renamed as Columbus Drive, the school was renamed as Robert E. Lee Elementary School.

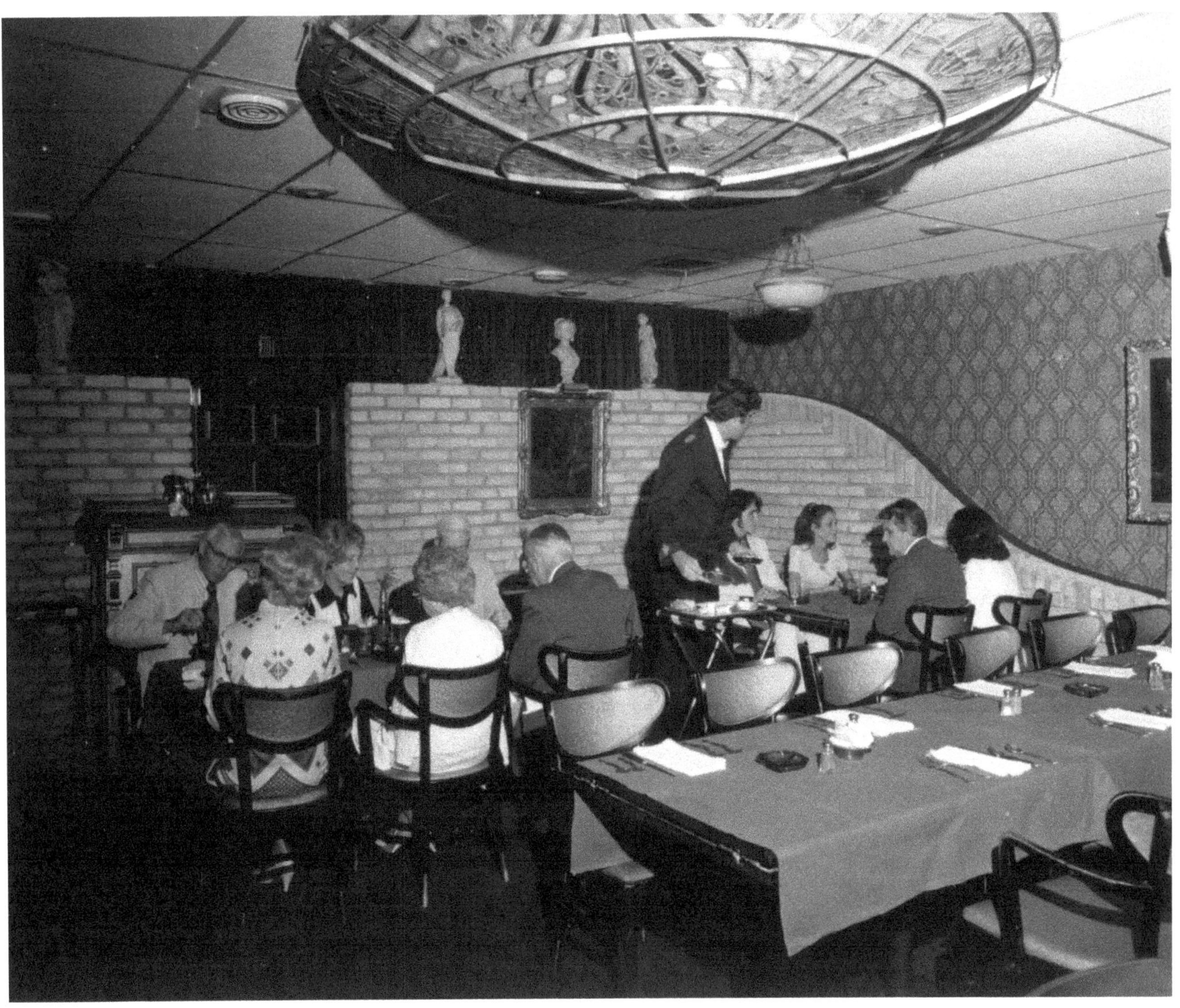

Bernard H. and Gertrude Laxer of New York founded their first Tampa restaurant, Bern and Gert's Little Midway, in 1953. In 1955, they opened Bern's, a hamburger joint in a strip shopping center, and they bought out the other stores so they could expand. Bern's Steak House was founded in 1956 and has grown into a Victorian showplace with an amazing wine selection, house-aged prime beef, live seafood, organic produce grown on its own farm, and an upstairs dessert room with a 65-page menu.

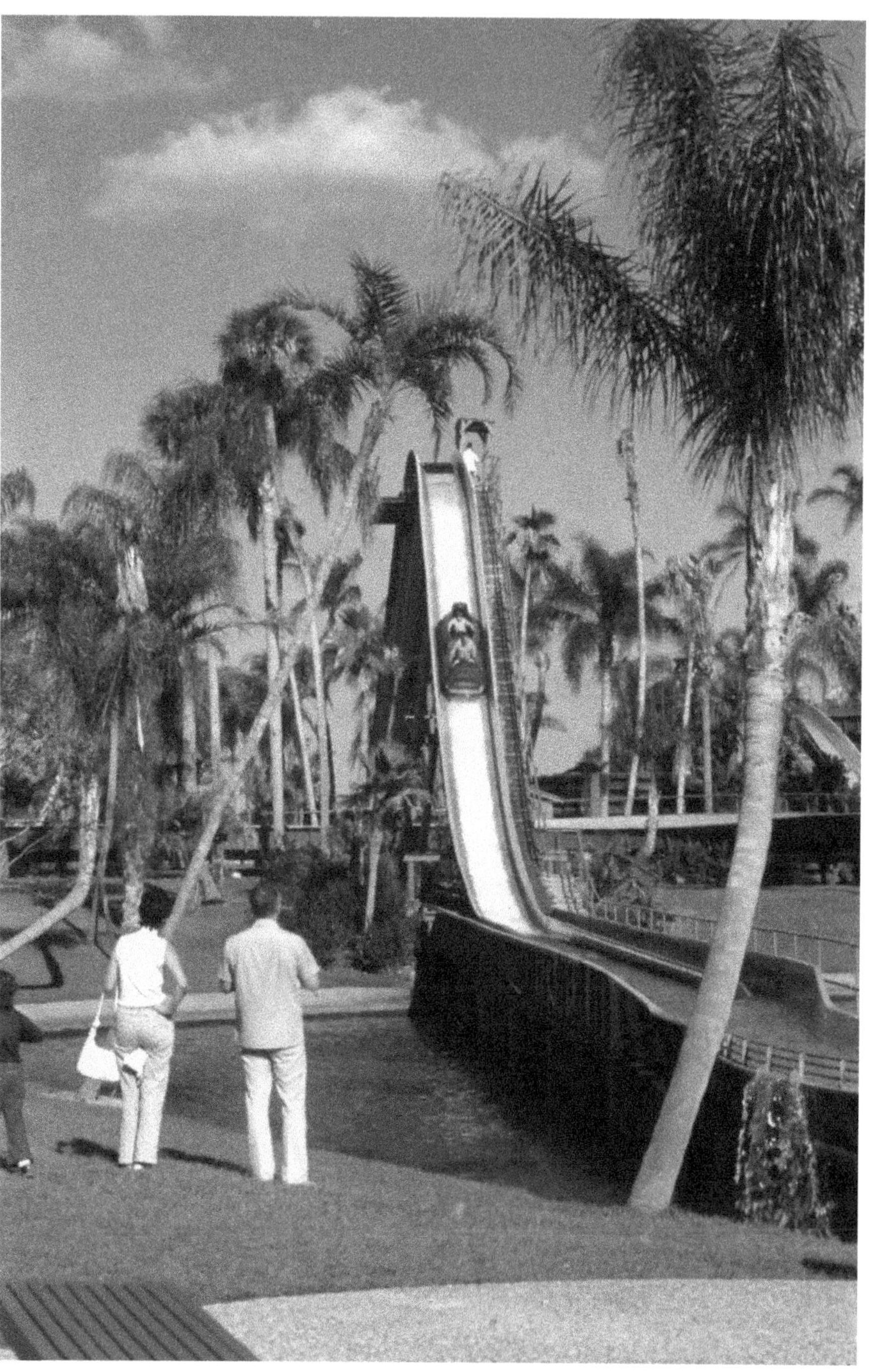

In 1973, in the section of Busch Gardens known as Stanleyville, this flume ride with a 43-foot drop opened with the name of the Stanley Falls Flume. It was the park's first, but not its last, water ride. Stanleyville also includes the Tanganyika Tidal Wave (formerly the African Queen Boat Ride) and dive coaster SheiKra.

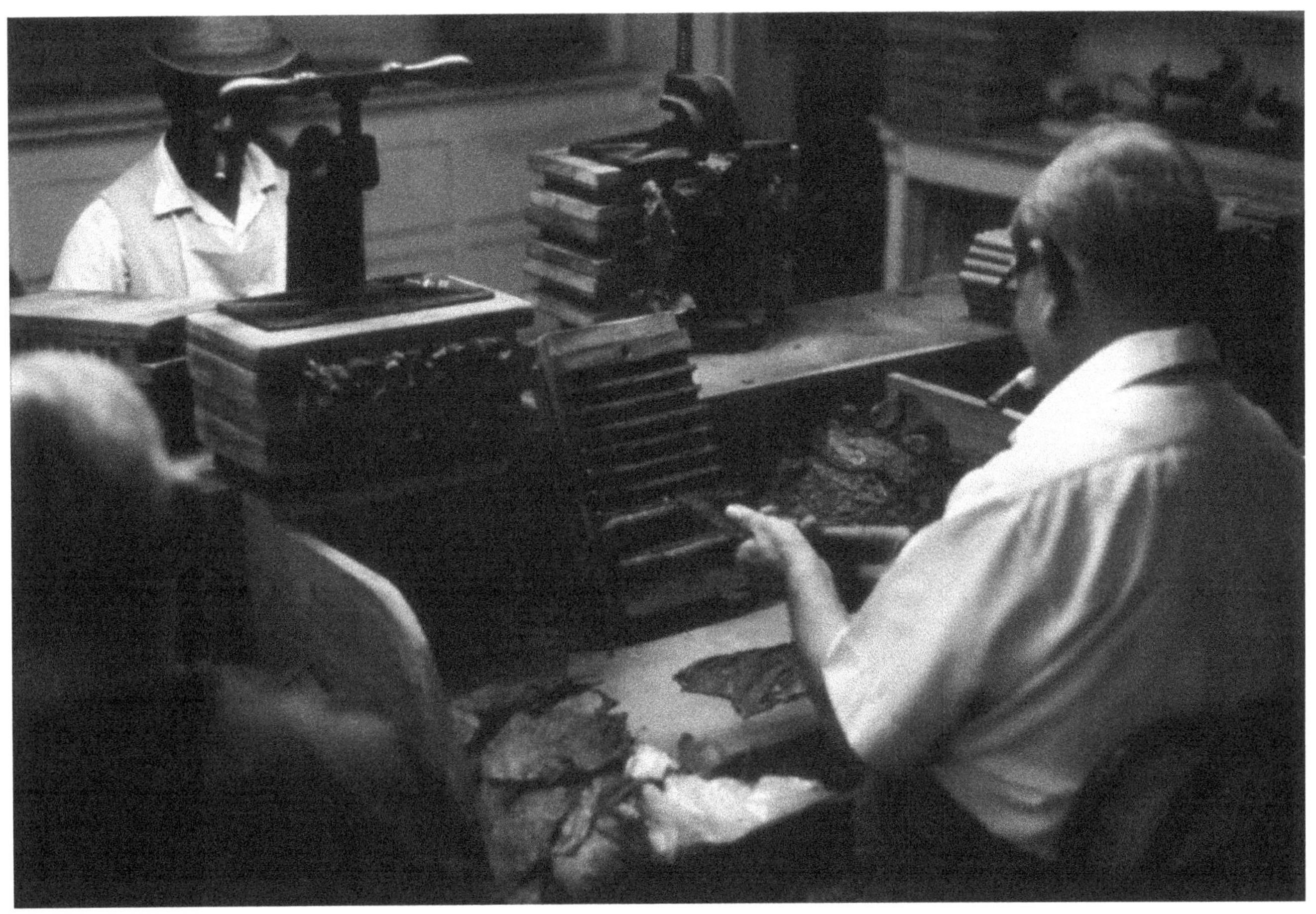

In the early days of the Tampa cigar industry, all cigars were made by hand. The first step in making one is to take a quantity of filler tobacco and roll it into the shape of a cigar, then place it into a cigar press. It remains there for 30 to 45 minutes while it takes on the desired shape. It is then wrapped and sealed with the tobacco patch and vegetable glue, and the head is cut to the correct size and shape. Today, hand rolling can still be observed, but as small-scale demonstrations that hardly resemble the large factories of yesteryear.

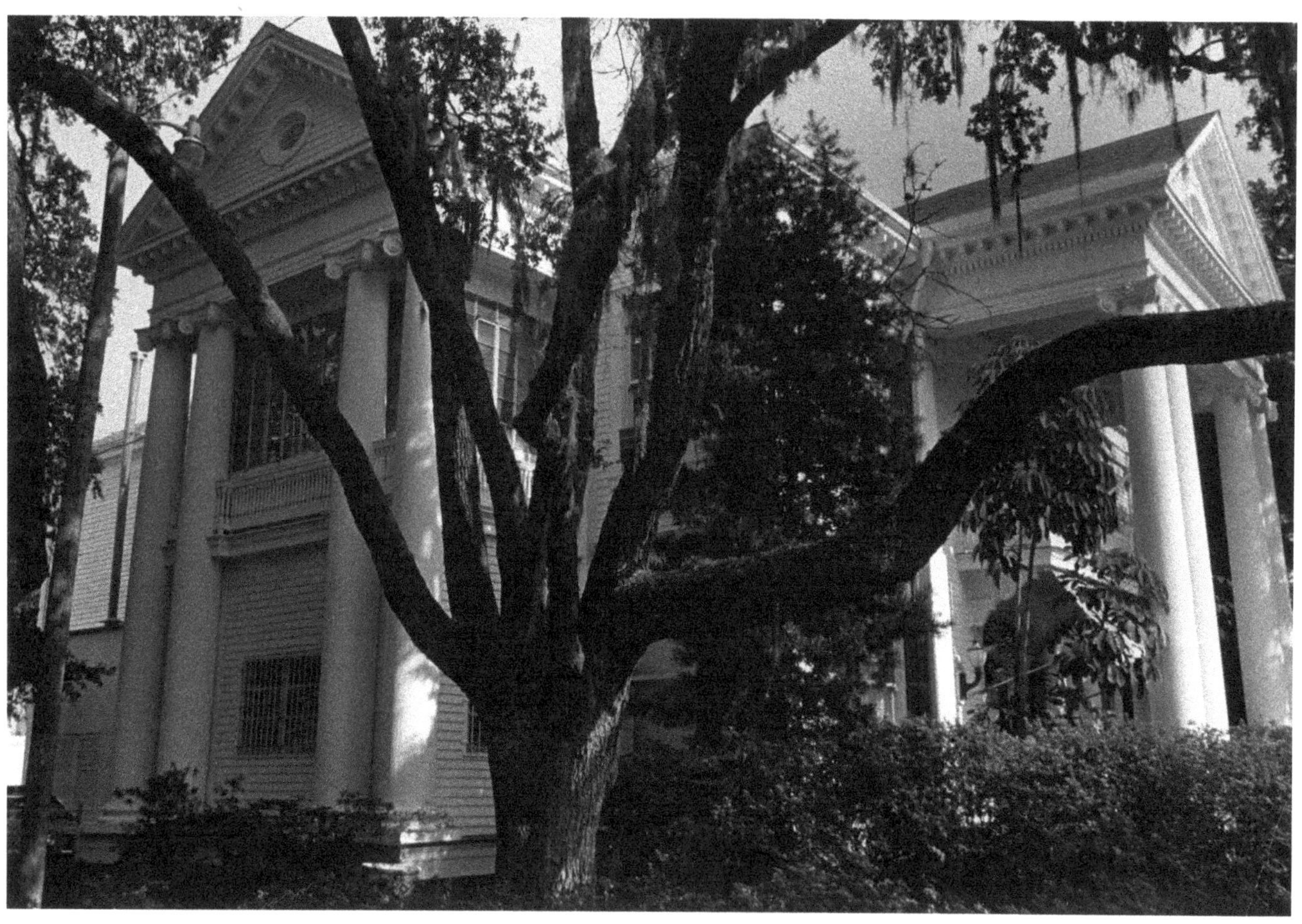

This home at 305 Hyde Park Avenue was built in 1890 for Thomas C. Taliaferro. It has a Classical Revival style and paired Ionic columns, and was added to the National Register of Historic Places on October 1, 1974. Taliaferro and his family founded the First National Bank and he was its head from 1903 until 1927. A later use of the home was as the Center for Women.

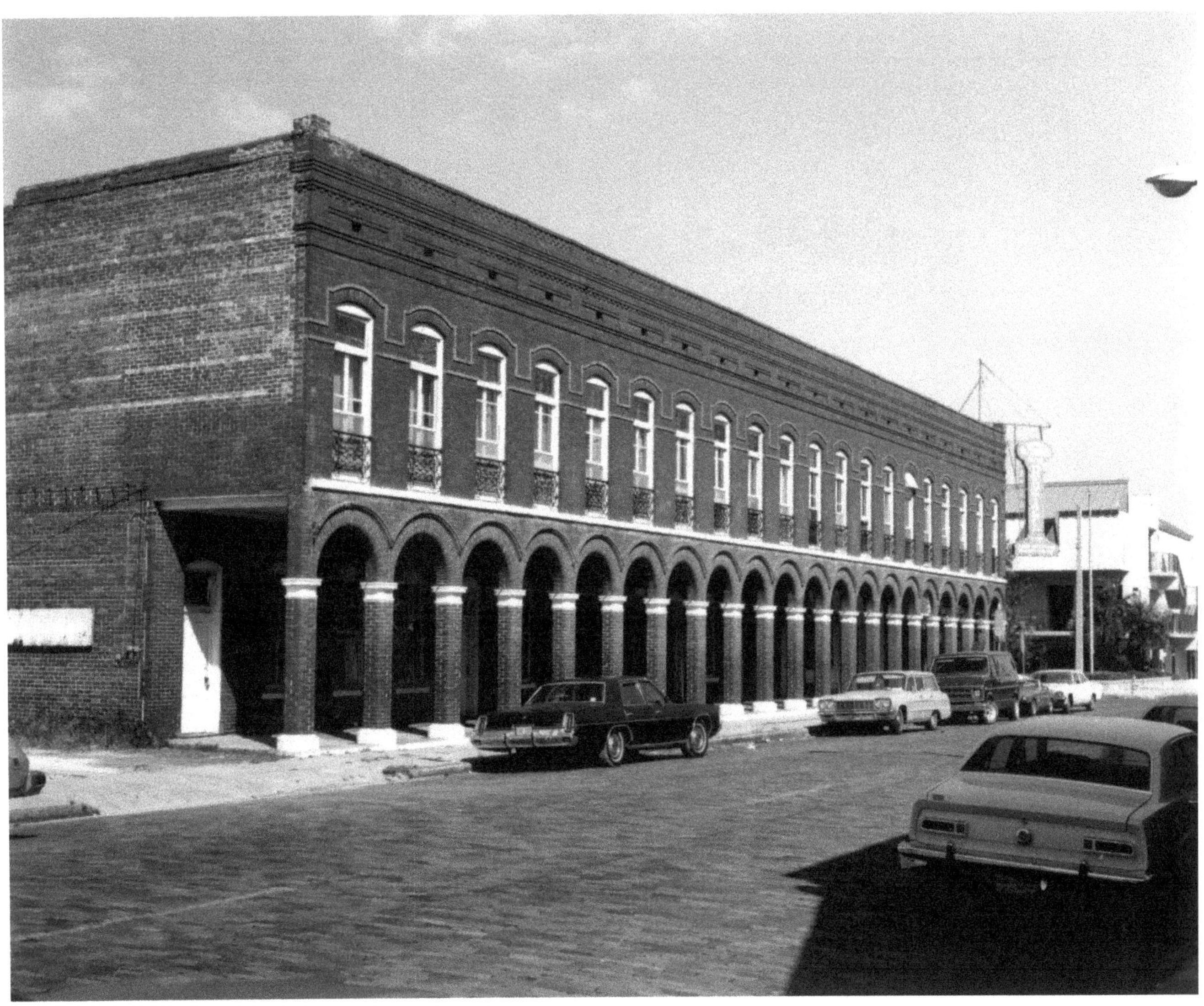

The building housing the Cherokee Club, nicknamed "El Pasaje" for the arched passageway along the south side, was built with money donated by Vicente Ybor. The Cherokee Club was established to provide a place for the interaction of cigar manufacturers and other prominent businessmen. It included a hotel and gambling casino. The building is eclectic in style and has some Italian Renaissance elements, and was modeled after an Italian villa. It was named to the National Register of Historic Places in 1972, two years before this photo was taken.

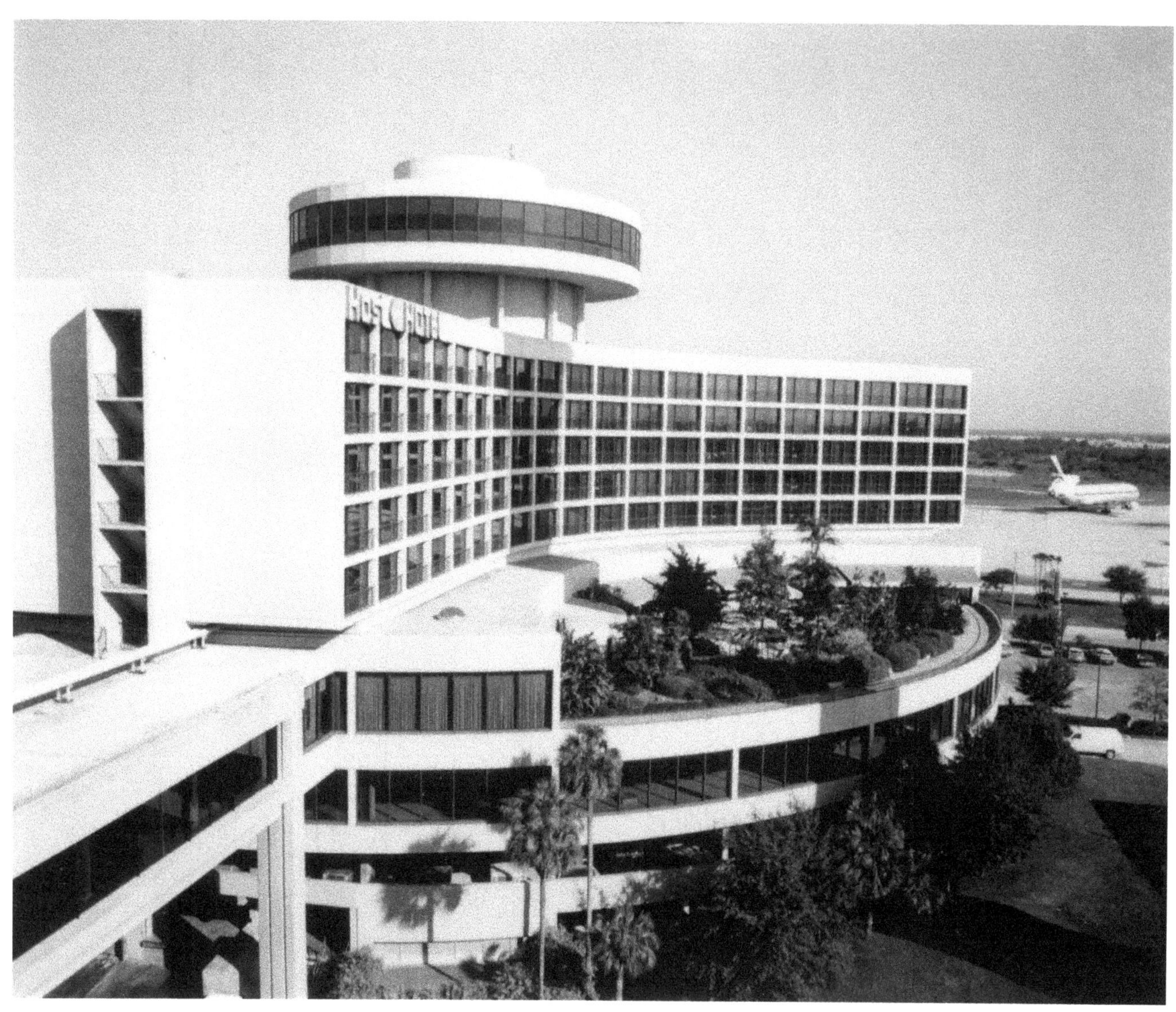

In 1971, construction began on the Host of Tampa Hotel at the Tampa International Airport. Its cost was estimated to be $11 million, and it opened for business in 1973, the year before this photo was taken. It later became known as the Tampa Airport Marriott Hotel.

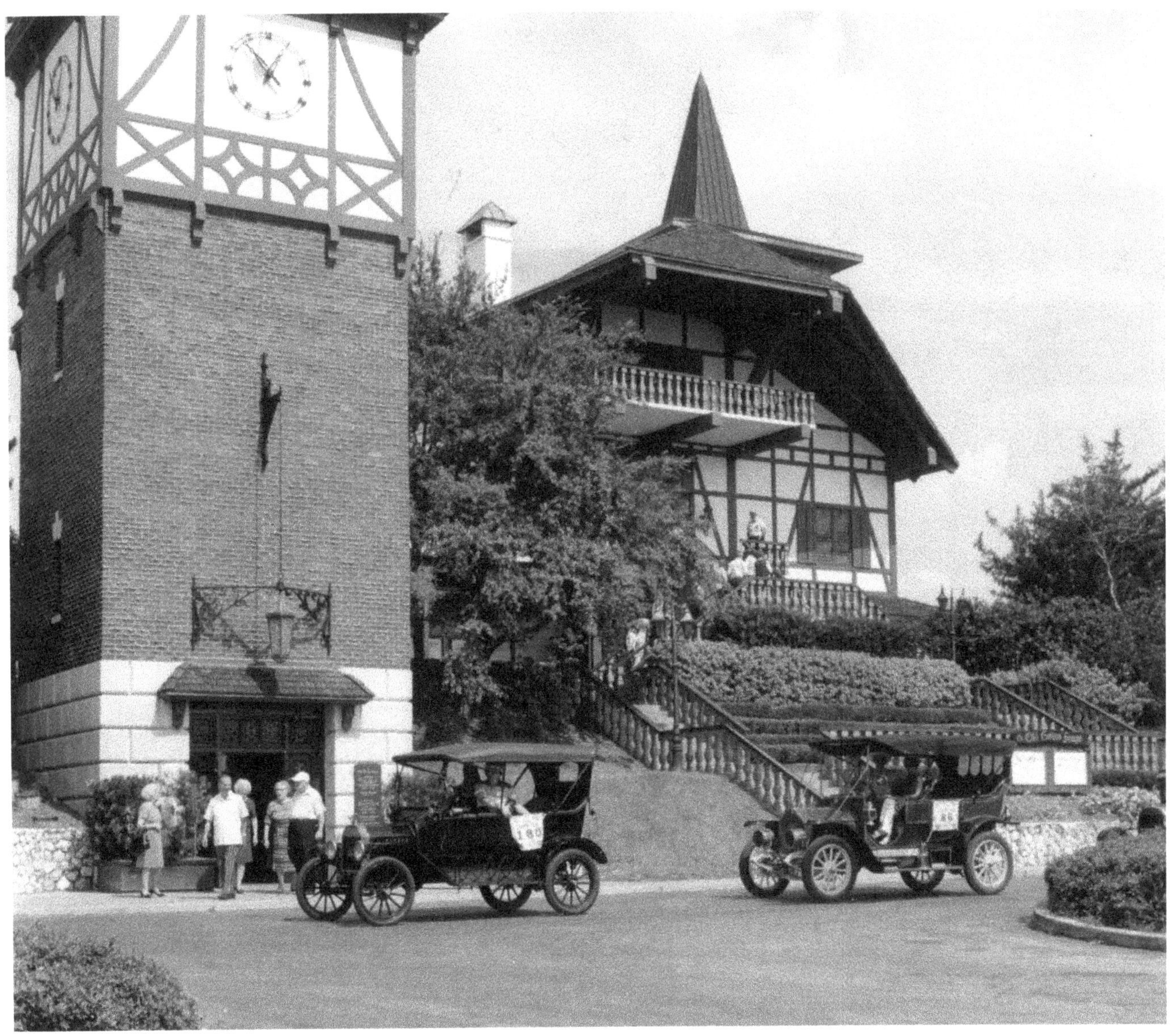

The Swiss House restaurant at Busch Gardens was considered to be one of Tampa's finest restaurants, but in about 1980 it closed and remained so until 1990, when it reopened as the Crown Colony House. The restaurant has both casual and fine dining, and along with a Skyline station and Budweiser Clydesdale Hamlet comprises the smallest separate section of the park. The original design of the structure was modeled after the Old Swiss House in Lucerne, Switzerland, owned by the brother of Adolphus Busch's third wife, Trudy.

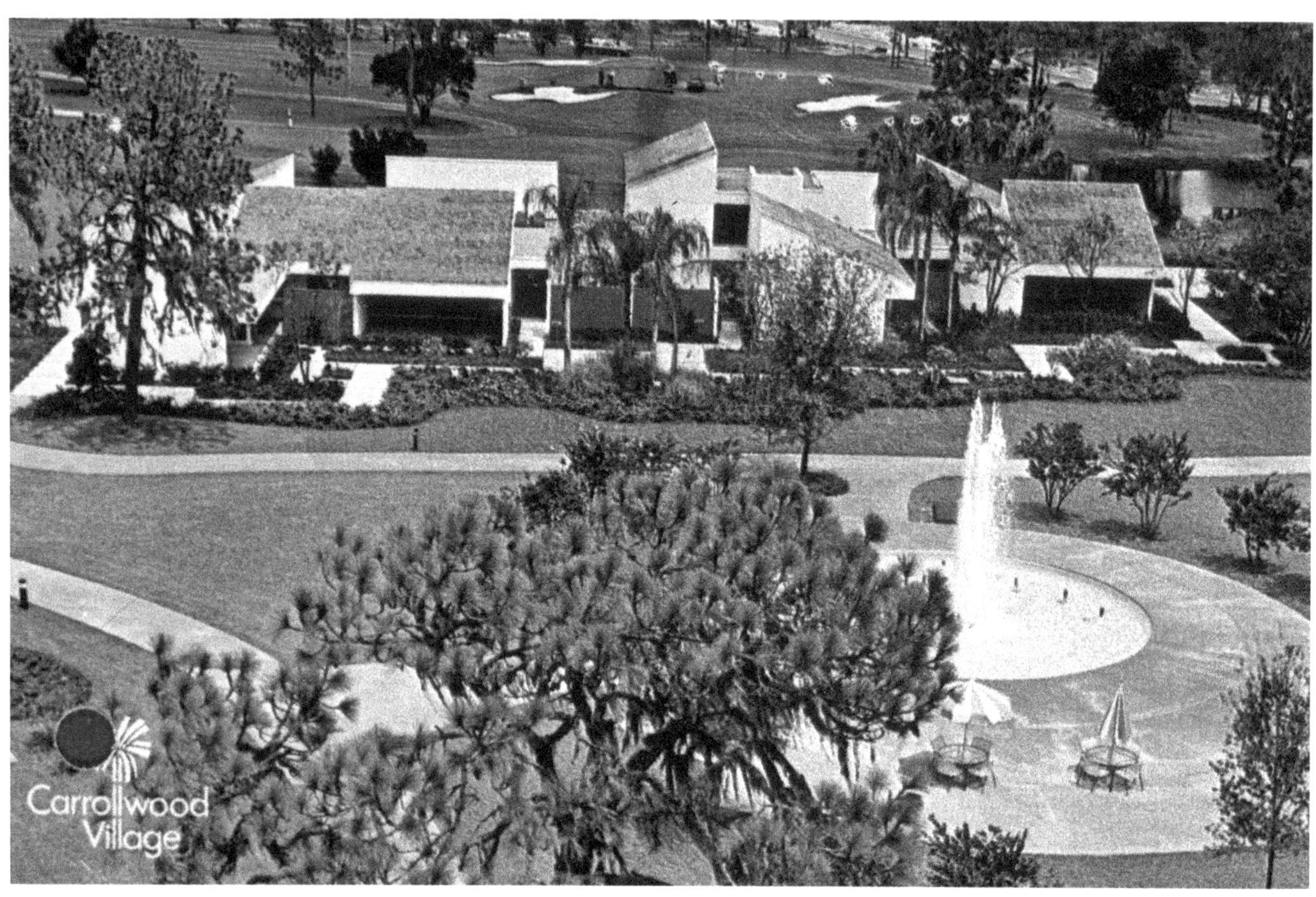

The Carrollwood area of Tampa was developed in the 1960s and became a destination for University of South Florida professors and administrators. By 1968, about 1,000 homes were located near Lake Carroll. In the early 1970s, developer Matt Jetton acquired 2,000 acres nearby and developed Carrollwood Village around a golf and tennis club. *Better Homes & Gardens* magazine presented Carrollwood Village with its Decade 70's award.

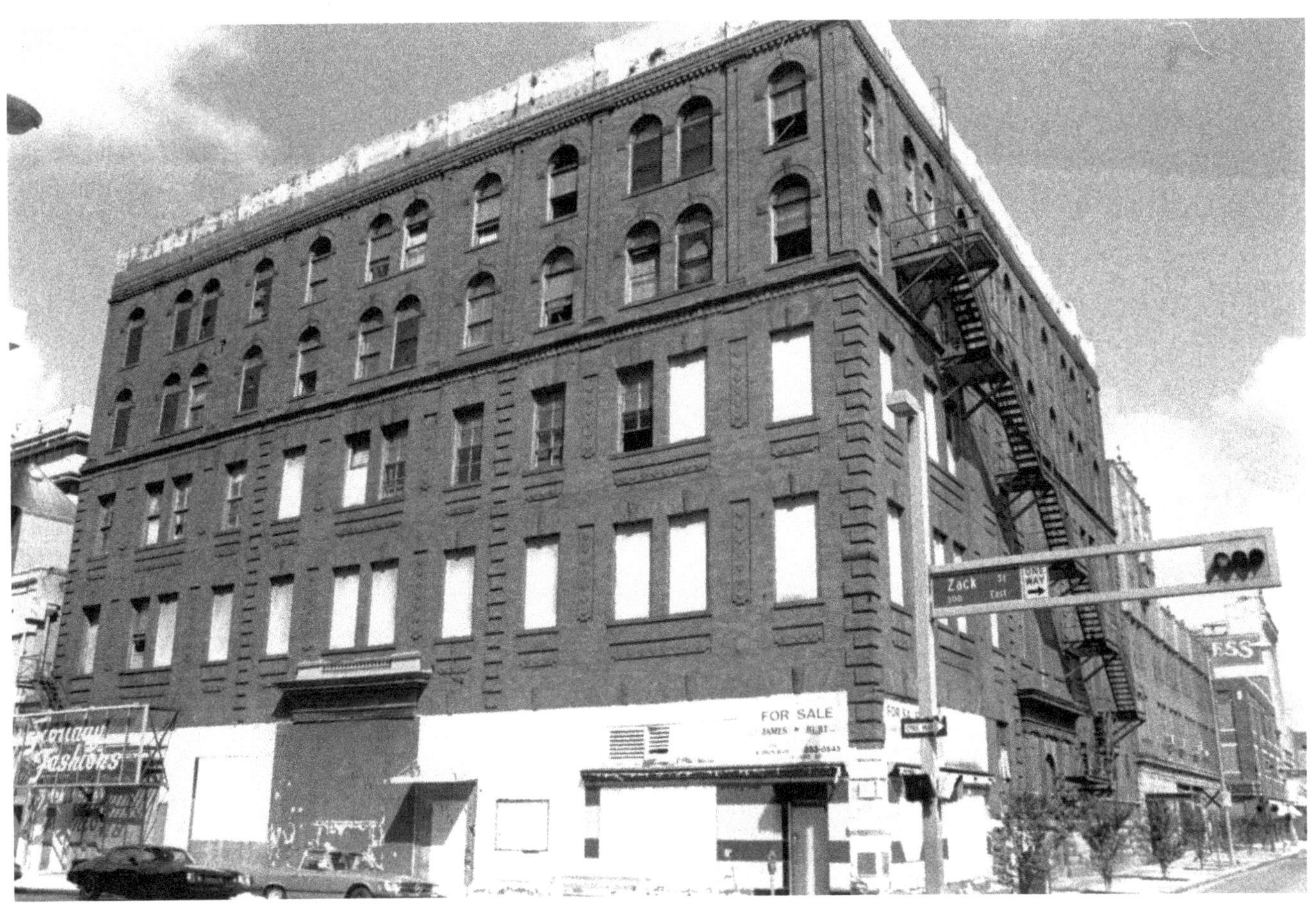

John Long donated the land at 314 Zack Street, and construction of the YMCA building began in 1908. During the early 1970s, the building was damaged by a fire and the boarded up windows are evident in this photo. It was razed in 1991.

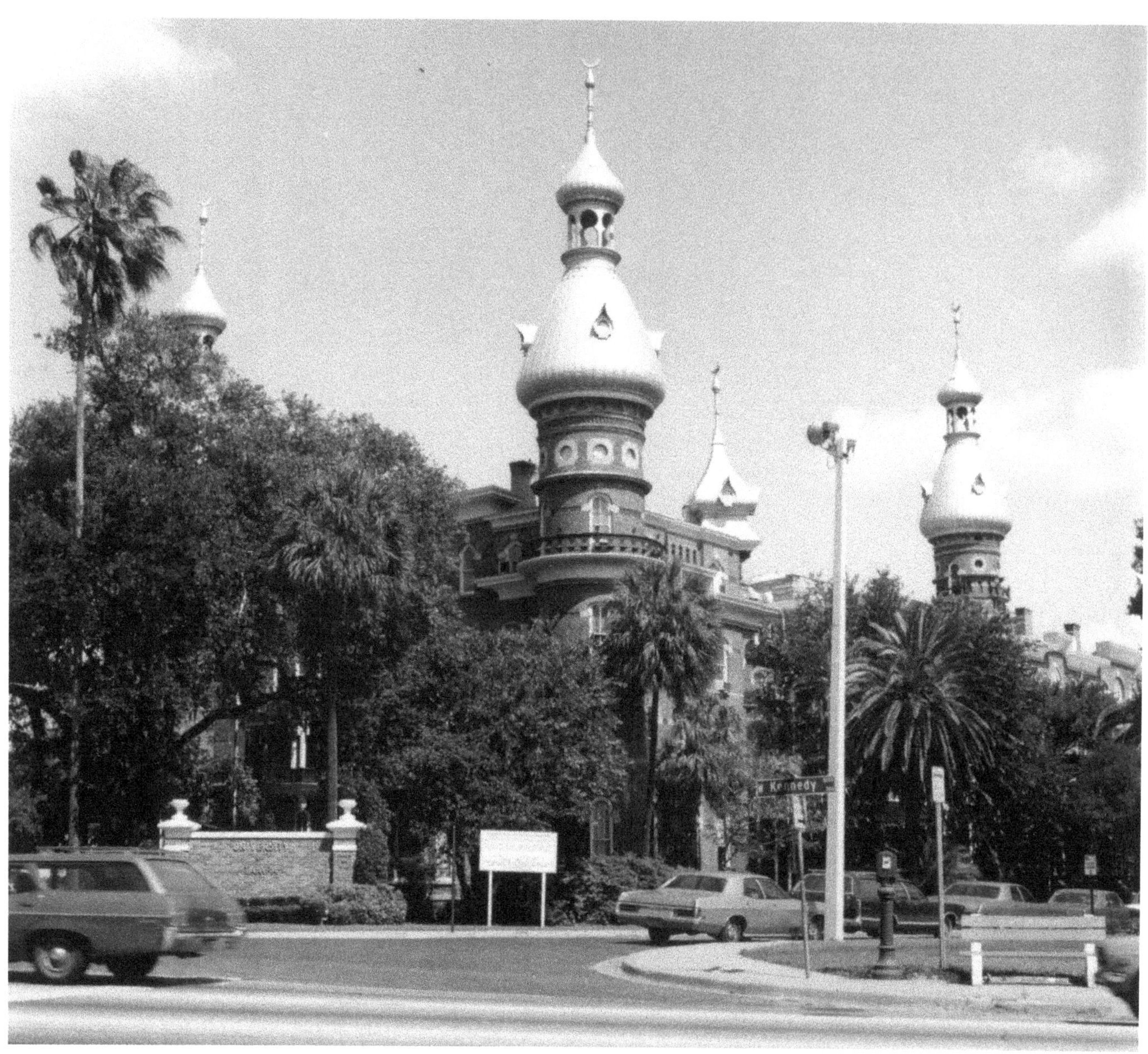

Frederic Spaulding, the principal of Hillsborough High School in 1931, founded Tampa Junior College to meet the needs of high school graduates who could not afford to go away to college. Classes met in the high school building for two years, then expanded to become a four-year university (University of Tampa) and moved to the former Tampa Bay Hotel. Shown here is the main hotel building, renamed as Plant Hall to honor its developer, Henry B. Plant.

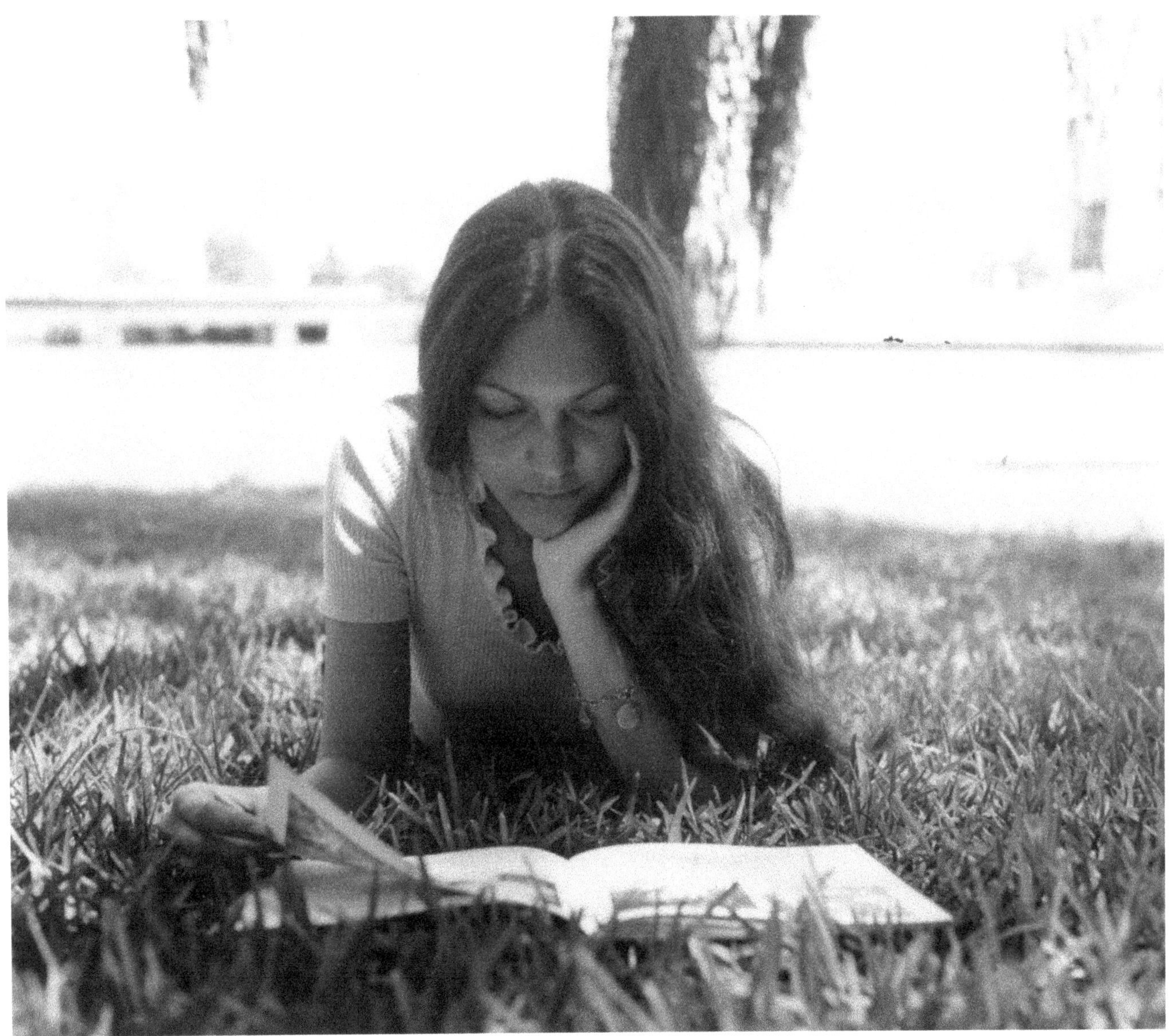

The University of Tampa started out with a student body mostly from the local area, but when the University of South Florida opened in 1960, the older school vigorously recruited students from across the country. By 1964, UT shifted from being mostly a commuter school to a residence university and had students from 38 states and 10 foreign countries. By the end of the 1970s, the student body was back to being predominantly from Florida. The school currently has about 5,700 students, the majority of which are female.

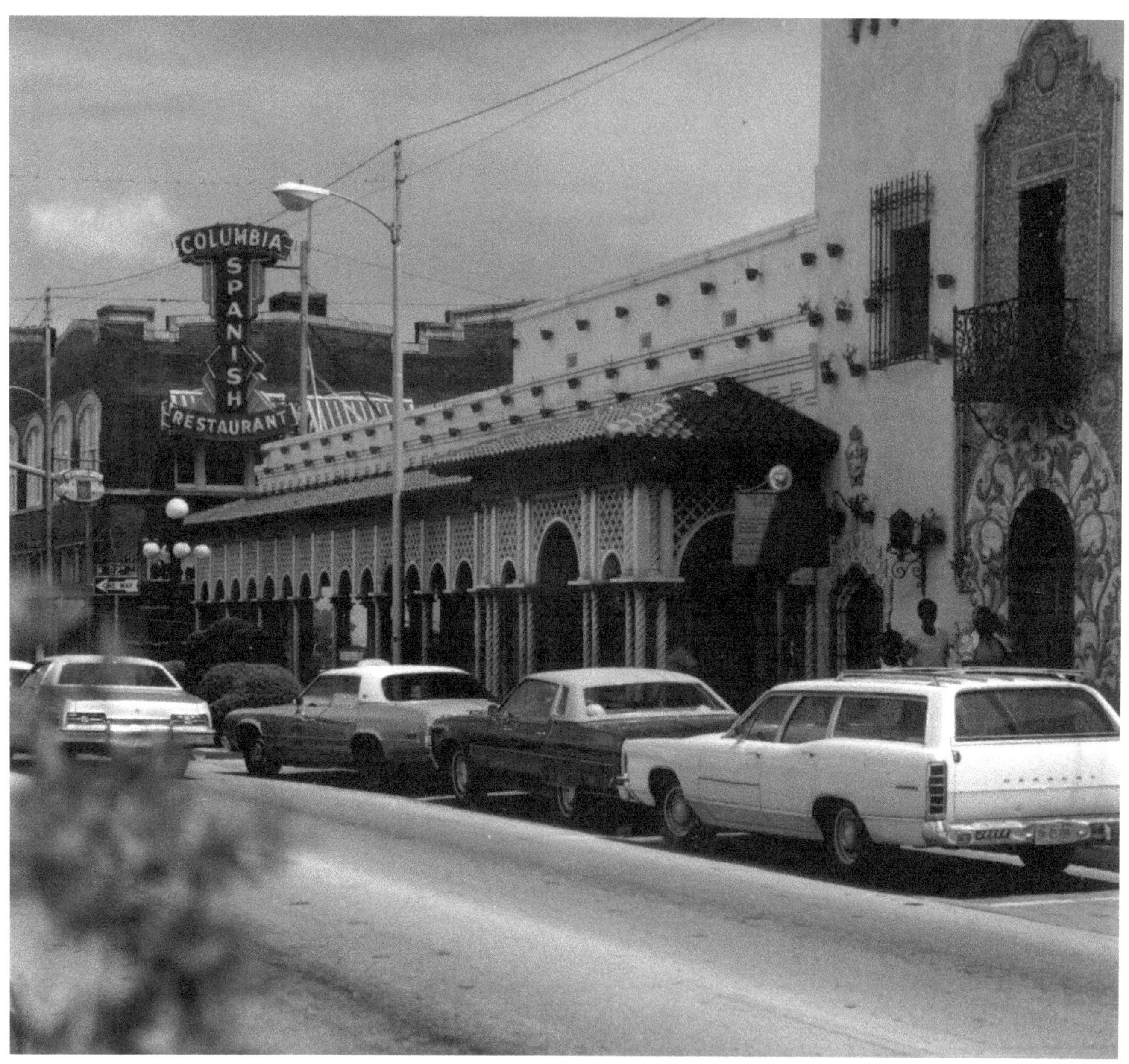

The Columbia Restaurant opened as a café for cigar makers. It was established in 1905 by Casimiro Hernandez, Sr., who chose the name from the song "Columbia, Gem of the Ocean." In 1927, his son took over its operation and at least five generations of the family have run the Columbia so far. This is a photo of some of its interesting architecture during the 1970s.

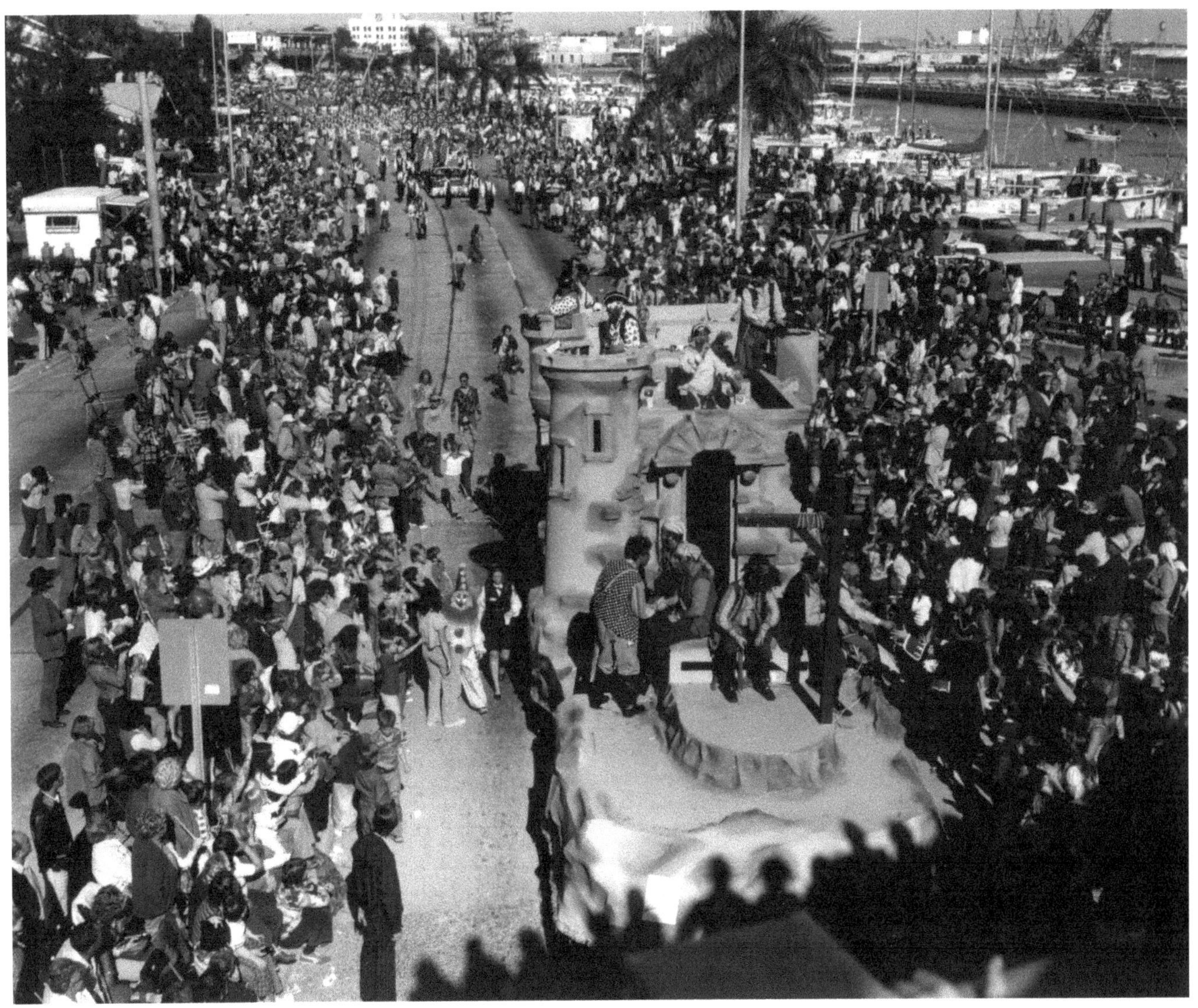

Ye Mystic Krewe of Gasparilla grew from its original 40 members to more than 700 prominent men who perpetuate the legend of a hearty old swashbuckler with courtly manners and prankful habits. An old tradition, which was not celebrated from 1965 through 2007, was for the pirates to ceremonially return the key to the city to the mayor, then board their ship and return to the sea, marking the end of Gasparilla Festival.

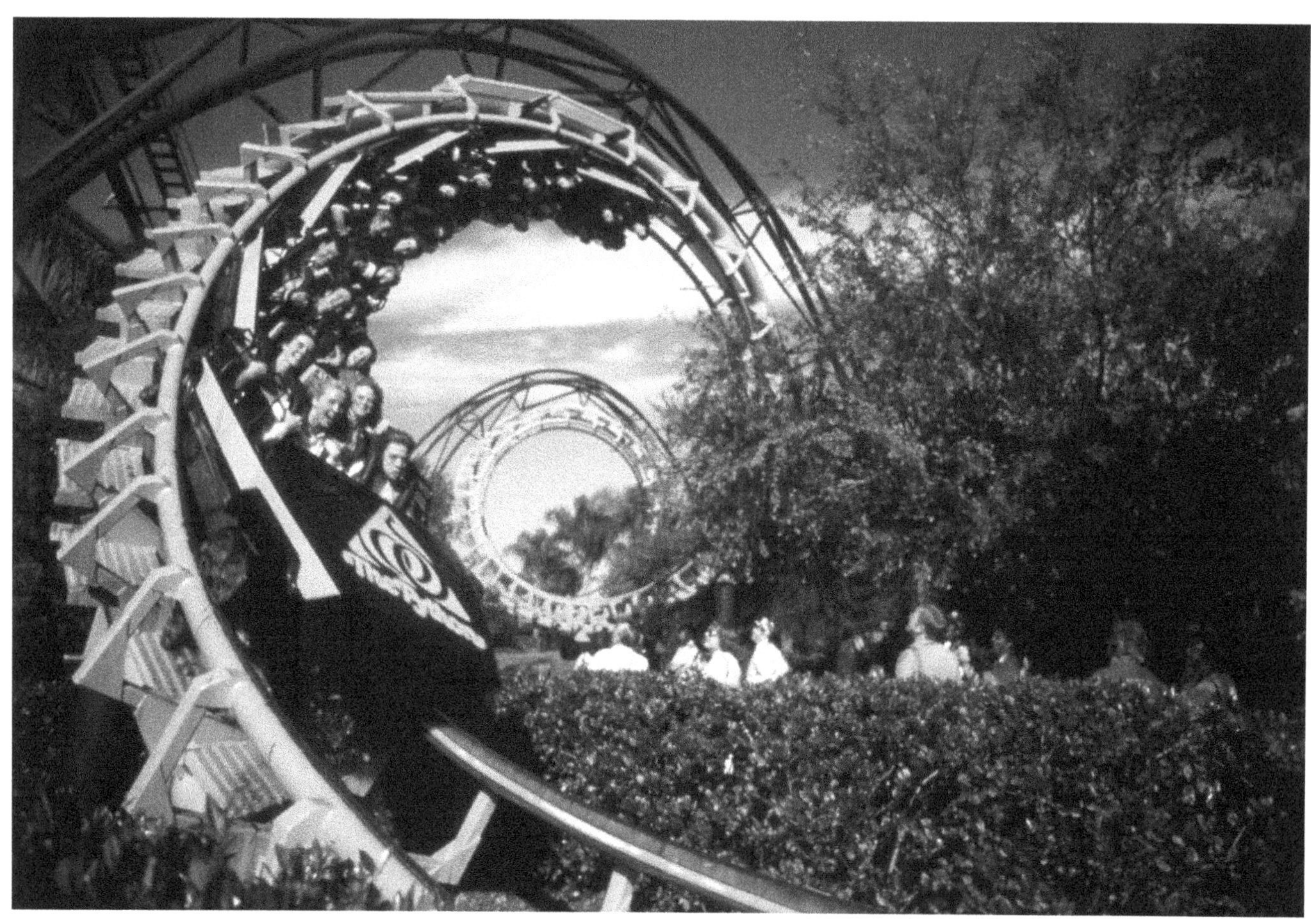

Shown here is Busch Gardens' spiral roller coaster, "The Python," which opened on July 1, 1976. It was the park's first roller coaster and lasted more than three decades before it was closed down on October 31, 2006. It was located in the Congo section of the park, which includes the Kumba roller coaster, the Congo River Rapids water ride, and the Ubanga Banga Bumper Cars.

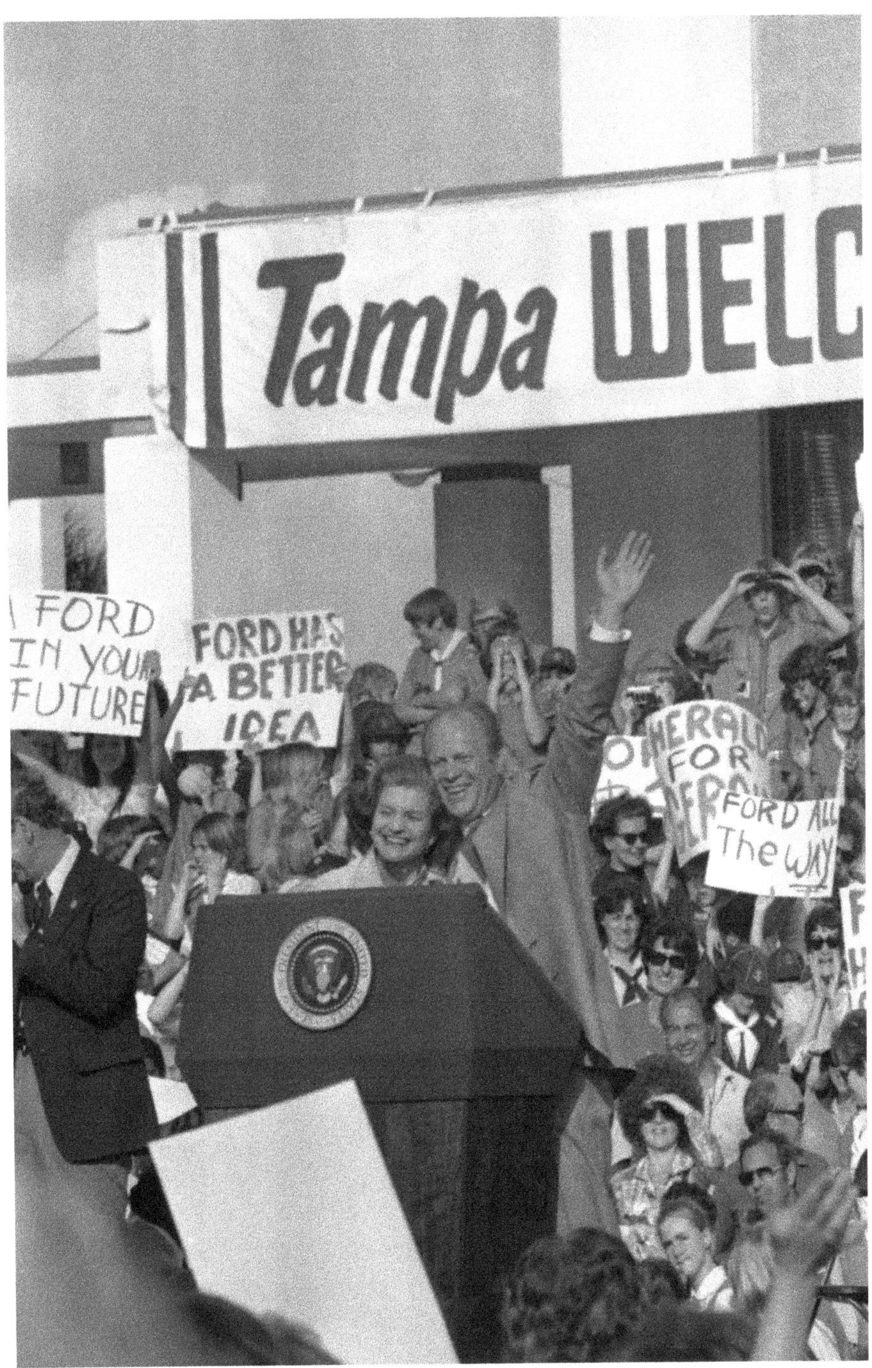

During the 1976 presidential campaign, Gerald R. Ford and his wife, Betty, stopped off in Tampa. He won the Florida primary election and became the party's candidate to run against Jimmy Carter. However, Ford lost the general election in Hillsborough County, Florida, and the United States, making him the only U.S. president to have served in such capacity without ever having been elected to a national office.

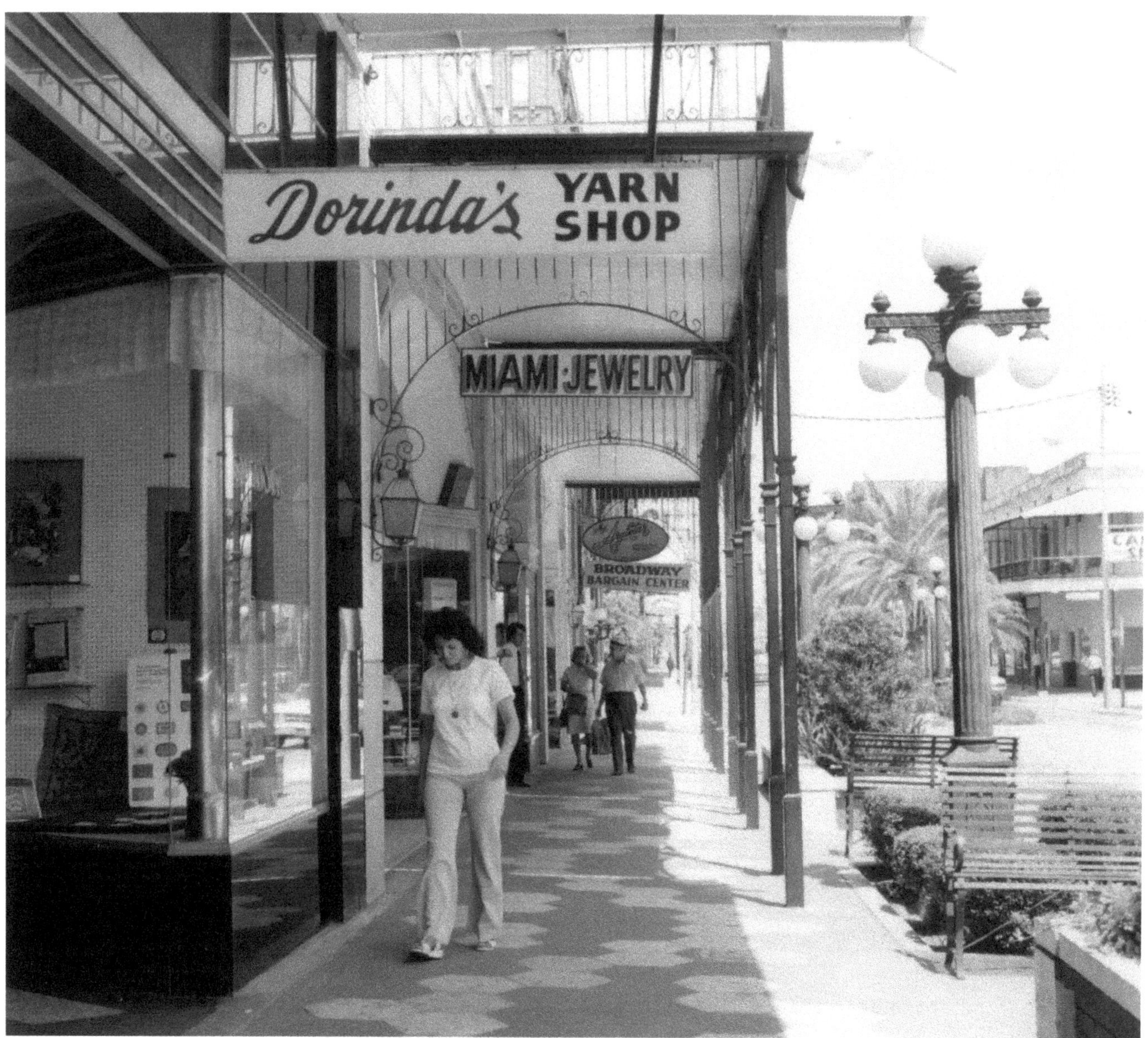

During the mid-1970s, a portion of Ybor City's 7th Avenue which, a half-century before, had been the home of many Jewish-owned businesses, turned into a collection of quaint little stores with a variety of subjects and owners. In this photo can be seen the signs of Dorinda's Yarn Shop, Miami Jewelry, and Sam Argintar's clothing shop, one of the dwindling number of Jewish-owned shops.

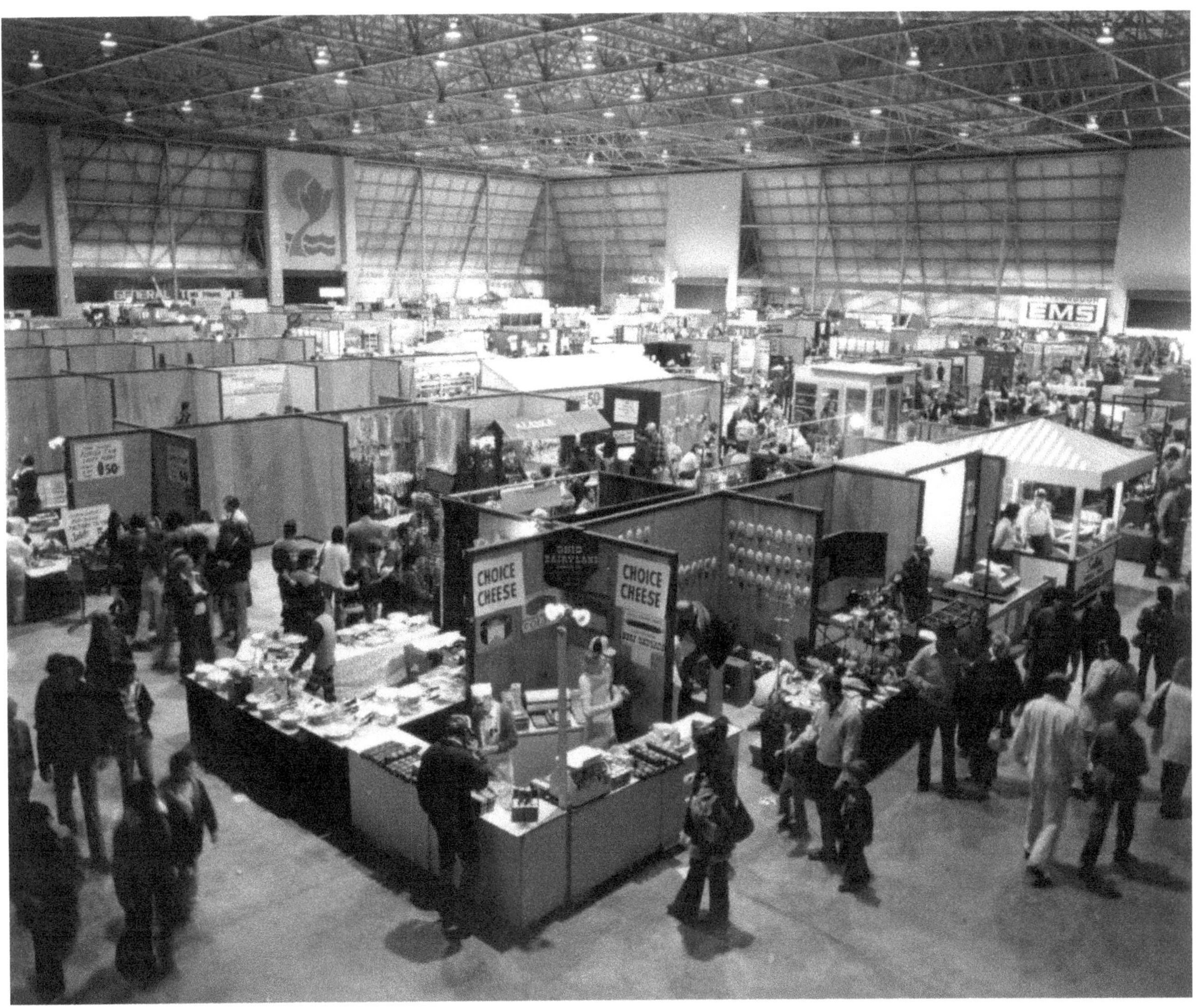

After the 1976 fair was held at a temporary site adjacent to Tampa Stadium, the annual event moved to its present 355-acre fairground at the junction of Interstate 4 and US 301. This is a photo from February 1977, the first state fair at a new location. Since 1995, the fair has operated under the auspices of the Florida Department of Agriculture and Consumer Services.

Currie J. Hutchinson built this home in 1908 at 304 Plant Avenue in Hyde Park, exhibiting a Second Empire style and tall Corinthian columns. It was added to the National Register of Historic Places on November 1, 1977, and became the office of Tampa Preservation, Inc. Hutchinson was a local merchant and served on Tampa's city council.

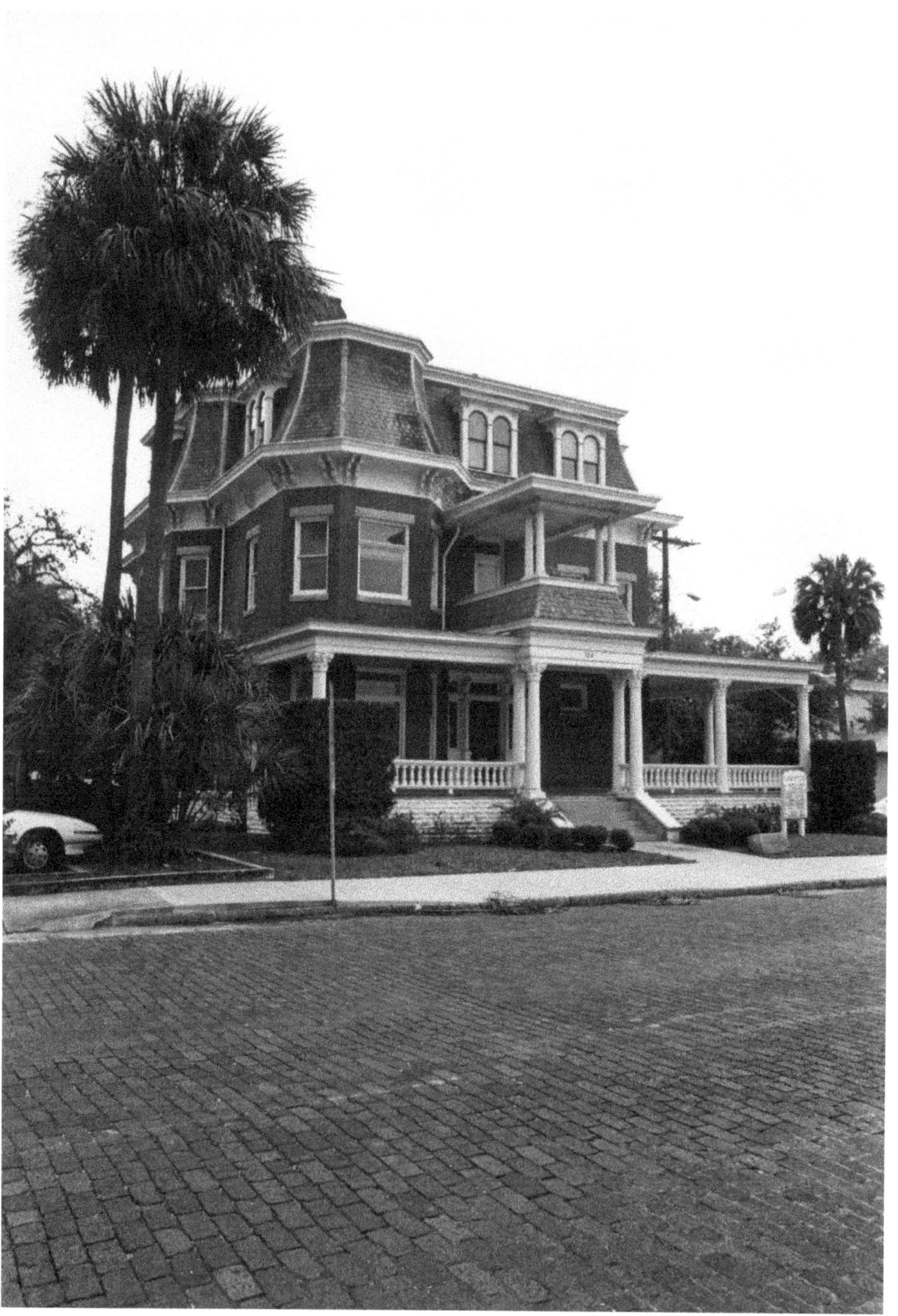

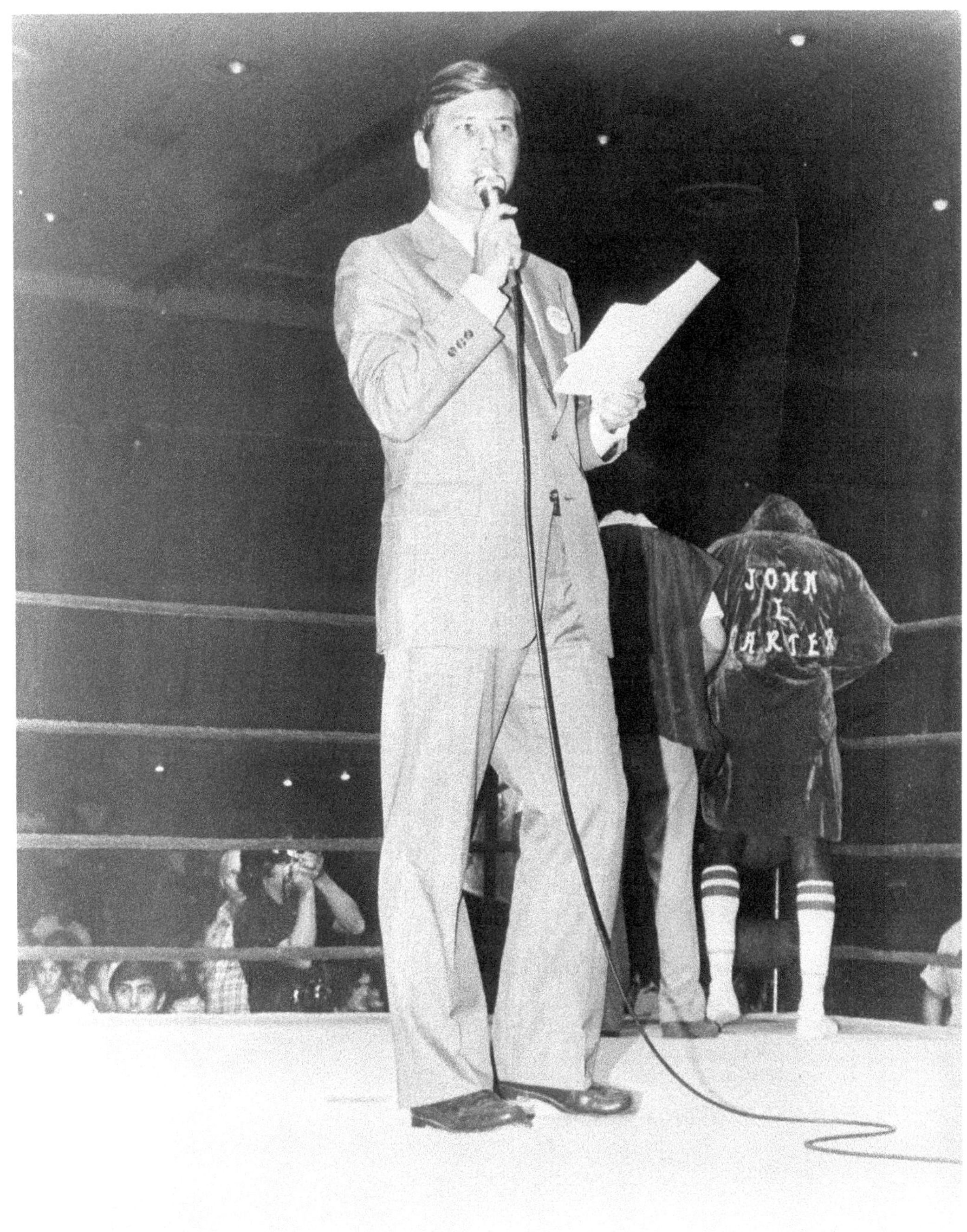

While serving as a United States senator, Bob Graham traveled throughout the state for a series of “workdays.” He performed more than 180 jobs including factory worker, policeman, social worker, teacher, railroad engineer, busboy, construction worker, sponge fisherman, and newsman. On August 10, 1978, in Tampa, he was the ring announcer for boxing matches.

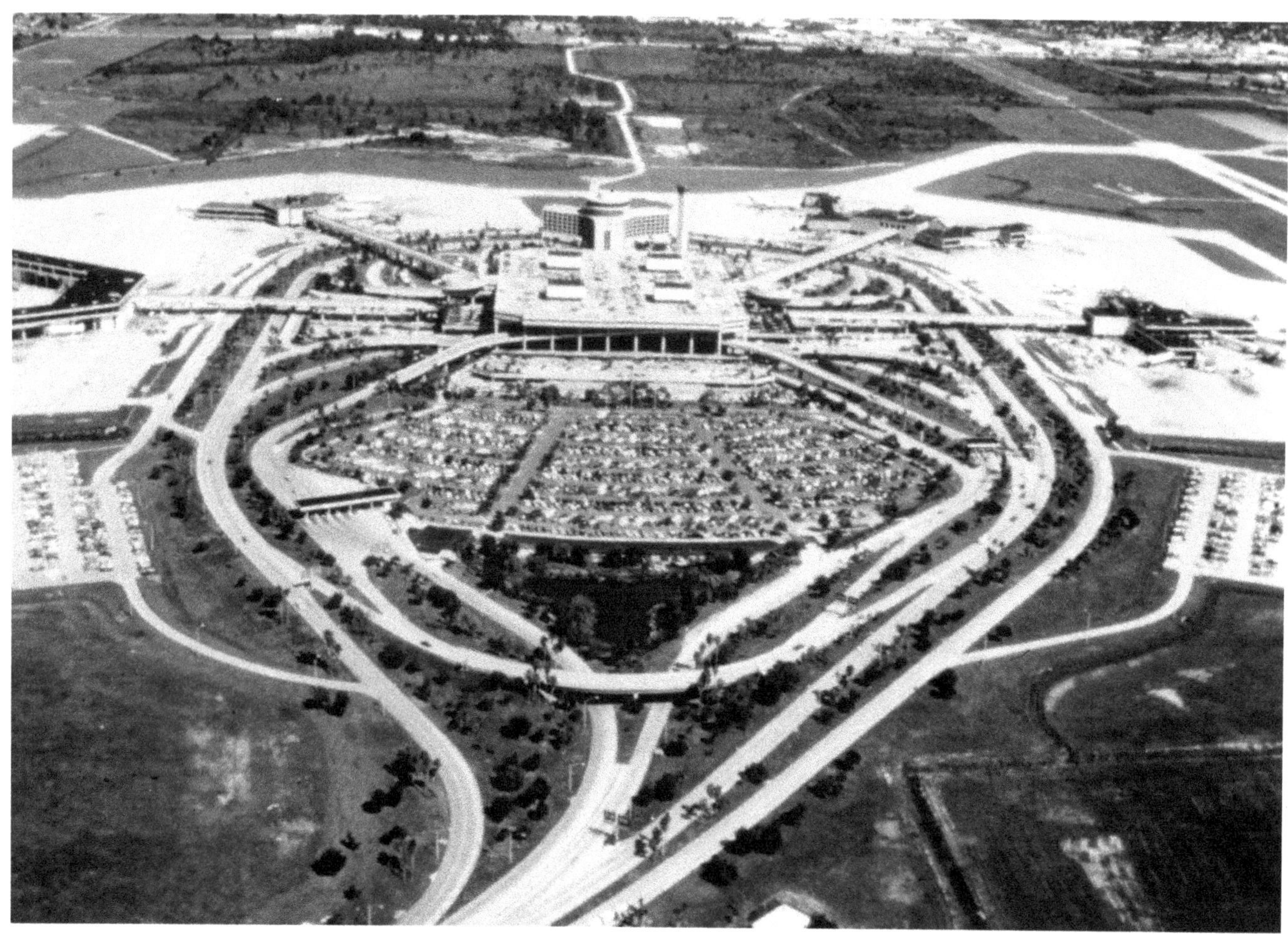

The Tampa International Airport greatly expanded in size with the construction of this new terminal. It was designed for passenger comfort and convenience, and when it opened in April 1971, it was recognized as one of the best-designed terminals in the world. It was the first to provide a people mover system of moving sidewalks for passengers. During 1979 alone, when this picture was taken, more than 8 million airline passengers passed through this airport.

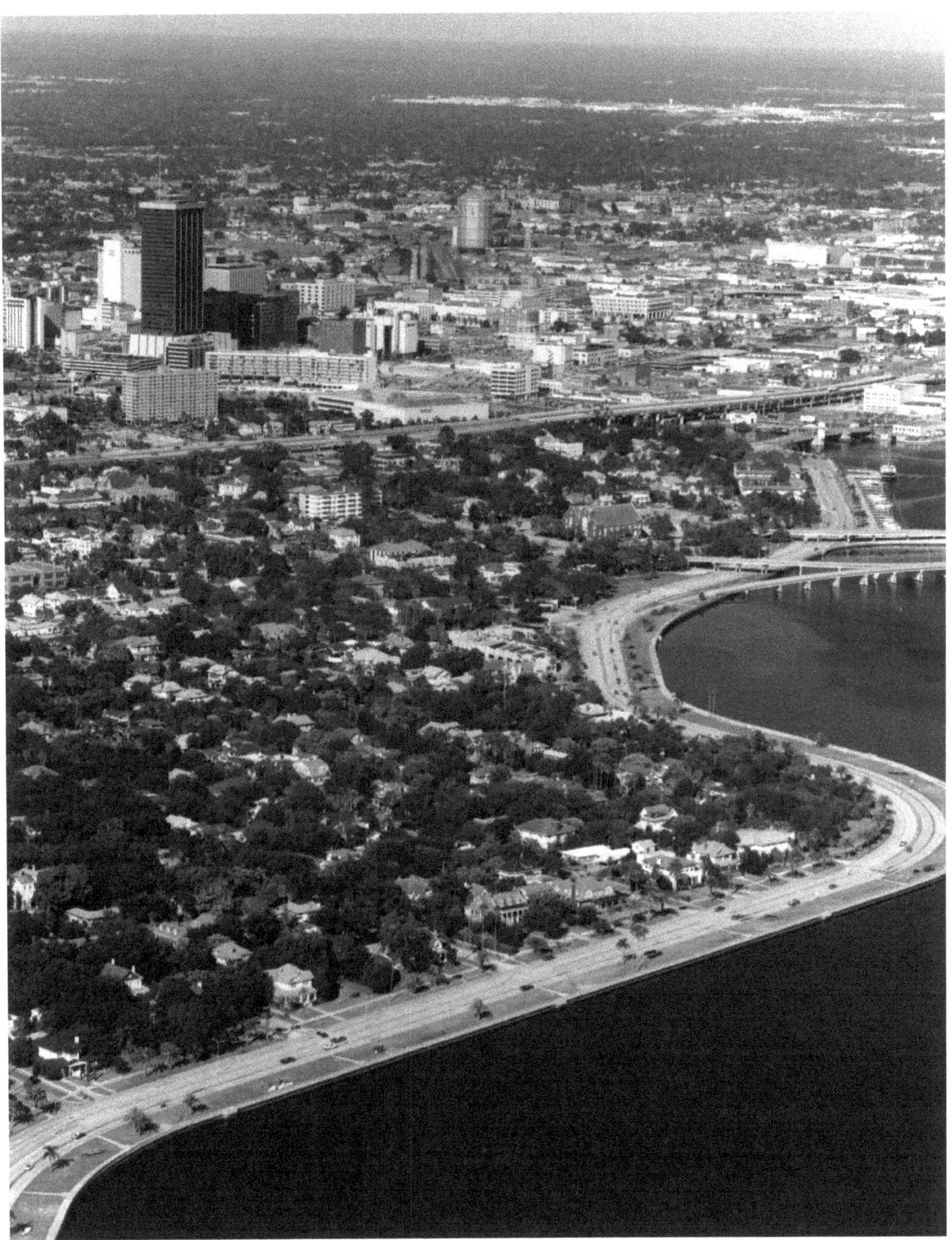

The bottom half of this photo, consisting mostly of large homes surrounded by trees, is Hyde Park, a portion of the farmland of Levi and Nancy Dixon Collier during the 1820s. Their daughter married Robert Jackson in 1834, and they made their home in an area known as Jackson's Point, a portion of which was sold in 1886 to Obadiah H. Platt of Hyde Park, Illinois. He named the 20 acres after his hometown and on it was built substantial homes.

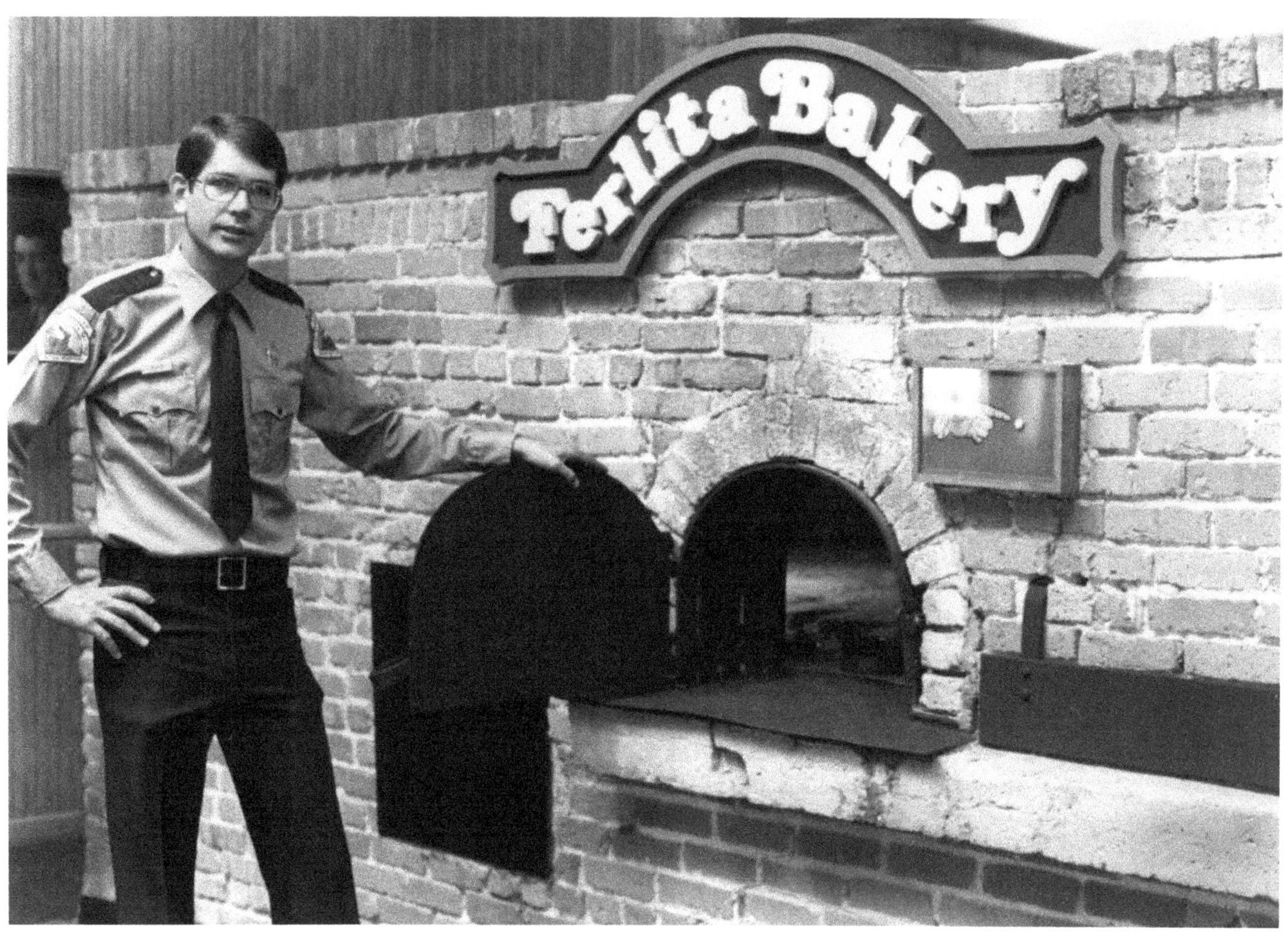

Park ranger Rob Heath stands by the ovens of the Ferlita Bakery. These ovens were used in the original wooden bakery founded by Francisco Ferlita in 1896. When it burned down, the ovens were salvageable so the new bakery building was built around them. This is how they appeared during the 1970s as the bakery was being turned into a state museum.

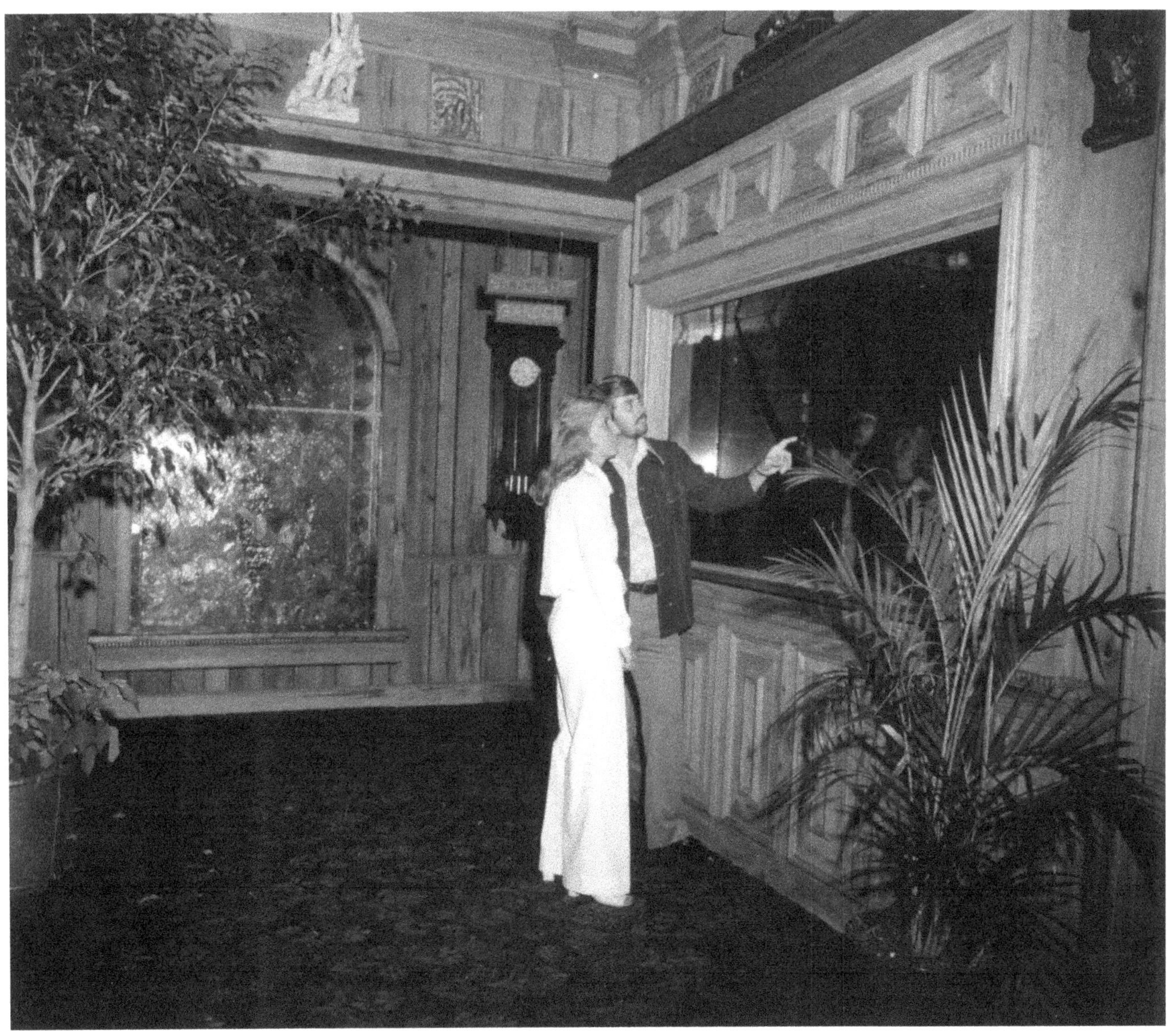

The Sea Wolf Restaurant was a multi-million-dollar project of Gene Holloway and occupied 14 acres across from Busch Gardens. It had a seating capacity of 500 but was so popular, it still often had waiting lines hours long. It opened in 1979 and quickly became one of the ten highest grossing restaurants in the country. After a messy divorce in which he was accused of burning down the house, plus a faked death and criminal charges (which included a five-year sentence for conspiracy), Holloway closed the restaurant and became a deep-sea treasure hunter. The former restaurant burned down in 1991.

Still standing at 2701 16th Street, the Regensburg Cigar Factory and its large clock tower is a familiar Tampa landmark. It was built in 1909 and was nicknamed El Reloj ("the clock") for its large clock faces on each side of the square seven-story water tower. Its first occupant was the Pendas and Alvarez Cigar Company, and on May 20, 1920, it became the home of cigar maker E. Regensburg & Sons, owned by Jerome Regensburg. It is now the home of the J. C. Newman Cigar Company, which continues to produce cigars including the brands of Cuesta-Rey and Arturo Fuente. Today, it is separated from the main portion of Ybor City as a result of the construction of Interstate 4.

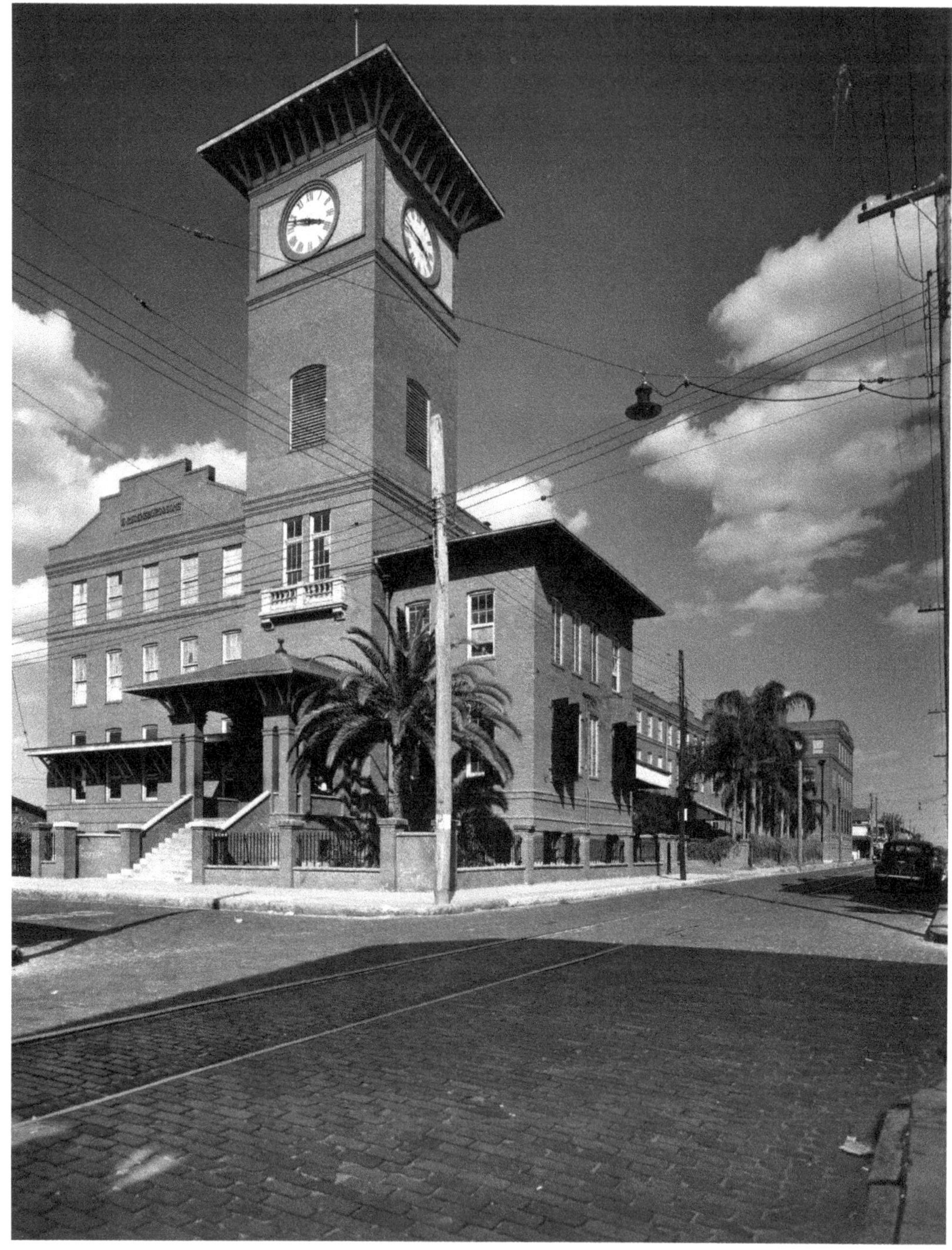

Notes on the Photographs

These notes, listed by page number, attempt to include all aspects known of the photographs. Each of the photographs is identified by the page number, photograph's title or description, photographer and collection, archive, and call or box number when applicable. Although every attempt was made to collect all available data, in some cases complete data was unavailable due to the age and condition of some of the photographs and records.

II **Park Tower**
C682620
Photo by Gaines

VI **Treasureland**
C673103

X **Rooftop View**
01/357
Photo by Burgert Brothers

2 **Gasparilla Festival**
C012729

3 **Pirate Float**
C012740

4 **Tampa Heights**
07/6651
Photo by Burgert Brothers

5 **Red Cross Flags**
12/11294
Photo by Burgert Brothers

6 **ROTC Ball**
MS25890

7 **Wolf Brothers**
07/6703
Photo by Burgert Brotehrs

8 **Episcopal Wedding**
15/14560
Photo by Burgert Brothers

9 **Hotel Puritan**
05/4209
Photo by Burgert Brothers

10 **Marion Street**
07/6858
Photo by Burgert Brothers

11 **Dime Stores**
12/11377
Photo by Burgert Brothers

12 **Pioneer Tire**
07/6870
Photo by Burgert Brothers

13 **Swanson's Candy Butcher Shop**
07/6486
Photo by Burgert Brothers

14 **Christmas Lights**
07/6253
Photo by Burgert Brothers

15 **County Courthouse**
03/2793
Photo by Burgert Brothers

16 **Cuesta-Rey Cigars**
07/6089
Photo by Burgert Brothers

17 **Peninsular Telephone Company**
07/6430
Photo by Burgert Brothers

18 **Fairground**
07/6501
Photo by Burgert Brothers

19 **Stunt Driving**
07/6505
Photo by Burgert Brothers

20 **School Band**
11/10432
Photo by Burgert Brothers

21 **Auto Racing**
11/10391
Photo by Burgert Brothers

22 **County Courthouse**
07/6902
Photo by Burgert Brothers

23 **Armory**
12/11476
Photo by Burgert Brothers

24 **Citizens Bank Building**
07/6776
Photo by Burgert Brothers

25 **Yacht and Country Club**
07/6800
Photo by Burgert Brothers

26 **Merry-Go-Round**
12/11509
Photo by Burgert Brothers

27 **Municipal Auditorium**
07/6916
Photo by Burgert Brothers

28 **Tampa Skyline**
C016451
Photo by Florida News Bureau

29 **Company Banquet**
RC20734

30 **Baseball Dinner**
GV016277

31 **Baseball Players**
12/11612
Photo by Burgert Brothers

32 **State Fair**
07/6507
Photo by Burgert Brothers

33 **Franklin Street**
06/5947
Photo by Burgert Brothers

34 **City Hall**
02/1395
Photo by Burgert Brothers

35 **Tampa Forge**
N043480

36 **WDAE Radio**
15/14716
Photo by Burgert Brothers

37 **Hillsborough River**
01/208
Photo by Burgert Brothers

38 **Sahlman Sea Food**
RC20090

39 **School Crossing**
07/6990
Photo by Burgert Brothers

40 **Woolworth's**
06/5915
Photo by Burgert Brothers

41 **Theaters**
12/11679
Photo by Burgert Brothers

42 **Tampa International Airport**
01/828
Photo by Burgert Brothers

43 **Hotel Hillsboro**
01/359
Photo by Burgert Brothers

44 **Carl Brorein**
RC20874

45 **Orange Grove**
12/11685
Photo by Burgert Brothers

46 **Aerial View**
12/11707
Photo by Burgert Brothers

47 **County Courthouse**
RC03371
Photo by Burgert Brothers

48 **Sailboat**
C018310
Photo by Francis P. Johnson

49 **Tropical Nursery**
C017364
Photo by Charles Barron

50 **Confederate Monument**
RC20785
Photo by Burgert Brothers

51 **Florida Avenue**
01/360
Photo by Burgert Brothers

52 **Bridge Construction**
DOT1929
Photo by Florida State Road Department

53 **County Courthouse**
06/5941
Photo by Burgert Brothers

54 **Madison Drug Store**
01/362
Photo by Burgert Brothers

55 **Tampa Terrace Hotel**
07/6145
Photo by Burgert Brothers

56 **Giddens Corner**
01/363
Photo by Burgert Brothers

57 **Central Business District**
01/946
Photo by Burgert Brothers

58 **Movie District**
12/11767
Photo by Burgert Brothers

59 **City Hall**
05/4215
Photo by Burgert Brothers

60 **Plant Field**
06/5971
Photo by Burgert Brothers

61 **Exchange National Bank of Tampa**
12/11811
Photo by Burgert Brothers

62 **Franklin Street**
12/11887
Photo by Burgert Brothers

63 **Florida Avenue**
07/6150
Photo by Burgert Brothers

64 **Franklin Street**
01/949
Photo by Burgert Brothers

66 **Franklin Street**
07/6151
Photo by Burgert Brothers

67 **Federal Building**
03/2399
Photo by Burgert Brothers

68 **Lafayette Street**
03/2696
Photo by Burgert Brothers

69 **Hotel Thomas Jefferson**
01/950
Photo by Burgert Brothers

70 **Platt Street Bridge**
01/952
Photo by Burgert Brothers

71 **Corral, Wodiska and Company**
08/7081
Photo by Burgert Brothers

72 **First National Bank**
03/2450
Photo by Burgert Brothers

73 **WFLA Television**
RC20823

74 **Plant Park**
01/364
Photo by Burgert Brothers

75 **Publix Supermarket**
15/14623
Photo by Burgert Brothers

76 **William Brooker**
15/14626
Photo by Burgert Brothers

77 **Hillsborough River**
RC20679
Photo by Blake

78 **Flagler Building**
13/12063
Photo by Burgert Brothers

79 **Hotel Hillsboro**
08/7402
Photo by Burgert Brothers

80 **Kress**
07/6159
Photo by Burgert Brothers

81 **Lafayette Hotel**
08/7177
Photo by Burgert Brothers

82 **WTVT Television**
GV035136

83 **First National Bank**
15/14641
Photo by Burgert Brothers

84 **Platt Street Bridge**
C025832
Photo by Florida News Bureau

85 **Gandy Bridge**
C024520

86 **Yacht Basin**
C025834
Photo by Hackett

87 **Sacred Heart Catholic Church**
C024491
Photo by Karl E. Holland

88 **Drive-In Restaurant**
11/10344
Photo by Burgert Brothers

89 **Louis Wohl & Sons**
MS25872

90 **Franklin Street**
08/7420
Photo by Burgert Brothers

91 **Group Singing**
NO39562

92 **Paint Plant**
C025591
Photo by Charles Barron

93 **Golf Course**
C026757
Photo by Charles Barron

94 **Tennis Players**
C026834
Photo by Charles Barron

95 **Hillsborough River**
13/12318
Photo by Burgert Brothers

96 **Jai-Alai**
C026496
Photo by Charles Barron

97 **Greyhound Racing**
C026485
Photo by Charles Barron

98 **Tampa Bay Hotel**
01/768
Photo by Burgert Brothers

99 Chapin House
RC20794
Photo by *Tampa Tribune*

100 Gasparilla Festival
C026990
Photo by Karl E. Holland

101 Cigar Factory
08/7510
Photo by Burgert Brothers

102 WEDU Television
PR12530

103 Snow Show
07/6044
Photo by Burgert Brothers

104 Roller Coaster
07/6541
Photo by Burgert Brothers

105 Roy and Dale
07/6539
Photo by Burgert Brothers

106 Tampa International Airport
07/6026
Photo by Burgert Brothers

107 Flood
RC16559

108 Hospitality House
C029646

109 Steel Foundry
C030451
Photo by Stokes

110 Aerial View
03/2507
Photo by Burgert Brothers

112 Gasparilla Festival
C031817
Photo by Karl E. Holland

113 Farris Bryant
RC19299

114 Cigar Queen
C032997
Photo by Charles Barron

115 Seminole Heights Baptist Church
NO43487

116 General Telephone Company
RC20937

117 W. L. Cobb
14/13167
Photo by Burgert Brothers

118 Fishing Tournament
C033469
Photo by Sandy Gandy

119 Grand Central Avenue
07/6169
Photo by Burgert Brothers

120 Tampa Skyline
01/956
Photo by Burgert Brothers

121 USF Convocation
RC21258

122 Parrots
C034382b

123 Monument to Mothers
RC20766
Photo by Hampton Dunn

124 Federal Building
03/2404
Photo by Burgert Brothers

125 John F. Kennedy
RC19370

126 Administration Building
C034406
Photo by Florida News Bureau

127 Pelota Maker
C035516
Photo by Stokes

128 Maas Brothers
C035524
Photo by Stokes

129 Rodeph Sholom Synagogue
MS25876

130 Sorting Tobacco Leaves
14/13242
Photo by Burgert Brothers

132 Aerial View
03/2405
Photo by Burgert Brothers

133 Ferlita Bakery
RC08736

134 Lykes Brothers
C620808
Photo by Charles Barron

135 Armory
15/14701
Photo by Burgert Brothers

136 Traffic Police
NO27378

137 Sorting Coconuts
14/13455
Photo by Burgert Brothers

138 Day Nursery
14/13463
Photo by Burgert Brothers

139 Banana Cart
14/13467
Photo by Burgert Brothers

140 Kennedy Boulevard Bridge
PR65885

141 Amusement Rides
C621010b
Photo by Karl E. Holland

142 Metal Shop
14/13480
Photo by Burgert Brothers

143 Brewster Vocational School
14/13841
Photo by Burgert Brothers

144 Nick Nuccio
RC17150

145 Centro Español
C650026
Photo by Hackett

146 Cherokee Club
RC20801
Photo by Hampton Dunn

147 Safety Village
C65198
Photo by Karl E. Holland

148 Cuban Sandwiches
C660503

149 Night Scene
C660502

150 Fairyland
660328

151 Card Players
C660501

152 Golden Gate Speedway
C660523
Photo by Bevis

154 Boat Parade
C672527
Photo by Karl E. Holland

155 Stovall House
PR65846

156 New Library
07/6099
Photo by Burgert Brothers

157 High School Football
06/5913
Photo by Burgert Brothers

158 Columbia Restaurant
C671727
Photo by Karl E. Holland

159 Tampa Library
07/6096
Photo by Burgert Brothers

160 Schlitz Brewery
COM05266
Photo by Florida Division of Tourism

163 Baseball Championship
MS26141

164 Seald-Sweet
PR65857

165 Phosphate
C676573
Photo by Hackett

166 Al Lopez Field
PR00651
Photo by *Jacksonville Journal*

168 Busch Brewery
C677345

169 Italian Club
PR12437

170 Curtis Hixon Hall
C678955
Photo by Murphy

171 Boma
C678789

172 Edmund Muskie
PT00120

173 Cigar Company
C678768
Photo by Murphy

174 Columbia Bank
C678765
Photo by Murphy

175 Guernsey City
NO43670

176 Water Tower
PC5724

177 Steam Train
C681096

178 Robert E. Lee Elementary
PR24349

179 Bern's Steak House
C680937
Photo by Karl E. Holland

180 Water Flume
COM01254
Photo by Fortune

181 Cigar Makers
FS85691
Collected by Ormond H. Loomis

182 Taliaferro House
PR65878

183 Cherokee Club
C000997

184 Host of Tampa Hotel
C000932

185 Swiss House
C682074
Photo by Karl E. Holland

186 Carrollwood Village
N043669

187 YMCA
PR65793

188 University of Tampa
C682652
Photo by Gaines

189 **UT Student**
C682653
Photo by Gaines

190 **Columbia Restaurant**
C683720
Photo by Tom McLendon

191 **Gasparilla Festival**
C683424
Photo by Karl E. Holland

192 **Roller Coaster**
COM01250
Photo by Florida Division of Tourism

193 **Gerald Ford**
DND0696
Photo by Donn Dughi

194 **Nostalgia Market Area**
C682632
Photo by Gaines

195 **Florida State Fair**
C683849
Photo by Karl E. Holland

196 **Hutchinson House**
PR65859

197 **Bob Graham**
N048741

198 **Tampa International Airport**
RC20779

199 **Hyde Park**
PR65886
Photo by Skip Gandy

200 **Ferlita Bakery**
FPS1511
Photo by Florida Division of Recreation and Parks

201 **Sea Wolf Restaurant**
C684325
Photo by Eric Tournay

202 **El Reloj**
RC07726

Bibliography

Bane, Michael and Marry Ellen Moore. *Tampa: Yesterday, Today and Tomorrow.* Tampa: Mishler and King Publishing, 1981.

Covington, James W. and C. Herbert Laub. *The Story of the University of Tampa.* Tampa: University of Tampa Press, 1955.

Deitche, Scott M. *Cigar City Mafia: A Complete History of the Tampa Underworld.* Fort Lee, NJ: Barricade Books, 2004.

Dunn, Hampton. *Tampa: A Pictorial History.* Norfolk, VA: The Donning Company, 1985.

Dunn, Hampton. *Yesterday's Tampa.* Miami: E .A. Seemann Publishing, Inc., 1972.

Lastra, Frank Trebín. *Ybor City: The Making of a Landmark Town. Tampa* (University of Tampa Press, 2006).

Mendez, Armondo. *Cuidad de Cigars: West Tampa.* Tampa: Florida Historical Society, 1994.

Mormino, Gary R. and Anthony P. Pizzo. *Tampa: The Treasure City.* Tulsa, OK: Continental Heritage Press, Inc., 1983.

Norman, Robert and Lisa Coleman. *Tampa.* Charleston, SC: Arcadia Publishing, 2001.

HISTORIC PHOTOS OF TAMPA IN THE 50s, 60s, AND 70s

In the ever-changing decades of the 1950s, 60s, and 70s, one could wander through the city of Tampa and experience a rich variety of architectural styles, business, languages, and traditions, all mixed in with first-class universities, hospitals, and museums. By the 1950s, the University of South Florida was founded, and Busch Gardens opened to locals and tourists alike. The 1960s ushered in a period of construction and entertainment, with residents visiting for the first time the Lowry Park Zoo, Curtis Hixon Hall, and "The Big Sombrero," or Tampa Stadium. Like the rest of the country, the 1970s in Tampa was a time of continued modernization and expansion.

Though not immune to crime or misfortune in this thirty-year span, Tampa is remembered as an attractive destination and place of residence, as seen through the lens of the camera, a modern city that continues to honor its historical roots.

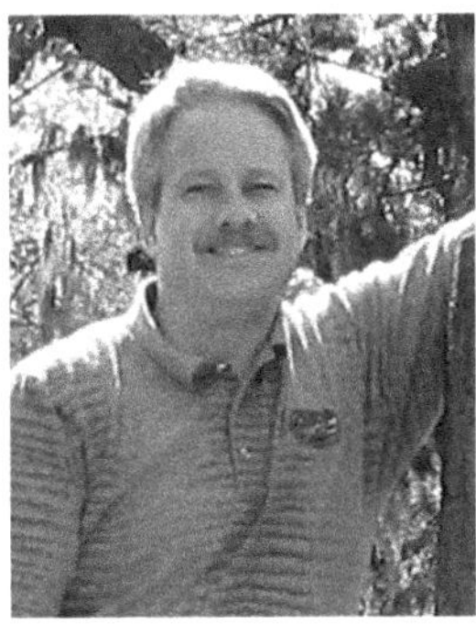

Steve Rajtar has over 20 books, each dealing with history, particularly that of Florida. Among these works are *Historic Photos of Florida Tourist Attractions*, *Historic Photos of Gainesville*, *Historic Photos of the University of Florida*, and *Historic Photos of Florida Ghost Towns*. Rajtar grew up near Cleveland, Ohio, and after graduating from the University of Central Florida and the University of Florida, he entered the practice of law. He continues in that profession today.

A love of the outdoors and a fascination with local history has resulted in one of his hobbies: leading historical tours in Florida's communities of today and yesteryear.

www.ingramcontent.com/pod-product-compliance
Lightning Source LLC
LaVergne TN
LVHW060614110826
845154LV00003B/84
9781684421336